W9-BXA-837

Cultural Models of Nature

Drawing on the ethnographic experience of the contributors, this volume explores the Cultural Models of Nature found in a range of food-producing communities located in climate-change affected areas. These Cultural Models represent specific organizations of the etic categories underlying the concept of Nature (i.e., plants, animals, the physical environment, the weather, humans, and the supernatural). The adoption of a common methodology across the research projects allows the drawing of meaningful cross-cultural comparisons between these communities. The research will be of interest to scholars and policymakers actively involved in research and solution-providing in the climate-change arena.

Giovanni Bennardo is Presidential Research Professor in the Department of Anthropology and Cognitive Studies and also works at the Institute for the Study of the Environment, Sustainability and Energy at Northern Illinois University, USA.

Routledge Studies in Anthropology

www.routledge.com/Routledge-Studies-in-Anthropology/book-series/
SE0724

Cultural Models of Nature
Primary Food Producers
and Climate Change

Edited by Giovanni Bennardo

Routledge
Taylor & Francis Group
LONDON AND NEW YORK

First published 2019
by Routledge
2 Park Square, Milton Park, Abingdon, Oxon OX14 4RN

and by Routledge
52 Vanderbilt Avenue, New York, NY 10017

Routledge is an imprint of the Taylor & Francis Group, an informa business

British Library Cataloguing-in-Publication Data
A catalogue record for this book is available from the British Library

Library of Congress Cataloging-in-Publication Data
A catalog record has been requested for this book

ISBN: 978-0-8153-5658-5 (hbk)
ISBN: 978-0-367-73109-0 (pbk)
ISBN: 978-1-351-12790-5 (ebk)

DOI: 10.4324/9781351127905

Typeset in Sabon
by Newgen Publishing UK

Contents

Figures

Tables

Boxes

Notes on contributors

Teferi Abate Adem is a research anthropologist with Human Relations Area Files (HRAF) at Yale University. His current research encompasses a variety of historical and comparative themes related to household- and community-level responses to climate-change-related extreme weather events, expanding state powers and volatile market forces.

Giovanni Bennardo is Presidential Research Professor in the Department of Anthropology, the Cognitive Studies Initiative, and the Environment, Sustainability, and Energy Institute at Northern Illinois University, DeKalb, IL. He conducted research on the linguistic, cognitive, and cultural representations of spatial relationships in Tonga, Western Polynesia. His current interest is the investigation of primary ontological categories as organized in foundational cultural models.

Leandro Mahalem de Lima is an associate researcher at the *Centro de Estudos Ameríndios* of the University of São Paulo, Brazil, where he received his PhD in social anthropology in 2015. He has conducted ethnographic research among indigenous and traditional riverine dwellers in Brazil's Central Amazon area since 2008.

Victor C. De Munck is professor at the Anthropology Center, sociology faculty at Vytautus Magnus University in Kaunas, Lithuania, as well as at the State University of New York, New Paltz. He is a cognitive, socio-cultural anthropologist who has written a number of books and articles on cultural models and on cross-cultural comparative works on romantic love.

Chisaki Fukushima holds an MA in environmental anthropology from the University of Kent and is currently a PhD researcher in Agriculture, Food and Rural Development at the University of Newcastle, UK. She has carried out fieldwork in Japan and Laos among rice producers and textile producers.

Eric C. Jones is assistant professor of social epidemiology at the University of Texas, Houston, School of Public Health. He has worked in Ecuador with farmers for more than two decades. Much of his work concerns cultural responses to extreme settings.

Stephen M. Lyon is professor of anthropology at the Institute for the Study of Muslim Civilizations, Aga Khan University in London. He has published widely on Pakistani conflict, kinship, social organization, and agriculture. He uses computational analyses to complement traditional ethnographic research.

Muhammad A. Z. Mughal is assistant professor of cultural anthropology at King Fahd University of Petroleum and Minerals and honorary research fellow at Durham University. His research interests include time, space, environment, rural social organization, and social change. Over the last ten years, he has carried out ethnographic and field-based research projects in rural Pakistan.

Anna Paini is associate professor of cultural anthropology at the University of Verona. She received her PhD from the Australian National University, Canberra. She has done extensive fieldwork in Lifou (Loyalty Islands) on gender issues and material culture and, more recently, in the Italian Dolomites on sustainability.

Hidetada Shimizu is associate professor of educational psychology at Northern Illinois University, Dekalb, IL. His research interests are cultural influences on personality and behavioral development in Japan.

Thomas Widlok is professor for cultural anthropology of Africa and currently head of African studies and of the research area Cultures and Societies in Transition at the University of Cologne.

Katharine L. Wiegele is a researcher in the department of anthropology at Northern Illinois University, Dekalb, IL. She has worked and done research in the Philippines since the 1980s on religion and civil society.

Wenyi Zhang is an associate professor at the Department of Anthropology and Center for Medical Humanities, Sun Yat-sen University, China. He is co-author of *Individual and Collective Memory Consolidation* (MIT 2012). He works at the intersection of medical and psychological anthropology and the cognitive sciences.

Introduction

Cultural Models of Nature of primary food producers in communities affected by climate change

Giovanni Bennardo

On March 12–14, 2015, at the Biblioteca Frinzi (Frinzi Library) of the University of Verona, Italy, a workshop was held entitled 'Local Knowledge and Climate Change: Fieldwork Experiences.' The workshop was organized by Giovanni Bennardo (Northern Illinois University) and Anna Paini (University of Verona) and was sponsored by the National Science Foundation (NSF) and by the Dipartimento Culture and Civiltà and the Biblioteca Frinzi, both at University of Verona. Twelve scholars from American, European, and Chinese institutions participated in the workshop. They reported on extensive fieldwork conducted in communities in twelve countries on five continents (see Figure I.1): China, Ecuador, Japan, Kenya, Italy, Lithuania, Namibia, Pakistan, the Philippines, Poland, the Kingdom of Tonga (Polynesia), and the United States.[1] The workshop participants pursued deeper understandings of the cultural models of Nature held in these communities.

The workshop represents a milestone for the project, 'Cultural Models of Nature Across Cultures: Space, Causality, and Primary Food Producers.' This project started in September 2011 with a first NSF-sponsored three-day workshop the results of which were published as a working paper of the ESE Institute at Northern Illinois University and titled *Proceedings of Workshop: Cultural Models of Nature and the Environment: Self, Space, and Causality* (Bennardo, 2012). In June 2013, the resulting research proposal was funded by NSF (BCS 1330637). During summer 2014,[2] the scholars involved in the project conducted research at their respective field sites and, once back at their institutions, systematically processed and analyzed the data. This volume contains the results of the analyses conducted by nine of the twelve scholars who presented and discussed their research in the workshop at the University of Verona. It also contains the results of the analyses of two additional scholars who had not completed their work yet—in Ethiopia and in Amazonian Brazil—when the workshop was held.

The NSF-sponsored research project

The NSF-sponsored research project entitled 'Cultural Models of Nature Across Cultures: Space, Causality, and Primary Food Producers' is

DOI: 10.4324/9781351127905-1

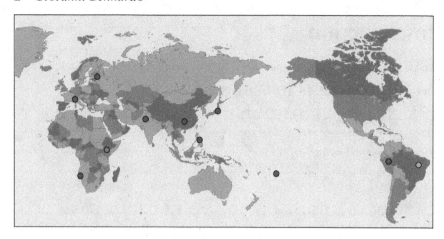

Figure I.1 Field sites.

investigating cultural models of Nature across several cultures held by populations/communities of primary food producers such as farmers, fishermen, herders, and hunter-gatherers all affected by climate change. I capitalize *Nature* when the word refers to the cultural model we are investigating. I want to draw attention to the fact that capitalized *Nature* and lower case *nature* have two distinct meanings. The latter is typically intended to mean a specific part and type of the environment (e.g., woods, rivers, mountains, etc.) or some biologically given aspect of existence (i.e., instinct), while the former may include all that exists. Capitalized *Nature* then is a concept that is close to what is traditional called a 'worldview.'

Evidence suggests that cultural models of Nature influence environmental actions in ways not necessarily predicted by more traditional ecological models (see Kempton, Boster, and Hartley, 1995; Atran and Medin, 2008). While traditional ecological knowledge typically tends to freeze knowledge in the past, cultural models affect attention, observation, reasoning, and understanding and therefore engage with the current situation.

Climate change is one of the most challenging issues we collectively face insofar as it threatens the survival of our species. Before long, extensive action will have to be implemented worldwide to minimize its potential and disastrous effects (such actions have already been initiated in the last two decades). The populations keenly aware of and most at risk from the effects of climate change are obviously those whose livelihood depends on daily contact with the changing physical environment. Primary food producers best represent these populations: farmers, fishermen, herders, and hunter-gatherers. Of course all humans are at risk, and we will eventually be obliged to change our behavior to make our presence on the planet sustainable (see Moran, 2006, 2010). However, primary food producers' daily and close contact with the physical environment makes them most directly affected by climate change. Besides, they will likely be asked to implement whatever new and/or radical remedial policies are proposed. Before carrying out any strategies directly impacting these populations, it would be prudent to understand their cultural models of Nature.

All primary food producers hold views—mostly out-of-awareness (Kempton, 2001), as most of our knowledge is (e.g., knowledge about language)—about nature and the physical environment, particularly in terms of how they are affected by and must adapt to changes in the latter. Such out-of-awareness knowledge structures are typically called cultural models (Holland and Quinn, 1987).

One of the most widely accepted ways of understanding the organization of knowledge in the mind is that of mental models (Johnson-Laird, 1980, 1999). When a mental model comes to be shared within a community, then one calls it a 'cultural model' (Holland and Quinn, 1987; D'Andrade, 1989; Shore, 1996; Strauss and Quinn, 1997; Quinn, 2005; Kronenfeld, 2008; Bennardo, 2009; Bennardo and De Munck, 2014). These out-of-awareness mental structures are used to make deductions about the world, to explain relationships in a causal fashion, and to construct and interpret representations from simple perceptual inputs to highly complex information. Importantly, they can also motivate behavior (D'Andrade and Strauss, 1992; Kempton, Boster, and Hartley, 1995; Atran and Medin, 2008), or more precisely, contribute saliently to the generation of behavior. In other words, we use cultural models to make sense of the world around us and at the same time they provide the basis out of which we plan our behavior (see also Paolisso, 2002).

A significant characteristic of this research project is the adoption of Cultural Models Theory and the use of the logically resulting methodology—for data collection and for data analysis—by all the participating scholars. One of the advantages of this fundamental feature of the project that generated the results reported in this volume is that the results for each community is comparable across all the investigated communities, that is, cultures.

Cultural Models Theory

We chose to look into the local knowledge of primary food producers affected by climate change through the lens of Cultural Models Theory. This theory allows us to address culture as knowledge, which is exactly the focus of our research. A fundamental assumption of Cultural Models Theory is that the locus of culture is the mind of the individual (Goodenough, 1957). A mind consists of operations and processes that work with a set of representations. Mental representations have content and, at the same time, they realize and induce processes. A mental representation, that is, a mental model, is a model of a part of perceived reality and as such it is a reduction of the part of the world it represents. These models/reductions by necessity retain aspects of the structures they represent (Johnson-Laird, 1980, 1983, 1999). Therefore, mental models are structured. Consequently, they are made out of units that have relationships to each other. These relationships vary in type, for example, sequential, taxonomic, or causal.

Another fundamental property of mental models is that they consist of core and periphery parts (Minsky, 1975). The periphery comes into contact with contexts that could change its value/s, while the core is less prone to change. If context does not provide sufficient input to set a new value of the periphery, then a default (previously obtained) value is assigned. Mental models are typically out-of-awareness and may participate in the construction of larger models via nesting. When a mental model is assumed to be held by members of a community, then it is a cultural model (D'Andrade, 1989, 1995; Strauss and Quinn, 1997; Bennardo and Kronenfeld, 2011). To be considered 'cultural,' models also need to be socially transmitted and carry some socially coercive force (Gatewood, 2014). From these assumptions, we can make a few deductions about cultural models:

- Cultural models are mostly out-of-awareness because mental models typically are;
- There are minimally two types of cultural models: (a) foundational, which are simpler and based on ontological domains (e.g., space, time, relationship, etc.), and (b) molar, which are complex and may include foundational ones and knowledge from other domains (Bennardo and de Munck, 2014);
- Individual variation in the construction of cultural models is a consequence of their nature and how they interact with context (ontogenesis);
- Cultural variation within communities is also a result of the nature of cultural models (their core and periphery structure) and how they interact with contexts, that is, group and/or individual experiences;
- A cultural model is considered the unit of investigation of culture.

Cultural Models Theory and methodology

Adopting Cultural Models Theory as a way of conceiving culture leads to a specific methodological path that requires the acquisition of three types of data: ethnographic, linguistic, and cognitive (see Figure I.2, also Bennardo and de Munck, 2014). All the authors in this volume have extensive ethnographic knowledge and ongoing experience of the community they have investigated. This knowledge has been supplemented by further participant-observation, nature walks, and open-ended interviews focusing on cultivated fields, subsistence gatherings areas, pastures or marine habitats depending on the type of food production, for example, horticulture, herding, fishing. During these walks or outings, the researcher conducts informal, thematically driven interviews. Through this activity, scholars focused the

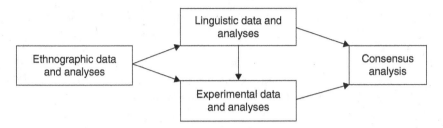

Figure I.2 Methodological trajectory (Bennardo and de Munck).

ethnographic lens on the topic at hand while eliciting language related to the natural environment. Ethnographic knowledge is considered a necessary prerequisite to the other methodological steps and an essential part of the data-analysis process.

Gathering linguistic data is justified by the common understanding that language represents the 'highway' into the mind (see Strauss and Quinn, 1997). Semi-structured interviews are administered to a sample of the community. The major justification for such a move is rooted in the nature of cultural models that by definition are shared within the members of a community. Then, asking the same questions to the chosen sample should make likely the elicitation of the model. The interviews are about daily food-producing activities because talking about them is supposed to activate the interviewee's cultural model of Nature as they explain the activities and their beliefs about them (see Bennardo, 2012: 126, and Appendix). In other words, we chose not to ask participants directly about the cultural model investigated (see D'Andrade, 2005). After all, also by definition, the interviewees hold cultural models mostly out-of-awareness.

As important as language is in exploring the mental organization of knowledge, that is, cultural models, analyzing linguistic production does not exhaust all the possibilities in exploring the mind. Cognitive tasks should be administered to obtain further data. Some tasks allow one to explore memory (free listing tasks), other tasks explore categorization (sorting tasks), yet other tasks allow one to investigate the organization of knowledge strategies (drawing tasks), and others the assignment and establishment of relationships (rating tasks), for example, causality. Free listing tasks were completed, and results of their analyses are reported by almost all the authors in this volume. Other tasks are planned to be used in the future when the research project is eventually continued and brought to its necessary conclusion.

A number of analyses of the ethnographic and linguistic data collected follow their acquisition. The scholars analyzed ethnographic data, including inferences about relationships that were not explicitly stated. For example, when a Tongan subsistence farmer states that *taro* (among other crops) must be planted with full moon, we infer that the moon (physical environment) and *taro* (plant) are related in some significant way. The same is true for Amazonian farmers who only plant during waxing moon.

The transcriptions of the semi-structured interviews[3] are analyzed at the word, sentence, and discourse level. The analysis strategies employed include the finding of key words via a frequency analyses of the words in all the interviews. The top most frequent and salient words—relevant to the topic investigated, that is, Nature in our case—are then used for a semantic role analysis (sentence level). That is, it is determined if each of the words selected is used in the 'agent' or 'patient' role. This analysis provides insights into the role(s) that various words—related to the six components of Nature, plants, animals, physical environment, weather, people, and supernatural or local adaptations of these components—play within the interviewees' construction of their linguistic production as molded by their cultural model of Nature. Thus, a first insight into the content and structure of the cultural model sought for begins to emerge.

The next linguistic analysis is about metaphors used (sentence level). The frequency of the various types of metaphor possible (see Lakoff and Johnson, 1980) provides further insight into the cultural model activated. Moreover, an analysis of the types of source and target of the metaphors used also increases the understanding of which aspects of Nature are most commonly mobilized to 'explain' those parts of the world addressed in their linguistic production. For example, is it animate beings who are used to 'explain' (i.e., source, hence, known) inanimate ones (i.e., target, hence, unknown) or the other way around? What type of animate beings are used? Insights into relationships between aspects of Nature can be obtained by the results of such analysis.

Finally, an analysis of reasoning passages (discourse level), especially those referring to causality, is conducted. The results of this analysis ensure the opportunity to ascertain important relationships established within components of Nature, for example, a plant and another plant, and across components, for example, plants and animals. Since causality is one of the most common type of relationships established among components of the world, it can become the focus of the analysis. Thus, a further insight into the content of the cultural model of Nature is achieved.

The results of the analyses conducted on the ethnographic and linguistic data already provide sufficient ground to formulate a hypothesis about the cultural model of Nature held by the populations under investigation. This hypothesis consists of a number of propositions about the way in which the major components of Nature stand in salient relationships to each other—a causal model could also be arrived at from such content.

The preliminary hypothesis about a cultural model of Nature can be refined and/or confirmed by the results of the analyses of cognitive data. The most frequent words (adjusted frequencies) obtained from the free listing tasks about the components of Nature provide the input for sorting tasks.

The latter are an effective way to elicit overall similarity judgments among a set of items. The sample's aggregate item-by-item similarity matrix is then analyzed using multi-dimensional scaling and cluster analysis. The results of these two analyses supply potential categories as salient constituents of the Culture Model sought for. In fact, they suggest relationships between items within a category or between categories. Thus, they contribute to a necessary refinement of the hypothesis arrived at from the analyses of the ethnographic and linguistic data obtained earlier.

A cultural model of Nature hypothesized by the results of these procedures consists of a list of propositions that need to be validated by other means (D'Andrade, 2005). The propositions form the basis of a fixed-format, 'strongly agree to strongly disagree' questionnaire. Validation of the hypothesized elements of the model is done by univariate analyses of the questionnaire's items. Finally, because culture is seldom distributed uniformly among individuals in a community (see Kempton and Clark, 2000; Gatewood and Lowe, 2008; Atran and Medin, 2008), the degree to which cultural models of Nature are shared, and the degree to which they differentially motivate people to act is assessed through a consensus analysis on the questionnaire data.

This methodological trajectory just presented represents an ideal one to implement when searching for cultural models in a specific community/population/culture (Bennardo and De Munck, 2014). Keeping this methodological trajectory in mind, the authors of the chapters in this volume have all conducted ethnographic, linguistic, and cognitive data collections and analyses, each representing a unique assemblage of a specific deployment of a number of methodological tools. All the authors end their methodological excursus by reaching enough insights into the community investigated such that a strong hypothesis about a commonly held cultural model of Nature could be advanced. We are convinced that additional research in the near future would add further support to the hypotheses formulated.

Causal models in Cultural Models of Nature

The authors in this volume hypothesize a variety of cultural models of Nature found in the communities investigated. These cultural models represent specific organizations of the ethically suggested constitutive categories underlying the concept of Nature, that is, plants, animals, physical environment, weather, humans, and the supernatural. Causal relationships are one of the major forces weaving together these categories. When presenting hypotheses about a cultural model of Nature in the communities investigated, many scholars characterize the internal causal structure of the cultural model by making reference to and at times refining one or more of the three causal models suggested by Bennardo (2014) (for causal models see also Sloman, 2009; Rips, 2011).

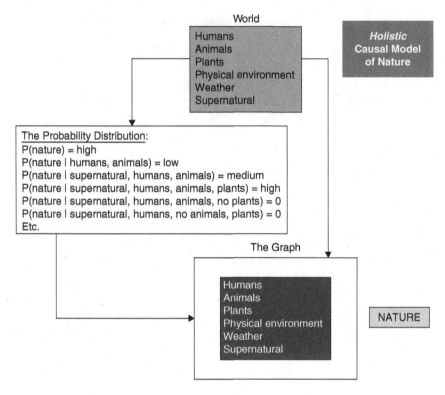

Figure I.3   Holistic CM of Nature (Bennardo).

The three causal models suggested in Bennardo (2014) are the *Holistic* model (see Figure I.3), the *God-Centered* model (see Figure I.4), and the *God-Humans-Centered* model (see Figure I.5). The *Holistic* causal model in Figure I.3 is based on 'The Probability Distribution'—obtained from descriptions of cultural models of Nature in Kempton, Boster, and Hartley (1995), Selin (2003), and Atran and Medin (2008)—of the six components[4] of Nature or the 'World.' Notice, that the more of the six components that are co-present, the higher the level of positive probability for the construction of the concept of Nature becomes. The causal model is then represented in the box labeled 'The Graph,' that is, the concept of Nature. For this holistic model, Nature includes all the six components insofar as no clear separation among them is conceived as probable: This conclusion is drawn from the content of 'The Probability Distribution.'

The *God-Centered* causal model in Figure I.4 is based on a different probability distribution. For example, the probability increases when the 'supernatural' is present, but it disappears when it is absent. The graph makes clear that the 'supernatural' component of the 'World' is separate from the other components when the concept of Nature is constructed.

The *God-Humans-Centered* causal model in Figure I.5 is based on a third type of probability distribution. The presence of 'supernatural' or both

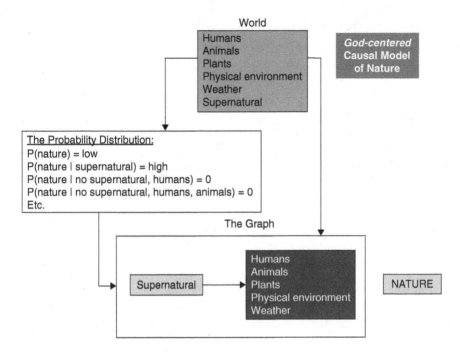

Figure I.4 God-centered CM of Nature (Bennardo).

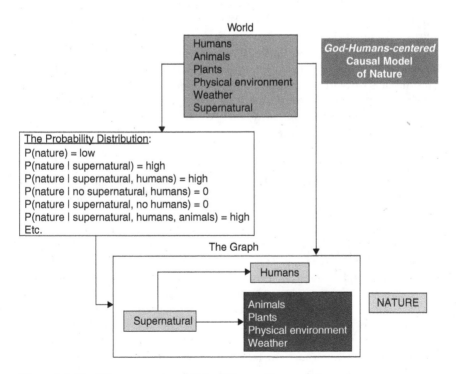

Figure I.5 God/Human-centered CM of Nature (Bennardo).

'supernatural' and 'humans' increases the probability while the absence of either of them makes the probability cease to exist. The graph makes clear that both the 'supernatural' and the 'humans' component of the 'World' are independently separate from the other ones when this concept of Nature is constructed.

The content of the cultural models of Nature hypothesized for the communities investigated by the contributors to this volume, have allowed us to expand this preliminary proposal. In fact, three new articulations of types of relationships among the basic components of Nature have emerged. The expanded typology of causal models is presented in the Conclusion chapter.

The chapters and the hypothesized Cultural Models of Nature

The chapters in this volume appear in alphabetical order by author. Each researcher first introduces the field site, that is, the community within which the collection of the data was conducted. Then, the methodology used is discussed in detail. Later, the results of the analyses on the data collected are presented and examined. Finally, the authors conclude by advancing a hypothesis about the cultural model of Nature discovered within the community investigated.

Before introducing the content of the various chapters, including the cultural models of Nature hypothesized by the authors, I want to point out that a number of commonalities emerged among the findings. First, members of all the communities investigated perceived changes in their climate-change-affected environment. Second, these changes were typically explained 'locally' and rarely related to 'global' causes. And third, many of the cultural models of Nature contained internal contradictions that often led the researchers to indicate the presence of two or more cultural models used within individuals or across individuals in any specific community. A more extensive discussion of these and other commonalities is presented in the Conclusion chapter.

In Chapter 1, Adem ethnographically explores the ways drought-prone farmers in Ethiopia's South Wollo region perceive and respond to increased variability in the timing, amount, duration, and spatial distribution of rainfall during the growing wet season. The vernacular explanation of farmers suggests a god-centered cultural model of Nature in which rainfall and all other economically useful natural resources, notably plants, animals, land and water, are perceived as divine gifts to humans from an all-powerful and omnipresent God, 'Allah.' This understanding has led a unanimous perception of the underlying causes of rainfall variability as divine acts. Yet, these farmers avoid fatalistic explanations of their vulnerability to perceived negative impacts by underscoring two complementary ways by which humans influence divine acts. The first involves pragmatic, household-level, agronomic responses fine-tuned to landscape-level variations in altitude, topography, biotic diversity, soil types, and moisture conditions. The other is seeking Allah's mercy through village-wide rain-making prayers and communal observances, as well as invoking the help of 'mediating agencies,' such as angels, saints, holy men, sheiks, guardian, and ancestral spirits, and other invisible sacred beings.

In Chapter 2, Bennardo suggests the following minimal content of the cultural model of Nature for Tongans:

(1) Humans, plants, animals (mammals, birds, and fish), physical environment, and weather belong together;

(2) While humans belong with these components of Nature, they may also act on them and change them;

(3) Supernatural/God is not separated from other components of Nature, but is everywhere and also Supernatural/God is separated from nature, and masters nature—that is, plants, animals, physical environment, weather, and humans.

This hypothesis contains some issues that need to be pointed out. First, humans seem to be thought of as belonging together with any other component of Nature. However, they are also conceived of as acting on and changing plants, animals, and the physical environment, thereby appearing to be thought of as separate from these latter. Second, the immanence of the supernatural, that is, being one with any other component of Nature, is contrasted with its 'separation' from the other components, which allows 'causing' within the expressed 'mastering.' Third, in pursuing a resolution to the above-stated issues, it would be useful to keep in mind the Polynesian (and Tongan) traditional concept of *mana* or 'vital force.' This concept was and is deeply related to a conceptualization of all the components of Nature as holistically related. In spite of a hundred and fifty years of Christianity, the persistence of such a way of thinking in Tonga has been documented (see Bennardo, 2009: 188–189).

In Chapter 3, De Lima hypothesizes a cultural model of Nature for Amazonians with the following contents: (1) God, father above all, created everything, it is everywhere, and punishes his creatures if they act badly; (2) Below god, what belongs to humans contrasts with what exists in nature; (3) Everything in nature have specific mothers or owners that live beneath water and soil environments, and may help/punish 'people' if they do not take care or destroy nature; (4) Within soil and water environments, humans live between the 'inside-outside' (of the river/lake), and 'center/periphery' (of the forest). The house is thought as a 'center' around which other human environments radiate from, in the midst of 'nature'; (5) Destructive acts upon nature are commonly described as caused by greedy people; (6) Climate changes are mainly attributed to deforestation, and its effects are being especially felt by plants because the soils are poorer, the days are warmer, the rains are scarcer, the droughts are harsher, the forests are drier, the manioc roots are weaker and threatened to cook under the now hot soil.

In Chapter 4, De Munck states that Lithuanian farmers have adapted to being subject to the regulations and benefits of belonging to the EU and points out their sense of identity in relationship to their farms and nature. In his research it became clear that farmers had a distinctive but overlapping model of farmland and nature. Their models of both overlapped in that farmland was also nature but nature was not only farmland. Farmers also had two distinctive identities in relation to these dual conceptions of nature. As farmers they conceived of themselves as industrious and feeders of the nation; in their non-farming role nature was viewed as it is for most all Lithuanians as all encompassing and revitalizing. Farmers noted that climate was changing but viewed it pragmatically and locally in terms of how to adapt to these changes rather than as ideologically and globally.

In Chapter 5, Jones hypothesizes a cultural model of Nature for people from a farming village near Cotacachi, Ecuador. He explores causality and relationships between humans, plants, animals, the supernatural, weather, and features of the biophysical environment, as well as the relative importance of each of those domains and their components. The goal is to understand through what cultural lenses these food producers understand environmental change. Results suggest that Nature—with care of soil, responsibility to others, and attention to the Earth Mother at its core—can exist without cities and without the Christian God. Dividing the spirit world between Christian spirits and Earth Mother, as well as dividing humans between urbanites and rural dwellers, may generate more than one cultural model of Nature, may cause cognitive dissonance and may be supported by common Christian and Western/urban dualisms. However, these divisions also allow people to switch from one way of life to another, and to invoke the cultural model that is appropriate for a given setting. This may also be a consequence of the social and ecological changes these farmers are experiencing.

In Chapter 6, Lyon and Mughal present a coherent cultural model that reflects local farmers' concept of nature in Attock District, Punjab, Pakistan. Local farmers in northern Punjab do not spontaneously articulate a bounded concept of 'Nature' (*kudruti mahole*), but have clear ideas about the relationship between the Divine (Allah), the natural resources around them and the moral, political and economic positions of people. This ideal relationship spells out the incumbent responsibilities and opportunities of people in their natural environments and provides explanatory narratives for good and ill fortune. Leveraging local knowledge to better implement agricultural interventions is challenging, but they argue critical for the development of sustainable food production and environmental stewardship at a time of steadily degrading environments with rising populations across Punjab. They conclude by arguing that understanding local interpretations of global doctrines of Islam, along with folk understandings of *kudruti mahole* 'Nature,' provides a valuable base model for a generative cultural model of Nature.

In Chapter 7, Paini discusses how the people of Vinigo, a mountain village situated in the Dolomites (Italian Alps), perceive changes in their environment. She also provides indications on how villagers interpret the effects of these changes. In their reasoning, they attribute agency to elements of the close physical environment and stress engagement, both symmetrical and asymmetrical, and interaction with them. They indicate the causes that have brought about these changes and the risks involved as well as their anxieties about the future. They perceive their environment as filtered by local knowledge which highlights salient reciprocal and asymmetrical relationships among fundamental components of Nature such as humans, plants, and animals. Paini suggests the following initial components of a cultural model of Nature for the Dolomitic community she investigated: (1) A reciprocal relationship between humans and woodland, this latter being a mixture of physical environment and plants—if humans take care of woodland, woodland gives back to humans; (2) A non reciprocal relationship between woodland and wild animals—increased woodland fosters the presence of more wild animals; (3) A unilateral relationship between weather and agricultural produce (plants) and human activities, that is, weather affects these latter, but these latter do not affect weather.

In Chapter 8, Shimizu and Fukushima state that the Japanese word for nature, *shizen* (自然), has two basic meanings: To be 'natural,' that is, to be 'spontaneously or naturally so' (Tucker, 2003: 161); and that which pertains to the natural world, that is, the environment and creatures in it (Tucker, 2003; Shimizu, 2012). Consequently, they generate a hypothesis about what constitutes 'natural' (meaning 1) ways to produce foods via 'nature' (meaning 2). Using both meanings, they propose a cultural model in which they state that 'nature' is not 'natural' until it is 'humanized.' An analogy here may be that of creating a *bonsai* tree, the art of producing miniature trees that 'mimic' the way they 'naturally' grow. This view contrasts with the two other alternative views, that nature is 'below' human to be used as *the means to* achieve utilitarian gain, or 'above' them in that it is too powerful and beyond human control (e.g., natural disasters).

In Chapter 9, Widlok reports on field research in Namibia, contextualized in the region of sub-Saharan Africa at large. Based on this empirical work with rural people in the region, the problems of connecting scientific interests in 'climate' and 'nature' with local experiences of weather and the environment are being highlighted. The case material suggests that local models of nature are not limited to the spatial dimension but also include ways of conceiving time and the future. Moreover, the distinction that is commonly made between the natural environmental change and man-made change is problematized. By revisiting the distinction between 'wild' and 'domesticated' in the light of the case study, the author also suggests that it is appropriate to broaden our understanding of 'cultivation,' 'culture,' and 'cultural models.'

In Chapter 10, Wiegele presents components of a cultural model of Nature held by fishermen in two communities in the Verde Island Passage,

Philippines. The components reflect the complex mix of traditions and contemporary situations of these people who have multiple historical and cultural influences. In addition, the fishermen in these two communities have vastly different experiences with their environments in terms of preservation, degradation, and changing weather patterns that present serious challenges to their livelihood in different ways. The cultural model she presents suggests that the major components of Nature (humans, plants, animals, weather, physical environment, and the supernatural) are related to each other holistically. In this approach humans are the source of a personification metaphor that explains how Nature in general and the earth (holistically) works—through cycles of life moving naturally from young to old (to death), or cycles of life that involve continuous regeneration. God may act through nature (especially the weather and the earth in general) and the weather or the earth may have a 'life' of its own; either way they have moods and emotions that parallel those of humans. Furthermore, people, God, and other supernatural entities are connected reciprocally in a variety of ways to the physical environment (geographical features, plants, and weather), and animals (including fish). Even global concepts such as 'the earth' and 'the climate' are at times conceived in human terms.

In Chapter 11, Zhang examines how the ethnic Kachin in Southwest China conceive of nature and environment. He begins with the local scheme of time that captures the causal relationships among people, the supernatural, and physical environment into a rhythmic pattern. The Kachin seek a synchronization between these rhythms and their activities: The seasonal rhythm defines their activities within a year, and the local divination table specifies those within a day. Such a synchronization can be easily broken by human desires that expand excessively. The Kachin have also developed techniques to maintain, or to make up, synchronization through the local tradition of animal sacrifice. In bad situations, when synchronization has been broken too deeply, nature will move away, and humans are left behind.

Relevance of the volume

The content of the chapters contained in this volume significantly contribute to and enrich the already conspicuous literature about cultural models. Specifically, they all focus on cultural models of Nature in many and diverse communities of primary food producers. This common focus allows comparison across these communities located in extremely different environmental contexts on six continents. Interesting similarities emerged and are presented in the Conclusion chapter. Local peculiarities in cultural models of Nature held also emerged and both findings point towards a rich and varied set of beliefs and behaviors that members of these communities hold when confronted with the effects of climate change.

The tripartite methodological trajectory required by the adoption of Cultural Models Theory and uniquely implemented by the researchers follows the suggestion by Bennardo and De Munck (2014: 286) that recommends such a trajectory as being the necessary procedure to discover cultural models. The results of the various projects conducted support that trajectory as appropriately conducive to that discovery. None of the researchers used the suggested trajectory in its entirety. However, relevant aspects of its content were implemented. Above all, the necessity of the acquisition of extensive ethnographic knowledge turned out to be of paramount importance. Similarly, the analyses (and their results) on the acquired linguistic data were the most productive methodological steps in arriving at solid hypotheses about cultural models of Nature. Cognitive data (e.g., free listing) as well showed how crucial they are in constructing, verifying, and validating hypotheses.

Scholars, policy makers, and lay individuals who actively conduct research on, and pursue solutions to, climate-change-induced-problems, a challenging species-survival issue, should benefit from the information on local cultural models of Nature contained in the chapters included in this volume. In fact, we are convinced that cultural models of Nature contribute to the generation of a variety of behaviors in response to environmental changes in food-producing communities worldwide. Then, it follows that this information should be regarded as highly valuable and can assist policymakers in their decision-making (see Kempton, 2001; Lauer and Aswani, 2009). Taking this knowledge into consideration is essential for the planning and implementation of any successful intervention projects in climate-change-affected areas. In other words, the research results presented can contribute in fostering sound policies based not only on decontextualized scientific notions, but grounded in the local knowledge of the people directly responsible for adopting any suggested modifications to their daily practices and very likely already engaged in the generation of solutions.

Appendix

Semi-structured interview

Questions about daily activities

Personal questions precede the following ones:
1. Describe your work/job (which relates to primary food production).
2. What is your typical work/work day?
3. What is the rhythm of work in this area ... or actual activities?
4. What are some of the essential knowledge, skills, experience you need to be a successful food producer?
5. What are considered 'productive activities'?
6. Which fields/sea areas/etc. are productive?
7. What affects productivity? What forces have an influence on production success?

8. What is meant by growth; why do plants grow?
9. What are the key decisions one must make to be successful?
10. What information do you need to make decisions?
11. How do you choose what crops to grow, what to fish, what to go after?
12. What are some of the constraints/problems you face as a food producer?
13. Who or what affects your environment (fields, forest, sea, etc.) the most?
14. What is the worst/best thing humans can do in fishing/farming/etc.?
15. What do you like/not like about what you're doing (satisfaction)?

Questions about climate change

16. What changes have occurred in your work/environment?
17. Why are there these changes/variations?
18. Weather change, how?
19. What can humans do about it?
20. Can humans/human activity affect nature/weather/wind/currents?

Notes

1 A 13th and a 14th site (Ethiopia and Amazon, Brazil) had been added later and the two scholars were not able to report about completed analyses. This volume, though, includes their reports (see Chapters 1 and 3). Also, three scholars are not contributing the results of their research to this volume (Kenya, Poland, and United States).
2 No field work could be conducted in summer 2013 because the NSF funds became available only in September.
3 These texts can be reduced to their gist—and care should be taken in using the interviewees' language when constructing the gist—before starting the linguistic analyses (D'Andrade, 2005). An added benefit of the gist analysis is that the researcher acquires an extensive familiarity with the texts. However, certain type of analysis, e.g., semantic role analysis, are better conducted on the original texts.
4 The components vary with each community investigated, thus making the content of the 'World' vary as well. The components presented are only suggestive of possible ones. The ones that each scholar eventually uses are the ones they discover in their community.

References

Atran, S., and Medin, D. L. (2008). *The Native Mind and the Cultural Construction of Nature*. Boston: MIT Press.

Bennardo, G. (2009). *Language, Space, and Social Relationships: A Foundational Cultural Model in Polynesia*. Cambridge: Cambridge University Press.

Bennardo, G. (ed.). (2012). *Proceedings of Workshop: Cultural Models of Nature and the Environment: Self, Space, and Causality*. Working Paper, 1. DeKalb, IL: ESE, NIU

Bennardo, G. (2014). The fundamental role of causal models in Cultural Models of Nature. *Frontiers in Psychology*. October 10, 2014, http://dx.doi.org/10.3389/fpsyg.2014.01140

Bennardo, G., and De Munck, V. C. (2014). *Cultural Models: Genesis, Methods, and Experiences*. Oxford: Oxford University Press.

Bennardo, G., and Kronenfeld, D. (2011). Types of collective representations: Cognition, mental architecture and cultural knowledge. In Kronenfeld, D., et al. (eds.), *A Companion to Cognitive Anthropology*. Chichester: Wiley, 82–101.

D'Andrade, R. G. (1989). Cultural cognition. In Posner, M. I. (ed.), *Foundations of Cognitive Science*. Cambridge, MA: MIT Press, 795–830.

D'Andrade, R. (1995). *The Development of Cognitive Anthropology*. Cambridge: Cambridge University Press.

D'Andrade, R. (2005). Some methods for studying cultural cognitive structures. In Quinn, N. (ed.), *Finding Culture in Talk: A Collection of Methods*. New York: Palgrave Macmillan, 83–104.

D'Andrade, R., and Strauss, C. (1992). *Human Motives and Cultural Models*. Cambridge: Cambridge University Press.

Gatewood, J. B. (2014). Criteria for regarding group-group differences in cognition as 'cultural' differences. Paper presented at the 10th Annual Meeting of SASci, Albuquerque, March 22.

Gatewood, J. B., and Lowe, J. W. (2008). *Employee Perceptions of Credit Unions: Implications for Member Profitability*. Madison, WI: Filene Research Institute.

Goodenough, W. H. (1957). Cultural anthropology and linguistics. In Garvin, P. (ed.) *Report of the Seventh Annual Roundtable Meeting on Linguistics and Language Study*. Monograph Series on Language and Linguistics No. 9. Washington, DC: Georgetown University Press, 167–173.

Holland, D., and Quinn, N. (1987). Culture and cognition. In Quinn, N. and Holland, D. (eds.), *Cultural Models in Language and Thought*. Cambridge: Cambridge University Press, 3–40.

Johnson-Laird, P. N. (1980). Mental models in cognitive science. *Cognitive Science*, 4: 71–115.

Johnson-Laird, P. N. (1983). *Mental Models: Toward a Cognitive Science of Language, Inference and Consciousness*. Cambridge, MA: Harvard University Press.

Johnson-Laird, P. N. (1999). Mental models. In Wilson, R. A., and Keil, F. C. (eds.), *The MIT Encyclopedia of the Cognitive Sciences*. Cambridge, MA: MIT Press, 525–527.

Kempton, W. (2001). Cognitive anthropology and the environment. In Crumley, C. L (ed.), *New Directions in Anthropology and Environment*. Walnut Creek, CA: AltaMira Press, 49–71.

Kempton, W., Boster, S. J., and Hartley, J. A. (1995). *Environmental Values in American Culture*. Cambridge, MA: MIT Press.

Kempton, W., and Clark, J. (2000). Cultural models of *Pfiesteria*: Toward cultivating more appropriate risk perceptions. *Coastal Management*, 28: 273–285.

Kronenfeld, D. (2008). *Culture, Society, and Cognition: Collective Goals, Values, Action, and Knowledge*. Berlin: Mouton de Gruyter.

Lakoff, G., and Johnson, M. (1980). *Metaphors We Live By*. Chicago: University of Chicago Press.

Lauer, M., and Aswani, S. (2009). Indigenous ecological knowledge as situated practices: Understanding fishers' knowledge in the Western Solomon Islands. *American Anthropologist*, 111(3): 327–329.

Minsky, M. (1975). A framework for representing knowledge. In Winston, P. H. (ed.), *The Psychology of Computer Vision*. New York: McGraw-Hill, 311–377.

Moran, E. F. (2006). *Environmental Social Science: An Introduction to Human Ecological Relations.* Oxford: Blackwell.

Moran, E. F. (2010). *People and Nature: Human-Environment Interactions and Sustainability.* Oxford: Wiley-Blackwell.

Paolisso, M. (2002). Blue crabs and controversy on the Chesapeake Bay: A cultural model for understanding watermen's reasoning about blue crab management. *Human Organization,* 61(3): 226–239.

Quinn, N. (2005). *Finding Culture in Talk: A Collections of Methods.* New York: Palgrave Macmillan.

Rips, L. J. (2011). *Lines of Thought: Central Concepts in Cognitive Psychology.* Oxford: Oxford University Press.

Selin, H. (ed.). (2003). *Nature Across Cultures: Views of Nature and the Environment in Non-Western Cultures.* Dordrecht: Kluwer.

Shimizu, H. (2012). Cultural model of nature and environment in an agricultural region in central Japan: A preliminary proposal. In Bennardo G. (ed.), *Cultural Models of Nature and the Environment: Self, Space, and Causality.* DeKalb: Northern Illinois University, Institute for the Study of the Environment, Sustainability and Energy.

Shore, B. (1996). *Culture in Mind: Cognition, Culture, and the Problem of Meaning.* Oxford: Oxford University Press.

Sloman, S. A. (2009). *Causal Models: How People Think About the World and Its Alternatives.* Oxford: Oxford University Press.

Strauss, C., and Quinn, N. (1997). *A Cognitive Theory of Cultural Meaning.* Cambridge: Cambridge University Press.

Tucker, J. A. (2003). Japanese views of nature and the environment. In Selin, H. (ed.), *Nature Across Cultures: Views of Nature and the Environment in Non-Western Cultures.* Boston: Kluwer.

1 Vernacular explanations of rainfall variability in highland Ethiopia

Teferi Abate Adem

Introduction

Small-holder farmers in the drought-prone Ethiopian highlands, like others living in the arid and semi-arid parts of Africa, have a range of economic strategies and communal rituals that help them, to varying degree of effectiveness, adapt to rainfall fluctuations (Rahmato, 1991; Castro, 2012). Along with a predicted increase in the intensity of climate-change-induced extreme rainfall events (IPCC, 2014), there is a growing concern that the adaptive limits of local responses will be reached, posing serious challenges to the well-being of rural peoples (Béné et al., 2012). With few exceptions, however, there is very little written about how farmers themselves perceive, and hope to mitigate, increased climate variability. This chapter addresses this question by focusing on the ways Amharic-speaking farmers in two South Wollo (Ethiopia) villages think and talk about variability in the timing, amount, duration, and spatial distribution of rainfall during, as well as across, their respective crop-growing wet seasons.

The broad thesis I examined in this research project is that farmers' perception of the causes of increased rainfall variability, as well as possible remedies, is quite different from the dominant global narrative of climate scientists and policymakers. Specifically, the chapter shows that most farmers, while acknowledging increased deviation from the expected normal in the onset, duration, and intensity of the growing wet seasons, do not think of this pattern as an outcome of meteorologically observable acts in global climate change and climate variability. Instead, they think of rainfall as a divine gift to humans from an omnipresent Creator, Allah, and understand the underlying causes of rainfall variability as beyond the ability of ordinary farmers.

The chapter traces this vernacular perception of rainfall to two complementary sources of knowledge that, together, comprise Wollo farmers' cultural model of Nature, broadly encompassing all six constitutive components of Nature, namely plants, animals, physical environment, weather, humans, and supernatural forces, which Bennardo suggested in the Introduction of this volume. The first source used to understand their cultural model of

DOI: 10.4324/9781351127905-2

Nature is farmers' cumulative phenomenological experience and intimate knowledge of rainfall variability and related weather events across local landscapes that vary in altitude, topography, biotic diversity, soil types, and moisture conditions. The second source is a more general, religiously colored, understanding of the biophysical nature as consisting of different landscapes, each imbued with supernatural forces. This understanding, which reveals continuity of elements of traditional Oromo-Amhara religious practices, suggests that rural communities are varyingly endowed, not just with economically valued natural resources, but also with degree of mystical protection they each enjoy from adverse rainfall and related climatic calamities. Presumed differences in mystical protection are in turn associated with variations in each community's ability to mitigate erratic rains by praying to the Creator, both directly and through the intercession of a hierarchy of mediators. The latter include angels, saints, *waliy* 'holy men,' *awaki* 'men of knowledge,' and *kole* 'guardian spirits of places and/or revered ancestors.'

Study area

Much of the data informing this study were collected during fieldwork among Amharic-speaking rain-fed farmers in the South Wollo area of Ethiopia. This area has long been part of Ethiopia's plow-based intensive agricultural system, which has sustained substantial populations over many centuries (McCann, 1995). Ironically, it was also the epicenter of cyclical famines including the tragic famines of 1973/1974 and 1984/1985 (Woldemariam, 1984; Rahmato, 1991). Famines of such magnitude have lately become rare, thanks to improved early-warning systems and government-provided safety-net and asset-protection programs (Berhane et al., 2011; Little, 2013). However, seasonal agricultural shocks—including prolonged droughts, poorly timed rains, frosts, and crop pests—remain important challenges to millions of farmers (Dercon et al., 2005; Castro, 2012).

The two South Wollo villages chosen for this study are located at different altitudinal gradients. The first village, hereafter called the 'highland' for shorthand, is located in a moderately cold zone locally called *dega*, 'Afro-alpine highland.' The second, hereafter called the 'lowland,' is nested in a low-lying isolated valley locally classified as *kola*, 'hot lowland.' The elevation ranges from about twenty-five hundred meters above sea level in the first to below two thousand in the second (Woldemariam, 1991).

This vertical difference is undoubtedly associated with further variation in other agro-ecological features, including timing and duration of the main growing season, plus crop diversity. In normal years, farmers in the highland village cultivate twice, using rains in both *belg*, 'spring,' from February to May, *kirmet*, 'summer,' from June to September. By contrast, the lowland village relies solely on summer rains. Compared to the highland, the topography in the lowland village is relatively flat and extensively cultivated. Although moisture-stressed, the soils are extremely fertile, conducive for cultivating a wide variety of crops, including teff, maize, sorghum, wheat, barley, horse beans, cow peas, chickpeas, lentils, and fenugreek. Separated from the neighboring village by a dry stream, the village consists of 60 household units, clustered into 4 neighborhood groups inhabited by closely related families.

The highland village consists of 56 homesteads, horizontally distributed along the middle slope of a low, rising mountain range. Each household owns patches of plots vertically scattered between swampy fields along the valley below the homesteads and the dry grounds on the summit above. As in other highland areas of South Wollo, a majority of these households suffer from chronic food insecurity, that is, they do not produce enough food to feed themselves year round (Negatu, 2006). Studies attribute this difficulty to many factors, most notably ill-advised rural development programs (Woldemariam, 1984). Yet, farmers and local government officials alike often single out erratic rains as the most important factor to blame. To an extent, this claim is valid. The rains in this village, as in some other parts of northeastern Ethiopia, tend to be unreliable for crop cultivation as they are too scattered and few in the spring (Mesay, 2006; Rosell and Holmer, 2007) and extremely heavy and intense in the summer (Bewket and Conway, 2007; Rosell and Holmer, 2015; Alemayehu and Bewket, 2017).

Despite these variations in their growing seasons and degree of food self-sufficiency, the two villages share many historical and sociocultural features in common. While Amharic-speaking and predominantly Muslim, residents of both villages are descendants of Oromo lineages that settled in the area as part of a larger northward expansion of various Oromo communities beginning in the sixteenth century.[1] More relevant for this study, each village comprises the smallest unit of an all-inclusive residence-based community, called *qire*, widely known outside South Wollo as *iddir*, and commonly translated in English as 'burial society' (Pankhurst and Hailemariam, 2000; Pankhurst, 2001; Hoddinott et al., 2009). While primarily concerned with helping members in times of death, the *qire* in both villages also functions as a collective action group that coordinates village-wide responses against common threats. In times of prolonged droughts or other rainfall=related threats, for example, the *qire*—led by an elected man addressed as *qire dagna* 'judge of the *qire*'—organizes communal prayers and sacrificial rites. Specific responsibilities of the *qire dagna* include collecting contributions from individual members and visiting *awaki* 'men of knowledge' on behalf of the *qire*. In doing so, the *qire dagna* relies on the support of knowledgeable neighbors and other helpers.

Data collection

Ethnographic fieldwork in two South Wollo villages was conducted for three weeks in 2016, from March 17 through April 6. Additional interviews were conducted in the summers of 2016 and 2017.[2] I chose these two villages for two main reasons. The first was the nature of the villages which, as mentioned above, vary in their growing seasons and crop diversity, while being similar in other features. The commonalities include type of agriculture (rain-fed crop cultivation using oxen-drawn plows), language (Amharic), and religion (predominantly Islam). Although hardly a perfect laboratory, this context provides unique opportunities for examining possible variations in farmers' perception of rainfall variability by minimizing other factors. The second main reason for the selection of these sites was the need to collect reliable data on otherwise intimately personal and communally guarded cultural practices such as prayers and sacrificial rites. I was raised in both villages, undertaking a range of agricultural activities expected of any child of my age and gender. More relevant to the goals of this research, I still maintain close relations with family members and relatives in both villages. As I show below, building on this unique experience has enabled me to develop a more nuanced understanding of the ways farmers think and talk about nature and the environment in general and rainfall variability in particular.

In each village, I employed three major data-collection strategies. The first strategy consisted of transect-walks around homesteads, as well as informal gathering places in each village to meet and greet as many people as possible. While inside a homestead, I used the opportunity to ask brief questions about many things that caught my attention, including animals in shady pens, straw from the latest harvest heaped in a corner, and activities in which specific individuals happened to be engaged at the moment. As it later became evidently clear while I was writing up my field notes that the responses I gathered were dominated by themes that have to do with the challenges households face due to negative impacts of climate variability, most notably extreme variability in the timing, duration, amount, and spatial coverage of the rainy season.

The second data-collection strategy combined both impromptu brief interviews and focused group discussions. Some of my informative conversations were with relatives and family friends—including some from outside the two villages—who came to greet me. As an expression of appreciation, I returned the visits, which gave me the opportunity to engage in follow-up conversations. Other conversations occurred when I joined neighbors and extended family members as they gathered to drink coffee together or sat in a common place to spend time. During my second and third visits, however, I ran focus-group discussions with members deliberately selected to include household heads who varied by age, gender, wealth, and participation in village leadership and community affairs. The purpose of each focus group was to understand the ways farmers talk and think about nature and the environment in general and rainfall variability in particular. I gathered such data from nine focus groups. Group members ranged from three to seven and the discussion lasted between thirty minutes and two hours.

The third data-collection strategy involved more detailed individual interviews with selected informants. I interviewed a total of 18 individuals in each village in the privacy of either their own home or in the place where I was staying. The interviewees were adult men and women, but an attempt was made to balance representation by paying attention to locally used wealth ranks, social standing, age, and degrees of participation in community affairs. As in the focus-group discussion, each interview started with broad questions about changes in the local landscape and the environment. I asked follow-up questions whenever rainfall or something important about the negative impacts of climatic factors were mentioned.

In each village, my interviewees included former and current *qire* leaders who provided me with rich data for reconstructing some of the communal rain prayers they helped organize. This information was especially helpful in the highland village where, as I discuss below, an annual 'spring prayer' has been regularly held on the first Thursday of January. In addition to answering specific questions uniformly asked of all other key informants, *qire* leaders in both villages kindly provided me with important information on the organization of village-wide periodic and aperiodic rainfall prayers, fasts, and sacrificial rituals.

Data analysis

To capture farmers' perceptions of rainfall variability within, as well as across, each wet season, I draw on analysis of key expressions and institutionalized practices I came across during interviews and discussions. Beginning with the wet season immediately prior to the study as a benchmark, I specifically focused on understanding the meanings, household-level coping strategies, and village-wide rain-making rituals respondents in both villages mentioned when answering three questions.

The first question asked about the timing of the normal wet season. Specifically, I asked the particular month or weeks in the month in which the wet season's rains are expected to start and end. The goal was to establish the expected rainfall cycle in each village. The second question encompassed a set of follow-up probes on whether farmers felt that the wet season deviated from the expected in its onset (starting time), duration (time span), cessation (manner of ending), and total amount of rain received. Overlapping with the above two, the third question specifically focused on farmers' perception of the frequency, intensity, and geographical distribution of individual rainfall episodes within the wet seasons.

Together, respondents' responses to these questions constitute their conscious and relatively top-of-the-mind perception of change and variability in local rainfall conditions. I first read all responses and discussion notes on the highland village where my fieldwork period coincided with a total failure of the spring rains. In doing so, I paid particular attention to the kinds of religious and emotional concerns, as well as specific temporal and spatial indicators, informants shared when talking about, and responding to, the drought they faced. In the same vein, I read all the responses and notes on the lowland village, narrowing my focus on understanding respondents' perception of rainfall change and rainfall variability. Finally, I compared perceived patterns, effects, and mitigation strategies of rainfall variability in both villages.

Perceived variability in the normalcy of the wet season

Not surprisingly, respondents in both villages emphasized that their season-to-season farming decisions are highly attuned to minimizing crop failure due to deviations in the expected onset, duration, intensity, and spatial coverage of rainfall in the growing wet season. Yet, each farmer also knew that a household head's ability to respond to, and recover from, the negative impacts of erratic rains greatly depends on the availability of sufficient information for quick and flexible decision-making. As a consequence, the beginning of each wet season is a time of deep emotional and religious concern to farmers in both villages.

Notable evidence of this concern was heard in the questions farmers pose to each other when meeting while travelling on the road or in other social situations. With the delay of the summer rains of 2016, for example, the greetings of farmers in the lowland village typically included the following questions: (1) *Kiremtu gebalacchihu?* 'Did the summer arrive for you?' (2) *Zinabu atigbual?* 'Did you get sufficient rain [to sow crops]?' (often asked after some knowledge of its arrival), and (3) *Kiremtu endet yizochihual?* 'How has the rainy season been [for you] so far?' (when inquiring as to how reliable the rains have been since onset).

In both villages, the most common answers I heard in responding to such questions suggest that the timing of the wet season has lately deviated from the normal it used to be. Informants in both villages insisted that some years the season was delayed significantly. Other years, it came too early. This perception was well articulated in the focus-group discussions, where the responses I received included the following fear-loaded expressions: *Ende durow aydelem*: 'It [the wet season] is not like in the past.' *Embiblual*: 'It has refused [to be normal].' *Ayastemaminim*: 'It is not reliable.' *Ayasdestim*: 'It disappoints.' *Tekeyrual*: 'It has changed.'

Absence of normalcy was further documented through in-depth interviews with key informants. In the lowland village, for example, a majority of older interview respondents recalled that back when they were young the wet season used to start in June, as expected, when farmers typically need optimal moisture for sowing crops. It then continued fairly evenly through July but without obstructing work on fields. The season's rain finally reached a peak in August to enable crops to reach maximum vegetative growth, and gradually subsided in September when crops started blooming and fruition. In normal years, respondents recalled, the village also regularly received a few light showers sometime in late October to mid-November that nurtured ripening crops without any damage.

In the highland village, too, informants perceived increased irregularity, especially in the timing, duration, and cessation of *belg* (spring) rains. The irregularity has been especially noticeable since the tragic 1972/1973 famine, as stated by an elderly informant:

> It [the spring wet season] used to start raining by the first week of February or end of January as expected. The soil was then sufficiently moist and we all sowed varieties of barley, wheat and lentils which we harvested before the summer rains started in June. Since [the] famine of 1972/73, and especially following the death of the emperor [Haile Selassie I in 1975], however, *belg* [spring] rains have become completely unreliable. Sometimes, the rain started too early, only to stop abruptly before crops ripen. Other times, it came too late when there is no enough time for the crops to mature before the onset of the *kirmet* [summer] rains. We have been forced to stop sowing in the spring.[3]

Interestingly, this pattern is broadly supported by Rosell's (2014) analysis of daily rainfall data for the years 1964–2012 from 13 stations, some of them in South Wollo. In addition to substantial variability in total rainfall amounts recorded across different years, decades, and meteorological stations, results show that cereal cultivation during the spring wet season has become increasingly risky.

Together with the above-discussed seasonal and inter-annual variabilities in the cycle of the wet season, a majority of farmers in both villages also perceived an increase in the frequency (occurrence) and intensity of extreme rainfall events. Sometimes, it rained violently for many hours, if not days. Other times, it rained only sporadically, even in the middle of the peak rainy months. In still other times, it rained only in pockets of places, leaving others completely dry. In yet other times, it rained at the wrong time, often destroying crops at critical periods of harvesting, transporting, or threshing.

To sum up, the many dimensions of rainfall change and rainfall variability can be summarized in the flow chart in Figure 1.1 adopted from Simelton et al. (2013). Simelton and colleagues developed a simplified version of this flow chart to systematize farmers' responses in Malawi and Botswana to two aspects of rainfall variability; (1) what aspects of the rainy season did change (see column 2, from left, of Figure 1.1), and how did it change (see column 3). While adopting the basic question (see column 1) and modifying these two questions (see columns 2 and 3), I added a fourth level to the chart to accommodate more nuanced responses on local indicators of perceived rainfall variability.

Perceived effects of rainfall variability

One of the follow-up questions I used in all the interviews, informal conversations, and focus-group discussions asked the farmers to provide as

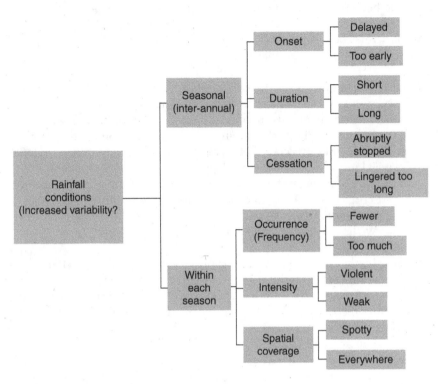

Figure 1.1 Flowchart for organizing Amhara farmers' perception of rainfall variability (adapted based on Simelton).

much qualitative evidence about rainfall variability as possible by considering certain benchmark years (e.g., after the coming to power of the present regime in 1991 vs. before), or particular growing seasons (e.g., the main rainy season of 2016 vs. the main rainy season of 2015). Not surprisingly, much of the concern relates to the impacts of erratic rains on long-standing farming practices and cropping systems.

In the highland village, for example, the loss of landrace crops due to erratic rains was the most important concern uniformly raised in focus groups and individual interviews alike. The list of reportedly lost crops includes two barley landraces that were highly valued for food, animal feed, beverage-making and roof thatching. One was a high-yielding landrace locally called *Ginbotie*, '[barley] of May,' after the month in which it used to be sown. The other was a nutritionally valued landrace locally called *Worqiye Sene*, 'golden [barley] of June,' after the month it was normally sown. Both varieties reportedly failed to do well when adjusted to rainfall variability. As a consequence, many households gradually gave up cultivating these crops in favor of adopting drought-resistance crops, including improved varieties distributed through Ethiopia's national agricultural extension program (Adem, 2012). Evidently, the net effect of these household-level weather-induced adaptations has been the increasing disappearance of landrace seeds from informal circulation among farmers.

Perceived solutions to rainfall variability

In this section, I will discuss the most important agricultural and religious responses through which Amhara farmers seek to mitigate the vagaries of erratic rains. The agricultural responses involve household-level flexibility in cropping decisions, timing, and labor allocation. Religious responses comprise village-wide rainfall prayers and sacrificial rituals to make the rainfall pattern normal by appealing to the Creator, Allah, either directly or through the help of mediating powers. The mediating powers include the guardian spirits of local landscapes, angels, patron saints, favored religious authorities, venerated ancestors, and other sacred powers.

Agricultural responses to rainfall variability

As in other arid and semi-arid parts of Ethiopia, farmers in both villages seek to mitigate the negative impacts of rainfall variability by adjusting their seasonal cropping decisions to fit changes in rainfall conditions.[4] In doing so, farmers rely on their *cumulative* phenomenological experience of landscape-level variation in soil types, proneness to moisture-stress, waterlogging, flooding, hails and frosts, and other climatic calamities. This knowledge helps them make pragmatic decisions that take account of which crops do better under what conditions. To this effect, a majority of farmers in the focus groups thought of their seasonal agricultural activities as hopelessly dictated by erratic rains. As one lowlander farmer put it, *Egna yeminwedewun sayhon, meretu yemodewun bemezrat new yemnitagelew*: 'We no longer [can afford to] cultivate what we want, but struggle [to do better] by sowing what the land wants.'

When I asked this man to explain this point with examples, he had the following to say:

> If the rain started too early in April or May, for example, we would utilize it by sowing long maturing crops like sorghum and maize. We say the land would like these crops because they germinate well with little soil moisture, continue growing with the often-sporadic showers of late May and early June, and dramatically flourish when summer rains rise to a peak later in July and August. When we encounter delayed summer, by contrast, we resort to short maturing crops like teff and legumes (especially chickpeas and fenugreek). From experience, everyone in the village knows that these crops can be sown as late as the end of July to mid-August and ripen for harvest in about three months.[5]

Another lowlander farmer recounted how he has been trying to cope with erratic rainfall patterns by sowing sorghum back-to-back, as opposed to rotating crops:

> One of my main plots is on the lower section of the village, which I inherited from my father. In the past, having a plot in that location was highly desirable. You can cultivate teff one season, sorghum in the next, and teff again or any other grain you want after that. The soil was suitable for growing any crop and we rarely faced rainfall constraints. Lately, however, that area has become highly moisture-stressed. You need at least three major raining events for the soil to be ready for planting. But in today's rainfall pattern, it is impossible to get this much moisture in the soils until almost the middle of the rainy season. By then, unfortunately, it will be too late for us to cultivate teff. It just doesn't work because if you sow teff that late the seedlings will dry a month or so later when the rain ceases. Sorghum is a better choice because you don't have to wait for the rains for planting. Sorghum does well even when sown by *mantef* [literally, spreading, but in this context 'ploughing the seeds into dry soil and waiting for the rains to come']. The seeds have this unique ability of withstanding a dry spell, and germinating with minimal moisture. For this reason, I have been sowing sorghum on that plot back-to-back for the past eight years. I sometimes laugh at what kind of farmer I have become. This would have been the lousiest thing to do in my father's time. But now, it will be foolish to try teff on the dry soils there. Although short maturing, teff needs more rain than maize does.[6]

Compared to the lowland village, farmers in the highland village do not have a large crop repertoire to choose from. For this reason, one of their noticeable agricultural responses has been adopting new crops that previously were rarely sown in the village. One such example is the rapid expansion of teff, Ethiopia's culturally favored staple that used to be cultivated only in hot and moderately hot areas in this and neighboring high-altitude villages. Another equally noticeable change has been the rise of fenugreek, which used to be a marginal drought-time crop, often planted for fodder, but now an important staple. Other new crops include maize and a variety of oats locally called *Selale* (named after its perceived place of origin). Interestingly, farmers have come to learn that maize does well even in drier months especially when sown on pockets of previously underutilized plots typically located along river banks and marshy areas. While waterlogged in the summer, these plots retain some soil moisture sufficient enough for growing maize, but not other crops, in the dry season.[7]

Prayers and mediations as perceived solutions to rainfall variability

In both villages, the above-discussed household-level agricultural responses are accompanied by supra-household religious responses. The most important of these are prayers and mediatory practices believed to protect the village against the vagaries of rainfall variability and other climatic calamities. Unlike agricultural responses that are attuned to landscape-level, empirically observable knowledge of distinct biophysical features, these religious responses draw on a vernacular perception of rainfall as a divine gift to humans of an all-knowing and omnipresent Creator, Allah. In this explanation, the onset, frequency, amount, and spatial coverage of seasonal rains or overall rainfall trends are all divine acts. To this effect, ordinary farmers are perceived as incapable of controlling these acts by themselves. They can, however, influence the pattern in two ways. One is through direct prayers to Allah as individuals, households, and village communities. The other is by invoking the mediation of .Allah-favored. supernatural powers.

In both villages, these mediating supernatural forces are believed to be vertically connected to each other.[8] At the bottom of the hierarchy live more person- and place-specific forces such as *kolle*, 'guardian spirits believed to be living in particular places,' and *wukabi*, 'spirits of particular ancestors.' The next level comprises middle-level powers such as *awuliya* 'ghosts of venerated personalities,' and patron saints associated with named geographical areas. The peak of the hierarchy, where the Creator himself is believed to live, consists of powerful angels and saints who have the power 'to carry rain onto,' or inversely 'chase away looming wet clouds from' particular places.

The ethnographic data I collected reveal the pervasiveness in both villages of this 'god-centered causal model' as part of their cultural model of Nature (see Bennardo, 2014 and the Introduction to this volume). Every morning, when neighbors meet to drink coffee at each other's houses in *tertib*, 'rotation,' they start with prayers that invariably include blessing the village with good rains. When the rainy season is delayed, or faced with erratically timed rains, adult men of each household meet at a central location believed to be the most favored abode of the village's *kolle*, 'guardian spirit,' to mitigate sufferings through intense prayers and sacrificial rites. The latter involve magical rites that need to be kept semi-secret from neighboring villages and/or some members of the village known for advocating a more purist Islam. During fear-ridden times, when extreme events like prolonged droughts, excessive rain, or outbreaks of crop pests threaten the livelihoods of entire communities, women and children organize their own gender and age-specific prayer groups. In the event the threat continues, residents of neighboring villages meet at a sacred place for much-larger, community-wide prayers and sacrificial rites.

Consistent with the perception of rain as a divine gift of the Creator, all these religious responses are believed to make the rains of the wet season start when farmers want rain and to stop when they are no longer needed. This optimism draws on the perception that the Creator has infinite amounts of rain divinely stored in a 'big jar' deep at the center of the heavens. In this understanding, rain events occur only by Allah's will when the jar is tilted down over a certain area. Evidence of this perception is a popular Amharic children's rain prayer chorus:

Azenbilew ganun	'Tilt the jar down'
Azenbilew ganun	'Tilt the jar down'
Yezinabun	'The jar of the rain'
Yezinabun.	'The jar of the rain'

It then follows that, in the eyes of Amhara famers, seasonal variations in the amount, frequency, intensity, and spatial distribution of rain events are outward manifestations of the degree that the heavenly jar has been mysteriously pointed down to, or held away from, different areas. The presumption is that by changing the positioning of the jar across time and space, Allah may apportion a greater or lesser share of seasonal rain to some communities rather than others. For this reason, one of the key expressions villagers use when praying for an ideal rainfall pattern goes as follows: *Zinabun begebere eji yadregew!* 'May [Allah make] the rain [jar] in the hands of the plowman.' Underlying this wish is the understanding that the plowman—whose culturally expected division of labor comprise the lion's share of all major outdoor agricultural activities, including preparing plots, sowing seeds, clearing and weeding fields, and finally harvesting, threshing, and storing the grain—is best positioned to know when rain is needed, in what amount, and for what type of crops.

The data I collected also show that the type and intensity of rainfall prayers in both villages greatly varies by the scale of perceived threats. In normal years, when signs show that the main growing season would likely start on time, organized prayers tend to be limited to neighborhood wards. In both villages, women of each household prepare coffee and snacks under a shade tree believed to be housing the neighborhood's *kolle*, 'guardian spirit.' The goal is to thank the spirits for preventing erratic rains.

When the season's rain is delayed, however, rain prayers involve more households and invoke help at different levels of the celestial world. In the following popular chorus, for examples, children hope to evoke Allah's pity:

Akolkuleh atayenim wey?	'Don't You pity our sorrowful sight?
Akolkuleh atayenim wey?	'Don't You pity our sorrowful sight?
Yantew wuchachoch wydelen wey!	'Aren't we all children of yours!'

In another song, children invoke the mediation of Mohammed, the Prophet, by chanting

Ante demena ...wured... wured ...	'Oh you [rain] clouds ... fall down. down'
Le Seid bileh Le Mohammed.	'In the name of the [great] Messenger,
Mohammed	Mohammed'

In addition to such emotionally loaded poems, prayers also include reciting rainfall-related miracles believed to have been performed by other mediators including revered saints, respected sheiks, and diviners. One such miracle involves a former *wali*, 'diviner/sheik,' known by name to farmers. By virtue of possessing special faculties Allah bestowed on him, the story goes, this *wali* mystically moved rain-bearing clouds across the sky. In the course of the movement, the story continues, the rain fell on villages and fields of loyal believers, bypassing those of disloyal followers.

When faced with even more severe threats, farmers rely not just on prayers and the help of mediators, but also on the use of rainmaking charms. In the highland village, for example, increased unreliability of spring rains has led to the institutionalization of a rather complex annual village-wide ritual that involves prayers, sacrifices, and rites. Every year, on the first Thursday of January (*Tir* in Ethiopian calendar), I was told, all adult men of the village gather at a hilltop locally called *Doro Marejaw*, 'place of slaughtering rooster,' for an organized ceremonial known as *yebelg wodaja*,[9] 'spring prayer.'

As recounted by informants, preparations for the event start some weeks in advance on the evening of the Ethiopian Christmas. On this date, which marks the imminent approach of normal spring season rains, the village *qire dagna*, 'judge,' accompanied by two other men, visits a known diviner looking for rain charms that would ward off hail and killer frosts while also putting spring rains into the hands of the plowman. As part of the preparation, the *qire dagna* also collects from each household a compulsory cash payment in the amount of five *birr* (about $ 0.30). In addition to honorary payment to the diviner, the money is used for purchasing a sacrificial black ram and coffee beans for the event.

The event opens with the *qire dagna* ceremonially presenting the black lamb and coffee beans to the assembly. To confirm acceptance, three elderly men speak on behalf of all the other event participants. Each elder blesses the *qire dagna* for organizing the event, while also praying for good rains and a bumper spring harvest. Following the blessing ceremony, the *qire dagna* instructs two unmarried men to carry the lamb on their shoulders and walk around all corners of the village territory as prescribed by the diviner who has been consulted. The young men are joined by a boy chosen to carry the secretly guarded rain charm. The goal of this rite is to guard the perimeters of the village from the negative impacts of erratic rains and related weather shocks.

When the young men return to the group, the three elders receive the lamb back by ceremonially rubbing and spitting on its forehead. Prayers continue for a while, invoking all perceived mediators and guardian spirits to witness the sacrificial ram. One of the elders finally slaughters the sheep and requests that the guardian spirits of the village receive their annual sacrificial gifts. The elder also instructs each farmer to soak the tip of his plowshare in the fresh blood of the animal. The meat is then roasted and shared on the spot. The prayer and feast also include a coffee ceremony and continue until dusk.

On the way down to the village, and under the cover of darkness, the *qire dagna* buries the rain charm deep in the ground. While the exact components and magical rites associated with this charm remain secret, many people seem to know that one of the objects would be a piece of bread, often baked from a mix of seven types of locally grown grains and pulses. Curiously, the evidence for this comes from knowledge of a 'reverse' magical rite occasionally held in both villages. When faced with heavy rains pouring non-stop for weeks, the *qire dagna*, under the instruction of a knowledgeable elder, seeks to stop it by digging out previously buried rain charms. While details of this ritual, too, would remain secret, the *qire dagna* needs to assure villagers that the ritual is performed properly by hanging a piece of bread baked from multiple above-mentioned crops on an *adbar* '(sacred) tree.'

Summary and conclusion

Ethnographic examples and key expressions provide important insights into South Wollo farmers' perception of where the rain comes from, who controls local rainfall patterns, and what ordinary people can do about erratic rains. The central theme of this chapter is that farmers' vernacular explanation of these issues draws on two complementary sources of knowledge. One source is intimate knowledge of empirically observable patterns in the onset, duration, intensity, and cessation of rainfall in each wet season across different sections of the local landscape that vary in bio-physical features. Cumulative lived experience of this variation has helped farmers develop landscape-level pragmatic cropping decisions and land-use patterns that, to varying degrees of effectiveness, enabled improved adaptation to erratic rains. The other source is farmers' perception of rainfall as one element of a larger cosmic order, divinely created and ruled by an all-powerful and omnipresent God, Allah (e.g., Manzoor, 2013; Lyon and Mughal, in this volume).

South Wollo farmers refer to this 'god-centered' (Bennardo, 2014) cosmic order, which is abundantly revealed in seasonal rainmaking prayers and rituals, as *tefetro* 'creation,' and they define it both broadly and narrowly. Broadly, *tefetro* encompasses everything in the realm that was created by the omnipresent Allah/God. Farmers often speak of this broad realm as divided into two. One is the sky, where supernatural beings and climatic forces live. The other is earth, consisting of humans, physical objects (such as landscapes, water sources, rocks, and other immortal things), plants, animals, and invisible guardian spirits associated with particular places (see Figure 1.2). Narrowly defined, however, *tefetro* refers to earth and its resources, most notably plants, animals, and water upon which humans rely for survival. 'Creation' in this sense of the term excludes humans and supernatural beings, but includes rainfall which, as an expression of Allah's kindness to humans, is the main source of water for cultivating crops and replenishing village wells and other water sources.

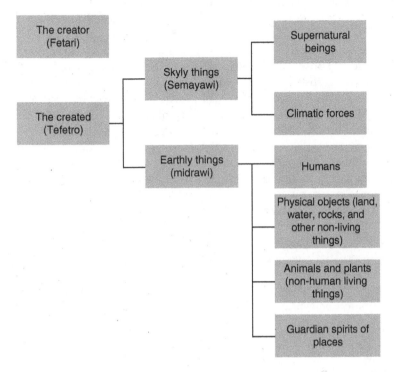

Figure 1.2 Perceived components and links in Amhara farmers' Cultural Models of Nature and the environment.

An interesting feature of this vernacular explanation of rainfall variability is that it encourages farmers to be less fatalistic even though they seem to believe that the pattern in each season is up to God/Allah. While apprehensive about increasing discrepancies in the timing, frequency, and spatial distribution of seasonal rains, farmers ultimately believe that the 'rain jar' above, in the center of the sky, has abundant rainfall to take care of all humans in all countries and villages.

Understanding that Allah may divinely apportion sufficient and timely rains to some villages while insufficient and adversely timed rains to others, farmers also believe that humans can obtain His mercy in two complementary ways. One is through direct prayers to Allah to gently pour the 'rain jar' when they want it and lift the jar away when they do not want it. The other is by invoking the help of 'mediating agencies,' such as angels, saints, holy men, sheiks, guardian ancestral spirits, and other invisible sacred beings, whose prayers, and/or magical acts God/Allah is likely to hear more than those of ordinary farmers (Girma, 2012; Mesay, 2006; Boylston, 2012).

Perhaps because of this sense of optimism in influencing divine acts, one finds strong complementarity between farmers' pragmatic, household-level agronomic responses to erratic rains, and their village-wide rain-making prayers and seasonal agricultural rituals. In both villages that provided ethnographic data for this chapter, farmers sought to minimize the vagaries of adverse rainfall not just by changing cropping decisions, but also through collectively enforced observances and sacrifices. On Sundays, which is devoted to guardian and ancestral spirits known by different names, villagers observe the day by refraining from seasonal agricultural activities. Strict enforcement of this restriction means that all able-bodied members of each household, as well as oxen and farm tools, rest on Sundays. To prove loyalty to the spirits, the restriction is especially severe during peak sowing and weeding times. In some cases, households honor spirits by adding optional observances such as not grinding grain, leaving the cattle kraal unswept, and refraining from engaging even in non-farm activities, such as marketing or visiting people.

As the discussion above shows, while sharing in common this .god-centered. cultural model of nature (Bennardo, 2014), the two villages slightly vary in the degree to which periodic communal rainfall prayers and related sacrificial rites are institutionalized. Perhaps because of their enigmatic survival in a region infamously called 'the buckle of Ethiopia's famine belt' (Little, 2013), highlander farmers have a regularly observed annual rain-beseeching prayers and sacrificial rites held in January, when the wet season is expected to start. By contrast, village-wide rainfall rituals in the relatively food self-sufficient lowland village come to life only when faced with serious threats like prolonged droughts or adversely timed, crop-destroying, rains.

Notes

1 For an ethnographic history of different Oromo lineages that settled in Borena, see Jorgi (2017). For Oromo groups that settled in other parts of Wollo, see, e.g., Gebremariam (1964) and Asfera (1973).
2 My spring 2016 fieldwork was supported by National Science Foundation (NSF) Grant (BCS#130637) to Giovanni Bennardo (PI). The summer trip was in part supported by Human Relations Area Files (HRAF). I also received additional travel support from the University of Texas Health Sciences Center at Houston, research grant to Eric C. Jones.
3 Head of HH#12, Interview, Highland Village, March 4, 2016.
4 For inventory of farmer-initiated climate-smart adaptive farming practices in highland zones, see Kidane et al. (2010). See also Rahmato (1991).
5 Head of HH#2, Interview, Lowland Village, July 23, 2016.
6 Head of HH#9, Interview, Lowland Village, July 23, 2016.
7 For maize's rapid expansion in Ethiopia and other parts of sub-Saharan Africa, see McCann (2005).
8 For a more recent work on the pervasiveness of vertical power in Amhara peoples' religiosity and other domains of life, see Boylston (2012) and Kebede (1999). Earlier works on the subject include Levine (1965), Weissleder (1965), and Hoben (1970).

9 In rural Wollo, w*odaja*, also interchangeably called *du'a*, is a generic name for organized prayers, whether directly to Allah or through the help of mediating forces. *Wodaja* maybe organized by individuals, households, neighborhoods, villages, or a group of villages for a number of reasons including safeguard against and disease and to treat patients suffering from certain diseases. According to the historian Assefa Balcha (2017), the practice can be traced to the arrival of Oromo settlers in Wollo in the sixteenth century.

References

Adem, T. A. (2012). The local politics of Ethiopia's Green Revolution in South Wollo. *African Studies Review* 55(3): 81–102.

Alemayehu, A., and Bewket, W. (2017). Local spatiotemporal variability and trends in rainfall and temperature in the central highlands of Ethiopia. *Geografiska Annaler: Series A, Physical Geography* 99(2): 85–101.

Asfera, Z. (1973). Some aspects of historical development in Amhara Wollo: ca. 1700–1815. BA thesis in History, Addis Ababa University.

Balcha, A. (2017). Wadaja ritual: Portrait of a Wallo cultural coping mechanism. *Eastern African Literary and Cultural Studies* 3(1): 40–52.

Béné, C., Devereux, S, and Sabates-Wheeler, R. (2012). *Shocks and Social Protection in the Horn of Africa: Analysis from the Productive Safety Net Programme in Ethiopia*. Brighton: Institute of Development Studies.

Bennardo, G. (2014). The fundamental role of causal models in cultural models of Nature. *Frontiers in Psychology*. October 10, http://dx.doi.org/10.3389/fpsyg.2014.01140.

Berhane, G., Hoddinott, J., Kumar, N., and Taffesse, A. S. (2011). *The Impact of Ethiopia's Productive Safety Nets and Household Asset Building Programme: 2006–2010*. Washington, DC: International Food Policy Research Institute.

Bewket, W., and Conway, D. (2007). A note on the temporal and spatial variability of rainfall in the drought-prone Amhara region of Ethiopia. *International Journal of Climatology* 27: 1467–1477.

Boylston, T. (2012). The shade of the divine: Approaching the sacred in an Ethiopian Orthodox Christian community. PhD thesis, London School of Economics and Political Science.

Castro, A. P. (2012). Social vulnerability, climate variability, and uncertainty in rural Ethiopia: A study of South Wollo and Oromiya zones of Eastern Amhara Region. In Castro, A. P., and Brokensha, D. W. (eds.), *Climate Change and Threatened Communities: Vulnerability, Capacity and Action*. Rugby, UK: Practical Action Publishing, 29–40.

Dercon, S., Hoddinott, J., and Woldehanna, T. (2005). Shocks and consumption in 15 Ethiopian villages, 1999–2004. *Journal of African Economies* 14: 559–585.

Gebremariam, A. T. (1964). *History of the People of Ethiopia (Amharic)*. Addis Ababa: Qedus Giyorgis Printing Press.

Girma, M. (2012). *Understanding Religion and Social Change in Ethiopia: Toward a Hermeneutic of Covenant*. New York: Palgrave Macmillan.

Hoben, A. (1970). Social stratification in traditional Amhara society. In Tuden, A., and Plotnicov, L. (eds.), *Social Stratification in Africa*. New York: Free Press, 187–224.

Hoddinott, J., Dercon, S., and Krishnan, P. (2009). *Networks and Informal Mutual Support in 15 Ethiopian Villages.* Washington, DC: International Food Policy Research Institute (IFPRI).

IPCC. (2014). *Climate Change 2014: Synthesis Report. Contribution of Working Groups I, II and III to the Fifth Assessment Report of the Intergovernmental Panel on Climate Change.* Core Writing Team, Pachauri, R. K., and Meyer, L. A. Geneva: IPCC.

Jorgi, Y. (2017). "Historical ethnography of Wollo-Borena: Identity, changes and continuities." Unpublished PhD diss., Addis Ababa University, Department of Social Anthropology.

Kebede, M. (1999). *Survival and Modernization: Ethiopia's Enigmatic Present: A Philosophical Discourse.* Lawrenceville, NJ: Red Sea Press.

Kidane, G., Alemneh, D., and Malo, M. (2010). *Agricultural-based Livelihood Systems in Drylands in the Context of Climate Change: Inventory of Adaptation Practices and Technologies of Ethiopia.* Environment and Natural Resources Management Working Paper, 38. Rome: Food and Agriculture Organization of the United Nations (FAO).

Levine, D. N. (1965). *Wax and Gold: Tradition and Innovation in Ethiopian Culture.* Chicago: University of Chicago Press.

Little, P. D. (2013). *Economic and Political Reform in Africa: Anthropological Perspectives.* Bloomington: Indiana University Press.

Manzoor, P. (2013). Nature and culture: An Islamic perspective. In Selin, H. (ed.), *Nature across Cultures: Views of Nature and the Environment in Non-Western Cultures,* vol. 4. Manchester: Springer Science & Business Media.

McCann, J. C. (1995). *People of the Plow: An Agricultural History of Ethiopia, 1800–1990.* Madison: University of Wisconsin Press.

McCann, J. C. (2005). *Maize and Grace: Africa's Encounter with a New World Crop, 1500–2000.* Cambridge, MA: Harvard University Press.

Mesay, A. (2006). The Onset, Cessation and Dry Spells of the Small Rainy Season (Belg) of Ethiopia. Addis Ababa: Meteorological Research and Studies Department, National Meteorological Agency.

Negatu, W. (2006). Determinants of small farm household food security: Evidence from south Wollo, Ethiopia. *Ethiopian Journal of Development Research* 28(1): 1–34.

Pankhurst, A. (2001). Natural resource management institutions in post conflict situations: Lessons from Mount Yegof, in South Wello, Ethiopia. In Pankhurst, A. (ed.), *Natural Resource Management in Ethiopia.* Addis Ababa: Forum for Social Studies, Ethiopia, 85–104.

Pankhurst, A., and Mariam, D. H. (2000). The iddir in Ethiopia: Historical development, social function, and potential role in HIV/AIDS prevention and control. *Northeast African Studies* 7(2): 35–57.

Rahmato, D. (1991). *Famine and Survival Strategies: A Case Study from Northeast Ethiopia.* Food and Famine Monograph Series No. 1. Uppsala: Nordic Africa Institute.

Rosell, S. (2014). Rainfall variability, oils and land use changes in the Ethiopian Highlands. PhD thesis, University of Gothenburg, Department of Earth Sciences.

Rosell, S., and Holmer, B. (2007). Rainfall change and its implications for Belg harvest in South Wollo, Ethiopia. *Geografiska Annaler: Series A, Physical Geography* 89(4): 287–299.

Rosell, S., and Holmer, B. (2015). Erratic rainfall and its consequences for the cultivation of teff in two adjacent areas in South Wollo, Ethiopia. *Norsk Geografisk Tidsskrift–Norwegian Journal of Geography* 69(1): 38–46.

Simelton, E., Quinn, C. H., Batisani, N., Dougill, A. J., Dyer, J. C., and Fraser, E. D., and Stringer, L. C. (2013). Is rainfall really changing? Farmers' perceptions, meteorological data, and policy implications. *Climate and Development* 5(2): 123–138.

Weissleder, W. (1965). The political ecology of Amhara domination. PhD thesis, University of Chicago, Department of Anthropology.

Woldemariam, M. (1984). Rural Vulnerability to Famine in Ethiopia 1958–1977. New Delhi: Vicas.

Woldemariam, M. (1991). *Suffering under God's Environment: A Vertical Study of the Predicament of Peasants in North-Central Ethiopia*. Geographica Bernensia.

2 Cultural Models of Nature in Tonga (Polynesia)

Giovanni Bennardo

Introduction

Climate change is affecting communities all over the world. Local populations perceive a number of changes in their environment due to climate change and explain them using the knowledge they have and the beliefs they hold about their world. We have labeled the encompassing knowledge structure—organized and related units of knowledge—about various components of one's physical, mental and spiritual world, a Cultural Model (CM) of Nature.[1] This CM is a major component of local knowledge, and it plays a fundamental role in the perception and interpretation of any phenomena related to changes in the environment, including climate change.

This chapter is about the results of the analyses conducted on data collected in the Kingdom of Tonga (henceforth, Tonga), Polynesia, in search of a Tongan CM of Nature. Tongan communities are deeply affected by changes in the climate such as weather unpredictability (including increasing number of typhoons and length and frequency of dry and wet seasons), the rising level of ocean waters (affecting their fresh-water supply), and the variability of fish supplies (changes in quantity and size, in their place, and in the time of year of their appearance).

This chapter is organized into several sections. In the first section, I provide a brief introductory description of Tonga and specifically of the small community I investigated. In the second, I describe the methodology—including both collection and analysis of data—resulting from the Cultural Model Theory (henceforth CMT) I adopted and illustrated in the Introduction of this volume. In the third section, I report about the results of the analyses. In the fourth section, I present a hypothesis about the Tongan CM of Nature, which I was able to infer from the results of the analyses. Then, I continue by looking at the internal causal structure of this CM. Finally, I look at possible future activities—data collection and analyses—that could answer some of the questions arising from the results presented.

DOI: 10.4324/9781351127905-3

Place of research

The Tonga archipelago lies on a south-west to north-east line in the South Pacific Ocean. Most of the islands are of coral, some are volcanic, and a few are atolls. Coral beaches lined with palm trees and emerald lagoons with luxuriant tropical vegetation are characteristic features. The kingdom consists of approximately one hundred fifty islands, thirty-six of which are inhabited and divided into three groups: Vava'u in the north (also the name of the major island in this group), Ha'apai in the center, and Tongatapu in the south (also the name of the major island in this group). The capital town, Nuku'alofa, is on Tongatapu island. The total population reached 103,036 according to the latest census (Tonga National Population Census, 2011), and more than a third (35,778) live in the capital.

Tonga is a constitutional monarchy headed by King Tupou VI. He is the direct descendant of King George Tupou I, who introduced the Tongan Constitution in 1875. Traditional Tongan society had at its top the *ha'a tu'i*, 'royal line,' followed by the *hou'eiki*, 'chiefs,' *ha'a matāpule*, 'talking chiefs,' *kau mu'a*, 'virtual or would-be talking chiefs,' and *kau tu'a*, 'commoners' (Gifford, 1929). All the titles were inheritable. The 1875 constitution introduced the figure of the *nōpele*, 'noble,' in an attempt to substitute that of the chief in some of its traditional prerogative (such as owning land), but this latter figure still exists. Moreover, an increasingly market-oriented economy and an expanding bureaucracy have lately added a middle class that spans some of the traditional strata from commoners to chiefs (Gailey, 1987; Linkels, 1992; van der Grijp, 1993; James, 2003).

Kinship ties are of paramount importance in Tongan society. The two major kin groups are *fāmili* and *kāinga*. A *fāmili* 'family' is made up of a married couple and their children living together in the same house, and it typically includes some male and/or female collaterals and affinals (usually, son-in-law or daughter-in-law). The *'ulumotu'a*, 'head,' presides over this group. The *kāinga*, 'extended family' is a group of people living in different households, mostly in the same village, but often including residences in other villages. They are related to one another by a bilateral relationship of consanguinity (cognatic system or kindred). A specific *'ulumotu'a* presides over this group besides his own family. In a changing contemporary Tongan society, membership to this kin group is not strictly following traditional guidelines, and inclusion is more and more restricted to closer relatives than in the past (van der Grijp, 1993: 135, 2004; Evans, 2001). The basic parameters that are applied in establishing hierarchy at any level are gender and age, with the former preceding the latter. A female is always considered higher in rank than a male.

Nobody visiting Tonga will fail to notice the overwhelming presence of Christianity throughout the kingdom. From the first failed attempt in 1797 by Wesleyan missionaries to Christianize the islands, the middle of last century saw an increasing presence of Christian religions (Lātūkefu, 1974).

The contemporary religious landscape of Tonga is characterized by many churches. The major one is the Free Wesleyan Church (37.3%), which is also the 'official' religion of the monarchy.

Tongan is an Austronesian language of the Oceanic subgroup. It belongs to the Western Polynesian languages, specifically the Tongic group. Seventy years as a British protectorate (until 1970) has resulted in the introduction of English. Much of the village population still knows little of this language. However, in Nuku'alofa and other major towns, most business transactions are conducted in English. While English is taught in elementary schools and is the language of most high school instruction, Tongan is the language commonly spoken on the streets and in shops, markets, schools, offices, and churches.

The first European visitors arrived in the late 1700s and spoke of a population scattered throughout a densely cultivated land (Ferdon, 1987). Contemporary Tongans are now concentrated in villages and small towns. Most villages lie around an empty area, called *mala'e,* used for social gatherings and games. Contemporary houses are usually rectangular and made of timber with corrugated iron roofs. The toilet and the kitchen are traditionally in separate huts, but modern houses have them indoors. Little furniture is used.

The village where I conducted the data collection is on the island of Vava'u, in the northern archipelago by the same name. It is a small village of approximately one hundred and seventy inhabitants living in thirty-six houses. In the village, there is one main church (Free Wesleyan Church) with an adjacent hall for communal activities and another smaller church (Latter Day Saints). The elementary school is placed outside the village perimeter. Junior high and older students go to school in the main town of Neiafu, site of the local government and governor.

The village lacks a noble, but it has a residing chief. A *mataāpule* 'talking chief,' is also in residence. The local Wesleyan minister is an important member of the community. Ministers, however, are rotated every four years, and only their office and not them as individuals is part of the long-lasting social fabric of the village. Another prominent figure is the elected '*ofisa kolo* 'town officer.' Thus, the village social structure suggests three formal positions—a chief, a ceremonial officer, and an elected town officer. One needs also to add the *'ulumotu'a* of the nine *kāinga* into which the population is divided. The main income of the villagers comes from subsistence farming, shell gathering, and fishing, the most common activities. However, there are also a number of wage laborers earning cash, and the cash economy has become more significant in the last couple of decades. Recently, cash and goods from relatives abroad—mainly New Zealand, Australia, and the United States—have also become a relevant source of income for the villagers.

The effects of climate change have not left this small Polynesian kingdom untouched. The level of the ocean water has raised, and tides are finding their way inland causing damage to cultivated plots. Typhoons have become more frequent, with occasional loss of lives in addition to the destruction of houses and vegetation, including numerous trees (almost all fruit-bearing, e.g., coconut, mango, papaya, and banana). A well-established weather pattern—alternating between rainy and dry seasons—has also been affected with longer drought spells and with rain that has become unpredictable in its quantity and distribution over the yearly cycle. The availability, quantity, and size of fish have also been affected in such a way that villagers rely less on their own fishing activities and more on the fish market[2] in the main town and port of the island.

Cultural Models Theory (CMT) and methodology

Cultural Models Theory (CMT)[3] provides a framework within which investigations are conducted using a specific methodological approach. The methodology employed within this project is a consequence of adopting a CMT perspective on culture. This methodology includes both data collection and data analysis. In 2015, I conducted field work in Tonga for five weeks, from May 8 through June 12. The village in the northern Tongan archipelago of Vava'u, where I collected the data, is very familiar to me because I have spent a total of more than 21 months there since my first visit in 1991.

Data collection. The data was collected using a variety of methods, including: Nature walks, open interviews, semi-structured interviews, free-listing tasks, and space tasks. Given the extensive familiarity I have with Tonga, and specifically with the community focused on, I started my data collection with a few nature walks and open interviews. The intention was to familiarize myself again with the Tongan physical environment, both spatially/visually and linguistically, while freely talking about it (in Tongan).

Later, I conducted semi-structured interviews (see Appendix 2.1 for content) with a sample (N=18) of the community/village population obtained, keeping in mind parameters such as age, gender, education, *kāinga* 'extended family' membership, occupation, and religion. All the interviews were video-recorded and later transcribed in the field with the help of native speakers.

I also administered free-listing tasks to 27 individuals—representing a similarly composed sample of the local population—about the major components of Nature: plants, animals, physical environment, weather, humans, and supernatural. I must add that the term *fangamanu* 'animals' did not elicit the intended comprehensive list, but only a few mammals. So, I administered three other free-list tasks about three other terms, that is, *manupuna* 'birds,' *ika* 'fish,' and *inisikite* 'insect.'

Data analyses. I conducted five types of analyses on the transcriptions of the semi-structured interviews: A gist analysis, a key words analysis, a semantic roles analysis, a metaphor analysis, and a reasoning/causality analysis. The first analysis is intended to obtain condensed versions of the interviews while maintaining the language used by the interviewees. The second analysis highlights the most frequent words used to refer to Nature during the interviews. These terms function as building blocks of the CM of Nature to be hypothesized.

The semantic roles analysis is conducted on the most frequent, and thus salient, key words and obtains which of them is used as agent or patient, thus indicating a specific relationship between terms/concepts. The analysis of metaphor follows wherein I counted all the metaphors used and classified them according to Lakoff and Johnson's typology (1980). I also detected concepts used as sources and/or targets of the metaphors found. Finally, I highlighted and classified reasoning passages and those implicitly or explicitly indicating causality. The intention of this last analysis is to acquire insights into the type of relationships—implicit or explicit—the interviewees establish between the various terms/concepts about Nature.

I analyzed the results of the free-listing tasks to obtain the frequency of occurrence of each item mentioned in all the lists obtained. The common assumption behind any free-listing task is that 'first listed' items stand for 'more salient' items. Thus, the lists obtained provide an excellent comparison/verification opportunity between the results of the analyses on the linguistic data and those on this cognitive/memory task.

Results of the linguistic analyses

In the following, I report first about the results of the analyses conducted on the data collected during nature walks and open interviews. Then, I report about the results of the five analyses on the transcribed semi-structured interviews.

What interviewees said about changes. During the nature walks and the open interviews, subjects often mentioned changes in their environments, and many of them happen to be related to climate change (many others referred to the composition of their social environment). The following is a list of locally perceived changes:

- Pattern of heat/sunny days;
- Pattern of rain/downpour;
- Pattern of typhoon occurrence;
- Rising level of ocean;
- Availability and size of fish;
- Availability and size of shellfish.

These same issues were found present also in the semi-structured interviews. I now introduce examples of sentences from the transcriptions and will later make some inferences from them that contribute to my hypothesis of a CM of Nature for Tongans. The sentences represent examples of statements often repeated across the sample of subjects interviewed.

    (1)   *tó 'a e 'ufi ('i) he mahina katoa*
           'plant yams with full moon'

koe'uhi:
'because'

ko e 'ufi ma'u ('a) e ivi mei ia
'yams get force from it'

I put *koe'uhi* 'because' on a separate line because it was not always explicitly included as a link between the two sentences in (1), but it was definitely implied. In (2), further salient propositions are introduced (only in English).

(2) 'when the moon is full, it gives energy to the soil and then the yams grow'
'yams get energy from sun, soil, and from water'
'soil gets energy from full moon and water'
'weeds get energy from soil'
'we must weed otherwise yams do not grow well'
'nature masters yams, etc.'

Some of the propositions were explicitly addressing the concept of Nature as in (3).

(3) 'humans belong to nature'
'humans cannot separate from nature'
'God, humans, nature belong together'
'when I see nature, I see God'
'God is in nature, but masters it'
'*they* [supernatural beings] are separated from nature because one cannot see them'

Inferences from what interviewees said. From the content of these shared ideas interviewees felt compelled to express linguistically in the interviews, I inferred a number of concepts that are presented individually in (4). These inferences (in italics) immediately follow the statements to which they refer more directly.

(4) 'when the moon is full, it gives energy to the soil and then the yams grow'[4]
physical environment (moon, soil) are related to plants (yams)

'yams get energy from sun, soil, and from water'
'soil gets energy from full moon and water'
'weeds get energy from soil'
energy is transferred among physical environment and plants

'we must weed otherwise yams do not grow well'
energy is limited

'nature masters yams, etc.'
nature is ruled by its internal laws

'humans belong to nature'
'humans cannot separate from nature'
nature includes humans

'God, humans, nature belong together'

'when I see nature, I see God'
supernatural is included in nature

'God is in nature, but masters it'
'*they* [supernatural beings] are separated from nature because one cannot see them'
supernatural is separated from nature

Gist analysis. I reduced the transcribed texts of the interviews to their gist by paying careful attention to using the words and sentences produced by the interviewees. This type of activity obtained an increased familiarity with the content of the texts while at the same time reduced the amount of interview content to be analyzed. In addition, the gist obtained for each interview functioned as a reference point for further analyses.

Key words analysis. I conducted a word-frequency analysis on the texts of the transcribed interviews.[5] For each text I excluded from the analysis the part in which I was asking questions or in any way producing language during the interview. The resulting list of words was greatly reduced (from 1170 to 495) by focusing on those, now key words, that were used to talk about Nature or nature-related activities. These key words were later classified as nouns (150), verbs (190), and adjectives (85), among other parts of speech (70) (see Appendix 2.2 for the first 60 of each type). I must point out that Tongan lexical items are not classifiable as nouns or verbs or adjectives, but they acquire a syntactic denomination by their appearance in a specific position in a syntactic structure. Then, the attribution of the key words to the various syntactic classes, that is, parts of speech, was done by typicality of occurrence: Each word was assigned to the most frequently occurring syntactic class in the texts analyzed.

Semantic role analysis of key words (Nouns). Out of the 150 nouns used by the interviewees, I selected 15 that were most frequent, while at the same time most topically salient, that is, they referred to Nature. I present these selected key words in Table 2.1.

While frequency and saliency were used to select the key words in Table 2.1, it remained to be seen what type of semantic role/s they played in the texts in which they were used. A semantic role is the role that a noun phrase (e.g., a noun) plays in the event that is described in an utterance. For example, an 'agent' is the noun to whom the speaker assigns the role of initiating or performing an action, while a 'patient' is the receiver of that same action. Such types of expressed relationships provide insights into the types of relationships among key words (i.e., concepts) that contribute to the structure of a CM of Nature. Thus, I conducted a further analysis in which I determined the semantic role, for example, patient or agent, of the selected 15 key words.

The results of the analysis in Table 2.2 indicate a slight preference (286 or 57% vs. 211 or 43%) for the use of the key words in the role of patient over that of agent. This finding is in line with a widespread Polynesian tendency to

Table 2.1 Salient key words

	Noun	Frequency
1	*Kelekele* 'soil'	120
2	*Tahi* 'sea'	114
3	*Vao* 'weed'	113
4	*'Akau* 'plant/tree'	80
5	*Kakai* 'people'	78
6	*Ivi* 'power/energy'	71
7	*La'ā* 'sun'	71
8	*Natula* 'nature'	64
9	*'Ea* 'weather'	63
10	*'Uha* 'rain'	46
11	*Vai* 'water'	40
12	*Mahina* 'moon'[6]	32
13	*Ika* 'fish'	28
14	*Fangamanu* 'animal'	26
15	*Puaka* 'pig'	20

Table 2.2 Semantic roles of key words

Key word	Frequency	Agent	Patient
Kelekele 'soil'	120	12	41
Tahi 'sea'	114	5	13
Vao 'WEED'	113	42	28
'Akau 'tree'	80	3	51
Kakai 'PEOPLE'	78	27	9
Ivi 'power/energy'	71	7	45
La'ā 'SUN'	71	28	11
Natula 'nature'	64	12	24
'Ea 'WEATHER'	63	14	9
'Uha 'RAIN'	46	13	7
Vai 'water'	40	8	19
Mahina 'moon'	32	7	7
Ika 'fish'	28	8	8
Fangamanu 'ANIMAL'	26	13	11
Puaka 'PIG'	20	11	2
Total		210	285

avoid expression of agency (Duranti, 1994; Bennardo, 2009). The key words most frequently used in the role of agent are the weather 55 (that is, sun 28, weather 14, and rain 13), followed by weeds 42, people 27, and animals 24 (that is, animals 13 and pig 11). The key words most frequently used in the role of patient are tree 51, power/energy 45, soil 41, nature 24, water 19, and sea 13.

When we consider that the interviews are about events related to daily subsistence activities, these results point toward a frequent assignment of agency to weather (55) over the 'living' environment, such as humans (27) and animals (24). The role of patient instead is most frequently assigned to the physical environment, 73 (that is, soil 41, water 19, and sea 13) and to plants, 51. These findings indicate the saliency assigned to weather as it comes into relationships with humans, animals, and plants. While at the same time the physical environment and plants are conceived as being typically acted upon by a number of agents, for example, weather, humans, and animals.

Metaphor (and source/target) analysis. Metaphors are significant rhetorical devices and, according to Lakoff and Johnson (1980), they represent a fundamental cognition building (i.e., knowledge) activity (see also Lakoff, 1987). An analysis of the metaphors used in the interviews conducted should provide further insight into the sought for CM of Nature (see Strauss and Quinn, 1997; Quinn, 2005; Bennardo, 2009).

I found 179 metaphors used in the texts analyzed. Each interviewee used an average of 9.94 and the range was 1–23. Using Lakoff and Johnson's (1980) typology, the metaphors found were classified into four different types: Ontological, 91 or 51 percent (either personification, 73 or 80%, or objectification, 18 or 20%); structural 81 or 45 percent; and orientational, 7 or 4 percent (see Table 2.3; in the same table, the first column refers to the interviewees indicated as a number).

The prevalence of ontological metaphors—an abstraction, for example, activity, emotion, or idea, is represented as something concrete, for example, object or person—seems to indicate a tendency to favor the rendering of

Table 2.3 Types of metaphor

	Ontological		Structural	Orientational	Frequency
	Personification	*Objectification*			
1	1	3	6		10
2	6		2		8
3		2			2
4	6	1	5		12
5	3	1	6		10
6	9	3	6	1	19
7	2	1	4	1	8
8	10	1	3		14
9	3				3
10			1		1
11	2	2	7		11
12	3		7		10
13	1	1	1	1	4
14	14		6	3	23
15	2		4		6
16	10		8		18
17			4		4
18	1	3	11	1	16
	73	**18**	**81**	**7**	**179**

abstract ideas as concrete things like a person or an object. Any metaphor is rooted in a 'source' domain or concept whose known content—including structural characteristics—are projected onto a 'target' domain or concept to make the latter familiar and often understandable and explainable. The various types of sources and targets used—especially those within ontological metaphors—may provide insights into the CM of Nature employed by the interviewees.

In Table 2.4, I present the results of a source/target analysis of the metaphors found. It is apparent from looking at the content of the table that the world/environment of living/animate entities (e.g., people and animals) is the preferred one that is used as source for metaphors (see types of sources under Ontological/Personification metaphors and under Structural metaphors). On the other hand, it is the physical environment/inanimate (e.g., weather, plants, physical objects) and abstract concepts (e.g., time, growth,

Table 2.4 Types of sources and targets in metaphors

	SOURCE	Frequency		TARGET	Frequency
	Ontological/ Objectification	18		Ontological/ Objectification	18
1	Physical object	18	1	Abstract/Responsibility	12
	Ontological/ Personification	73	2	Weather	5
1	Family/Son/Child	32	3	Time	1
2	Person	29		Ontological/ Personification	73
3	Command	12	1	Nature/Plant/Weather	52
	Orientational	7	2	Place	10
1	Something in front	3	3	Physical object/ Chemical	9
2	Something up	2	4	Abstract concept	1
3	Something in back	1	5	Activity	1
4	Something inside	1		Orientational	7
	Structural	81	1	Past	3
1	Animals, birds, people	55	2	Action	1
2	Living thing	20	3	First (Beginning)	1
3	Rest/Die (activity)	3	4	Future	1
4	Gold	1	5	Inside	1
5	Plants	1		Structural	81
6	Water	1	1	Plant	31
			2	Physical object/ Environment/ Chemical	22
			3	Abstract/Health	12
			4	Activity/Growth	11
			5	Time	3
			6	Weather	2
	Total	179		Total	179

and action) that are targeted by metaphors in order to find possible ways to be explained and understood (see targets under Personification metaphors, under Structural metaphors, and under Objectification metaphors).

These findings dovetail with those of the previous section about the semantic role analysis in which agency was predominantly assigned to the weather. In fact, for any aspect (or object) of the physical environment, for example, weather, to be assigned agency it needs to be treated as a living entity. Since we have just found out that living entities are the principal sources for targeted aspects of the physical environment, we can now understand even better why this latter is spoken about and thought of as having agency.

Reasoning (including causality) analysis. I organized the results of the reasoning analysis on the texts of the semi-structured interviews according to the topics the interviewees chose to reason about (a total of 615). In Table 2.5, the 15 topics are presented and ranked according to frequency of occurrence, while in Table 2.6 they are ranked according to frequency of use by subjects (N=18).

The most frequent topics happen to be also the most highly distributed among subjects. The only relevant difference I feel obliged to mention is that all subjects (18) reasoned about the 'salience of humans/group'—thus, it ranks first in Table 2.6—while this same topic is only 4th in the frequency by topic ranking in Table 2.5.

Looking more carefully at the frequency by topic, a preference for a focus on humans is detected—'relationships between humans and results' 213, 'salience of humans/group' 69, 'humans affect/change Nature' 42, 'relationship humans/nature' 13, 'separation humans/nature' 3, that is, a total of 340/615 or 55 percent.

All the other topics about plants, animals, weather, and physical environment appear to be also relevant—'relationship time/weather and plants' 79,

Table 2.5 Reasoning topics

213	*Relationships Humans/Results*
79	*Relationship Time-Month-Weather/Plants*
76	*Relationship Physical environment/Plants*
69	*Salience of Humans/Group*
42	*Humans Affect/Change Nature*
32	*Power/Energy in trees/Soil*
29	*Relationship Seed/Growth*
25	*Relationship God/Humans/Nature*
23	*Animals/Insects Positive/Negative*
13	*Relationship Humans/Nature*
5	*Relationship Weather/Fishing*
3	*Relationship Fish/Plants (Limu)*
3	*Separation Humans/Nature*
2	*Shellfish/Fish/Plants internal growth*
1	*God is Nature*

'relationship physical environment and plants' 76, power/energy in trees/ soil' 32, 'relationship seed/growth' 29, 'animals/insects positive/negative' 23, 'relationship weather/fishing' 5, 'relationship fish/plants' 3, 'shellfish/fish/ plants internal growth' 2, that is, a total of 249/615 or 41 percent. The remaining topics do not appear to have an overall salience as the previous ones. In fact, topics such as 'relationship between God/humans/nature' 25 and 'God is nature' 1, total only 26/615 or 4 percent.

At times, frequency of occurrence need not to be taken at face value. That is, the nature of the questions asked might be considered an 'influential' factor in the prevalence of certain topics over others. However, since all interviewees were asked the same questions, the fact that some of them chose to or did not choose to 'reason' about certain topics (see Table 2.6), should be a result to be considered with attention and care. That is why these results about topics most frequently reasoned about contribute to the description of the CM of Nature I will present later.

Another factor that needs to be pointed out is that 'reasoning' may typically involve expressing causes or 'causality' and this fact might often make the topic about which the reasoning is conducted less revealing than the causality structure articulated. Causality relationships are one of the most significant types of relationship that bind concepts and events together in mental constructions that are at the core of the structure of any cultural model (see Bennardo, 2014).

According to the results of the reasoning analysis 'humans' seems to be conceived as one of the major foci of the subjects' thinking about Nature. In addition, humans may cause changes in their surroundings that include animals, plants, and physical environment. Causal relationships among plants, animals, and the physical environment are very prominent, too, for example, phases of the moon cause optimal plants' growth. Weather is also significantly related to plants' growth and it is conceived as bringing

Table 2.6 Reasoning topics by interviewees

18	69	*Salience of Humans/Group*
18	79	*Relationship Time-Month-Weather/Plants*
18	76	*Relationship Physical environment/Plants*
15	42	*Humans Affect/Change Nature*
14	32	*Power/Energy in trees/Soil*
11	25	*Relationship God/Humans/Nature*
10	13	*Relationship Humans/Nature*
9	29	*Relationship Seed/Growth*
7	23	*Animals/Insects Positive/Negative*
5	5	*Relationship Weather/Fishing*
2	2	*Shellfish/Fish/Plants internal growth*
2	3	*Relationship Fish/Plants (Limu)*
2	3	*Separation Humans/Nature*
1	1	*God is Nature*

about fishing success (see Wiegele's Chapter 10 for a similar concept among Filipinos). Furthermore, a type of power/force is thought of as characterizing the physical and botanical environment, for example, soil and trees, thus causing growth in its own terms.

Finally, and in a less-frequent manner, one type of supernatural, that is, God, is talked about as being necessarily intermingled with any aspect of Nature, but also standing in a commanding position. While not overtly expressed, 'commanding' includes 'causing' other elements to be/behave in specific ways. Thus, God is a causal agent for the whole of nature. This idea, though, is also shortened in the expression 'God is nature' and no causality, not even commanding, is expressed.

Hypothesis about the Cultural Model of Nature in Tonga

The results of the analyses presented so far provide an extensive set of concepts, that is, propositions, about Nature and at the same time they introduce a good set of relationships among these concepts.

PROPOSITIONAL CONTENT *of Tongan CM of* NATURE	FROM *type of analysis*
1. *Nature is ruled by its internal laws and it includes humans*	GA
2. *Humans are related to all other components*	GA
3. *Weather is related to (affects) physical environment, plants, and humans*	GA
4. *Sun/moon/soil are related to plants via transfer of energy*	GA and CRA
5. *Supernatural/God is separated from nature, it masters nature*	GA and CRA
6. *Supernatural/God is not separated from nature, it is everywhere*	GA and CRA
7. *Plants (weeds), people, sun/moon, weather, and animals (pigs) are agents*	SRA
8. *Plants (trees), power, soil, nature, water, and sea are patients*	SRA
9. *Ontological metaphors are 51% (of which personification are 80%)*	MA
10. *Structural metaphors (concrete to explain abstract) are 45%*	MA
11. *Animate things are known and used to explain inanimate things*	STA
12. *Humans are salient/central and are related/affect nature*	CRA
13. *Plants are related to time and weather*	CRA
14. *Internal growth (essence) of seeds, fish, shellfish, plants*	CRA
15. *Fish are related to plants and weather*	CRA

Each proposition listed above has been arrived at from the results of a specific type of linguistic analysis indicated under the 'FROM type of analysis' column. This is the key used for the types of analysis: GA stands for Gist Analysis; SRA stands for Semantic Role Analysis; MA stands for Metaphor Analysis; STA stands for Source/Target Analysis; and CRA stands for Causal and Reasoning Analysis.

From these results, I feel confident to hypothesize the following basic/core content for the CM of Nature[7] for Tongans:

(a) **Nature** is ruled by its internal laws (essence), and it includes humans;
(b) **Humans** are salient and central, and they are related to (affect) all other components;
(c) **Plants** are related to time (seasons) and weather;
(d) **Fish** are related to plants and weather;
(e) **Weather** is related to (affects) physical environment, plants, and humans;
(f) **Physical Environment (sun/moon/soil)** is related to plants via transfer of energy;
(g) Physical environment, weather, plants, and **animals** belong together;
(h) **Supernatural/God** is separated from nature, it masters nature;
(i) Supernatural/God is not separated from nature, it is everywhere;
(j) In order to know/talk about inanimate and abstract things knowledge about animate things (via personification) is used because these latter are known;
(k) Plants, humans, physical environment (sun/moon), weather, and animals (pigs) are agents;
(l) Plants **(trees)**, **power**, **soil**, nature, **water**, and **sea** are patients.

The major components of Nature—plants, animals, weather, physical environment, humans, and the supernatural—seem to be thought of as related to each other in a holistic manner (see propositions *a-g*). Interestingly, though, different types of causal relationships exist among these components (see propositions *f* and *d*). In addition, the detected focus on humans makes them stand out from other components of Nature insofar as they are pointed out as capable of acting and changing the quality of the other components, they are agents (see proposition *b*). However, they are also acted upon 'agentively' by elements such as the weather (see proposition *e*). The supernatural, for example, God, is also addressed as belonging together to all the other elements of Nature (see proposition *i*). Often, though, it is talked about as being in a commanding role, thus, in a 'detached' position (see proposition *h*).

This preliminary hypothesis contains some issues that need to be pointed out. First, the internal relationships among the elements making up nature—excluding humans and the supernatural—need to be investigated further. The role of animals, that is, mammals, has been talked about very little, except for that of pigs. Similarly, the relationship between fish, birds, and mammals with plants, weather, and physical environment has been under-addressed and thus requires more attention in the future.

Second, there is a contradiction in the model regarding the relationship between God and all the other components of Nature, and it needs to be clarified. The immanence of the supernatural is contrasted to its being 'separated.' This latter separation allows to infer causality (from God to everything else) within the linguistically expressed 'God masters nature.' At the same time, humans too appear to be treated as 'separate' from the other components and thus thought of as capable of acting on and changing them (excluding the supernatural).

Third, in pursuing a resolution to the above-stated issues, it would be useful to keep in mind the Polynesian (and Tongan) traditional concept of *mana* or 'vital force.' This concept was and is deeply related to a conceptualization of all the components of Nature as holistically related. The persistence of such way of thinking in Tonga has been widely documented in spite of a hundred and fifty years of Christianity (see Bennardo, 2009, 188–189)

Causality structure of CM of Nature

In Bennardo (2014), I suggested that any CM of Nature would include a causality structure that can be represented by a causal model (see Sloman, 2009; Rips, 2011). In the same work, I introduced three possible causal models that eventually could be found across cultures. Which of those three suggested causal models can be hypothesized as being an appropriate one to represent causality within the hypothesized Tongan CM of Nature just introduced?

It appears that the Tongan CM of Nature includes the *Holistic* causal model (see Figure 2.1). In fact, all the components of Nature—or the 'World' in the causal model—are conceived as in reciprocal relationships. Notice—in *the Probability Distribution* box—that the more of the six components are co-present, the higher the level of positive probability for the construction of the concept of Nature becomes. In addition, even the place of the supernatural, that is, God, is often explicitly addressed as an essential constituent of Nature. Thus, the content of the concept of Nature seems to be accurately represented by the graph in the *Holistic* causal model (Figure 2.1).

At the same time, the presence of a *God-Centered* causal model (see Figure 2.2) was also detected. In fact, the wholeness and the inherent intra-relationships among the components of Nature are explicitly denied on several instances when God is assigned a 'master' position (see the graph in Figure 2.2).

The presence of this contradiction about the position of the supernatural in Nature both within (at different moments of the interview) and across subjects (subjects expressing different positions) points toward the possibility of two CMs of Nature co-existing within each individual and across the community at large. Further investigation should and could provide the opportunity to obtain insights into this matter.

Results of the free-listing tasks

Obtaining ethnographic data (from participant observation)[8] and linguistic data (from nature walks, open, and semi-structured interviews) followed

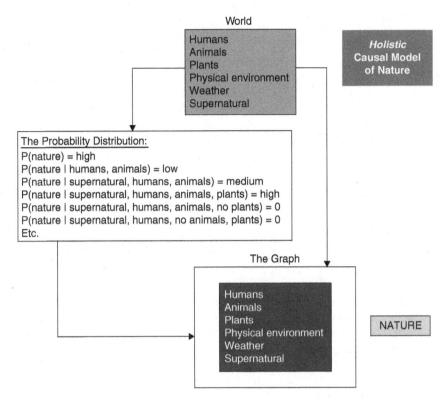

Figure 2.1 The *holistic* causal model.

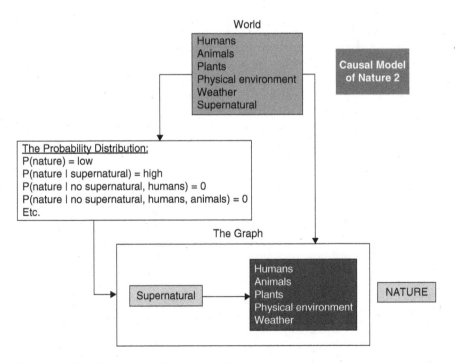

Figure 2.2 The *God-centered* causal model.

by an extensive set of analyses represents only two parts of the tripartite methodological trajectory suggested by Bennardo and De Munck (2014) as necessary when investigating cultural models. The third part of the methodology includes the use of cognitive tasks such as free-listing, sorting tasks, rating tasks, ranking tasks and also consensus analyses—this latter includes the use of structured questionnaires.

I have only administered free-listing tasks about the fundamental components of Nature—plants, animals (and fish, birds, and insects), weather, physical environment, humans, and supernatural—to 27 subjects, 14 males and 13 females, ranging in age from 28 to 80 (females range 28–76; males range 30–80). In Table 2.7, I indicate the free-listing categories I used—notice that the category 'animals' had to be emically divided into animals (mammals), birds, fish, and insects, since the word for animals in Tongan (*fangamanu*) refers only to mammals. In the same table, I indicate for each category the total number of words obtained across subjects, the average number of words produced by each subject, and the range.

Words for plants and fish top the chart with an average of 30.07 (15–66 range) and 20.85 (9–37 range), respectively. Remembering on average more than 30 names for plants and more than 20 for names of fish is to be considered very significant results. The interviewees are subsistence farmers, but their engagement with their environment is gendered biased—males typically do most of the fishing and farming activities, from preparation of soil to planting and harvesting—then the results are even more significant when one keeps this factor in consideration (memory performance of female might lower results). In the end, these results tell a story about the keen attention (and memory space) members of the community devote to these two components of their environment.

Table 2.8 contains the same results of the free-listing tasks with the categories changed as to reflect those that were originally suggested by the research group. That is, they represent the etic view of those components of Nature. I present these data so that they could possibly be used later for a

Table 2.7 Results of free-listing tasks

Category	Frequency	Average	Range
Plants	812	30.07	15–66
Fish	563	20.85	9–37
People	385	14.26	7–28
Birds	279	10.33	5–18
Weather	261	9.67	5–17
Physical environment	243	9.00	2–15
Animals	224	8.30	5–15
Supernatural	167	6.19	2–13
Insects	38	1.40	0–10
Total	**2972**		

cross-cultural comparison among all the results obtained in the various field sites for this research project.

The content of the various lists obtained was adjusted,[9] and frequencies were aggregated. Thus, it could be determined which specific words within each emic category are collectively privileged (remembered and mentioned more often) over others co-present in the lists. The most frequent words for plants (top 48) appear in Table 2.9. The length of the list of top words varies

Table 2.8 Adjusted results of free-listing tasks

Category	Frequency	Average
Fish/birds/animals/insects	1,104	40.88
Plants	812	30.07
People	385	14.26
Weather	261	9.67
Physical environment	243	9.00
Supernatural	167	6.19
Total	**2,972**	

Table 2.9 Results of free-listing task for plants

	PLANT	Cum. salience	Salience		PLANT	Cum. salience	Salience
1	mango	**24.56**	0.91	25	'ai	**4.65**	0.17
2	niu	**18.95**	0.70	26	kalosipani	**4.58**	0.17
3	mei	**15.79**	0.58	27	fau	**4.46**	0.17
4	lesi	**15.07**	0.56	28	fiki	**4.03**	0.15
5	vavae	**12.64**	0.47	29	siale	**4.03**	0.15
6	painí	**10.38**	0.38	30	'ovava	**3.89**	0.14
7	tava	**10.07**	0.37	31	manonu	**3.81**	0.14
8	tavahi	**9.12**	0.34	32	lo'akau	**3.78**	0.14
9	kuava	**8.20**	0.30	33	talo	**3.78**	0.14
10	toi	**6.96**	0.26	34	'āvoka	**3.72**	0.14
11	moli	**6.93**	0.26	35	futu	**3.43**	0.13
12	motou	**6.74**	0.25	36	tongo	**3.37**	0.12
13	ifi	**6.69**	0.25	37	ngatae	**3.35**	0.12
14	fekika	**6.15**	0.23	38	loupata	**3.33**	0.12
15	ngatata	**5.84**	0.22	39	mo'ota	**3.29**	0.12
16	toa	**5.39**	0.20	40	'āpele	**3.17**	0.12
17	pua	**5.34**	0.20	41	kape	**3.07**	0.11
18	mo'osipo	**5.07**	0.19	42	koka	**3.06**	0.11
19	siaine	**5.07**	0.19	43	feta'u	**2.96**	0.11
20	pua tonga	**5.02**	0.19	44	'ufi	**2.96**	0.11
21	hopa	**4.81**	0.18	45	sipaisi	**2.80**	0.10
22	vī	**4.77**	0.18	46	kava	**2.79**	0.10
23	nonu	**4.76**	0.18	47	manioke	**2.77**	0.10
24	ahi	**4.73**	0.18	48	sinamoni	**2.53**	0.09

for each category, and it was determined by considering saliency (to the topic of Nature) and occurring gaps in the frequencies, either in the cumulative saliency ranking (sum of all individual saliency rankings) or in the actual final saliency ranking or in both.

For example, in Table 2.11 (see Appendix 2.3) containing the top words in the list obtained from a free-listing task about fish, there are significant frequency gaps between number 2 and number 3, between 4 and 5, between 6 and 7, and between number 23 and number 24 (and others). I did not consider these gaps appropriate to stop the list because I considered the words following the gaps salient to the topic. However, I stopped the list for inclusion at number 36 because I regarded the gap occurring between 36 and 37, even though small (only .22), as significant. In addition, only 4 people had mentioned number 37 when compared to 5 (25%) people for number 36 (consider that the average number of fish recalled by subject is 20.83).[10]

In Appendix 2.2, I present the most frequent words used as verbs, nouns and adjectives during the interviews. Among these words, a good number appear in the hypothesized CM of Nature I outlined in the section titled *Hypothesis about the Cultural Model of Nature in Tonga*. I have indicated in bold those words in the CM and I have highlighted in gray the words in the list in Appendix 2.2. I regard as a positive output of the two results that such a cross-referencing could be obtained. After all, the key words used represent loaded indexes to more complex systems of ideas/concepts as they are presented in the list of propositions that may represent the whole highly structured and appropriately coherent Tongan CM of Nature.

Can the results of the free-listing tasks contribute in a similar manner to the clarification and/or elicitation of the content of the Tongan CM of Nature? I am convinced that they can, but further activities need to be conducted. In fact, the top listed words in each of the categories making up Nature can be used in sorting tasks—obtaining relationships within the members of each category—and rating tasks—obtaining relationships across categories. The former type of task will elucidate salient 'concepts,' that is, more abstract categories, used to group members of the various lists. The latter type of task will highlight perceived 'relationships' among members of the various lists, thus, providing further indications about possible causal (or other) relationships among the components of Nature. The results of both activities, then, can contribute in refining the content of the CM already hypothesized.

For example, by looking at the content of the free-listing results about plants (see Table 2.9), it is apparent that many of them are edible and widely present in the village environment, for example, mango, *niu* 'coconut,' *mei* 'breadfruit,' *lesi* 'papaya,' *kuava* 'guava,' *hopa* 'plantain,' and so forth. Similarly, another large category regards medicinal trees—bark, leaves and fruit are used in *fai to'o* 'traditional medicine'—such as *tavahi* 'rhus taitensis Guillemin,' *toi* 'alphitonia zizyphoides,' *motou* 'criptocarya hornei Gillespie,' *ngatata* 'elattostachys falcata,' *nonu* 'morinda citrifolia L.,' and so forth. These two categories of trees, edible plants and medicinal plants, might play a role in the CM of Nature. They may instantiate a close reciprocal relationship between humans and plants where both play an agentive role insofar as humans use these plants and the plants provide relief from diseases.

Conclusion

In order to discover the Tongan CM of Nature I collected a large amount of data. Ethnographic data was collected over more than two decades of field-work in a small community in Tonga whose livelihood is being threatened by several effects of climate change. The new data collection focused mainly on the acquisition of linguistic data by using nature walks, open interviews, and semi-structured interviews. Finally, some cognitive (memory) data was also collected by means of a number of free-listing tasks.

These different types of data were then analyzed in depth, especially the linguistic data. A gist analysis, a key words analysis (including a semantic role analysis), a metaphor analysis (including a source/target analysis), and a reasoning/causality analysis were used to analyze the texts of the semi-structured interviews. Frequency analyses were used to analyze the results of the cognitive (memory) tasks. All the results pointed towards the existence of a specific set of relationships among the various components of Tongan Nature, such as humans, plants, animals, fish, birds, insects, physical environment, weather, and supernatural. A list of propositions was presented as summarizing the content of the CM.

Further activities are already planned that would enhance the validity of the CM hypothesized in this work. In addition, since we axiomatically assume that variation is the existential condition of any culture, I am convinced that the distribution within the community of the CM presented in this work—and the refined one that will eventually be obtained—needs to be ascertained by means of a consensus analysis.

Thus, in addition to the mentioned sorting and rating tasks, I plan to conduct a consensus analysis in the community investigated about the CM suggested. For this analysis I will use a questionnaire generated from the final CM of Nature suggested. The results of such an activity may eventually elucidate/ highlight and support the presence of one specific (or more than one) CM and/ or culture. Finally, if more than one CM is discovered, their distribution within the community would highly enhance our understanding of the various type of local knowledge used by community members once climate change effects impact and modify their traditional expectations about how Nature works.

Appendix 2.1

Semi-structured interview

Questions about daily activities

Personal questions precede the following ones:
1. Describe your work/job (which relates to primary food production).
2. What is your typical work/work-day?

3. What is the rhythm of work in this area ... Or actual activities?
4. What are some of the essential knowledge, skills, experience you need to be a successful food producer?
5. What are considered 'productive activities'?
6. Which fields/sea areas/etc. are productive?
7. What affects productivity? What forces have an influence on production success?
8. What is meant by growth, why do plants grow?
9. What are the key decisions __x__ must make to be successful?
10. What information do you need to make decisions?
11. How do you choose what crops to grow, what to fish, what to go after?
12. What are some of the constraints/problems you face as a food producer?
13. Who or what affects your environment (fields, forest, sea, etc.) the most?
14. What is worst/best thing humans can do in fishing/farming/etc.?
15. What do you like/not like about what you're doing (satisfaction)?

Questions about climate change

16. What changes have occurred in your work/environment?
17. Why are there these changes/variations?
18. Weather change, how?
19. What can humans do about it?
20. Can humans/human activity affect nature/weather/wind/currents?

Semi-structured interview translated in Tongan

Questions about daily activities

Personal questions precede the following ones:
1. Fakamatala'i Mai Ho'o Ngaue
2. Ko e ha´ Ho'o Ongo'i Ki Ho'o 'Aho Ngaue Tu'uma'u?
3. Ko e ha´ ´ e Hokohoko Ho'o Ngaue Faka'aho/Uike/Mahina? (Toota'u = Planting)
4. Ko e ha´ Ho'o 'Ilo, Poto Ngaue, Mo Ho'o Taukei 'Oku Fiema'u Ke Hoko Ko Ha Fefine Ngaue Tu'umalie?
5. Ko e ha´ e Ngaahi Me'a/Ngaue 'e Fai Ke Hoko' (Ngaahi Me'a) Ke Fakatu'umalie?
6. Ko e ha´ e Ngaahi Mala'e'I he Ngaue' 'Oku Hoko Ko e Fakatu'umalieanga?
7. Ko e ha´ e Me'a 'Oku Nau Fakafe'atungia'i?
8. Ko e ha´ e Me'a 'Oku Tupu Ai e 'Akau´?
9. Ko e ha´ e Me'a 'Oku Ke Fakapapau'i 'e Hoko Ko E Fakatu'umalie Kiate Koe ('I Ho'o Ngaue)?
10. Ko e ha´ 'a e Taukei/'Ilo 'Oku Ke Fiema'u Ke Fai'aki Ho'o Tu'utu'uni?
11. Anga Fefe´ Ho'o Fili 'a e Fala Ke Ngaue: Lalanga/Fingota?
12. Ko e ha´ e Ngaahi Palopolema 'Oku Ke Fetaulaki Mo Ia 'I Ho'o Ngaue?

13. Ko Hai Pe´ Ko e Ha e Me'a 'Oku Ne Fakafe'atungia'i Ho 'Atakai?
14. Ko e ha´ e Me'a Lelei Taha Pe´ Kovi Taha 'Oku Lava Fai 'e Ha Fefine 'I He'ene Ngaue?
15. Ko e ha´ e e Me'a 'Oku Sai'ia Lahi 'I Ho'o Ngaue?

Questions about climate change

16. Ko e ha´ 'a e Ngaahi Liliu 'Oku Hoko 'I he 'Atakai Ho'o Ngaue?
17. Ko e ha´ e Uhinga 'Oku Hoko Ai e Ngaahi Liliu Ko Ia´?
18. Kuo 'I Ai Ha Ngaahi Liliu 'I he 'Ea?
19. Ko e ha´ e Me'a 'E Malava e Tangata Ke Fai Ki Ai?
20. ´E Lava e Ngaahi Ngaue 'a e Tangata 'o Fakafe'atungia'i 'a Natula, ea, au, La'a, Havili, Afa´?

Appendix 2.2

Results of the key words analysis (first 60 for verbs, nouns, and adjectives).

	VERB	Frequency	NOUN	Frequency	ADJECTIVE	Frequency
1	tó 'plant'	328	taimi 'time'	374	lahi 'big'	246
2	alu 'go'	251	ngoue	307	lelei 'nice'	140
3	lalanga 'weave'	225	me'a 'thing'	306	mo'ui 'alive'	91
4	ma'u 'get'	183	ufi 'yam'	223	kovi 'bad'	54
5	lava 'can'	182	lo'akau	169	kehekehe 'different'	47
6	osi 'finish'	170	kelekele 'soil'	120	si'isi'i 'small'	45
7	ngaue 'work'	153	tahi 'sea'	114	kehe 'different'	41
8	fai 'do'	148	aho 'day'	89	poto 'smart'	37
9	kai 'eat'	117	ta'u 'year'	86	kotoa 'all'	36
10	fiema'u want'	96	vao 'uncoltivated land'	113	tokotaha 'one'	33
11	liliu 'change'	95	akau 'tree'	80	matu'a 'old'	29
12	sio 'see'	92	kakai 'people'	78	momoko 'cold'	28
13	ha'u 'come'	87	fala 'mat'	76	faka'ofo'ofa 'beautiful'	27
14	huo 'hoe'	78	ivi 'test'	71	hangatonu 'straight'	26
15	tupu 'stand'	78	la'á 'sun'	71	lalahi 'big'	24
16	pau	69	ma'ala 'lot'	70	hala 'wrong'	23

	VERB	*Frequency*	NOUN	*Frequency*	ADJECTIVE	*Frequency*
17	nofo 'live'	61	natula 'nature'	64	mafana 'warm'	23
18	foki 'return'	53	ea 'weather'	63	uluaki 'first'	21
19	mate 'die'	52	famili 'family'	60	vave 'fast'	21
20	tauhi 'take care'	50	api 'village lot'	58	vela 'hot'	21
21	ave	48	kape 'yam'	51	fakapikopiko 'lazy'	19
22	fakatau 'buy'	46	tangata 'man'	49	momoa	18
23	tuku	44	palopolema 'problem'	47	fakataha 'first'	17
24	sa'ia 'like'	41	uha 'rain'	46	hinehina 'white'	17
25	palau	40	konga 'piece'	45	mokomoko 'cold'	17
26	hoko 'add'	39	uta 'land not village'	45	afá 'typhoon'	16
27	ilo 'know'	35	pule 'boss'	44	fakanatula 'natural'	16
28	to'o	35	tá 'picture'	40	puke 'sick'	14
29	omai 'give me'	34	vai 'water'	40	fo'ou 'new'	13
30	tu'u	34	talo 'taro'	36	fuoloa 'long time'	13
31	tokoni 'help'	33	ma'ala'ala	34	mamaha 'far away'	13
32	keli	32	manioke 'manioke'	34	ofi 'close'	13
33	tui 'follow'	31	pa'anga 'T currency'	34	tokolahi 'a lot'	13
34	kamata 'start'	29	foha 'son'	33	totonu 'right'	13
35	hanga	28	mahina 'moon'	32	malohi 'strong'	12
36	tau	28	me'akai 'food'	32	si'i 'small'	12
37	utu	28	vesetapolo 'vegetable'	32	fakatonga 'Tongan'	11
38	ngaue'aki	25	mali 'spouse'	30	fakaheka	10
39	ta'utu 'sit'	22	fangota 'shell fish'	29	ma'olunga 'superior'	10
40	a'u	20	holo	29	molú	10
41	tala 'tell'	20	lau	29	uli'uli 'dark'	10
42	fafanga	19	atakai	28	faingofua 'easy'	9

	VERB	Frequency	NOUN	Frequency	ADJECTIVE	Frequency
43	manatu'i 'remember'	19	ika 'fish'	28	loloa 'long'	9
44	ako'I 'study'	17	pulopula	28	avaava	8
45	mole	17	ta'ovala 'wearable mat'	27	mahu'inga 'important'	8
46	tofi	17	fangamanu 'animal'	26	tonu 'right'	8
47	fua 'grow'	16	kava 'kava'	26	aonga	7
48	fili 'choose'	15	fonua 'land'	25	malu	7
49	teuteu	15	feitu'u 'place'	24	maumau	7
50	fai'aki	14	fale 'house'	23	nounou 'short'	7
51	feunga 'try'	14	haka 'boil pot'	23	fiefia 'happy'	6
52	ta'ofi	14	kemikale 'chemical'	23	manifi	6
53	ui 'call'	14	tu'umalie	23	tokamui	6
54	ako 'study'	13	ā 'fence'	21	vaivai 'weak'	6
55	fie 'want'	13	kavenga 'duty'	21	afu 'hot and humid'	5
56	fusi	13	kolo 'village'	21	faka'ofa 'lovable'	5
57	hu	13	talanoa 'story'	21	fakahela	5
58	kaka	13	kumala 'yam'	20	fakalakalaka	5
59	faito'o 'cure'	12	puaka 'pig'	20	fefeka 'hard'	5
60	feinga 'try'	12	fingota '	18	i'iki 'tiny'	5

Appendix 2.3

Results of free-listing tasks.

Table A.2.3.1 Results of free-listing task for animals

	ANIMAL	Cum. salience	Salience
1	puaka 'pig'	22.63	0.84
2	pulu 'cow'	18.57	0.69
3	hoosi 'horse'	17.37	0.64
4	kulī 'dog'	14.5	0.54
5	kosi 'goat'	9.13	0.34
6	pusi 'cat'	7.46	0.28
7	kumā 'mouse'	5.78	0.21
8	sipi 'sheep'	5.43	0.20

Table A.2.3.2 Results of free-listing task for fish

	FISH	Cum. salience	Salience		FISH	Cum. salience	Salience
1	ngatala	16.02	0.59	19	pone	5.07	0.19
2	'anga	15.01	0.56	20	fai	5.03	0.19
3	tofua'a	13.09	0.48	21	tuna	4.79	0.18
4	lupo	12.30	0.46	22	'ume	4.69	0.17
5	tanutanu	10.85	0.40	23	sifisifi	4.42	0.16
6	sokisoki	10.34	0.38	24	paka	3.29	0.12
7	te'efō	8.92	0.33	25	te'ete'e	3.24	0.12
8	matu	8.61	0.32	26	hohomo	3.21	0.12
9	toke	7.84	0.29	27	'unomoa	3.09	0.11
10	manini	7.79	0.29	28	pōse	2.87	0.11
11	sipesipa	7.31	0.27	29	ō	2.81	0.10
12	fua	6.79	0.25	30	tenifa	2.74	0.10
13	palu	6.32	0.23	31	feke	2.73	0.10
14	nofu	5.94	0.22	32	fate	2.63	0.10
15	hakulá	5.86	0.22	33	ali	2.59	0.10
16	fonu	5.32	0.20	34	koango	2.42	0.09
17	kanahe	5.29	0.20	35	tolo	2.41	0.09
18	hapatū	5.18	0.19	36	fangamea	2.22	0.08

Table A.2.3.3 Results of free-listing task for birds

	BIRD	Cum. salience	Salience		BIRD	Cum. salience	Salience
1	sikiviu	18.08	0.67	17	kokí	3.22	0.12
2	lupe	17.91	0.66	18	ngongo	3.19	0.12
3	peka	15.12	0.56	19	pato	2.42	0.09
4	sikotā	11.52	0.43	20	pekepeka	1.36	0.05
5	lulu	8.86	0.33	21	manu'uli	1.26	0.05
6	kulukulu	7.03	0.26	22	manutea	0.75	0.03
7	tala	7.03	0.26	23	toloa	0.70	0.03
8	moa	6.92	0.26	24	ngutulei	0.67	0.02
9	kiu	6.57	0.24	25	lofa	0.61	0.02
10	motuku	6.47	0.24	26	helekosi	0.55	0.02
11	kalae	6.07	0.22	27	malau	0.48	0.02
12	misi	6.03	0.22	28	'ikale	0.45	0.02
13	veka	4.70	0.17	29	tavake	0.44	0.02
14	fuleheu	4.45	0.16	30	fata	0.25	0.01
15	misi'uli	4.25	0.16	31	kapatoka	0.16	0.01
16	henga	3.53	0.13	32	ngutuenga	0.09	0.00

Table A.2.3.4 Results of free-listing task for weather

	WEATHER	Cum. salience	Salience		WEATHER	Cum. salience	Salience
1	momoko 'cold'	21.24	0.79	16	fakapōpō'uli	1.65	0.06
2	māfana 'warm'	19.47	0.72	17	mālohi	1.42	0.05
3	afā 'typhoon'	9.98	0.37	18	malū	1.36	0.05
4	'afu 'humid'	9.36	0.35	19	matangi	1.35	0.05
5	la'ā 'sunny'	8.86	0.33	20	'alotāmaki	1.27	0.05
6	havili breeze'	8.70	0.32	21	tafitonga	1.20	0.04
7	vela 'hot'	8.47	0.31	22	langi 'clear sky'	1.00	0.04
8	'uha 'rain'	8.40	0.31	23	pupuha	1.00	0.04
9	mokomoko	7.67	0.28	24	'uho'uha 'drizzle'	1.00	0.04
10	hakohako	3.96	0.15	25	'alomālie	0.97	0.04
11	'ao'aofia 'cloudy'	3.95	0.15	26	hahau	0.74	0.03
12	'ahiohio	2.81	0.10	27	matamata'uha	0.38	0.01
13	mofuike	2.52	0.09	28	mana 'thunder'	0.22	0.01
14	havilivili 'breezy'	1.83	0.07	29	fatulisi	0.11	0.00
15	hako	1.67	0.06	30	pakukā	0.06	0.00

Table A.2.3.5 Results of free-listing task for physical environment

	PHYS. ENVIRON.	Cum. salience	Salience		PHYS. ENVIRON.	Cum. salience	Salience
1	kelekele 'soil'	18.95	0.70	17	'ea 'air'	1.61	0.06
2	tahi 'sea'	16.73	0.62	18	kele 'mud'	1.60	0.06
3	maka 'rock'	16.07	0.60	19	tele'a	1.51	0.06
4	'one'one 'sand'	15.69	0.58	20	makamaka	1.47	0.05
5	vai 'water'	6.82	0.25	21	mo'ungaafi	1.35	0.05
6	mo'unga	5.55	0.21	22	loloto 'bottom of sea'	1.29	0.05
7	hakau	5.12	0.19	23	moana 'deep sea'	1.17	0.04
8	lilifa	3.61	0.13	24	'ulu'ulu	1.13	0.04
9	fonua 'land'	3.59	0.13	25	liku	1.11	0.04
10	feo 'coral barrier'	3.17	0.12	26	vaitafe	1.04	0.04
11	matātahi 'beach'	3.06	0.11	27	tāfea	1.00	0.04
12	langi 'sky'	2.38	0.09	28	vao 'bush'	1.00	0.04
13	māhina 'moon'	2.22	0.08	29	efu	0.92	0.03
14	fetu'u 'star'	1.82	0.07	30	ngoue 'garden'	0.89	0.03
15	'ao 'cloud'	1.73	0.06	31	vavā	0.87	0.03
16	la'ā 'sun'	1.62	0.06				

Table A.2.3.6 Results of free-listing task for supernatural

	Supernatural	Cum. salience	Salience		Supernatural	Cum. salience	Salience
1	'Otua	25.85	0.96	16	kalaisi	0.50	0.02
2	tēvolo	12.12	0.45	17	Palōfita	0.44	0.02
3	sētane	9.25	0.34	18	me'akehe	0.43	0.02
4	Sīsū	7.33	0.27	19	'afiona	0.40	0.01
5	laumalie	6.48	0.24	20	fili	0.40	0.01
6	Sihova	4.80	0.18	21	satulō	0.36	0.01
7	'angelo	2.34	0.09	22	laumālie kovi	0.33	0.01
8	Ta'ehāmai	1.47	0.05	23	tafeuni	0.23	0.01
9	lusefā	1.45	0.05	24	fakapouli	0.20	0.01
10	'Atonai	1.43	0.05	25	'ata	0.17	0.01
11	laumaāie 'uli	1.16	0.04	26	laumaāie ma'a	0.17	0.01
12	pinono	1.16	0.04	27	felehuhuni	0.15	0.01
13	Sātai	1.16	0.04	28	laumālie lelei	0.13	0.00
14	tēmeniō	0.85	0.03	29	angahala	0.09	0.00
15	palepalengākau	0.75	0.03	30	taufatahi	0.08	0.00

Notes

1 I capitalize Nature when the word appears as defining a CM. I also want to draw attention to the fact that capital letter 'Nature' and small letter 'nature' have two distinct meanings. The latter is typically intended to mean a specific part and type of the environment (e.g., woods, trees, rivers, etc.) or some biological given aspect of existence (i.e., instinct), while the former may include anything that exists (e.g., humans, plants, animals, weather, physical environment, and the supernatural).

2 The fish sold in this market is sometimes caught locally, but it often comes from larger commercial fishing boats.

3 See the Introduction to this volume for an exhaustive treatment of CMT.

4 For a similar belief see De Lima's chapter about native Amazonian in Brazil.

5 I conducted the same word frequency analysis on the gist texts and results were extremely similar. This result supported the validity of the gist constructed out of each interview.

6 The word *mahina* 'moon' also means 'month.' I report only the uses with the meaning of 'moon.'

7 I indicate in bold words that appeared as very frequently used after the key words analysis was conducted (see Appendix 2.2).

8 My personal ethnographic knowledge about Tongan culture and the village within which I collected the data spans more than 25 years, since 1991, and comprises a total of more than two years of residence.

9 For the formulas used, see Bennardo, 2009: 289 (these formulas were developed independently of Smith, 1993 and they turned out to be the same).

10 The results of the free-listing tasks about animals (mammals), fish, birds, weather, physical environment, and supernatural are found in Appendix 2.3.

References

Bennardo, G. (2009). *Language, Space and Social Relationships: A Foundational Cultural Model in Polynesia*. Cambridge: Cambridge University Press.

Bennardo, G. (2014). The fundamental role of causal models in Cultural Models of Nature. *Frontiers in Psychology*. October 10, http://dx.doi.org/10.3389/fpsyg.2014.01140.

Bennardo, G., and De Munck, V. C. (2014). *Cultural Models: Genesis, Methods, and Experiences*. Oxford: Oxford University Press.

Duranti, A. (1994). *From Grammar to Politics: Linguistic Anthropology in a Western Samoan Village*. Los Angeles: University of California Press.

Evans, M. (2001). *Persistence of the Gift: Tongan Tradition and Transnational Context*. Waterloo, ON: Wilfrid Laurier University Press.

Ferdon, E. N. (1987). *Early Tonga: As the Explorers Saw It 1616–1810*. Tucson: University of Arizona Press.

Gailey, C. W. (1987). *Kinship to Kinship: Gender Hierarchy and State Formation in the Tongan Islands*. Austin: University of Texas Press.

Gifford, E. W. (1929). *Tongan Society*. Honolulu: Bernice P. Bishop Museum.

James, K. E. (2003). Is there a Tongan middle class? Hierarchy and protest in contemporary Tonga. *The Contemporary Pacific* 15(2): 309–336.

Lakoff, G. (1987). *Women, Fire, and Dangerous Things: What Categories Reveal about the Mind*. Chicago: University of Chicago Press.

Lakoff, G., and Johnson, M. (1980). *Metaphors We Live By*. Chicago: University of Chicago Press.

Lātūkefu, S. (1974). *Church and State in Tonga*. Honolulu: University of Hawai'i Press.

Linkels, A. (1992). *Sounds of Change in Tonga*. Nuku'alofa, Tonga: Friendly Islands Book Shop.

Quinn, N. (2005). *Finding Culture in Talk: A Collections of Methods*. New York: Palgrave Macmillan.

Rips, L. J. (2011). *Lines of Thought: Central Concepts in Cognitive Psychology*. Oxford: Oxford University Press.

Sloman, S. A. (2009). *Causal Models: How People Think about the World and Its Alternatives*. Oxford: Oxford University Press.

Smith, J. J. (1993). Using ANTHROPAC 3.5 and a spreadsheet to compute a free-list salience index. *Cultural Anthropology Methods* 5(3): 1–3.

Strauss, C., and Quinn, N. (1997). *A Cognitive Theory of Cultural Meaning*. Cambridge: Cambridge University Press.

Tonga National Population Census. 2011. *Preliminary Count*. Nuku'alofa, Tonga: The Statistics Department.

Van der Grijp, P. (1993). *Islanders of the South*. Leiden: KITLV Press.

Van der Grijp, P. (2004). *Identity and Development: Tongan Culture, Agriculture, and the Perenniality of the Gift*. Leiden: KITLV Press.

3   'Plants are cooking under the soil'

Food production, models of Nature, and climate-change perceptions among indigenous peasant communities (Amazonia, Brazil)

Leandro Mahalem de Lima

Introduction

To acknowledge that the disturbing tendencies of climate change measured by natural sciences are valid[1] is to recognize that people are already perceiving and producing knowledge about these trends in their own terms. To understand different ways of thinking and acting upon changes in small-scale environmental systems is to describe analytically how different minds and cultures conceive what the world is and what are the entities that exist in it, how they relate to each other, and upon which ontological grounds they are based. This is where and how the relevance of social sciences, specifically anthropology, comes to the fore.[2]

I present here an ethnographic contribution to a cross-cultural research project coordinated by Giovanni Bennardo, in which ethnographers of small-scale communities in six different continents have agreed to use a common blended methodological protocol that includes qualitative and quantitative strategies to analyze samples of linguistic and cognitive data (see Introduction to this volume). Primary food producing is proposed as a cross-cutting criteria because it is assumed that people whose livelihood depends on constant engagement with a changing environment are very likely to have extracted from their daily observation a logic and meaningful understanding of causes and consequences of climate and environmental degradation, as well as possibly already developed strategies on how to respond to these threats.

In 2015 I conducted fieldwork and collected data samples among the Tapajo and the Arapium, in two small riverine communities located in the zone of confluence between the Arapiums, Tapajos, and Amazon rivers, in Santarem, western Para State, Brazil (see Figure 3.1). Among these peoples, daily food production is based on a variety of agricultural and gardening practices, centered in the cultivation of manioc, and associated with fishing and hunting. Their ways of producing food delineates a typical tropical forest mixed strategy, whose basic features constitute a clear actualization of resilient Amerindian practices that date back to pre-Columbian times.

DOI: 10.4324/9781351127905-4

This pattern, shared among many colonists who were incorporated into native settlements, is also associated with activities introduced by farmers and other incomers, as some do cattle ranching of their own, or work for the farmers (e.g. Moran, 1974,1993; Harris, 2000).

The samples of information generously provided by the Tapajo and the Arapium consist of 18 semi-structured interviews, complemented by a series of free-listing tasks about constitutive categories of Nature. In the collected corpus of interviews, key topics such as deforestation, soil impoverishment, climate warming, disruption of periodical weather patterns, and over-fishing/ hunting appear among other issues of everyday life and food production. The preliminary findings I present here are not about ways to deal with these problems, but about the categories that underlie the linguistic production of the interviewees and how those categories relate to each other.

I have organized this chapter into six sections. In the first, I provide a brief introduction to the region and the small communities concerned. In the second section, I introduce the theoretical assumptions and the specifics of the methodological protocol that guide the construction of this and other ethnographic contributions to the 'Cultural Models of Nature across Cultures' research project. In the third, I present a snapshot of basic constitutive categories and relations that exist in the world and which the interviewees talked about. I arrived at this by means of the analysis of frequent key words in the interviews. In the fourth section, I detail components of Nature, relations among them, and assumptions about them obtained by the analysis of free-lists focused on basic cultural domains that exist in their world. In the fifth section, I analyze the gist of propositions in the interviews that directly mention the emic word, *natureza*, Nature. In the sixth, I introduce their ways of understanding how and why the weakening of crops cultivated in slash-and-burn gardens index effects due to climate change caused by humans. In the conclusion, I recapitulate some basic features of cultural models of Nature and climate change perceptions among the Arapium and Tapajo—representatives of the many indigenous peasant communities along the Amazon basin.

Place of research

The villages in focus, Caruci and Garimpo, were selected for this research because they are two of the main places on which I had conducted participant observation and structured data collection between 2010 and 2012 (for one year, in three visits). I reported about the results of this research mainly in my doctoral thesis (De Lima, 2015). Caruci and Garimpo are located on an isthmus that separates the Amazon and Arapiuns Rivers and ends in the zone of their confluence with the Tapajos, in front of the city of Santarem (see Figure 3.1).

The city was built upon the old Tapajo mission, established in the seventeenth century by the Portuguese Jesuits among densely populated

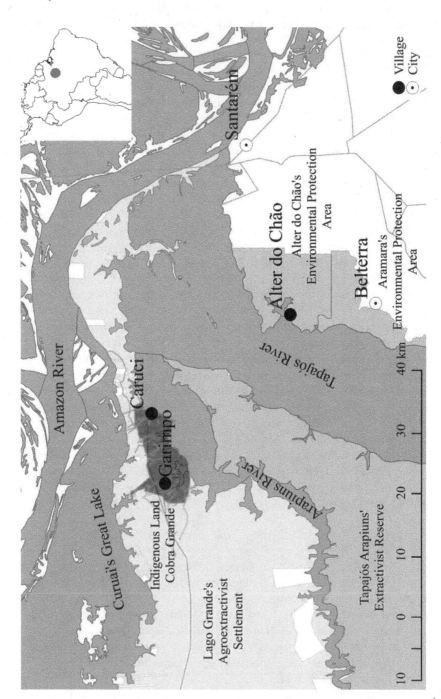

Figure 3.1 Map of the area of research.

permanent settlements, as were several others in the region, dating back to 1300 BP (Gomes, 2017). These were wrongly reported to have been abandoned by the mid-1800s, while they continued to exist as *tapuios* 'civilized indigenous' communities, commonly referred to as '*Caboclo* societies' (e.g., Nugent, 1993).

During a recent period of military dictatorship in Brazil (1964–1985), the region passed through radical socio-environmental changes that scholars have named as the 'second conquest of the Amazon' (e.g., Maybury-Lewis, 1984; Parker, 1985). In the 1940s, according to the official census (IBGE), Santarem had over 47,000 inhabitants. Seventy years later (2010), the reported population was six times larger, but in a territory reduced to less than half of its previous extension because of the rise of new municipalities (cf. IBGE, 2010). Most of the incomers—73 percent of its population (215,000)—live in the city's urban area or along the adjacent roads. In the 1970s, the areas along the Lower Tapajos and the Arapiuns were kept reserved to exploration projects conducted by the federal government and private corporate groups. As an indirect effect, this strategy kept new incomers relatively away from the vicinities of the rivers and contributed to the survival of indigenous peasant villages.

In 2010, over eight thousand people were recorded as living in the district of Alter do Chao, which covers most of the zone of confluence between the Tapajos and the Arapiuns Rivers. Of these, at least 60 percent (4,800) live in the homonym small town, the old Borari mission, which is currently growing fast because of tourism activities. The other 40 percent live either in Vila Franca (500), the old Arapium mission, or in several smaller clusters of houses formally organized in communities in the last four decades, as those I focused on for my research.

Since the 1990s, after the proclamation of a democratic constitution (1988), traditional riverine dwellers began to be generically recognized as 'traditional peoples,' with collective territorial rights granted in protected areas for sustainable use. Currently, at least four thousand people (over sixty villages) in the banks of the Arapiuns and the Lower Tapajos identify themselves as mixed-blood indigenous peoples associated to at least 13 ethnonyms (e.g., Arapium, Borari, Tapajo) and claim the recognition of land rights (see Ioris, 2005; Vaz, 2010; Bolaños, 2010; Stoll, 2016). These various territorial claims are defended as a means to contain processes considered to be the main drivers of environmental degradation such as deforestation and over-fishing/hunting.

The riverine communities in the region speak a variation of Portuguese, largely influenced by the Nheengatu (or the Amazonian general language), a Tupi idiom spread in the Amazon Basin over Aruak and Karib in the eighteenth century, with the contribution of the Jesuits. In the Lower Tapajos region, communities are considered to have abandoned the use of that language in the early part of the twentieth century. In the last decades, many of those who value the indigenous culture have begun to study it again.

The Indigenous Land where the communities concerned are situated— named Cobra Grande (or Anaconda), a reference to an aquatic enchanted being they claim lives at the bottom of the river (more in following sections)— covers five villages and over 650 inhabitants (in 8,900 hectares). This area neighbors and overlaps with a settlement (Lago Grande) that, since 2005, formally guarantees collective territorial rights to traditional communities.

The households, typically occupied by conjugal families, are grouped in clusters formed by cognatic kindreds and distributed along interconnected hydrographical bodies, that is, the Arapiuns River, several lakes and *igarapés*, streams. As I reported (De Lima, 2015), the territory Cobra Grande is formed by over 18 clusters with a mean population of 32 inhabitants. Each community is formed as the result of an alliance among over four clusters (see Figure 3.2). The communities are administered by a *cacique*, 'chief,' also called the 'president,' but each cluster and chief of a kindred have large autonomy over others.

To collect linguistic data for this research, I conducted fieldwork in 2015 at the beginning of the Amazonian summer (June 22–July 15). I was accompanied and assisted by Dr. Ana Cecilia Bueno, a colleague anthropologist (and my wife), who collaborated to transcribe the interviews and assisting the analyses. We spent 20 days among the Arapium in Caruci and the Tapajo in Garimpo. Later, for five days, we conducted interviews and free-listings in Alter do Chão, with members of one of the dominant kindreds in Caruci, who had recently established a cluster of houses there.

Constructing the informants sample for the research in Caruci and Garimpo was an edifying process because it brought to the fore differences between living in forest areas—near the headwaters of small *igarapés* (as is the case for Garimpo)—and living in the vicinity of a major lake (as is the case in Caruci). Collecting data on an isthmus with over 5.5 miles of extension also highlights the important contrast between the white, muddy waters of the Amazon, born in the Andes, richer in nutrients and life, and the black clear waters of the Arapiuns–Tapajos, drained from senile sandy soils of the Brazilian Shield (e.g., Raffles, 2002).

In total, 35 individuals associated with four different residential clusters provided the 18 audio-recorded semi-structured interviews and the 14 free-lists with 24–32 respondents each. The participants were selected according to the following basic criteria: gender—male and female (as no other gender category was ascertained)—and age, with respondents distributed in three groups: young adults from 20 to 40 years old (born in the 1980s to 1990s); elder adults from 40 to 60 (1960–1979), and senior, between 60 and 80 (1930–1959). If part of the older adults and senior cohorts, all interviewees are married (or widowed) with children or grand-children and occupy positions of prominence in the cluster and in the multi-communitarian space.

Among the 18 interviewees, 11—all the seniors (6), most of the adults (4), and one young adult—have no formal education or attended school for

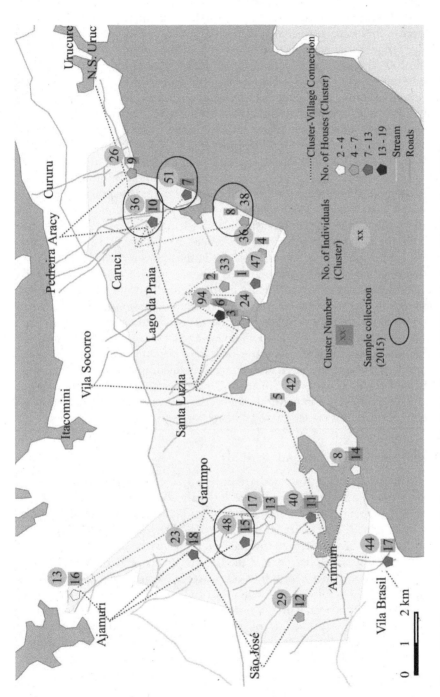

Figure 3.2 Clusters of houses in Indigenous Land, *Cobra Grande* (2012), with sites of fieldwork in 2015.

no more than three years. Among the younger interviewees, three completed secondary school, and two went to university. This points to an important difference in access to formal education across generations. In fact, it is a consequence of the construction of schools in the communities by the end of the 2000 decade, and the establishment of inclusion programs in a public federal university founded in Santarem in the same period.

Among the four residential groups that contributed to the sample, three claim Black ancestry, whereas one claims having white Portuguese ancestry— besides the common Amerindian ground. These foreign ancestries are commonly considered to have been incorporated by natives in their settlements. Although linked to different ethnic and communitarian associations, the different residential groups recognize sharing a common cultural heritage.

All respondents reported as Catholics, despite the expansion of Protestant churches in the region. The Tapajo have constructed a church of their own, conducted by a local ceremonialist, whereas the Arapium are making efforts to build theirs in Caruci. Although this village does not have a church, it has a resident *pajé-sacaca* 'shaman.' He is not in the audio-recorded sample, but he described his 'work' as a result of his connection with 'god above all' and the 'mothers'/'enchanted' that exist in the *fundo* 'bottom.' Local religious and cosmological thinking constitutes a variation of common Amerindian– hybrid systems, firstly described in, by now classic, ethnographies of the mid-twentieth century (e.g., Wagley, 1953; Galvão, 1955). As will be detailed in the next sections, interviews and free-lists show that cultural categories such as mothers/enchanted, shared among many indigenous people in Amazonia (e.g., Viveiros de Castro, 1998; Fausto, 2008; Lloyd, 2007; Descola, 2014), are of key importance in cultural models of Nature that frame perceptions of environmental degradation and climate change.[3]

Assumptions, theories, and methods

As already mentioned, I use a shared protocol established within the field of cognitive anthropology to collect linguistic data and analyze them at the word, sentence, and discourse levels, with the aid of computer tools. Cognitive data is also collected and analyzed. The analyses are conducted considering the broad picture provided by long-term participant observation.

Within Cultural Model Theory, the theoretical frame here adopted, cultural models are conceived as out-of-awareness shared mental structures (e.g., Holland and Quinn, 1987; Bennardo and De Munck, 2014). The mind is assumed to be engaged with the current situation—in addition to including bodily experience—as in acts of observation, reasoning, and understanding, and being associated with feelings and other motivations. To an individual conceived as a person who possesses a human body, thoughts expressed in words are modes of ordering perception and which provide mutual understanding in a common language. This ordering, that is, knowledge, is accomplished by mental organizations commonly called mental models, or frames, schemas, or schemata. When shared among several minds, these models may be said to be cultural out-of-awareness structures that function in the same way as the 'rules of language that people use without being aware of what they are' (Bennardo and De Munck, 2014: 282)—as C. Lévi-Strauss (1945) and W. H. Goodenough (1957) had proposed, even if differently, in the mid-twentieth century.

In this perspective, concepts represent sets of objects in the world, but also sets of possible objects and worlds, or, the actual and the counterfactual. In Bennardo's proposal (see the Introduction to this volume), a 'cultural model of Nature' is the way in which a community understands what the world is and how it works. This analytical concept of Nature, written with 'N' capitalized, refers to integrated models of everything that exists in the world, from a shared point of view. Based on contributions to cognitive anthropology of the environments (e.g., Atran and Medin, 2008), the author proposes that what exists in Nature may be synthesized in an etic framework composed of six constitutive categories: plants, animals, weather, physical environment, humans, and supernatural. These components are intended to guide the ethnographic and cross-cultural study of emic assemblages of knowledge. Cultural models that emerge from the relationship between these components include the establishment of both intra-categorical (e.g., between kinds of people or of animals) and cross-categorical causal relations (e.g., between people, animals or plants).

Bennardo (2014) discusses causal relations as part of cultural models and the likelihood that the resulting models generate reasoning strategies. From ethnographic data, he formulated three causal models: (1) the holistic way in which the existing world and its components form realities with no privileged agents; (2) the supernatural/god-centered that implies a separation of a supernatural being from all other elements of the world; and (3) the human centered, in which both supernatural/God and humans occupy a privileged position over other beings and entities that exist in Nature. In the analysis that follows, I will build causal models from what emerges of the analysis of the semi-structured interviews and the free-listing tasks.

The protocol for linguistic data collection follows suggestions by D'Andrade (2005) and Quinn (2005). It proposes to have informants talk about activities related to food production because it is assumed that an interviewee needs to activate one's unconscious model of Nature to talk about it. Issues of environmental degradation are covered when mentioned by the interviewees (see Introduction to this volume).

The semi-structured interviews were complemented by free-lists of terms provided by the respondents to questions as 'list all the _____' with the slot content varying according to the basic emic constitutive categories proposed, that is, plants, animals, weather, physical environment, people, and supernatural. These cognitive tasks are of key relevance because they provide a snapshot of a cultural domain: defined as a group of categories that members of a community/culture conceptualize as belonging together.

Problems and misunderstandings in cross-cultural translation and levels of abstractions are expected to come up in the conduction of the tasks and are important material to be explored in the analysis of the results.

In this research, most of the interviews were conducted in the kitchen of the interviewees' houses. When referred to, individuals will appear in the form of a short name. This procedure safeguards privacy and provides a means for respondents and acquaintances to identify themselves when they read this work, avoiding the use of numbers.

To retrieve every time a word (or sentence or concept) appears in a set of texts—that is, this specific set of interviews—I used *MaxQDA* 12, a qualitative and mixed-methods data-analysis tool developed by Verbi (2017). The answers to the free-list questions were recorded on paper by me or by the assistant anthropologist and were later processed with *Anthropac*, a free program for cultural domain analysis developed by Borgatti (1996).

Snapshot of basic categories in Nature from key words in interviews

As concepts represent sets of what exist, frequent words that emerge in a set of interviews addressing the same topic constitute the building blocks of underlying cultural models used by the interviewees. Therefore, extracting and ordering frequent words is to provide a valid, simple, and rich snapshot of the basic constitutive categories of the world interviewees talked about. The aim of this section is to arrive at these results from the linguistic data provided by the Arapium and the Tapajo in the 18 semi-structured interviews.

Table 3.1 contains the 15 most salient words distributed in nine groupings. The first column contains the most frequent words overall. The other eight columns represent smaller sub-groupings formed by the crossing of the gender categories (male and female), age (senior and young), and place of residence (lake border or central forest). Describing these sub-groups is of key importance in the analytical effort to elicit basic shared categories, because they bring to the fore words that are salient within different social segments.

In Table 3.1, the word 'people' is the most frequent, both overall and in the subgroupings. In the overall list, it is followed by 'garden' and 'fish,' facts that highlight the saliency of this basic pair in food production and consumption. The domain of gardens directly connects to four other words: 'plant,' 'manioc plant,' 'manioc root,' and 'flour.' 'Soil,' and 'water' appear as key terms. The saliency of the category 'moon' highlights the importance of the 'force of the moon' in fishing, hunting, and agricultural activities. The presence of the sun is indexed by the terms 'day' and 'summer,' which also index basic cyclic 'times,' as does the moon. The overall list also highlights the two words 'labor' and 'home.'

The subgroups in Table 3.1 indicate that 'fish' and 'game' are more salient among male respondents, as 'plant,' 'garden,' and 'home' are among women.

Table 3.1 Key words in interviews for all respondents and sub-groupings

	Overall (N=18)		Male								Female							
			Young (N=3)		Senior (N=3)		Lake border village (N=2)		Central forest village (N=2)		Young (N=3)		Senior (N=3)		Lake border village (N=2)		Central forest village (N=2)	
	Word	N	Word	N	Word	N	Word	N	Word	N	Word	N	Word	N	Word	N	Word	N
1	people	790	people	170	people	91	people	75	people	112	people	200	people	79	people	70	people	124
2	garden	265	fish	94	fish	54	moon	75	game	45	garden	65	garden	49	plant	29	manioc root	60
3	fish	219	moon	82	garden	40	fish	67	garden	36	manioc root	63	soil	33	garden	27	garden	54
4	soil	219	game	54	time	39	force	43	time	28	soil	44	plant	27	year	25	manioc plant	34
5	manioc root	195	hours	52	soil	25	day	39	path	25	flour	40	time	20	manioc root	25	soil	27
6	moon	188	force	49	day	20	hours	35	manioc root	20	manioc plant	38	house	19	soil	23	mother	26
7	plant	153	day	43	flour	20	water	24	moon	18	labor	35	manioc root	17	house	19	plant	25
8	time	148	time	35	water	19	lake	23	forest	18	house	32	beach	16	corn	16	flour	24
9	day	121	garden	33	moon	19	manioc root	23	soil	18	mother	29	year	13	flour	13	moon	21
10	flour	119	manioc root	28	manioc root	18	time	22	hours	17	summer	29	lake	13	time	13	labor	19
11	labor	119	forest	28	house	16	soil	21	manioc plant	15	stream	28	god	12	water	12	forest	18
12	manioc plant	109	fishing	26	month	16	fishery	20	day	14	moon	27	flour	12	*bicho* animal	13	house	17
13	home	107	path	26	plant	16	money	19	labor	14	year	26	mother	11	god	13	stream	15
14	water	99	labor	25	*curupira*	15	morning	18	law	12	plant	26	water melon	10	rain	12	*capoeira*	13
15	summer	98	soli	22	lake	14	plant	18	border	11	garden	24	fish	10	moon	12	family	12

It is interesting to observe that 'fish' is more salient among men in the village situated alongside a lake, whereas 'game' is more salient in the village in the central forest. Note also that, in a male's daily life, 'fish' and 'game' appear together with 'gardens,' 'plants,' and 'manioc,' which underlines the complementarity of these activities. These findings emphasize the idea that a male's self-construction is strongly framed by the logics of animal predation, whereas self-construction among women and the cross-gender relations are more closely linked to cultivation.

In the following list, I group the frequent key words in Table 3.1 according to the six proposed cross-cutting domains of Nature (see Introduction to this volume by Bennardo). This way of organizing the words is not intended to be a final and unique frame, but only a situated one that may be refined and reordered in several ways, and this may depend on context of use. At the same time, as in the presented sub-groupings, it is intended to provide a simple and rich image of basic components and relations within the world interviewees talked about.

(1) *Gente* 'people,' *família* 'family,' *casa* 'home,' *trabalho* 'labor,' *dinheiro* 'money;' *pesca* 'fishing';
(2) *Floresta* 'forest,' *capoeira* 'anthropogenic forest,' *roça* 'garden,' *planta* 'plant;' *maniva* 'manioc plant'; *mandioca* 'manioc root,' *farinha* 'flour,' *milho* 'corn,' *melancia* 'water-melon';
(3) *Peixe* 'fish,' *caça* 'game,' *bicho* 'animal';
(4) *Terra* 'soil,' *água* 'water,' *lago* 'lake,' *praia* 'beach,' *igarapé* 'stream,' *lua* 'moon';
(5) *Deus* 'god,' *mãe* 'mother,' *curupira* 'mother of forest/game';
(6) *Tempo* 'time,' *força* 'force,' *dia* 'day,' *verão* 'summer,' *horas* 'hours.'

To provide a general picture of the basic relationships between these salient categories, I constructed the model in Figure 3.3. I used a visual tool in the qualitative data analysis software (MaxQDA) to draw it. I configured each word as code and, if the case, included one code into another (e.g., 'beaches' are a kind of 'soil' environment; 'manioc' is a kind of 'plant'). The oriented lines (asymmetrical) highlight a clear relation of inclusion and causality between terms, while the non-oriented (or symmetrical lines) are aimed to highlight that the two codes are only related to each other (e.g., 'animals' and 'fish')—within this specific ordering of domains. The difference in the size of the words (large or small) indicates whether they appear in the 15 most frequent overall list (large) or in the subgroupings (small). The difference in thickness of the lines that connect two words represents whether they co-occur (thicker) or not (thinner) in one or more sentences within the set of interviews.

In the diagram, I placed 'people' in the center because this is the most frequent word, both overall and in the subgroupings. The image clearly

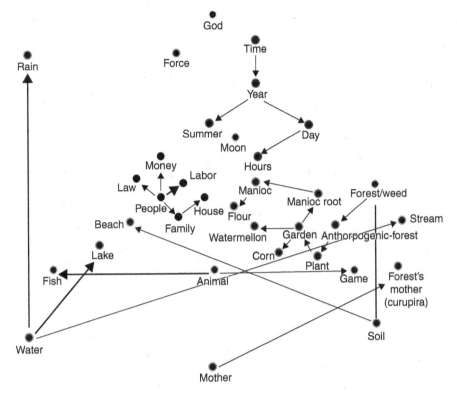

Figure 3.3 Relationships between salient categories from key words in interviews.

shows 'soil' and 'water' as the two basic environmental categories, and they include specific inhabited landscapes: 'beach,' 'lake,' 'forest,' 'brook,' and so forth. 'Forest' and 'plants' are placed between the 'anthropogenic forests'—a transitional category between humans ('plants') and nature ('forest')—and 'gardens' where 'people' cultivate 'plants.' The representation highlights the cultural saliency of 'manioc' with specific words for its 'plant,' its root and its 'flour.'

In addition to 'soil' and 'water,' two other domains appear implicit in other frequent words: one is 'sky'/'air' implicit in 'moon,' 'rain,' and 'summer' [sun]; the other is *fundo* 'bottom,' a cosmological domain that exists underneath 'soil and water,' implicit in the category 'mother.' In its turn, 'God,' was placed at the top of the representation because 'He' is reported to be the 'creator above everything that exists.' The diagram also highlights that 'time' and 'force' were the most frequently used categories to talk about the phenomena of weather and climate.

These findings show that constructing the diagrams was a useful analytical strategy because the image reduces complexity and brings to the fore the basic constituents of the world that interviewees talked about: water and soil; moon, sun, and rains; lakes and forests; plants, manioc, gardens; fish, game; bottom, sky; god, mothers; people, family, house; labor and money. Problems affecting the community– for example, deforestation, soil impoverishment, over-fishing and hunting, weaker and more unpredictable rains, warmer days and summers—these occur within the basic constituents presented in Figure 3.3. Once diagrams like this have been constructed, they can be brought back to the field, and their content discussed with respondents. More refined versions may also contribute to cross-cultural translation and comparison, especially when specific key words vary across cultures.

Detailing basic cultural domains from the analysis of free-lists

In this section, I present and comment on the results of the free-listing tasks I administered. The lists explore four etic cultural domains: animals, plants, physical environment, and supernatural. As shown in Table 3.2, I have conducted nine tasks about plants and animals, with 32 to 24 respondents, respecting the sampling criteria already suggested.

In the interviews, the etic concept of 'physical environment' demanded further explanations that led to the necessity of giving exemplifications. Although giving an example produces a bias, I felt it necessary to use 'forest' as a general example of a kind of environment (this might have contributed to its higher relative saliency). Despite this bias, the exemplification induced a clear understanding about the domain of interest. In Table 3.3, I present the 21 most salient types of environment listed, and I follow with some

Table 3.2 Free listings and respondents

	Category		N° of respondents	N° of items	Average	Range
1	Animals	'Forest/Game'	32	90	13	5–29
2		'Birds'	32	107	11	3–27
3		'Fish'	32	108	13	4–39
4		Wetland/Game	28	61	5	2–14
5		Poisonous animals	6	12	4	2–7
6		Domestic animals	24	26	5	2–13
7	Plants	'Plants'	32	144	16	6–40
8		Maniocs	32	59	6	2–18
9		Weeds	32	120	9	2–27
10	Environment		24	95	8	4–16
11	Supernatural/'Mysterious'		30	96	6	1–21

Table 3.3 Free-list results about kinds of environments

	Item	Frequency (F)	Saliency (S)
1	*Mata* 'Forest'	20	0.525
2	*Beira* 'Border'	10	0.318
3	*Lago* 'Lake'	12	0.287
4	*Igapo* 'Flooded lands'	17	0.281
5	*Rio* 'River'	10	0.26
6	*Ponta* '[Beach] tip'	6	0.188
7	*Igarape* 'Brook'	7	0.149
8	*Cabeceira* 'Headwaters'	5	0.148
9	*Rio-Grande* 'Big-River'	4	0.134
10	*Praia* 'Beach'	5	0.121
11	*Peral* 'deep waters'	3	0.107
12	*Lajeiro*	4	0.089
13	*Comunidade* 'Community'	2	0.073
14	*Cabeceira-Do-Lago* 'Headwaters of the lake'	2	0.067
15	*Beira-Do-Lago* 'Border of the lake'	2	0.063
16	*Roça* 'garden'	2	0.063
17	*Fora* 'Outside'	3	0.062
18	*Enseada* 'Inlet'	2	0.06
19	*Boca-Do-Lago* 'Mouth of the lake'	3	0.057
20	*Centro* 'Center'	3	0.055
21	*Campo-Da-Natureza* 'Natural field'	3	0.051

comments on the results. The list of answers given by 24 respondents provide 85 items, with an average of 8 items per respondent.

In Table 3.3, 'forest' is followed by 'border,' 'lake,' and another ten categories that refer to specific aquatic environments. The profusion of words for this domain highlights that people are fundamentally oriented in space by the hydrography. In the overall list, 'border' also appears in three composite categories: 'border of the lake,' 'the beach' and 'outer-border,' which refers to the 'border of the river.' This last term indicates that the pair 'outside'–'inside' is commonly used to express the contrast between the 'border' and the 'forest.' These interrelations may be clearly observable in the model that resulted from frequent words in the interviews (Figure 3.3).

The inner terrestrial areas are directly associated with the category 'center,' which is also referred to as 'center of the forest.' It is important to observe that although the 'center' is closely connected to the forest, it is also associated with environments as the savanna-type areas they call 'natural fields.' Note that they use a different category, *peral*, to refer to what could be defined as the center of the river/lake. All these features imply the occurrence of a spatial model based on three distinct complementary oppositions: the 'front-back' (of the river), the 'inside-outside' (of the forest or the river), and 'center-periphery' (of the forest). In this scheme, humans live between the inner and the outer, in front of the main aquatic bodies, with their backs to the center of the forest.

Although not as salient as the border–forest contrast, the free-lists also elicited several terms for the most common humanized spaces: 'community,' 'garden,' 'village,' 'town,' 'house,' 'home garden,' 'harbor,' and 'church.' These categories are also complemented by the contrastive categories *limpo*, 'cleaned up' and 'natural,' which point to the contrast between domesticated and non-domesticated landscapes. It is also worthy to note that one subject listed the common expression 'close to the house,' in which the house operates as a point of reference for what is close or distant. In this scheme, ego's house is thought as being in the 'center' from which all other environments radiate.[4]

Note also that although the free-lists are focused on 'water' and 'soil' environments, they also elicited culturally salient spatial concepts such as 'bottom,' and 'sky' and 'air.' It is important to highlight that neither in the free-listing, nor in the interviews, were 'environments' described as living creatures, with intentionality and conscious thoughts.

The category *bicho* is the most commonly used category to talk about animals, more than *animal* 'animal,' and may refer to 'people,' 'enchanted,' 'birds,' 'fish,' but not 'god,' creator of all these categories. Even though used in these various meanings, the free-listing tasks show that a *bicho* is typically a 'forest animal'—mammals that are most commonly referred to as *caça* 'game.'

Because of that, I conducted complementary free lists about *peixes* 'fish' (see Table 3.4) and *animais de casa* 'domestic animals.' Motivated by the interest shown by the respondents, I also conducted complementary free lists on 'game' animals that exist in 'water'/'flooded' areas. For the same reason I also conducted an exploratory free list on what interviewees defined as *bicho venenoso* 'poisonous animals,' a category in which 12 kinds of 'snakes' and 'insects' appear altogether. In total, the lists bring an average of 51 kinds of *bichos* per person, a total of 404 items, and highlights the deep knowledge and close relation 'people' maintain about these categories.

It is important to highlight that the category 'plant' was commonly and emphatically restricted to the ones 'planted by human hands,' while those that 'exist in nature' were associated to terms as *matos* 'weeds.' Because of that (and following the same procedure adopted for animals), I used different free lists for 'plants' and 'weeds' that were conducted after a specific one about types of 'manioc,' given the cultural salience of this family of species in their livelihood. Each person listed an average of 31 items—25 names for plants (16) and weeds (9), plus 6 kinds of manioc—and the lists contain a total of 264 items (323 if types of manioc are considered).

Observe in Table 3.5 that the number of plants per respondent (16) is almost double the number of weeds (9), which once again highlights the cultural saliency of the cultivation of plants. Note also that these correlations

Table 3.4 Animals, birds, game, and fish in free lists (only 10 most frequent/salient items)

	Domestic		Birds			Game			Fish		
		F	S		F	S		F	S		F	S
1	'Chicken'	18	0.61	Inambu 'wild Chicken'	19	0.47	'Armadillo'	31	0.65	Jaraqui	30	0.81
2	'Duck'	16	0.42	Jacu 'wild Chicken'	16	0.35	'Agouti'	30	0.64	Tucunare	30	0.70
3	'Dog'	10	0.33	'Hawk'	15	0.33	'Deer'	26	0.57	Caratinga	26	0.59
4	'Pig'	13	0.32	'Parrot'	16	0.27	Paca	29	0.56	Pacu	20	0.38
5	'Cat'	8	0.22	'Big inhambu'	12	0.26	'Monkey'	19	0.41	Jutuarana	17	0.33
6	'Bull'	6	0.21	Santacruz 'Pidgin'	12	0.24	'Forest pig'	15	0.34	Aracu	18	0.32
7	'Goat'	8	0.18	Inambu Sururina	12	0.21	Guariba 'Monkey'	18	0.27	Charuto	19	0.30
8	'Sheep'	7	0.16	Juruti 'Pidgin'	10	0.2	Prego 'Monkey'	16	0.24	Traira	15	0.27
9	Picote 'Chicken'	7	0.13	'Macaw'	11	0.19	Catitu 'Pig'	9	0.23	Jacunda	12	0.23
10	'Horse'	6	0.1	BemTe Vi 'Kiskadee'	9	0.17	'Coati'	15	0.23	Pescada	16	0.21

Table 3.5 The 10 most frequent/salient types of plants, maniocs, and weeds in free lists

	Plants			Manioc			Weeds		
		F	S	Item	F	S	Item	F	S
1	'Mango'—fruit	25	0.44	Caratinga	21	0.58	Sucuba—med.	14	0.35
2	'Banana'—fruit	20	0.36	Macaxeira	18	0.32	Copaiba—med.	11	0.23
3	'Orange'—fruit/tree	12	0.27	Achada—Preta	13	0.23	Itauba—log/wood	12	0.21
4	'Herb—of—grace'—medicinal/weed	13	0.24	Manicoera	10	0.14	Jutai—med.	8	0.15
5	Nanche—fruit/tree	17	0.24	Curuazinbo	9	0.19	Andiroba—med.	7	0.14
6	'Guava'—fruit	18	0.23	Brebe—Zolbuda	8	0.14	Pororoca—fruit	6	0.13
7	'Cashew'—fruit	14	0.23	Roxinha	8	0.18	Piquia—fruit	7	0.13
8	'Lemon'—fruit	12	0.21	Sao—Jose	7	0.11	Bacaba—fruit/palm	5	0.12
9	'Coconut'—fruit	11	0.21	Massarico	7	0.1	Marupa—wood/log	5	0.11
10	Cupuaçu—fruit	14	0.21	Perereca	5	0.11	Unka—De—Gato—medicinal weed	4	0.11
11	Açai—fruit/palm	11	0.18	Jaraqui	5	0.08	Uixi—fruit/tree	5	0.1
12	'Avocado'—fruit	11	0.18	Inambu	5	0.08	Açai—fruit/palm	5	0.09

appear inverted in the case of 'animals,' as the number of 'forest animals'/ 'game' (13) is almost three times that of 'domestic animals' (5) elicited from each respondent—reinforcing the cultural saliency of relations with animals mediated by the language and the logic of predation. These findings also reinforce the central importance of the contrast between 'what pertains to people' and 'what exists in "nature"' in their strategies to classify the cultural domains of 'plants and animals.'

The results of the free lists point out how the shared knowledge about plants is very detailed and nuanced among the Arapium and Tapajo. Among the ten most frequent/salient plants out of a list of 144 there are 9 kinds of fruits, one kind of medicinal plant, and no vegetables, an important family of plants grown in 'black-soils' (more in section 6). The absence of 'vegetables' among the most frequent members of the list probably reflects the fact that the free lists were conducted in people's houses, so they first picked home-garden species. Had the interviews been conducted in a slash-and-burn garden the results might probably have been inverted. This finding shows that 'fruits' are common as 'home gardens' species whereas 'vegetables' are connected to 'slash-and-burn' activities in more distant areas.

In the list with the ten most frequent kinds of 'weeds,' the two most commonly mentioned are *Sucuba* and *Copaíba*—described as big trees from which they extract 'milk' and oil for medicinal purposes. They are followed by a common fast-growing tree, *Itauba*, whose wood is used in the construction of houses, commonly classified a kind of *pau* 'log.' It is also interesting to observe that the only item that appears in both 'plants' and 'weeds' lists is *Açai* 'palm tree.' This points out the fact that this and other palm tree fruits occupy an ambivalent or transitional position in the minds of the respondents, as they are planted by humans, but not cultivated as the ones planted near home or in slash-and-burn gardens. This also points to the importance of the dissemination of plants—commonly palm trees—in the natural environments. Since the plants that exist in nature are not cultivated by people, they are cultivated by someone else, that is, the enchanted mothers/owners.

About the ambivalent position occupied by the *Açai*, it is also significant to note that ecological and archaeological studies highlight the importance of the cultivation of 'anthropogenic forests' among the Amazonian indigenous peoples. This has been true for millennia before 'first contacts' in the sixteenth century and provides a way to measure the extent and the specifics of Amerindian occupation of the Amazon river valley area in pre-Columbian times (e.g., Petersen et al., 2001; Heckenberger et al., 2007; Balée, 2013).

The lists about kinds of maniocs produced 59 items, with an average of 6 per respondent. The species *Caratinga* is far more salient than any other type. It was described by several respondents as 'a resistant manioc that grows in the sand and matures in six months.' It is followed by *Macaxeira*, also described as a resistant type, with softer roots cooked to eat in the same way as for yams and potatoes.

Table 3.6 The 15 most frequent words about 'mysterious entities' in free-lists

	Item	Frequency (F)	Saliency (S)
1	*Curupira* 'mother of forest/game'	14	0.389
2	*Encantado* 'Enchanted'	13	0.301
3	*Boto* 'Dolphin'	14	0.285
4	*Merandolino* (Name of an 'enchanted person')	12	0.251
5	*Cobra Grande* 'Anaconda'	8	0.184
6	*Visagem* (spectrum/ 'mysterious presence')	7	0.16
7	*Mãe do igarape* 'mother of the brook'	6	0.122
8	*Bicho do fundo* 'Animal from the bottom'	4	0.119
9	*Espirito* 'Spirit'	5	0.105
10	*Invisivel* 'Invisible'	2	0.067
11	*Jurupari* 'forest beast'	5	0.058
12	*Misura* 'mysterious presence'	2	0.049
13	*Mãe* 'Mother'	2	0.043
14	*Dona da boca* 'Owner of the mouth'	1	0.033
15	*Mulher da boca do lago* 'Women of the mouth of the lake'	2	0.033

It is important to note that, although the Arapium and Tapajo speak Portuguese, the category *sobrenatural* 'supernatural' did not generate responses. And in the set of interviews, it was not mentioned, not even once. In free-listing tasks, when I asked about meanings for this word, the most common answer was to say that it literally meant 'about nature,' because the Portuguese preposition *sobre* also has this meaning ('about'). Two subjects described the contrast natural/supernatural by the opposition between what exists in nature and what is brought about by humans. A young female provided an interesting explanation about this understanding: 'Supernature is to nature,' she said, 'as the chicken is to the *inhambu* 'forest chicken,' or the fan's wind is to the natural wind.'

Such thinking is far from alluding to what is 'beyond scientific understandings or the laws of nature,' as formulated in the common definition for 'supernatural' in English dictionaries (e.g., Oxford online, 2017). To conduct free listings considering an emic definition of 'supernatural,' I asked 30 subjects to mention to me things, beings, or forces they considered to be in some way mysterious. The resulting free list was productive and elicited 95 items, ranging from 1 to 21 items per subject, with an average of 6 items per person.

The categories that emerged are focused on, but not restricted to, the domain of the 'enchanted'—a term that appears in the second position in saliency. Among the 15 most salient categories (Table 3.6), 10 or 66 percent refer to items associated with this domain. As my participant observation and the preliminary analysis of the interviews indicate, an 'enchanted' may be contextually associated to several of these categories, as it is the case of *Merandolino,* a character reported by several ethnographers (Bolaños, 2010; De Lima, 2015; Stoll, 2016):

> *Merandolino* is the name of a *sacaca* 'shaman' whose 'spirit' (50th) became 'enchanted.' He lives in *fundo* 'bottom' (16th) and *se gera* 'turns into' (31st) or uses the *formatura* 'bodily form' (80th) of 'anaconda' (5th) to travel through 'water' and get to 'soil' in the form of an 'animal' or 'human.' He is the 'owner'/'mother' of a *ponta* 'beach tip' (*Toronó*) in the Arapiuns River. Commonly, he is perceived and felt as a *misura* 'mysterious presence' (12th), but not seen. He appears typically during 'stormy times.' He protects the 'fish' and the 'river,' but responds to threats if rules of respect are not met.

The basic themes of this narrative that informs the saliency of this specific name *Merandolino* in the free lists, highlight that 'enchanted,' 'spirit,' 'owner'/'mother,' and *sacaca* 'shaman' are connected in their capacity to use specific kinds of bodies. This brings to the fore that, among respondents, the human body is only one of the many bodies that spiritual beings can use as clothes when they act upon people.

In the set of interviews, the name *Merandolino* appears twice, once as a quick reference and another in a more comprehensive example of an 'enchanted' being that may change or affect the force of winds and rains, provided by an adult woman: 'I heard that if *Merandolino* gets angry, it becomes stormy, with *swirls* in the "water"' (Deni). This proposition highlights the presence in the cultural model shared among respondents of events such as storms, winds, and swirls that may be intentionally caused by these kinds of spiritual beings who occupy the position of mothers/owners of animals/fish/weeds/soils, and waters.

Additionally, the first entry on the list, the *curupira* 'mother forest/ game,' typically assumes the bodily form of animals or of a small 'Black/ Indian man.' He/she tricks hunters and loggers, making them lose orientation, if they destroy nature (animals, trees) excessively. This implies that these spirits are embedded with intentionality and have power to act upon humans (more in the next section).

In closing this section, I would like to emphasize that eliciting constitutive categories, relations, and assumptions from the analyses of the results of free lists has proven to be an important strategy for the clarification of shared knowledge about the specifics of the world people live in.

Analysis of propositions that mention the word 'Nature'

In this section, I explore how the Portuguese word *natureza,* nature, appeared in the responses provided by the interviewees. It is assumed that direct mentions of the term may bring important insights into the underlying cultural models. To conduct this exploration, I combine frequency, semantic roles, causal relations, and reasoning analyses.

In total, 'nature' was mentioned 18 times by 9 respondents of different ages; but mostly by four young adults (12 times out of 18 or 66%). Although the concept was more commonly used by young adults—which may suggest an association with subject matter learned in school—the content of the interviews and of the free lists show that nature is a relevant category among all respondents.

Regarding its semantic role, 'nature' plays a 'patient' role in most of the sentences (13 out of 18 or 72%). In the majority of the 'patient' role cases (10/13 or 76%), it refers to situations in which humans act destructively upon nature, notably in discourses about problems with deforestation, as in the following sentence offered by an elder male: 'The forests, the nature is diminishing because people are destroying it too much' (Francisco). Common statements as these imply a separation between humans and nature.

A related sentence framing a contrast between people and nature was stated by a young woman: 'If people destroy nature, nature punishes people' (Lucia). This proposes a reciprocal relation such as nature acts upon humans and humans act upon nature, which implies an understanding that nature responds to people's acts of aggression.

A statement proposed by an adult woman correlates nature's will with God's will: 'God created nature for people to use, not destroy so, if he gets angry, he may take it back' (Deni). This implies a separation between God (the supernatural creator), nature, and humans. As already highlighted in the analysis of the free-listing tasks, natural responses to aggression provoked by humans may also be caused by the 'enchanted.'

Two sentences connect the word 'nature' with the words *curupira* 'mother of forest/game' and *cobra grande*, 'anaconda,' 'mother of the river/ fish,' because for respondents these creatures exist in nature, that is, they are not thought as being supernatural. An adult male explained that 'in stormy nights, the "anaconda" gets out of the bottom, and that is what nature is' (*Peroba*), which implies that the appearance of this 'water animal,' 'enchanted,' 'mother' is related to the presence of storms (weather) and is understood as part of nature. The other sentence is provided by his father: 'An experienced hunter knows nature and therefore he can feel the presence of the *curupira* and will not let her make him get lost in the middle of the forest' (Francisco).

In another group of sentences from the interviews, the concept of nature is used to highlight the contrast humans vs. nature. This is the case of a sentence in which an adult woman contrasts the forests (in nature), with the *capoeiras* 'anthropogenic forests': 'Here in our community, nobody can slash the *mato alto* "big forest," the nature, only the anthropogenic forests' (Ana). 'To live in the community is different than to live in the city because there we can use what exists in nature and here we need money for everything,' said another young woman (Lucia) who had recently moved from one of the communities investigated, Caruci, to a small city, Alter do Chão. These statements imply a separation between nature and humans, but also suggest that the communities are closer to nature than the cities where usable things may only be accessed with money. These sentences also underlie the fact that money appears as one of the key human drivers and leads to the destruction of nature.

The analysis of these sentences and their contexts of enunciation, within the set of interviews in which respondents mentioned the word 'nature,' reinforces the hypothesis that 'nature' is a relevant category in the respondents' way of understanding what the world is. 'Mysterious' entities, such as the 'enchanted,' not only exist in 'nature,' but act as keepers of its laws and see that it is functioning well. In fact, they share with God the responsibility to punish people if they destroy what exists in nature: environments, animals, fish, forests, and so forth. The establishment of rules to forbid slashing and burning the forests brings to the fore native reflections about a way of life that is becoming more distant from nature, more connected with the greed for money, the influence from 'city lives,' thus leading to more and more destruction of nature.

Time, force, plants, and perceptions of climate change

As shown previously in the frequency analysis of key words the categories 'time' and 'force' are the most frequently used to talk about the phenomena of weather, climate, and changes caused by humans. In this final section, I present some findings about how climate change (warming) and soil depletion are directly affecting the lives of plants. This is to be added to a shared perception among the Arapium and the Tapajo that the destructive actions caused by humans are already provoking disturbing changes in nature that are impacting their daily livelihoods. The respondents' descriptions of the causes and effects of these impacts were fundamentally framed by the perception that periodical cycles of cultivation are becoming, year by year, more and more deregulated and unpredictable. To understand the problems that arise, it is fundamental to describe how people conceive the regular functioning of periodical cycles within different complementary time frames: days and nights, weeks and months, seasons and years.

In the interviews, when asked about forces or factors that are important for plants to grow, most of the respondents highlighted first that 'plants are affected by the force of the moon' or 'the growth of the moon makes plants grow.'[5] This common knowledge, also highlighted in hunting and fishing activities, guides the organization of monthly calendars of cultivation: 'As the moon changes and makes plants grow, people here plant by the force of the moon,' many said. Interviewees agreed that planting during the waning moon should be avoided because it is weak, and most of them also proposed that the full moon should be avoided because it is too strong. 'If the moon is too strong it can even burn the tips of the leaves of the *maniva*,' explained two interviewees. One male adult used a metaphor to name this effect: 'The burned leaves become as the *rabo de mucura* "possum's tail"' (Peroba).

For most interviewees, the best time to plant is during the new or waxing moon, so that the sprouts may follow the moon's cycle of growth and profit from the full moon when already in the soil. 'The new moon makes plants grow; when it begins, they start growing, growing, growing, and therefore planting at this moment makes the *maniva* grow beautiful and strong.' This common knowledge, which surfaced in the interviews, emphasizes not the peak of the force of the moon, but the process of growing and gaining momentum until that peak. It is important to point out that interviewees did not associate the 'force of the moon' with climate change effects, since they described it as a very regular and predictable force. The effects of climate change are instead perceived in the 'forces' of the rain (lesser) or of the sun (stronger) and the quality of soils (weaker).

As indicated in previous sections, *terra* 'soil' is linked to 'forest'/'weeds' and 'plants.' The term encompasses terrestrial landscapes (as forest and beach in the diagram in Figure 3.3), but also different types of soils that are basically classified by the crossing of two criteria: (a) sandy *(areiento)* or muddy (*barrento*), (b) associated or not with the *terra preta* 'black soil.' The 'black soil' is used in two composite categories: 'black soil of sand' and 'black soil of mud.' Because of their fertility, respondents highlighted the association of these types of soil with the cultivation of crops like corn, potatoes, yams and fruits such as watermelon, banana, and sugar-cane. These same soils are alternatively named as 'crop soil,' whereas 'sandy soil' appeared as 'manioc soil,' because this species is the only one that typically grows everywhere.

In the interviews, three senior adults (two males and one female) mentioned the local understanding, validated by pedologists and archaeologists,[6] that 'black soil' is the best for plants to grow because it was made in ancient times by indigenous peoples, using ashes to fertilize the soil: 'It is good for plants because they were created by indigenous peoples in old times, they worked/prepared it. It is true because many clay ceramic pieces are found in it when gardening' (Luiza). Because of this association, 'black soil' is also named 'black soil of Indians' (although this formulation does not appear directly in the interviews).

'Mud soil' and 'sand soil' contrast because of differences in looseness/ thickness that explains their distinct capacities to retain water, as in the common sentence: 'Sandy soils are less fertile, take too long to turn wet and too fast to dry out.' As a result of this, the 'center of the forest' is the best place to cultivate because it has more weeds to be cut off and burned to fertilize the soil. The scarcity of 'forest soils' caused by deforestation and the scarcity of free land has led to regulations that allow gardens to be started only in *capoeira* 'anthropogenic forests.' However, 'because soils are getting poorer, the plants are becoming weaker,' several respondents stated.

Interviewees also emphasized the general understanding that to have success in plant cultivation, it is fundamental to take advantage of the 'forces' of the rain, the moon and sun. It is because of their daily observations that most of the people perceive changes induced by humans as local climate warming and disruption of periodical cycles. For plants to grow, as many interviewees stated, they need the force of the moon, the sun and the water, but in the right measure. The climate has changed, and locals perceive it as being warmer than it was in the past, which also explains why the plants are having more difficulty growing. As already mentioned, deforestation is pointed out as the main driver of that change.

Disruption of seasonal cycles is mentioned by most of the respondents, as in the following line of argument. Deciding about the best time to slash and burn the weeds depends on the quality of the soil and the presence of water. As plants do not grow in dry soils, people have to plant in the forest when the rain comes. Typically, the rainy season (a) begins in November-December, (b) intensifies in January through February, (c) loses force by March-April, and (d) reaches drought level by August through September. In this typical calendar, slashing must be done some time before the rains come, typically in December through January, so that the plants are already strong and high in the peak of the summer. But now things have changed, as in the argument presented by one adult and reiterated by other respondents: 'We used to plant in December, but because it is warmer, and it does not rain as much as it did before, we are planting in January, even February.'

Some respondents indicated also the understanding, as stated by a senior woman, that 'some years ago, it used to rain the whole day and during the night in the winter, but it is not like that anymore.' In the village of Garimpo, located in the 'center of forest,' a young male corroborates this fact, stating that 'there used to be mist/haze in the forest during the night even during the summer, but now it does not happen anymore. The forests are dry and ready to catch on fire' (Saba). A senior woman synthesized this idea with the following reasoning: 'Because the rains are getting weaker,' she explained, 'the summers are becoming too hot, which is making the plants dry out and grow smaller, if they do not cook and rot under the soil' (Luiza).

The same phenomenon may be observed in daily rhythms of labor in the gardens. More than one respondent used a metaphor to explain how the force of the sun influences daily life: 'By midday, the sun is so hot that the garden turns into fire.' Because of this, daily activities (a) begin by dawn, (b) are paused for lunch when the sun gets too hot, (c) reinitiated when the sun cools down, and d) goes on until the sun sets or the job is done. The underlying intention is to benefit from the light of the sun and to avoid the time when its force is too strong. These changed routines of labor in outdoor spaces are used by the Arapium and the Tapajo as an important index to explain why the climate is warming up. For example, Vico, an adult male stated (and the same idea appeared in other interviews): 'We used to work in the gardens from 7 a.m. to 11 a.m., when the sun used to become too strong. But nowadays, there are times when at ten, even nine, no one can stand it anymore, because the sun is already too hot.'

These perceptions about climate change, extracted from daily experience in the cultivation of plants, points out that people—in small riverine communities such as Caruci and Garimpo—have established clear, simple and valid shared evidence to describe and explain why the climate has changed: The plants are weaker, the soils poorer, the climate warmer, the rains more scarce, the forests drier and more susceptible to catch on fire.

Conclusion and final remarks

The results of my analysis of the interviews and the free lists collected in 2015 that I have presented provide an extensive set of propositions about what the world is and how it works, bringing to the fore fundamental modes of relationships between constitutive categories of Nature.

- God created the world; including people and everything that exists in nature—environments (water, soil and sky; rivers, lakes, streams, forests, moon, sun), animals, fish, weeds, and spirits.
- Once God created the world, 'he' masters it; he is everywhere, and may destroy everything if his creatures act badly.
- People vs. Nature. What belongs to people does not pertain to Nature; therefore, cultivated/domesticated environments, animals and plants contrast with the ones that exist in Nature.
- The 'mothers'/'enchanted' own and master what exists in Nature. Everything that exists in nature has specific mothers or owners who live in an enchanted 'world'/'city' beneath water and soil.
- The mothers/enchanted think and act as people because they are animated by a human spirit. As masters and owners, they can use (as clothes) different bodies—people, animals, and fish—and may help/punish people if they do not take care of or if they destroy nature.

These results suggest that different causal models proposed by Bennardo (2014)—introduced previously—coexist within the cultural models that structure the knowledge I elicited from the Arapium and the Tapajo. The propositions about [the Christian] god imply that 'he' is as a 'father' and occupies a privileged position above everything that exists. This suggests a 'god-centered causal model.'

At the same time, results highlight the occurrence of a salient contrast between humans and nature. The 'nature'/'people' opposition points toward a 'human-centered model' in which people are placed in a privileged position over everything that exists in nature. The nature/people opposition also points to a causal model in which 'enchanted mothers' occupy a privileged position in nature and over people, thus I suggest the possibility of an 'enchanted'-centered causal model. But as people and mothers think, feel and act the same way, and are animated by a human spirit, the relationship between them appears to be one that characterizes a holistic causal model, in which people and other beings in nature share a common condition.

The assumption that everything that exists in nature has a 'mother'/ 'owner'—this concept repeatedly appeared in the results of the different analyses conducted—indicates a cultural model vastly shared among the indigenous peoples of lowland South America, and that scholars have named an animist/perspectivist ontology (Descola, 1996, 2014; Viveiros de Castro, 1998; Lloyd, 2007; Fausto, 2008). In this cultural model, categories of 'mother' *dono* 'owner' transcend specific domains of application to constitute a 'generalized mode of relating that characterizes interactions' that operates at 'different scales, ranging from the micro-constitution of the person to the macro-constitution of the cosmos' (Fausto, 2008: 1, 18). In this cultural model, ownership denotes not domination and private ownership, but motherhood. The act of taking care with love, as mothers do of their children, connects with the cultural saliency of the cultivation of plants and contrasts with relations mediated by the idiom of predation, as those established with animals, fish, and enemies.

The key-word analysis and the results of the free lists about environments pointed out a spatial model of orientation framed by three distinct complementary oppositions: the 'front-back' (of the river), the 'inside-outside' (of the forest or the river), and 'center-periphery' (of the forest). In this scheme, humans live between the inner and the outer, in front of the main aquatic bodies, with their backs to the center of the forest. Within this spatial frame, the house is thought a 'center' around which all other human environments (gardens, harbor, paths, communities) radiate from, in the midst of nature.

Destructive acts upon nature are commonly described as caused by greedy people who have no respect for mothers and their children. Within this frame, people argue that deforestation is causing climate changes for a series of interconnected reason associated to the perception that 'plants are being hardly impacted.'

- For plants to grow they need the force of the moon, the sun, the water and the soil, but in the right measure.
- The best time to plant is during the new or the waxing moon because the growth of the moon makes plants grow.
- Unlike the moon, whose force is regular and fixed, the forces of the sun, rains, winds and soils are more unstable, and have changed a lot and for worse lately.
- The climate is warmer because nowadays when it gets to 9–10 a.m., no one can work in open spaces (e.g. gardens) anymore, whereas in the past people were able to stay until 11–12 a.m.
- Lesser and unpredictable rains are causing harsher droughts, that are making people confused about when to plant. In the past, people used to slash, burn and plant from September to December, when the rains used

to begin, but now people are having to farm their gardens in January and February.

• These changes are making many people lose their crops because the plants are growing weaker and end up dying. In that context, many people are complaining that the manioc roots are more frequently 'cooking and rotting under the earth.'

In a world like this, the conclusion is that 'people need to stop destroying nature,' because if not, humans will end up dying 'cooked and rotted' in their houses, just as it is already happening to plants, but as a righteous punishment for their wrong deeds. It is not deforestation that is problematic, in fact, it is fire and ashes that can make soils as fertile as the black soils of Indians. The problem is a bad attitude that combines disrespect toward life and makes people forget that everything has a 'mother' and needs to be taken care of. Greed for money and things that come from the cities makes people forget about nature.

Notes

1 In the last two decades, according to Cook et al.'s (2016) estimate, natural scientists have reached a strong consensus, expressed in 97% or more of agreement in specialized peer-reviewed articles, that intensive human activities and fossil fuels burning are the root causes of local and global climate changes that began to occur in the last century.

2 Acknowledgment. This material is based upon work supported by a National Science Foundation Grant (BCS 1330637). Any opinions, findings, conclusions or recommendations expressed in this material are those of the author and do not necessarily reflect the views of NSF. I am very grateful to Giovanni Bennardo for bringing me into this research project, and for the comments and editing. Last but not least, I am very grateful to the Arapium and the Tapajo for the open interest in sharing their knowledge for this research.

3 Relations of mothership/ownership are of key importance because they structure the cosmos and inform human actions regarding nature. 'Mothers' and 'enchanted' are also referred to as synonyms to concepts as *dono* 'owner,' *mestre* 'master,' *chefe* 'chief' or *bicho do fundo* 'animal of the bottom.' It is assumed that these non-human persons are enchanted because they live in an *encante* 'enchanted domain' situated at the 'bottom' and 'own'/'master' everything that exists: physical environments, animals, fish, plants. It is a position that involves relations as control, protection, engendering, possession, domestication, or cultivation. Within that framework nature is thought of as domesticated by these non-human persons who have the ability to use different specific bodies as clothes—humans, animals, fish— to circulate in the aquatic and terrestrial environments among the species they 'own.' A true *paje-sacaca* 'shaman' is a 'human,' but also an 'enchanted' because he/she has the ability use bodies as clothes to circulate among his/her enchanted 'partners'/'masters' at the 'bottom.' During controlled shamanic sessions, these partners/masters may also use his/her body to dispense cures, healings, or aggression, if it is the case of what they define as *feitiçaria* 'sorcery.'

4 The two models dovetail with the discussion of the back-front model and the radial model proposed by Bennardo (2009, 2014) in Polynesia. I hypothesize that the back-front model is the most salient, but it coexists and is complemented by a radial model.

5 For a similar belief in Tonga, see Chapter 1 by Bennardo.

6 Statements such as those provided by the Arapium and the Tapajo, informed scholars who, in the 1980s, confirmed that 'black soils' are generated by humans as the result of intensive sedentarization and substantial alteration of the environment throughout several millennia (e.g., Petersen et al., 2001).

References

Atran, S., and Medin, D. L. (2008). *The Native Mind and the Cultural Construction of Nature*. Boston: MIT Press.

Balée, W. (2013). *Cultural Forests of the Amazon: A Historical Ecology of People and Their Landscapes*. Tuscaloosa: University of Alabama Press.

Bennardo, G. (2009). *Language, Space, and Social Relationships: A Foundational Cultural Model in Polynesia*. Cambridge: Cambridge University Press.

Bennardo, G. (2014). The fundamental role of causal models in cultural models of nature. *Frontiers in Psychology* 5: 1140.

Bennardo, G., and De Munck, V. (2014). *Cultural Models: Genesis, Methods and Experiences*. New York: Oxford University Press.

Bolaños, O. (2010). Reconstructing indigenous ethnicities: The Arapium and Jaraqui peoples of the Lower Amazon, Brazil. *Latin American Research Review* 45(3): 63–86.

Borgatti, S. (1996). *ANTHROPAC 4.0*. Natick, MA: Analytic Technologies.

Cook, J., et al. (2016). Consensus on consensus: A synthesis of consensus estimates on human-caused global warming. *Environmental Research Letters* 11(4): 8.

D'Andrade, R. (2005). Some methods for studying cultural cognitive structures. In Quinn, N. (ed.), *Finding Culture in Talk: A Collection of Methods*. New York: Palgrave Macmillan, 84–104.

De Lima, L. M. (2015). No Arapiuns, entre verdadeiros e -ranas. Sobre as lógicas, as organizações e os movimentos dos espaços do político. PhD thesis, Universidade de São Paulo.

Descola, P. (1996) Constructing natures: symbolic ecology and social practices. In Descola, P. and Palsson, G. (Orgs.), Nature and Society: Anthropological Perspectives. London: Routledge, 82–102. www.routledge.com/Nature-and-Society-Anthropological-Perspectives-1st-Edition/Descola-Palsson/p/book/9780415132169

Descola, P. (2014). Modes of being and forms of predication. *Hau: Journal of Ethnographic Theory* 4(1): 271–280.

Fausto, C. (2008). Too many owners: Mastery and ownership in Amazonia. *Mana* 14(2): 329–366.

Galvão, E. (1955). *Santos e visagens: Um estudo da vida religiosa de Itá, Baixo Amazonas*. São Paulo: Nacional (Coleção Brasiliana).

Gomes, D. (2017). Politics and ritual in large villages in Santarém, Lower Amazon, Brazil. *Cambridge Archaeological Journal* 27(2): 275–293. www.cambridge.org/core/journals/cambridge-archaeological-journal/article/politics-and-ritual-in-large-villages-in-santarem-lower-amazon-brazil/C7CAE8B472A0650EBDB6801ACF2A47D6.

Goodenough, W. (1957). Cultural anthropology and linguistics. In Garvin, P. (ed.), *Monograph Series on Language and Linguistics*, n. 9. Washington, DC: Georgetown University Press, 167–173.

Harris, M. (2000). *Life on the Amazon: The Anthropology of a Brazilian Peasant Village*. Oxford: Oxford University Press.

Heckenberger, M., et al. (2007). The legacy of cultural landscapes in the Brazilian Amazon: Implications for biodiversity. *Philosophical Transactions of the Royal Society: (Biological Sciences)* 362(1478): 197–208.

Holland, D., and Quinn, N. (1987). Culture and cognition. In Holland, D. and Quinn, N. (eds.), *Cultural Models in Language and Thought*. New York: Cambridge University Press, 3–40.

IBGE. (2017). Cities and States in Brazil: Surveys, Infographs and Maps. Available at: https://cidades.ibge.gov.br/.

Ioris, E. (2005). A Forest of Disputes: Struggles over Spaces, Resources, and Social Identities in Amazônia. PhD diss., University of Florida, Gainesville.

Lévi-Strauss, C. (1963 [1945]). Structural analysis in linguistics and in anthropology. In *Structural Anthropology*. New York: Tempo Brasileiro, Basic Books, 31–55.

Lloyd, G. (2007). Nature and culture reassessed. In *Cognitive Variations: Reflections on the Unity and Diversity of the Human Mind*. Oxford: Clarendon Press, 131–150.

Maybury-Lewis, D. (1984). Demystifying the second conquest. In Schmink, M. and Wood, C. H. (eds.), *Frontier Expansion in Amazonia*. Gainesville: University of Florida, 127–134.

Moran, E. (1974). The adaptive system of the Amazonian Caboclo. In Wagley, C. (ed.), *Man in the Amazon*. Gainesville: University of Florida Press, 139–159.

Moran, E. (1993). *Through Amazon Eyes: The Human Ecology of Amazonian Populations*. Iowa City: University of Iowa Press.

Nugent, S. (1993). *Amazonian Caboclo Society: An Essay on Invisibility and Peasant Economy*. Oxford: Berg.

Parker, E. (ed.). (1985). *The Amazon Caboclo: Historical and Contemporary Perspectives*. Williamsburg, VA: College of William and Mary.

Petersen, J. B., Neves, E. G., and Heckenberger, M. J. (2001). Gift from the past: terra preta and prehistoric occupation in *Amazonia*. In McEwan, C., et al. (eds.), *Unknown Amazon: Culture in Nature in Ancient Brazil*. London: British Museum Press, 86–107.

Quinn, N. (2005). *Finding Culture in Talk: A Collections of Methods*. New York: Palgrave Macmillan.

Raffles, H. (2002). The Arapiuns Basin. In *In Amazonia: A Natural History*. Princeton, NJ: Princeton University Press, 23–33.

Stoll, E. (2016). La fabrique des entités: Récits sur l'enchantement d'un riverain extraordinaire en Amazonie brésilienne. *Cahiers de littérature orale* 79: 23–50.

Vaz, F. (2010). A emergência étnica do povos indígenas no baixo rio Tapajós (Amazônia). PhD thesis, UFBA, Salvador.

Verbi (2017). *MaxQDA 12: Reference Manual*. Berlin.

Viveiros de Castro, E. (1998). Cosmological perspectivism in Amazonia and elsewhere. In *Hau Masterclass Series*, vol. 1. Cambridge: Hau Books. Available at: https://haubooks.org/cosmological-perspectivism-in-amazonia/.

Wagley, C. (1953). *Amazon Town: A Study of Man in the Tropics*. New York: Macmillan.

4 Lithuanian farmers in a time of economic and environmental ambiguity

Victor C. De Munck

Introduction

These are unusually ambiguous, even turbulent, times for Lithuanian farmers. The main reasons for this are related to recent history and present instabilities. Lithuania was and continues to be a land of relatively small independent farmers. This profile was interrupted, of course, during Soviet times (from 1945 to 1991), when lands were collectivized. In the period after independence, farmers gradually returned to the pre-Soviet conditions, though a few managed to buy and gain title to large farms (over 200 hectares in size). Joining the European Union in 2004 has led to yet another cycle of adaptations to new regulations and expectations that shape not just the economic lives of farmers, but also their own sense of autonomy over their farms. As this study shows, the Lithuanian farmer does not perceive her or his farmland, nature, and their own sense of self as disconnected domains of value and meaning. These domains are distinct and distinctively interwoven. Describing the cultural model(s) of Nature and identifying their role in the life of Lithuanian farmers is the subject of this study.

Let me assert here from our findings, primary producers (i.e., farmers in this case) do have a cultural model of Nature (i.e., *gamta*) that is holistic and semantically equivalent to the model of Nature discussed in the Introduction of this volume, *but* they also have a functional cultural model of nature (little 'n') they refer to as 'soil' or 'ground' (*žemė*) and it is synonymous with Nature (see the chapters by Widlock and Wiegele for a similar portrayal of Cultural Models (CMs) of Nature depending on perspective or context). In this sense, as I show Lithuanians have a dual vision of nature, and the two are the same just seen from different perspectives.

When I started this field work on cultural models of nature, I had not expected that the cultural model would be part of a web of cultural models, each of them contingent and being in an interactive, dynamic relationship with each other (and probably with other cultural models as well). While the goal of this study is to focus—in a good way—on the cultural model of nature, this CM emerges from and at the same time partially constitutes the farmer's understanding of himself and his perceptions of the dynamic

DOI: 10.4324/9781351127905-5

forces (both natural and social) that motivate his actions. As our work (my Lithuanian assistants and I) progressed, it became clear to me (the assistant knew this already) that farmers have a double vision of nature: one that is particular to the farmer and one that is culturally normative (that is, held by almost all Lithuanians). Elucidating these two visions of how to look at nature is a main goal that is developed through the introduction and analyses of different data sets. These two visions, while distinct, do overlap so that the farmers' actions and perception of farmland are shaped by both CMs. I will show how one is foregrounded and the other backgrounded depending on context, but neither ever disappears. Through this study, I intend to persuade the reader that these two visions (or CMs) of nature have an ontological reality, serving as 'living tools' (Holland et al., 1998) used by farmers to make decisions, shape their view of themselves, and engage with the complex nexus of social and natural forces that impact her/him.

A brief history

In March 1990, Lithuania emerged from a long period of socialism, when farms were collectivized during Soviet times (1944–1990). Scholarly writings about the newly independent Eastern European states framed them as post-socialist. Indeed, there was a dismantling of Soviet social structures and institutions, but sometimes there were no resources in place to replace them. Besides the dismantling of Soviet institutions and structures, there was an equal push, if not a rush, toward what Knudsen (2012) has accurately labeled 'EUropeanization.' EUropeanization is a particularly ambiguous term because on the one hand farmers are encouraged to be more autonomous and, on the other hand, policies and socioeconomic–environmental goals are largely set by EU and national (i.e., Lithuanian) policies. In a recent study on farmers, Karpavičius (2016) analyzed the bottom-up, top-down tensions by noting that farmers viewed it as an extension of the time of *kolukas* (collectivized farms) in which form replaced content. Similarly, contemporary farmers consider the requirements to form communities and to work independently of government/bureaucratic input a kind of charade. Nonetheless, farmers now have their own land and their own farms, a far cry from Soviet times, as they readily acknowledge.

In May 2004, Lithuania joined the EU. It was in many ways a brief time of millennial dreams and exuberance matched only by independence. When Lithuania joined the EU, there was literally dancing in the streets with buses and signposts painted with the words *Mes Europaičai* (often translated as 'we Europeans'). This joy was not simply because they identified as Europeans, but because Europe held out the promise for wealth, modern living, and individual freedom. It was Heaven on Earth and, as one older woman said to me in 2004, 'We will all leave and go to Europe.' I asked, 'But who will stay, just the *pensioninkai* "retirees"?' 'No,' she said, 'the last one will leave and lock the door behind them.' We laughed, but indeed since EUropeanization,

Lithuanians have emigrated in the hundreds of thousands; the population being reduced from around 3.5 million to 2.7 million by 2016. Figures for 2010 show that Lithuania had by far [the] highest rate of emigration in Europe—with a net migration rate of -23.7 percent, the second highest was Ireland at a -7.5 percent net rate.[1] This puts pressure on farmers because by far most emigrants are youths and able-bodied people who are looking for work in Europe. Hence, there are fewer good farm laborers for farmers to choose from. All farmers complain about being unable to find good seasonal laborers, even though the pay rate seems significantly higher than other sectors of the economy (around 45 euros per eight-hour day for farm labor in 2016, I was told by different sources). The number of farms has shrunk by about 25 percent since 2003, but the size of the average farm has increased by the same percentage. Further, the age structure of farmers is significantly different than that of other European countries—approximately a third of farmers in 2010 were 65 years or older—for the rest of Europe the average is ten years lower.[2] The percent of Lithuanian farmers in their sixties has likely increased significantly since 2010.

The traditional CM of the farm has been and continues to be that of the family farm. In 2010 approximately 60 percent of farms were less than 12 acres in size even with a 25 percent increase in the average size of farms.[3] These figures indicate a growing bifurcation in land holdings and types of farms, with most being small family farms and a second sector of large agribusiness-style farms.

Foreign incursions into farming seem relatively insignificant. The government has made it difficult for foreigners to buy farm land. Foreigners must meet a number of requirements, including permanent residence in Lithuania, three years of prior work as a farmer in Lithuania, keeping the land as farm land for a minimum of five years, and not exceeding 300 hectares (or under special circumstances 500 hectares) of land. Nonetheless, foreign agribusiness personnel, especially from Poland and Germany, have leased large areas of land from poor villagers. Thus, while small farms remain typical, there is pressure to increase farm size. Government policies on the environment and the possibilities of obtaining subsidies to repair and buy machinery and other technologies as well as subsidies for a kind of process of re-collectivization, albeit referred to as 'community building,' also situates the farmer in multiple fields of ambiguity where form and content are not easily disentangled.

It is against this backdrop that farmers must adapt to a recent history of collectivization, EUropeanization, emigration, small-scale family farming, with the rich–poor division (always perceived and mostly real) between them and other European farmers. As emphasized, farmers conceive of the farm as a 'family' farm and not as incorporated into a global or national agribusiness complex. All Lithuanians also have a rich, historically rooted conception of nature (i.e., *gamta*) that is an integral part of the public-education system. Farmers do not live in an isolated localized ethnographic present, but in various historical, demographic, social, and economic fields that I have briefly outlined above. They interact with nature in multiple ways or, as Bourdieuan scholars might note, intersecting social fields. While it is too much to zoom in on all these factors and how they affect CM constructs and implementation, the reader will recognize when these factors seem especially entangled in the construction and use of CMs by farmers. These social fields—conceiving nature as a small farmer, as a vacationer, or as a Lithuanian patriot—are also instrumental in the construction of diverse CMs of nature. As noted in the Introduction by Bennardo, a CM consists of generic, relatively fixed conservative attributes or features, and other more peripheral ones. It is this conception of CMs that allows for flexibility and consistency at the same time, allowing them to be relative to context while still maintaining their core features.

Fieldwork site and participants

Fieldwork was conducted in Lithuania and was multi-sited (see Figure 4.1). I had originally thought to conduct single-sited research in the rural area around Telsiai in Northwest Lithuania. I had previously conducted fieldwork in that region (2002–2004). However, for both pragmatic and methodological reasons I decided to extend the research to different areas of Lithuania. The main pragmatic reason is that I had hired three Lithuanian graduate students in anthropology to help with collecting data. We worked in a number of villages in different areas of Lithuania. Methodologically, I had wanted to extend the study to include a variety of different farmers from different areas so that we could be confident in our ability to generalize from our sample to the target population of Lithuanian farmers. Our samples are of sufficient lengths and variability (in terms of land size and cattle versus crop farming) that the samples for the free lists (N = 32), and semi-structured interviews (N = 37), are sufficient to meet the requirements for cultural domain sampling as described by Weller and Romney (1988), Handerwerker and Wozniak (2002), and Bennardo and De Munck (2014).[4]

Methods for data collection

Two methods of data collection were used: free lists and semi-structured interviews. I have worked extensively in Lithuania since 2002, living there for approximately two years up to 2005, making annual trips there, and living and working in the country for a second two-year period (2014–2016). My working knowledge of the Lithuanian language suffices for basic communication and reading comprehension. Three graduate students from the Anthropology Center at Vytautas Magnus University were hired to assist in collecting data and were also trained to collect data on their own.[5] This allowed the research to be conducted at different field sites so that local field site biases might be eliminated, and the results could be more generalizable than it would otherwise be. We have information from a range of farmers

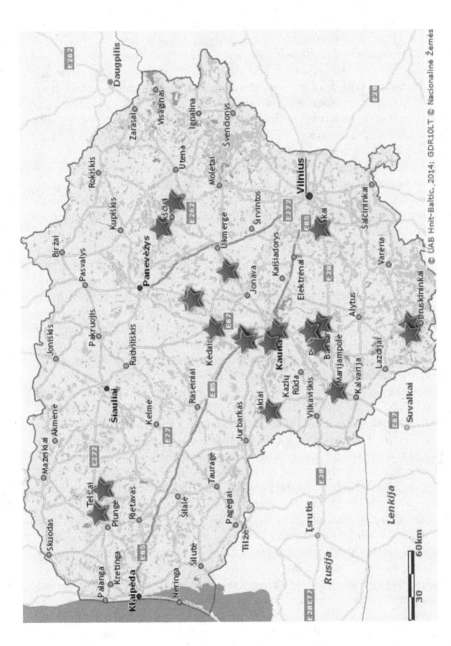

Figure 4.1 Map of research sites in Lithuania.

from different areas of Lithuania and with different sizes and types of farms, ranging from 200 to 500 hectares of land. All discussions of farmer–research interactions will be confined to those engaged in by the author.[6]

Bennardo and De Munck (2014) identify a methodological strategy for conducting research on finding and describing cultural models. Two initial stages of that model, not counting ethnography, include conducting free lists to familiarize the researcher with the key words (and concepts) that are shared among a sample of the population and, second, to conduct interviews that are partially constructed from the free-list results. For instance, if the term *pollution* is mentioned frequently in free lists (over 50% of informants cite the term), then interview questions can focus on what people identify as pollution and how people reason about pollution.

By conducting free lists, the researcher discovers (a) the words or phrases that the sample of informants identify with a cultural domain such as nature and (b) the relative saliency of these terms through cumulative frequency percentages (i.e., what percent of the people cited the term) and their average rank in the aggregated list (the higher the rank the more culturally important a term is likely to be) a saliency index (a combined rank and frequency index for each term). Free lists provide data on the important concepts of a particular cultural domain by giving data on the cumulative frequency (among other statistics) of words or phrases cited by informants independently on their respective free lists. Interviews provide ways to both correlate the free-list words with their usage by respondents in interviews. For example, if a word such as *pollution* is cited by 50 percent of respondents to a free-list question on how humans interact with nature, then these results can shape interview questions and also discover what contexts these words refer to and how they reason about these concepts. All free lists and semi-structured interview tasks took place in the residences of the farmers and at a time convenient to them. All were told they could halt at any time and that they would not be identified nor would information that could be used to ascertain their identity be reported. All the farmers were sympathetic, willing to participate and understood that they could quit whenever they wanted without any ill will or problems. Each of the data-collection methods is described below.

Free lists were typically conducted in the kitchen or living room and the free-list frame was either to 'list all the _____' or 'what are the _____?' with the content of the slot (i.e., ___) varying according to question. Informants were to write their responses on provided paper. For the free-list questions, respondents tended to provide phrases or short commentaries (usually less than one or two sentences long, and mostly three to four words). After all the free lists were collected, the primary investigator with one or two assistants, would work to shorten the responses to keywords. These are presented in the free lists presented below. Thus, the free-list words and phrases also serve as shorthand for the 'keywords in context' (KWIC) that aided in the analysis of the free lists.

D'Andrade has argued (2005) that it is better to ask indirect questions than direct, but this was recommended when he was studying American cultural values and already had specific dimensions in mind. Our knowledge of Lithuanian conceptions of Nature lacks this sort of initial sophistication. Furthermore, in his earlier work on contagious diseases and kinship (which are concrete nouns: e.g., cough, flu; mother, son rather than conceptual nouns: e.g., aggressive, liberal) he used direct elicitation techniques (e.g., 'List all the diseases/kinship terms you know'). Thus, on many occasions direct questions may also be used to elicit information for constructing CMs. Given that this is exploratory research in which we are gathering data from which to build a CM of nature (or more than one), any data that contributes to this process is useful. Hence, I decided to use a series of questions directly related to the concept of Nature (i.e., *gamta*) and that had been intended for semi-structured interviews.[7]

Gamta 'nature' is frequently mentioned by Lithuanians as important to their sense of national identity. In an earlier, unrelated study, *gamta* was the most frequently mentioned term in a free list asking Lithuanians, 'What characteristics of Lithuania are you most proud of?' ('*Kuo Jūs kaip lietuvis/ lietuvė didžiuojatės?*'). For that study 112 informants were used, equally distributed between males and females and rural and urban residents. The denotative meaning of the Lithuanian word *gamta* is semantically equivalent to the denotative meaning of the English word *nature*. However, as will be shown, it appears that the connotative understanding of *gamta* generates intimate-relational responses that differ from the usage of the term *nature* among Americans. I also suggest that it is a core feature of Lithuanian national cultural identity.[8] All Lithuanians recognize an emotional, intimate affinity with *gamta*, which appears absent in the normative conception of *nature* in the United States.[9]

The free lists questions used to analyze and induce a CM of Lithuanian farmers' conceptions of nature are presented in List 1, below; each question is followed by the Lithuanian translation.[10]

Box 4.1 List 1 Free-list questions

1. List all typical farm tasks that you do over the year?
    Surasykite visus tipiškus darbus, kuriuos dirbate savo ūkyje metų bėgyje?

2. List everything that comes to your mind when you think about nature
    Kokios mintys ateina į galvą kai pagalvojate apie gamtą?

3. In what ways do humans use nature? In what ways are humans a part of nature?
    Kaip žmonės naudojasi gamta? Kuria prasme zmones yra gamtos dalis?

4. List some of the bad things humans do to nature.
    Kokius įvardintume blogus dalykus žmonių daromus gamtai?

5. List all the problems you have as a farmer
    Su kokiomis problemomis susiduriate ūkininkaudamas.

6. What are the effects of climate change on your farm work and productivity?
    Kaip klimato kaita įtakoja jūsų ūkininkavimą ir produkciją/ produktyvumą?

In addition to the free lists, semi-structured long interviews were conducted with a (mostly) different sample of farmers. Like the free lists, interviews were conducted in the compound, and usually in the kitchen area of the farmer's residence. Often interviews were conducted with both spouses present. All interviews were between one and two hours long and conducted in Lithuanian. The informants were commonly pleased to participate and were relaxed and thoughtful during the interviews. All the interviews have been transcribed into Lithuanian and 12 have been translated into English. All informants were given the same set of questions. The interviewer felt free to pursue new lines of inquiry when it seemed worthwhile to do so. The interview material is quite detailed and informative. The interviews translated into English were coded using NVivo10-11.

The remainder of this chapter is organized in the following way: The next three sections present abbreviated outputs and brief analyses of the results of the free lists and interviews respectively. This is followed by a discussion and a conclusion. In the conclusion future research goals are suggested.

Free-list results and analysis

My discussion will focus on the six free lists mentioned above. To save space and confusion, words have been translated into English, and Lithuanian words have been minimized. Lithuanian speakers were used to back-translate ambiguous words unfamiliar to the author in order to assure accuracy. Words that are in bold are keywords in the development of a CM of nature. The words in bold are further discussed in the section in which I report about the results of the metaphor analysis I conducted on the long interviews.

Free-list Task 1: List all the typical tasks you do on a farm

For the first free list we asked farmers to list farming tasks. The cumulative data are as follows: N = 32; number of responses = 417; individual terms = 287; average responses per person = 13.031.[11]

Table 4.1 Free-list Task 1: List all the typical tasks you do on the farm

Item	Frequency	Resp PCT
1. Fertilizing	13	41
2. Sowing	9	28
3. Harvesting	9	28
4. Weeding	9	28
5. Ploughing	7	22
6. Care of garden	7	22
7. Soil cultivation	6	19
8. Haymaking	6	19
9. Spraying	6	19
10. Crop care	6	19
11. Take care of animals	5	16
12. Take care of flowers	5	16
13. Potato harvest	4	13
14. Cut grass	4	13
15. Fodder preparation	4	13

The top 15 responses are presented in Table 4.1.

The 287 total individual responses indicate that Lithuanian farmers have many year-round tasks to do. The farmers are unanimous in stating that they work all year round, and they take pride in their industriousness. Many note that to be a good farmer and continue being a farmer, 'It has to be in your blood.' They implied quite explicitly, that a lot of labor is involved as well as a lot of knowledge and adaptability to external natural, social, and institutional forces. Farmers work from morning to evening, some stating that they often work till eight or ten p.m. They frequently complained about difficulty in getting good workers. With only a few exceptions of small farms (three or less hectares), the farmers interviewed use machines, fertilizer, and spray their fields, considering this as mandatory if they are going to have good or even reasonable yields. Most want more modern machinery. *In sum:* the farmers think of themselves as hard workers (i.e., industrious or, in Lithuanian, *darbstumas*); they think that to be a good farmer, farming has to be *in your blood*. Informants are *pragmatic* in their approach, proud of their *autonomy* in dealing with the various outside and changeable forces, and think *knowledge* of farming, laws, people, technology, and markets are necessary in order to succeed.

Free-list Task 2: What thoughts come to your mind when you think about Nature?

For the second free-list task we asked farmers 'What comes to your mind when you think about Nature (i.e., *gamta*)?' The cumulative data are as follows: N = 32; Number of responses = 340; Individual terms = 285; average responses per person = 10.625. The top 16 responses are presented

Table 4.2 Free-list Task 2: What thoughts come to your mind when you think about Nature?

Item	Frequency	Resp PCT
1. Rest	15	16
2. Peace	12	22
3. Beautiful	10	19
4. Forest	9	13
5. Animals	9	13
6. Lake	10	9
7. Fresh air	3	9
8. Trash	3	9
9. Birds sing	2	6
10. Countryside	2	6
11. Pollution	2	6
12. Rain	2	6
13. Health	2	6
14. Childhood	2	6
15. Soil	2	6
16. Crops	2	6

below (in Table 4.2). A sixteenth term was added because it indicates, I believe, a shift to a second CM or at least a mode of perceiving nature. I need to stress that this question was not initially a scheduled free-list question, but was added to obtain basic thoughts about nature, to add a scaffolding of keywords that could be used for developing CMs.

Recent writings about cognition and studies of farmers and ordinary folks and how they think about climate change (Kahan, 2012, 2014; Rejesus et al., 2013; Hameed, 2014) demonstrate that information in general and specifically about climate change is processed in terms of cultural ideals and identity. Thus, information about climate change may be evaluated one way in one cultural context, and another way in a context that presupposes (or triggers) another cultural identity. I should add that the term '*gamta*' is an unambiguous word that refers to the physical, organic, not human-made environment in which we live. Emotionally and in terms of normative reference, *gamta* refers to the countryside (*kaimas*), not to cities (or city parks).

The answers are somewhat surprising as there is a disconnect between these terms and farming tasks. It can be inferred that when farmers think about nature they do not think of the farm and its immediate environs. Instead, they first think of it as distinct from the farming eco-niche. This is evidenced by the fact that the first 14 terms have nothing per se to do with farming. These terms are commonly used by city folk as well and reference a general emotional orientation, an ethos if you will, that Lithuanians have toward *gamta*. Only after what I would call the national default CM of nature do the farm-related terms *soil* and *crops* appear.

There were 285 individual responses. Many responses were phrases that we shortened for analysis. The default national conception of nature is signaled by terms such as *childhood*, *peace*, *rest*, *health*, and *fresh air*. These concepts are linked by respondents to the *countryside*, which is contrasted with Vilnius or urban living by quite a few of the informants. As a recent Lithuanian intellectual, poet, and former minister of education commented (in Lithuanian) during an interview, 'There is little or no *gamta* in the city, you have to go to the countryside (*kaimynas*) where you find lakes, forests, fresh air.'[12]

There appear to be two modes of thinking about nature: one is through the identity lens of a farmer and the second is through the identity lens of a Lithuanian. Both modes view nature as a force that causes something— nourishment—in terms of food and for the soul. Nature is agented as it provides vital resources that keep us alive and enhance well-being. Nature is associated with childhood, kinship, the countryside, and is integral to the Lithuanian concept of the 'good life.' 'Fresh air,' 'relaxation,' 'peace,' and other such terms are quite commonly associated with *gamta*. In the farm mode, nature is perceived as a resource that provides material needs, mainly food; in the national identity mode, it is perceived as a supernatural resource that provides nourishment for the soul. In either case the core feature is that nature provisions humans with either a natural or supernatural (i.e., for the soul) bounty. More evidence for the proposed two modes of perceiving nature is presented in responses to the third free-list question.

Free-list Task 3: List all the ways you use Nature

For this free list (see Table 4.5) the cumulative data are as follows: N = 32 number of responses = 287; individual terms = 256; average per person = 8.969. The top 15 responses are presented in Table 4.3.

Table 4.3 Free-list Task 3: How do people use Nature?

Item	Frequency	Resp PCT
1. Rest	20	63
2. Pollute	16	50
3. Take from Nature	14	44
4. Protect/take care	12	38
5. Pick mushrooms/etc.	12	38
6. Make a living	11	34
7. Litter	9	28
8. Work	9	28
9. Live in/part of	8	25
10. Nature gives	8	25
11. Grow grains	8	25
12. Get water	7	22
13. Destroy	7	22
14. Depend on	7	22
15. Fish	6	19

Twenty-seven percent (N = 77) of terms mentioned suggest a relationship between humans and nature; terms number 3, 4, 9, 10, and 14 are examples of terms expressing a relationship. The notion that we are dependent on nature is greater than the notion of us as the caretakers of nature. Nature is perceived as the more powerful partner; still, humans have an obligation to care for nature. We also destroy and take from nature; thus, humans exploiting nature is a powerful and pervasive theme in both the second and third free-list tasks. The terms *fishing* and *mushroom* included many other similar terms (e.g., *trout, berries*).[13] Most of the high-frequency free-list terms suggest that humans are perceived as threats rather than as caretakers of nature (e.g., *littering, destroy,* and *pollute*). That our lives depend on nature is reflected by key terms such as: *depend on, get water, nature gives, live in, work,* and *take from.*

Nature is thought of as possessing an *animating* force with particular characteristics. On the one hand humans are the stewards of nature, on the other hand, nature is the steward of humans. Nature is both animated and a biosphere in which we live and which provides resources for life as well as from which resources are taken by force. Though nature gives, it is also seen as whimsical and unpredictable. This viewpoint is expressed in comments expressed with regard to this question, such as: 'farmers are dependent on the pranks of nature'; 'nature rewards if used wisely'; and 'however much effort you put [into farm work], if summer is bad your harvest is bad.'

Free-list Task 4: What are the bad things people do to Nature?

For this free list we asked farmers to list the 'bad things people do to nature.' The cumulative data are as follows: N = 32; number of responses = 186; individual terms = 112; average per person = 5.812. The top fifteen responses are presented in Table 4.4.

Comments related to the top three items (e.g., Trash, Pollute, and Waste Resources) are usually made in relationship to specific kinds of trash (plastic bags, empty bottles, etc.) or pollution (of lakes, rivers, forest) rather than made as general statements.[14] With reference to trash, people commented on such as 'cigarette packages,' 'trash after fishing,' 'plastic,' 'broken buckets' and so on. The focus is overwhelmingly on small-scale rather than large-scale activities that the informants had personally observed and were irritated about. Their recollections are triggered by their emotional responses to their experiences of people 'not caring about nature.'

Chemicals, fertilizers, and dungwash are acknowledged by farmers as 'bad,' but also as 'necessities' ('*būtina*'). For the most part, farmers ignore industrial large-scale pollution (see Wiegele's chapter for a similar analysis). Six of the informants (18%) said they themselves 'do not do bad things, others do.' They attribute these bad things to people 'not thinking' or 'caring' and that this thoughtlessness leads to 'bad' actions. Farmers acknowledge

Table 4.4 Free-list Task 4: What are the bad things humans do to Nature?

Item	Frequency	Resp PCT
1. Trash	16	50
2. Pollute	1	47
3. Waste resources	13	41
4. Chemicals	11	34
5. Fertilizers	10	31
6. Cut forests	10	31
7. Don't recycle	10	31
8. Poachers	8	28
9. Burn grass	8	28
10. Don't think	7	28
11. Destroy ecosystem	6	22
12. Don't take care of nature	6	22
13. I don't do bad things	6	22
14. Dung wash	4	13
15. Destroy animals	4	13

Table 4.5 Free-list Task 5: What problems do you encounter in farming?

Item	Frequency	Resp PCT
1. Bureaucracy	25	78
2. Pests	16	50
3. Unstable weather	15	46
4. Unstable produce prices	12	38
5. Plant diseases	9	28
6. Shortage of good workers	9	28
7. High taxes	8	25
8. Financial money problems	7	21
9. Can't be lazy	7	21
10. Laws change frequently	7	21
11. Not knowing what EU payments will be next year	5	16
12. Expensive repair	5	16
13. Events in the Ukraine	4	13
14. Theft	4	13
15. Poor soil	4	13

that they also do bad things, but they are a result of necessity and have to be weighed in terms of the greater good—provisioning the country with food. Thus, one type of bad thing is done volitionally and without thought; the other is done out of necessity and with thought. Their assessments of actions are shaped by their cultural identity as farmers and being caught up in a capitalist modern system that requires massive yields using fertilizer and other methods for maximizing yields.

Free-list Task 5: What problems do you encounter in farming?

For this free list the total number of informants = 32; total number of terms = 107; total number of responses = 129; average number of responses per person = 3.909.

Bureaucracy is the most frequently cited term. Many of the other terms in the above list are also related to bureaucracy (see for example, items number 7, 8, and 10). These comments signal quite clearly the farmers' frustration with many newly implemented bureaucratic policies. Many of the policies and requirements simply seem unreasonable and make no sense to the farmers. EU policies are seen as separate from those of the Lithuanian government. The EU is said to provide some benefits in terms of subsidies and various incentives to create associations, implement sound environmental policies, and obtain new technologies.

As with the free-list question on 'bad things,' responses tend to be local and experiential, focusing on problems the farmers personally encounter. For instance, a sample of statements regarding the bureaucracy are: 'too much paperwork'; 'difficult to understand the paperwork'; 'unpleasant government employees'; 'changing paperwork requirements.' The difficulties encountered with bureaucracies are linked to an unstable economy and to complaints about the shift in their work ratio from being behind the plow to being in front of a computer. Sapir wrote about 'spurious cultures': 'The great cultural fallacy of industrialism ... is that in harnessing machines to our uses it has not known how to avoid harnessing the majority of mankind to its machines' (Sapir, 1924: 411). Farmers like their work and view farming as something 'in their blood,' but this feeling does not extend to the perceived increase in bureaucratic restrictions and work. Many note the general rise in prices of machinery, the instability in prices for crops after harvest, and the unpredictability of the economy.

Farmers also note changes in the weather and in a consequent increase in pests. Not all make this relationship explicit in free lists, but some do. For instance, statements related to bugs and weather frequently follow each other in free lists (I have not yet analyzed this quantitatively). Farmers write and speak as follows, 'There has been an increase in Colorado beetles,' 'there are now more ticks because in winter they don't freeze,' 'it is hard to predict the weather,' 'nature has become unstable.'

Farmers complain about the instability of prices and do not seem to know how much things will cost them or how much return they will receive from their harvests. In the interviews complaints about unstable prices and higher prices for machine repairs, and about government and EU environmental policies that increase the prices are extensively and energetically expressed. In terms of employee shortages, the farmers complain that workers drink too much, are lazy, unreasonably high unemployment benefits that exceed wages. Though what is surprising is that unskilled farm labor wages are quite high compared with wages for other unskilled jobs, averaging around 30 euros per day. However, the labor is usually difficult to do, and workers complain that farmers make them work overtime without paying them. All farmers complain about the shortage of laborers as well as the laziness and high alcohol consumption of those workers they hired. A few farmers note that they have steady laborers who had been with them for a number of years; these farmers consider themselves lucky and pay higher wages as a result.

Another dimension the farmers' problems is the people in the community. Farmers not only do not trust the government, they mostly do not trust their neighbors. They complain about a lack of 'community support,' and 'theft.' A common Lithuanian saying, oft repeated by farmers is that 'a neighbor is never so happy as when they see their fellow neighbor's field [or house] burning.' In many years of collecting free lists asking Lithuanians to list the main character traits of Lithuanians, jealousy (*pavydas*) always comes up first or second, the other being industriousness (*darbstumas*). The farmer views him or herself as isolated. One can only count on family and, indeed, of our sample, approximately 50 percent were joint parent–son/daughter farms.

Farmers view themselves as fighting the government, the weather, the economy, and their neighbors. As a consequence, they present themselves as industrious, honest, unpretentious, and (though not directly) heroic. It is a model of the self as farmer that is also elaborated on in the interviews.

Free-list Task 6: What are the effects of climate change on your farm work and productivity?

For this free-list task the total number of informants = 32; total number of terms = 103; total number of responses = 114; average number of responses per person = 3.563.

The question received fewer responses than previous questions as most of the farmers reject the fact that there is climate change on a global level. There are also few single-word or short-phrase answers. The list was more difficult to 'clean up' than others simply because it is difficult to combine gists of sentences into single categories, particularly when there is a lot of overlap in meaning, but not necessarily semantic equivalence. However, the gist of the findings I am confident in are presented below in Table 4.6. It may also have been a problem that the question as asked is perhaps too leading, since it takes the existence of climate change as a given. However, the responses of the farmers are quiet interesting in most of their explicit rejection of this assumption. Also, some would answer that there is climate change and later that there is not. I only list the top ten terms simply because the range of variation is not so great, and the answers are almost always presented in sentences.

Most of the farmers make comments acknowledging particular changes in the weather. These responses refer to local observations based on personal experiences. Common responses are, 'Everything happens earlier'; 'doesn't

Table 4.6 Free-list Task 6: What are the effects of climate change on your work and productivity?

Item	Frequency	Resp PCT
1. Warmer/Snowless winters	13	25
2. I_don't feel climate change	11	36
3. Climate changing very much	10	33
4. No effect	8	25
5. Childhood weather very different	8	25
6. Unstable weather	8	25
7. More droughts than before	7	22
8. Diseases	6	19
9. Hard to tell in which direction changing	5	16
10. Plant/Harvest rot	5	16

affect me much because I have a small farm'; 'the hot evenings are bad for spraying.' Further, many answers are expressed phenomenologically, as personally experienced: 'The weather was colder during my childhood;' 'the winters are snowless.' But when asked about climate change more globally, most would deny it as a global phenomenon: 'I don't feel climate change;' 'I don't worry;' 'Hard to tell.' The rejection of global climate change is particularly evident in the interview material, which we will turn to shortly.

Farmers think locally and, while they are quite cognizant of local changes in the weather and adapt to them, they are hesitant to generalize their immediate understandings to more global and permanent changes in the climate. Further, the effects of climate change have been inconsequential largely because they have adapted with different or better fertilizers, more spray (i.e., insecticide), and crop rotation strategies. They also talk of planting different types of seeds, ones adapted to warmer temperatures. In short, while they notice the effects of climate change, they see it through their own experiential lenses. What overwhelms them most are the changes occurring in government and EU policies, changes in technology and market prices for what they want and need to buy and the price of their crops on the market place.

Semi-structured interviews

The series of questions asked all 37 farmers interviewed are in List 2.

List 2: Topics and questions for semi-structured interviews.

About daily activities

(1) Describe your work/job (which relates to primary food production).
(2) What is your typical work/work-day? What is the rhythm of work in this area?

(3) What are some of the important skills and experience you need to be a successful food producer?

(4) What kinds of lands are most productive for farming (meaning lowlands/highlands/dark soil/light soil, etc.)? What kinds of things do you need to do to make your fields most productive? Are there material things you need to make your fields more productive (meaning equipment/fertilizer/seed types, etc.).

(5) What forces besides human and material things can affect your productivity (meaning supernatural forces such as gods, or nature, climate)?

(6) What makes plants or animals grow healthy?

(7) What are the key decisions in farming one must make to be successful? What information do you need to make decisions? How do you choose what crops to grow or animals to raise?

(8) What are some of the constraints/problems you face as a food producer?

(9) Do you believe there are supernatural forces that affect your farming success?

(10) How does the government (or NGOs) help or hinder your farming?

(11) What do you like/not like about what you're doing (satisfaction)?

(12) Are there things you have to do that are not good for the environment but are necessary for successful farming?

About climate change

(1) What changes have occurred in your work over the last 10 years? What changes have occurred in your environment over the last 10 years?

(2) What are the reasons for these changes?

(3) Can you suggest what humans can do about the changes that you mentioned above?

In this section my goal is to extend the analysis begun with the free-list data.[15] I expand the key points developed through the free-list tasks, particularly with regard to the two modes of perceiving nature: one based on a general national ethos of *gamta* as a place for leisure, peace and recuperation from city life; the other being an occupationally derived model of nature as a valued and unpredictable resource one uses and wrestles with to be a successful farmer. The metaphor analysis I use is similar to the one used by Quinn (1987, 1992, 2005) and Bennardo (2008, 2009).

My analysis below is subdivided into three sections: ethos, eidos, and relational. The configuration of ethos developed below comes largely from the interviews themselves and is focused on the farmers' conception of their own self-identity and general world view (Kearney, 1984). Each provides different aspects or 'views' of cultural 'models of nature.' This approach owes its inspiration to Bateson's analysis of the Naven ceremony among the Iatmul of Papua New Guinea (Bateson, 1958) and is not intended to segment and separate as much as to seek an integration of different vantage points farmers use in discussing nature in the context of their lives as farmers.

Let me clarify three concepts briefly. CMs are shared mental configurations that are activated in the relevant contexts. The self is, in part, a diffuse 'self symbol' that organizes CMs into larger sociocultural identities (De Munck, 2013). A world view is a macro-cultural frame, as noted in the Introduction to this volume, that delimits the range of feasible interpretations. For instance, the importance and high value placed on industriousness, the sense of a fused identity as farmers, and the low value placed on bureaucracy by Lithuanian farmers (all three of these world view components are discussed below). These three concepts are seamlessly integrated into the whole person. Ethos, then is simply shorthand for the emotional configuration or stance that farmers take as part of their cultural identity as farmers. As Bateson defined it, ethos is 'the system of emotional attitudes which govern what value a community shall set on some satisfactions or dissatisfactions which the contexts of life may offer' (1958: 220). It is important to recognize that this system of emotional attitudes is, in this context, a property of the person's sociocultural identity as a farmer and not necessarily other identities the person may take on.

Ethos: Farming is in the blood

For farmers, farming is *in their blood*, a good farmer is *born to farm*. In this sense the farmers perceive their role and purpose as an organic, natural, development of their lives. Farming is not just an occupation that one turns to, like plants or animals, it grows into the person from birth. All farmers come from rural areas and have experience with farming from childhood. However, given Soviet times when there were only collective farms (*kolūkis*) and land was divided into fairly small parcels after independence (in 1991), most of the large farmers 'grew' their farms as a result of their own ambitions as land has, and continues to be, quite cheap and often can be leased from the government for nominal prices.[16] Farmers, thus, see themselves as enterprising, hard workers, free from the constraints of collective farmers, and in short autonomous proud human beings.

Audriui, a 57-year-old farmer sitting side by side with his wife, described the ethos and conception of self that most of the farmers hold:

> You have to be born [a farmer] (*laughing*). Or to study it well and have a lot of practice because a farm is not some kind of a store—here you bought this, resold it and you have a profit. It is hard to even calculate that profit here. Because so many things depend on the climate and on the fertility, on the breeds and cultures ... also on the time you choose to sell your grains, whether you will be able to wait, and how you will predict changes in price. And finally, it also happens that they foist on you bad quality stuff, just like it happened to me one year, they sold me an

unconditioned seed. So instead of rapeseed I see that there is something else (*garstukas*) growing. ... So here you go, 'big money and no return,' as they say. So you can be very successful in farming but one year it cuts you and you can go bankrupt in a year.

Other farmers make similar kinds of comments, such as this one by Donatas: 'During the winter I look at the fields and wait for the spring to come faster, thinking how I will cultivate the land. That is inside a person. That is what I like.' Rimantas says, 'You have to like everything, you know, if you are farming. If you do it, you have no other choice. If you don't like, then you cannot work at all.' Yet another of the interviewees says,

> here is the beautifully tilled earth, sprouting crops, growing. So, you contribute everywhere, you know what your hand has touched upon. You can somewhat change the course. I would say it is like hunting, it is not just for making a living but also it gives a lot of this ... such, well probably no one, if he really does not like it, he does not farm, does he?

None of the farmers interviewed say they do not like their work. All imply, if not directly state, that farming is what they do and their identity as farmers seems to be, as Whitehouse and Lanman (2014) write, 'fused.' By *fused* they mean that the specific fused identity is not one of many identities a person shuffles through depending on context. If an identity is *fused* then among other things 'individuals demonstrate a significant willingness to sacrifice themselves for their groups' (ibid., 676). A fused identity is not perceived by the person as a role to play, a performance that is somehow not connected to one's core self, the fused identity is an essential feature of that core self.[17]

The farming ethos presented by the farmers entails a fusion of the self with the farm and the biosphere within which this identity operates. This particular cultural identity emphasizes hard work, providing for one's family, caring for one's land and animals, doing a good job that is done thoughtfully and with attention to detail, and also a sense of serving or provisioning the country. Industriousness and a sense of personal autonomy, self-determination, and competency are core components of their ethos. Here, by ethos I do not mean a general emotional configuration that is supported through primary and secondary cultural institutions, though this may occur. Rather, as noted above, I mean a general sense of themselves and their place in society as farmers that entails an emotional configuration of *rational stoicism*. Further, nature provides the context in which this identity is enacted and embodied.

Eidos: Without knowledge you will fail

I choose to use the term *eidos* (coined with reference to cultural configurations by Gregory Bateson, 1958) as a complementary contrast with ethos.[18] Eidos is the logical machinery through which humans think about how to behave and make decisions. It is distinct from the intuitive and emotive basis for action in that it is reflective, intentional, and involves applying cultural models to reason with. Bateson writes that Iatmul culture (his fieldwork site in Papua New Guinea) had 'some internal tendency to complexity, some property which drives it to fabricate and maintenance more and more elaborate constructs' (1958: 216).[19] This is what the farmers also point out—a general evolution to increasing complexity in doing farming resulting from the rapid turnover of technological innovations and ever more bureaucratic penetration in their work. Eidos, then, is an underlying culturally normative adaptation encouraging and rewarding a focus on intellectual/cognitive activity.

Our farm sample does not reflect the more classical portrayal of 'peasants' as conservative and tradition bound. Farmers valorize the pursuit of knowledge, are not reflexively averse to change, and many rue their own lack of knowledge. For instance, Linas, a relatively new ecological farmer says:

> The main problem is that we do not have experience. We do not have correct experience and little knowledge. Those would be our personal problems. And also that we want things fast, that everything would happen here and now, and would be perfect.[20]

The acquisition of knowledge is a major theme for all farmers. The importance of knowledge is emphasized eloquently by Jonas.

> Your knowledge needs to be applied everywhere—it is like the driving force that allows you to improve yourself. Anyway each year is different. And that knowledge every year needs to be applied differently. Or also it happens that you need to oppose your own beliefs and knowledge. There is not one year that's the same like before (*states firmly*). And each year you have to look at your knowledge and continuously add to it, so that ... Each year opens something new. And it is very joyful to see ... that you make progress. And ... Yes, indeed it is fun.

Milda provides a good account of the many levels and kinds of knowledge required to be successful:

> So you go into the fields and look. Depending on different species of plants: some species ripen earlier. It depends on soil. Also, when certain chemicals were applied to that soil. So you see, you can see from a grain. You carry them, look at the moisture ... if it is dry then all is good. You start threshing from that field. You decide everything yourself—when to spray, when to sow, when to do anything. You have to make the decisions yourself. Because nobody will tell you from the consulting service when to sow your field. Maybe it is still wet in my field. I would go

to work in that field but it is still a puddle there, so I start with another field this year. Or when to thresh. The same species can ripen faster in one soil but later in a different soil. Maybe soil is different there. Sometimes ... mmm...even two days difference in sowing makes a difference when to thresh. Every decision needs to be made on the spot and in time.

Some farmers signal their knowledge competency indirectly by noting their lack of knowledge. This lack is then connected to the increasing demands for the acquisition of new skills and knowledge just to keep up with the new innovations and policies. The quantification of knowledge (i.e., having more or less) is directly correlated to vectors of unpredictability: the national and EU bureaucracies, the global market place, and the weather. Petrus, who recently has expanded his farm lands to over 100 hectares says:

I think we lack knowledge. But really, I don't know, it seems that you accumulate a lot of knowledge in so much time. Sometimes I ... maybe I look funny but sometimes I compare that what I studied and what knowledge I received [as a student] and I think that if my professors had taught me back then [what I know now] I would have really become a rich man.

Implied is that while Petrus has a lot of knowledge it is not enough. His knowledge now is like a professor's, but he is not a rich man; he accumulates knowledge, but still there is a lack. Rimantas, a 48-year-old farmer, makes a similar comment:

Well, knowledge ... perhaps none of us has too much knowledge. Specialization is not so important now anymore. The most important thing is choosing the right technologies. So, for example, if you grow grains or potatoes or the same crops for animal fodder production, then it depends on each plant and it is different in the case of each plant, it depends on the area where you live, on the terrain, on ... Really, I would say it is a very individual thing. It depends on the structure of soil, on its shape, the fields. One cannot know all these things.

Petrus's statement suggests the Faustian nature of knowledge—there is never enough, and rising complexity outstrips our capacity for acquiring knowledge. Technology mediates the relationship between the farmer and external factors: the plants, soil, and weather (in short, Nature). Making good decisions entails knowing how to use the new technologies and why and when they should be used. The increasing complexity and reliance on technology add another layer of information one needs to be knowledgeable about in order to be successful. As in the quote by Petrus, no matter how much knowledge you have, there is never enough.

In a similar vein, Aldona speaks about the importance of knowledge and acquiring up-to-date information in order to succeed as a farmer. She and her husband own a cattle farm/ranch of 60 hectares.

> I am not a specialist from that field, but I have become a quite good specialist in cattle farming. Quite good. My husband does not intervene in what I order, what minerals [I buy] nor ... nothing ... nothing—I do everything myself. There is plenty [of information] now. If you want to know. If you don't want to know that you can know nothing. But if you are interested, not so much interested but if you need to know because you will not be able to do something properly otherwise. Because if you don't know anything, you are not interested in chemical substances then how will you apply them properly with plants?

The instabilities in the natural, political, and economic environments—both natural and human-made—promote a kind of Faustian feedback loop in which change is ever more varied and affects qualitatively different factors, thus knowledge acquisition never ceases. The pressure to 'keep up' increases and leads to feelings of anger and frustration, reminiscent of Lakoff's (1987) metaphor analysis of anger as represented by pressure increasing inside a container (as in the statements, 'pissed off' and 'boiling mad'). This Faustian bargain results from change or rather, instabilities in three qualitatively distinct systems: the climate, the market place, and the government.

While the acquisition of knowledge and hard work are taken as positive values, implementing them on a meta-system of instabilities leads to frustration. The farmers' responses are captured in the following two quotes, the first by Rimantas and the second by Jonas. In the first quote, Rimantas says:

> Well, with farming ... (pause). You know, finances sometimes do not match. Maybe the right farming branch has not been chosen or what the hell? But, what do I know, we work a lot, we work. We have pretty good machinery that we bought ourselves. We work a lot, we work consistently. ... We need to try harder. So, for example, this year I made a mistake with those winter [crops] and it is going to be a little bad for us. So. But anyway, we sell our cattle and everything. Well, right, (sighs) the stability of prices today ... Eee. Prices are very unstable. What concerns the cattle farming—last year we sold maybe seventeen bulls. ... But this year the price suddenly plummeted to four litas, fifty cents (approximately, 1.5 Euros). So we lost somewhere about one litas fifty from each kilogram. Or one litas thirty somewhere. ... And the same with grains. And, for example, the prices of fuel or fertilizer do not drop.

Here, the complaints are related to the government and the market, and the changes seem to be due to environmental instabilities that cannot be anticipated through knowledge. The farmer is at the whim of these vectors of instabilities. The second quote reflects more the climactic instabilities. Linas says, 'The climate is changing so the new seeds, you know I think are intended for warmer weather, but it froze, and the new seeds are not so resistant to the freezing as the old seeds, so the plants died.'

In a similar vein with regard to new seed types, Rimantas says that the weather is changing and that 'We used to have really big crops coming from fall and they would not rot. But now breeds are not very resistant. And all kinds of diseases attack them.' Almost all the farmers complained about an increase in ticks, aphids, beetles, and various other bugs, as well as the unpredictability of the weather (e.g., 'snowless winters,' 'rain downpours when there should be snow'). Knowledge regarding the weather and reading the signs no longer work as they once did.

All the above quotes emphasize the individual as an independent agent: Jonas says that 'you have to look at your knowledge and continuously add to it.' Milda notes, 'You decide everything yourself.' Rimantas notes that knowledge is 'an individual thing;' Petrus reflects on how he 'could have been a rich man' if he had the knowledge back then that he has now. It seems to me, and here I also use my familiarity with Lithuanian culture and people, that there is a difference between this sort of autonomy and an autonomy that refers to a condition of unconstrained freedom to act as one pleases (one often associated with US individualism). The speakers are all aware of constraints and forces that act on them and on the land. Within this changeable, unpredictable, fluid world they must make decisions autonomously but rationally and with knowledge. Autonomy in this sense is constrained by knowledge of critical, real natural and social forces that one must adapt to and engage with in order to be a successful farmer.

Relational metaphors

In all the questions about farming, farmers discussed soil, plants, seeds, farm animals, pests, and so on, but they do not refer to any of this as *gamta*. However, in our metaphor analysis of the interview material, nature is seen as the *container* we and everything else is 'in.' This 'container' metaphor is the master or dominant metaphor used by farmers when talking about nature. Thus climate, people, animals, weather, and so on are all in a *part to whole relationship* to nature. Second this part-whole relation is seen as a specific type of relationship. One aspect of the relationship is causal; with nature being the *primary cause* for either farming success or failure. The farmer's success depends on, or is determined by, nature and there is not much humans can do about this.

A second aspect of the relationship is that nature is not simply a resource or force; it is *animated* as is indicated by many of the quotes provided above and also in the list below. Sometimes, it is given a *personality* as being 'friendly' or 'whimsical,' but usually it is seen in the role of provisioning humans. A third aspect of the relationship is that humans can and often do *exploit* nature, often by befouling it. Fourth, many indicate that the ideal relationship between humans and nature is one of *balance*. Some argue that such a balance exists, others that it does not: All, however, use the metaphor of balance in their talk about the relationship of nature (or climate or weather) and making farming decisions. The lack of a balance is mostly, if not always, blamed on man's exploitation of nature. These metaphorical types of relationships are apparent in the 15 quotes presented below.

Box 4.2 List of metaphorical statements about nature and its relationship to humans and farming

(1) I know that it is good all this being green and the nature being green and beautiful but again *you don't need to force too much into nature* ... [metaphor—container]

(2) Also the spread of diseases. Because *if there are too much of something in nature*, then it has to be destroyed (referring to the bugs that germs and insects spread and cause diseases). [Metaphor—container, balance]

(3) Everything is grown *in and [its success] is determined by nature's conditions.* [Metaphor container and cause]

(4) Nature *cleans out itself, [it will clean out] what is not necessary.* So if there are more animals of one kind, then some disease appears and they die out. [Metaphors—balance, but also as a superorganism that strives for homeostasis]

(5) So, again there is no emptiness in nature. If... We've seen what is good from the land that's left to shrubs—clouds of ticks have appeared, we can't exit from nature. [Metaphors—container of all that exists and causal—life only emerges in the state of nature and not outside of it].

(6) The new farms somehow better fit into nature. [Metaphors—container and fit]

(7) It is the only friend and the only enemy. Nature. Only nature. You can wish for whatever. [Metaphor-animated, personality in relation to human]

(8) Everything depends on nature. Everything. The main factor. Nature and government! Nature on one side and government [on the other side]. [Metaphor—primary cause, opposite of government or culture]

(9) But you know, you can't regulate much with nature. [Metaphor—primary cause that we have little control over]

(10) Nature does a lot ('*gamta daug ką daro*'). You may raise an animal well and take care of him but if nature does not allow ('*jeigu gamta neleis*') then you may even have a loss, losses start from that. [Metaphors—animated, primary cause, personality]

(11) Well, you know, there is nothing good for nature in what we use. I think that our land is too saturated and all those ... fertilizers are not very ... I don't now, they are mainly all kinds of polyethylenes ... I think, that soil has been exhausted too much, maybe. I would think so. [Metaphor—exploitation of nature, nature as animated, and humans in a destructive relationship with nature].

(12) Nature has changed a lot. And so, as I say, all the consequences start with nature. If nature does not give much, you know, a farmer cannot do much sometimes. ('*Jeigu gamta nelabai ką duoda ir, žinokit, čia nelabai ką tas ūkinikas ir gali padaryt kartais.*') [Metaphor—personality, animated, primary cause, container]

(13) First of all, what we lack and what we need is wisdom about nature, understanding laws of nature and seeing because there are a lot of hidden dangers that we did not see in the beginning. There are such small creatures as ticks and worms. They did not seem very dangerous to us, but it turned out to be bigger enemies than we thought. Yes, little worms in water. For example, we walk and there seems to be a clean spring, but you need to know whether it is really clean: you walk all the way to the source to see. Because most often the source is in arable land. We look for springs by searching for yellow leaf thistle and cuckoo flower. If they grow, then we go all the way upstream and see where it comes from, and then we drink that water. So, these small creatures are such ... that is the first thought that comes to my mind. And this year we started seeing nature as our provider. It is our food and even our medicine. [Metaphors—animated, personality, primary cause, container, balance; complex provider that we do not know well].

(14) Goats are not good for nature because they graze everything, down to nothing, and the place where goats grazed for a few years looks like a wasteland. [Metaphors—exploit nature, balance]

(15) I think that we are a part of nature and a very natural, very natural part, very blending it, it's only that there's a lot of us. But perhaps that's natural, too, and nature will naturally take care of that sooner or later. We are a part of nature and everything is kind of okay. [Metaphors—container, balance, primary cause, animated, personality].

My metaphor analysis suggests that, for Lithuanians, a CM of nature is founded on a relational view that connects humans with nature. Thus, there is no CM of nature that does not somehow or other include humans and pertains to human motives. This, in itself, is an important finding and should strengthen the vision of CMs, or more generally the relationship between the individual, culture, and cognition propounded so forcefully and convincingly by Hutchins in his book, *Cognition in the Wild* (1995). CMs are constructed from daily life and, therefore, are never isolated from human desires, anxieties, and understandings of themselves, others and their relationship to those others and their physical environment (or nature). This point was also propounded earlier by Hallowell (1955), who combines others and nature in his concept of 'behavioral environment.' Most recently this idea has been developed and given further support by Bennardo and De Munck (2014), and the work of Kahan and his colleagues in the Yale culture and cognition project (2008, 2010, 2012, 2014).

In the ethos subsection I discussed, nature's and humanity's relation to it can be viewed in terms of an ethos that binds or fuses the individual to farming and through farming to land, plants, animals, weather, as well as social, political and economic forces. Farming is in 'her/his blood.' As a consequence there is no leaving. It is, in Sapir's (1924) words, a 'genuine' cultural–work relationship rather than a 'spurious' one. In brief, what Sapir means by 'genuine' in relationship with the case of Lithuanian farmers is that no act is without meaning; the 'major activities of the individual must directly satisfy his own creative and emotional impulses, must always be something more than [a] means to an end.' He contrasts this with jobs such as his famous 'telephone girl' example in which the individual is harnessed to a machine, and the activities of the job are inherently meaningless and do not engage the telephone operator (Sapir, 1924: 411). Her work, as Sapir notes, is highly efficient and at the same time 'an appalling sacrifice to civilization' (ibid., 411). The fused farm identity motivates the farmer to work hard and take care of things directly as best s/he can—her actions are meaningful.

However, the (forced) relationship with the bureaucracy disengages the farmer from farming. In this sense one can say that the Lithuanian farmer is caught in a dialectic in which life is out of balance in two ways: First exploitation of nature creates an imbalance between the farmer's capacity to make good decisions and the increasing whimsy of the weather; and, second, the increase of paperwork in proportion to actual farm work creates a further imbalance between the genuine culture of farm work and the spurious work demanded by the bureaucracy. In part, as a consequence of the fused identity with her farm and the perceived instabilities of the various external forces around her (e.g., market, government, nature), the farmer sees herself as an autonomous agent who can only rely on her own abilities. But these abilities are to be engaged in genuine work rather than in spurious cultural work.

In the eidos section, this analysis is extended so that the farmer privileges her knowledge and acquisition of new knowledge in order to be successful at the task of farming. The idea of farming being in the blood articulates neatly with the importance of knowledge, because the knowledge the farmer needs is about that skill and field of knowledge which he is naturally motivated to learn about. Acquiring knowledge about farming is also viewed as a necessity because nature is changing and unpredictable. Without this 'natural' motivation to learn how to anticipate and respond to nature, the farmer will fail.

Farmers do not talk disparagingly about acquiring knowledge concerning farming, and they are eager to discuss their knowledge and dispense with kernels of wisdom about farming. The only knowledge type that farmers speak disparagingly of is that related to paperwork. But the paperwork stems from the government and not from nature. Thus, it is fair to say that knowledge about farming fuses the farmers' identity with nature in a secular analogue to Whitehouse's (2004) conception of an imagistic mode of religiosity while their relationship to government generates aspects of farming that are more doctrinal and routinized, born out of bureaucratic necessity. It is this fusion of eidos and ethos that is reflected in my description of the farming ethos as *rational stoicism*.

Conclusion

There is a Lithuanian *gamta* that is conceptually distinct from the 'farming *gamta*.' In the former, nature is generally talked about and conceived as a biosphere separate from urban areas and located in the countryside which Lithuanians enter in order to get rejuvenated and to find emotional and cognitive balance. Nature is both distinct from humans and, yet, humans are 'inside of it,' a 'part of it.' From the farming perspective *gamta* is also seen as *zème* 'soil.' In both cases nature is a resource that improves the lives of humans, but in the former it improves our spiritual life, our sense of well-being, and rebalances us; in the second mode, it provides food that we need to live and stay physically fit. It also provides a sense of duty and meaning to the lives of farmers. In both these modes people are fused to nature and view nature as a supernatural, or sacred, entity that provides humans with nourishment. People act badly when they neglect, or seek to exploit, nature's bounty. The relationship is dynamic because both human institutions change and nature changes. Nature changes mostly though its own mechanisms and not as a property of humans, but humans also can affect nature through their negligence and greed. The relationship is usually cast as synthetic. Humans attempt to fit into nature and see this process as uncertain since nature is a prankster and changes in ways we cannot predict.

As we have seen, when farmers think of nature—here referring to their relationship to the land as farmers—they have a remarkable sense of connection to this type of labor. There is an affinity that creates what I have labeled a fused identity between the farmer and nature. That is, as a part–whole relationship where both the part (humans) and the whole (nature) are animate and have agency to both harm and do good. 'Good' is understood as evident in the notion of balance, harm in the notion of exploitation and negligence. It is easy to refer to this part–whole relationship as one of struggle, because indeed it is dialectic, but it appears that farmers view the relationship more complexly, for they enjoy their work. It is the very difficulties and intellectual attention needed to be a successful farmer that wed them to their farm and to the labor involved. While they do not find 'rest,' they do find 'meaning'—and a sense of their own self-identity as pragmatic, virtuous, hard-working humans useful to their family and their country. Nature provides a sense of a genuine cultural identity for both modes of 'being': as a farmer and as a Lithuanian.

Notes

1 Data obtained from http://vilnews.com/2011-07-lithuania-has-the-by-far-highest-emigration-rate-in-all-of-europe.

2 Data obtained from https://ec.europa.eu/agriculture/sites/agriculture/files/policy-perspectives/policy-briefs/enlargement/lt_en.pdf.

3 Data obtained from http://ec.europa.eu/eurostat/statistics-explained/index.php/Agricultural_census_in_Lithuania#Agricultural_holdings.

4 I sometimes bifurcate the respondent's gender as s/he or him/her but often opt for varying the gender, alternatively calling the farmer 'she' and then 'he' and using 'man,' 'woman' or human. My goal in using these pronouns and nouns is to minimize sexist language, but also to create fluent sentences. It is also the case that most farms where we conducted interviews are run equally by males and females (husbands and wives).

5 I have been teaching on a part-time basis in the anthropology master's program since 2005.

6 'We' (when used) refers to the author and assistants and is also used in the royal sense to refer to decisions made by the author.

7 In any case, informants mostly answered the free-list questions in sentences and short commentaries, which we then culled into key words.

8 In fact, the idea of linking *gamta* with national cultural identity is propagated in the public educational system, as we will later discuss and there would be, I believe with almost a hundred percent certainty, consensus by Lithuanians on the statement that 'nature is a core concept of Lithuanian identity.'

9 I must add that this observation is based on anecdotal evidence for the United States, though as a US citizen and resident for the vast majority of my life, I have not experience a corresponding stated affinity to nature among US citizens as is found among Lithuanians.

10 Other free-list questions were asked but are not relevant to this report. The English translations were worked out by the author and native Lithuanian speakers.

11 I eliminated average rank and Smith's S for now because the data requires more cleaning up, and these data would be inaccurate at present. However, I intend to use both, since they are important in determining collective cognitive (or cultural) salience of terms.

12 This is not quite an exact quote but certainly is the gist of the commentary.

13 We decided for brevity to include berry picking under the 'mushroom picking' since it does not affect the analysis, and mushroom was the most frequently listed item.

14 Please recall that the free lists are cleaned up, so *pollute* refers to many different statements informants wrote down or said to the researcher, while the free list was

being conducted. Free-list questions tended to elicit short phrases or comments rather than just a list of keywords. The shortening of commentaries was conducted by the researcher in collaboration with just one other Lithuanian assistant.

15 This is not to say other questions or materials are to be dismissed, but that this is the first of these data to go through, and I'm focusing on only that which stands out and segues with the analysis of the free-list materials.

16 The 'farmers land-holding' laws said that one cannot hold more than 80 hectares; however, farmers could lease land from the government to add to that. In 2015 an amendment was passed that legalized the buying of Lithuanian land by foreigners. This bill was strongly opposed by Lithuania's richest farmers, nationalists, and also the Green Party and Green Party types. Farm land had been quite cheap in Lithuania, and farmers could easily expand their holdings if they were ambitious and hard-working.

17 A word of warning: I am not implying that all farmers feel this way, or even all we interviewed; however, many did assert this without us looking for it, thus this data came voluntarily, from 'left field' so to speak. It was not part of the research agenda to consider identity and conception of the self.

18 We are indeed aware that the term has a lineage back to the Ancient Greeks. However there it was used, as Bateson notes, in a far different way than he uses it (1958: 212fn).

19 The passage has been slightly modified, while retaining the gist, to make it slightly more intelligible.

20 Linas and his wife had been 'regular' farmers for most of their time as farmers but switched for ideological and economic reasons.

References

Bateson, G. (1958). *Naven*. Stanford: Stanford University Press.

Bennardo, G. (2008). Metaphors in Tongan linguistic production about social relationships: '*Ofa* "Love" is Giving.' *Anthropological Linguistics* 50(2): 174–204.

Bennardo, G. (2009). *Language, Space, and Social Relationships: A Foundational Cultural Model in Polynesia*. Cambridge: Cambridge University Press.

Bennardo, G., and De Munck, V. (2014). *Cultural Models: Genesis, Typology and Experiences*. Oxford: Oxford University Press.

D'Andrade, R. G. (2005). Some methods for studying cultural cognitive structures. In Quinn, N. (ed.), *Finding Culture in Talk: A Collection of Methods*. New York: Palgrave Macmillan, 83–104.

De Munck, V. (2013). Theory of self, identity and cultural models. *Culture and Cognition* 13: 179–200.

Hallowell, Irving (1955). *Culture and Experience*. Philadelphia: University of Pennsylvania Press.

Hameed, S. (2014). Making sense of Islamic creationism in Europe. *Public Understanding of Science* 24: 1–12. Available at: http://pus.sagepub.com/content/early/2014/11/05/0963662514555055.

Handerwerker, W. P. and Wozniak, D. E. (1997). Sampling strategies for the collection of cultural data: An extension of Boas's answer to Galton's problem. *Current Anthropology* 37: 869–875.

Holland, D., Lachicotte, W., Skinner, D., and Cain, C. (1998). *Identity and Agency in Cultural Worlds*. Cambridge, MA: Harvard University Press.

Hutchins, E. (1995). *Cognition in the Wild*. Cambridge, MA: MIT Press.

Kahan, D. M. (2008). *Cultural Cognition as a Conception of the Cultural Theory of Risk*. Public Law Working Paper No. 222. Yale Law School.

Kahan, D. (2010). The communications failure. *Nature* 463: 296–297.

Kahan, D. (2012). Why we are poles apart on climate change. *Nature* 488 (7411): 255.

Kahan, D. (2014). Making climate-science communication evidence based: All the way down. In Boykoff, M. and Crow, D. (eds.), *Culture, Politics and Climate Change*. New York: Routledge Press, 203–221.

Kahan, D. M., Jenkins-Smith, H. C., Tarantola, T., Silva, C. L., and Braman, D. (2012). Geoengineering and climate change polarization: Testing a two-channel model of science communication. *Annals of American Academy of Political and Social Science* 658: 193–222.

Karpavičius, D. (2014). *Can the Local be Europeanized? A Case of Lithuanian Farmers' Responses to EU Policies and Promises*. Kaunas: Vytautus Magnus University, Anthropological Center.

Kearney, Michael (1984). *World View*. Berkeley: University of California Press.

Knudsen, I. H. (2012). *New Lithuania in Old Hands: Effects and Outcomes of Europeanization in Rural Lithuania*. London: Anthem Press.

Lakoff, G. (1987). *Women, Fire, and Dangerous Things: What Categories Reveal about the Mind*. Chicago: University of Chicago Press.

Quinn, N. (1987). Convergent evidence for a cultural model of American marriage. In Holland, D. and Quinn, N. (eds.), *Cultural Models in Language and Thought*. Cambridge: Cambridge University Press, 173–192.

Quinn, N. (1992). The motivational force of self-understanding: Evidence from wives' inner conflicts. In D'andrade, R. and Strauss, C. (eds.), *Human Motives and Cultural Models*. Cambridge: Cambridge University Press, 90–126.

Quinn, N. (2005). How to reconstruct schemas people share, from what they say. In Quinn, N. (ed.), *Finding Culture in Talk: A Collection of Methods*. New York: Palgrave Macmillan, 35–81.

Rejesus, R. M., Mutuc-Hensley, M., Mitchell, P. D., Coble, K. H., and Knight, T. O. (2013). U.S. Agricultural producer perceptions of climate change. *Journal of Agricultural and Applied Economics* 45(4): 701–718.

Sapir, E. (1924). Culture, genuine and spurious. *The American Journal of Sociology* 29(4): 401–429.

Weller, S., and Romney, A. K. (1988). *Systematic Data Collection*. Newbury Park, CA: Sage.

Whitehouse, H. (2004). *Modes of Religiosity: A Cognitive Theory of Religious Transmission*. Walnut Creek, CA: AltaMira.

Whitehouse, H., and Lanman, J. A. (2014). The ties that bind us: Ritual, fusion, and identification. *Current Anthropology* 55(6): 674–695.

5 Ecuadorian Quichua-speaking farmers' cultural models of climate, change, and morality

Eric C. Jones

Introduction

As part of a larger study, this research in a village in northern Ecuador sought to gain insight into the ways in which farmers conceive of their relationships to various aspects of their sociocultural and biophysical environments (i.e., the Nature of being), and how they understand changes in their climate and their environment along with consequential aspects of their relationships to Nature. This research occurred as part of the project "Cultural Models of Nature across Cultures: Space, Causality, and Primary Food Producers."[1] The project conducts research in over a dozen countries, with at least one investigator per country, to learn how primary producers understand Nature and environmental change. One basic assumption of the project is that human agency in Nature has spiritual, moral, and behavioral facets. While each investigator is using the same data-collection techniques, the interests and concerns of the local people resulted in different coverage of the topics from country to country. In Ecuador, what was most important to the informants was how much more difficult agricultural production is these days compared to the past. As one of the 12 sites we studied in order to understand how local cultural models (CMs) of Nature were involved in interpreting ecological changes, the research site, near the small city of Cotacachi, is a 40-home village inhabited by agriculturalists who speak a non-dominant language, and who have lived in the same place for hundreds of years.

Background and site description

A decade ago, farmers interviewed in northern Ecuador listed climate change as the most prominent factor causing transformations in agriculture in the early twenty-first century (Campbell, 2006). Indeed, glaciers on Mt. Cotacachi that rises above their farms stopped being permanent sometime between 1997 and 2004, based on longitudinal aerial photographs (Rhoades, Zapata Rios, and Aragundy, 2006). Since our interest in this project is in how weather, climate, and environmental change are interpreted

DOI: 10.4324/9781351127905-6

through the demands of daily production activities, this perception of, and concern about, climate change makes this group of farmers an interesting focus for research on CMs of Nature.

The current research involves this single village, called Alambuela, to the north of the city of Cotacachi in the state of Imbabura in north-central Ecuador. The village stretches westward up the slopes of Mt. Cotacachi from close to the north-flowing Alambi River. The larger *canton* or county of Cotacachi lies between the two Andean ranges in a valley 2,500 km above sea level, where average temperatures have historically had a narrow range, yearlong, at 15–20 degrees Celsius (59–68 degrees Fahrenheit). The region was conquered by the Inka, but not much later, in 1544, was again conquered and settled by Spaniards. The city of Cotacachi itself currently has around 9,000 residents and is known for its colonial architecture, its leather crafts, the annual festival *Inty Raymi*, and as a tourism destination because of its crafts, colonial architecture, and farm-dotted landscape between two dormant volcanoes just an hour and a half north of Ecuador's capital city, Quito.

I chose this site because people continue to speak Quichua in addition to Spanish, which is the predominant language in Ecuador. Within the larger project, we sought to represent a diversity of languages that had not been used for colonization in the past few hundred years (although Quichua was previously a language of colonization by the Inka). Not only is language an important facet of identity to this site, but the Peasants and Indigenous People's Association (UNORCAC) is an active supra-community organization that helps maintain collective action and collective identity in the rural areas outside Cotacachi town. The study site was also intriguing because it was small enough for nearly the entire village to be surveyed and thereby capture the range of cultural models in one community. Finally, I had already worked on sustainable agriculture and natural resource management in many of the communities around Cotacachi and knew that agricultural, environmental, and weather changes were on the top of people's minds.

As a precursor to the current research, from the mid-1990s to mid-2000s I was part of the multi-year interdisciplinary Sustainable Agriculture and Natural Resource Management–Andes project led by the late Robert E. Rhoades (Rhoades, 2002, 2006). In that work, we compared Andean Cotacachi with other human-inhabited ecological zones in terms of people's perceptions of the landscape and the role of migration in creating rootedness and agricultural continuity (Rhoades, Martinez, and Jones, 2002; Flora, 2006; Jones, 2002). We found a type of rootedness in Cotacachi that was associated with circular migration, compared to the stepwise and chain migration to the Ecuadorian agricultural frontier, and the permanent out-migration from a relatively densely populated rum-producing rural area that had been an agricultural frontier a generation before the other one. The type of connection to place in Cotacachi appears to be associated with a strong and salient beliefs about various facets of the biophysical environment,

Figure 5.1 A typical herd of cattle pasturing on the side of Mt. Cotacachi.

which subsequently led me to choose this site for the current study regarding cultural models generated by people experiencing environmental change—particularly changes to their agricultural livelihoods.

In the Cotacachi area, indigenous and non-indigenous smallholders mainly intercrop corn and pulses, and also grow potatoes, alfalfa for hay, peppers, and squash for household use and sale, a few pigs, cows, sheep and goats, as well as some vegetables and citrus for household use (see Figure 5.1). Up higher on Mt. Cotacachi, people pasture their animals and grow wheat and barley. Just under half the smallholders have access to irrigation for their fields, based on a survey by the local Peasants and Indigenous People's Association (Skarbø and VanderMolen, 2014). Farmers are losing some traditional crops, while adding others (Skarbø, 2006; Skarbø et al., 2012) such as Cape Gooseberry for making raisins for urban consumption and export, plus quinoa.

Methodology

Data collection. A resident of Alambuela village and I conducted this research with Quichua-speaking farmers. We interviewed them about their daily activities—particularly related to food production—with 23 individuals from different families from among the village households. Many homes were empty due to circular migration or anticipatedly temporary out-migration. All these families engage in farming activities, although farming is not the only productive activity for some of the families. We stratified the sample by the following characteristics and attempted to have equal numbers of each: irrigated and not irrigated, young and old, male and female, and smaller landholdings vs. larger landholdings. These are relevant for the following reasons:

- Irrigation is likely to be affected by climate-induced hydrological changes (Viviroli et al., 2011), and because water distribution is inequitable;
- Age is a proxy for cosmopolitan interests, a greater desire for cash/money, and loss of ecological knowledge;
- Gender is a basis for a moderate division of labor in agriculture in this area, plus men are more likely to work off-farm for pay;
- Land size is a proxy for the degree of financial investment in agriculture and also for financial resources for dealing with change.

In order to access explicit knowledge (e.g., facts, details, stories), as well as implicit knowledge (e.g., general perceptions, senses of things) and unconscious knowledge, our research into cultural models of Nature employs several data-collection techniques. This report only contains data collected through the semi-structured interviews. The team members used the semi-structured interview guide (see the Introduction to this volume) in each of the sites, but tailored the interviews to follow up on issues important to locals as well as to gather data concerning additional interests of the investigators in each site. My colleague conducted all but one of the interviews in Quichua, and I conducted the other interview in Spanish. We digitally recorded the interviews, and my colleague also transcribed the interviews and translated them into Spanish so we could compare our understandings of their responses. *Data analysis. Word, phrase, sentence and paragraph-level analyses supported the development of the cultural model in this chapter.* I conducted word counts of nouns and verbs using MaxQDA on the same linguistic data used for the thematic analysis and the causal analysis. This was followed by a metaphor analysis. I present results of the word-level analysis (word counts) and other linguistic sentence-level analysis (metaphors) in the section, 'Linguistic Indicators of Environmental Change,' followed by the thematic results and the more general building of the cultural model.

To capture the most important facets of these Cotacacheños' understanding of environmental change, I conducted thematic analysis at the phrase/sentence level, and causal analysis at the paragraph level. For thematic analysis, I counted whether a theme was present in each of the interviews. I mainly examined presence/absence of themes that came from the questions covering changes and challenges in agriculture, effects of weather changes, the nature of weather changes, and the agency of humans. For any identified theme, I counted each individual a maximum of one time per theme; thus, the maximum count for each theme being expressed is the same as the total sample size (n = 23). For example, in 14 of the interviews, I found mention of the 'timing of rainfall'—whether as a general shift or specific mention of months/seasons. I mainly report on themes counted among at least 10 of the

23 informants. In a few cases, to be illustrative, I included some subthemes that are not present in 10 or more interviews when its overarching or general theme was present in at least 10 interviews.

The other major analytical approach I used was a causal analysis, typically occurring at the paragraph level. I looked for co-occurrence of the themes encountered via thematic analysis, and particularly when one theme was described as a cause of another theme.

The sections 'Linguistic Indicators of Environmental Change, Perceived Environmental Changes', and 'Perception of Human Agency in Environmental Change' are the more descriptive parts of the manuscript in an attempt to report summary thematic and linguistic data plus locally perceived causality without my interpretations. The later section, 'The Structure of Causality and Hypothesized Cultural Model of Nature.' relies on my interpretation of these data in order to begin to capture an emic understanding of a cultural model of Nature (as distinguished from nature as the biophysical environment), and to synthesize the major causal statements made by the informants.

Results

Linguistic indicators of environmental change. I conducted an analysis of the most frequent key words, that is, nouns and verbs, in order to see how they relate to the domains of agriculture and environmental change. I also conducted a metaphor analysis. These analyses—which drew from the same semi-structured interview data as did the thematic and causal analyses— help the researcher to discover less overt or less top-of-the-mind responses about Nature or the way their world works (especially regarding how farming works). The assumption is that the frequency of terms indicates the importance of the concepts they express; and that metaphors capture one's relationships to Nature without directly answering questions about those relationships.

The frequency count of nouns and verbs across the 23 interviews generated over 100 nouns and verbs with total counts of 10 or more each. The top three were each over 300—'to do,' 'farmer,' and 'to have' were by far the top three words. Although 'to do' and 'to have' are common forms of speech in many languages, these words suggest that human agency or one's own agency is very important in understanding a cultural model of Nature. The frequency count put a relatively high emphasis on 'being' (e.g., have, do, to be, should be, live, need, can, want—all within the top third of terms). Some of these words are required in everyday speech, but nonetheless are important regarding the discussion of daily activities. Looking at these words in their contexts suggests that they are used in ways that helps one to define what it means to live rightly or 'to be' in the correct ways.

Next, after the words for being, there is a high frequency of words referring to the things going into agriculture (e.g., crops, land, weather, seeds, the day, wind, rain), which are slightly more numerous than agricultural activities undertaken by people (e.g., production, work, activity, cultivate, harvest). Specific words for plants and animals are not very common, but the word plants is among the top five words, and animals in the top 15.

The metaphor analysis revealed relatively few metaphors that were used to talk about the nature of daily activities and the ecological changes associated with food production. The two main metaphors—mentioned by a few people each—were about the gendering of parental figures in Nature, and about the centrality of the soil for good living on a healthy and productive farm:

(1) The moon and the sun, the two volcanoes that lie on each side of the village, and God and Mother Nature were personified respectively as mother and father who take care of the people and from which most all things come. The sun, moon, God, Mother Nature, and the dormant volcanoes are personified as parents. This may be because they are always present and stable, regardless of season or turmoil, just as parents should be. However, making all of these into supernatural parents—both mother and father—suggest the centrality of parenthood in this rural farming life. If we identify the source of the metaphor, it is the knowledge that community members have about how parents are supposed to be. And to identify the target of the metaphor, the target or the thing needing explaining would be these massive celestial, earthly, and supernatural entities with an unchanging nature.

(2) The soil is tired. The soil was portrayed as either living and/or, more frequently, as an embodiment of Mother Nature. The soil has been neglected and abused and does not have the energy that it should. The source of the metaphor is the people's knowledge that living things can get tired. The target of the metaphor is the soil, and the explanation of why the soil is the way it is currently.

These two metaphors contribute to the hypothesized cultural model of nature, which I present later, in two fundamental ways. First, the splitting of God and Mother Nature may constitute two separate cultural models of Nature held even by a single individual. Second, the soil is the key dynamic in environmental changes that people experience in daily activities. As an aside, it is interesting that the only two major metaphors I was able to discover in my analysis are metaphors of personification, and are not metaphors using nature, machines, and so forth as the source.

Perceived environmental changes. Without fully defining what is part of the environment in the minds of these Quichua-speaking highlanders, I want to note that my use of the word 'environment' in this study is my analytical concept, not theirs. We sought to get the interviewees to talk—in relation to their agricultural activities— about how they think about the six pre-selected domains of interest to our larger comparative effort, which were plants, animals, weather, landscape features (i.e., physical environment), supernatural, and people. Through the semi-structured interviews about agriculture and the changes in their lives, the broad kinds of things about which they talked were weather, plant/animal pests, people (knowledge, labor, symbolic activities), chemicals, soil, fire, the mountains (dormant volcanoes), and the wild grassland on Mt. Cotacachi.

When discussing changes in agriculture and problems with these changes, people's dominant focus was that the soil no longer produces like it used to, with a few people more graphically referring to the soil being worn out or tired. Thinking of production somewhat more broadly, and including this concern about soil, my thematic analysis found that people note major changes as:

- Soil has decreased in productivity;
- A diminishing supply of water;
- More extreme weather (heat, cold, rain, wind—each mentioned several times);
- An increase in microbial and insect pests;
- And shifts in the timing of the weather.

When the interview conversation covered why these changes were occurring, the informants provided a variety of answers which were almost exclusively regarding human behaviors. Next, in the section on 'Perception of Human Agency in Environmental Change,' I introduce my approximations or summaries of the informants' statements, and I avoid interpretations of these summaries in this section—such interpretations come more in the following section 'Causal Relationships among Themes.'

Perception of human agency in environmental change. Causal analysis of the themes highlighted suggest that causality typically flows from humans to the environment; however, weather, pests, and soils all have influences on food production. In the minds of the interviewees, the major factors bringing about environmental change include

- Cutting down trees that would otherwise hold back desertification;
- Burning trees and grassland and crop residues, which all protect soil moisture;
- Pollution of the planet by factories and cities;
- Poisoning of humans, animals, soil, and water through the use of agrochemicals poisons, although agrochemicals are beneficial by supporting good levels of production;
- Disposing of waste and garbage into the waterways and on the ground.

Interviewees also discussed the more moral side of human agency in environmental change. This is what I characterized in the title of this work as living respectfully. "We are to blame," or some version of this refrain, was offered by almost everyone in the sample as to why climate and other environmental changes were occurring. Not everyone characterized this moral blame in the same way, however. More specifically, a few to several people claimed each of the following were at play in the environmental changes they are experiencing:

- We have been lazy;
- We are egotistically doing whatever we want;
- We are teaching children poorly;
- We are getting on poorly with others;
- We have not been treating Mother Nature well.[2]

While fewer than 10 people stated so, I also found it noteworthy that a few people said, "Only our God knows why these changes are happening." Thus, a potentially significant minority includes in their explanations a disposition to be unable to explain why the environment was changing. Kempton, Boster, and Hartley (1996: 43) reported about a US cultural model of nature and one of its characteristics is, similarly, that people believed humans cannot fully know nature.

Causal relationships among themes. I organized the themes presented in the above sections on environmental changes, people's perceptions of those changes, and linguistic cues to their thinking about environmental changes, putting the themes into a summary graph that makes clear the causal relationships among them (Figure 5.2). Three types of enclosure symbols—rectangles for human behaviors, diamonds for climate, and ovals for pests—help differentiate the two major types of influence from the results of their impact.

The soil is affected by lack of water—because of humans burning crop residues and cutting trees and a shortage of organic matter, also because of burning—and the soil is affected by pollution. Factories and pollution seem to be cited to some degree as part of the more global dialogue on climate change, but also based on the idea that people are disrespecting the earth, Mother Nature, and soil through pollution. However, agrochemicals are cited directly as killing microbes in the soil by pesticides, reducing organic matter with herbicides, and more generally poisoning the soil.

Finally, both the timing and the extremes of weather have changed. These may or may not directly affect soil fertility for the informants, but decreased output is noted—some say because their prior farming knowledge is now less useful because of the changes that have occurred (see also Skarbø, 2006). At the center of the model is the key role of the soil, and this result of the causal analysis is clearly buttressed by the metaphor that the soil is tired.

Thinking more generally about the graph in Figure 5.2 and its significance for the hypothesized cultural model of nature to be discussed in the next section, I want to point out the relationship of these themes to the six etic components of Nature we sought to explore in this project.

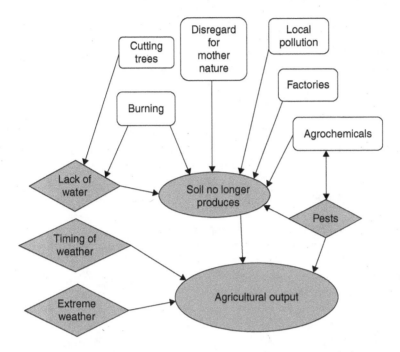

Figure 5.2 Graphic Model of Causal Relationships. Human behaviors (in white rectangles) largely impact soil productivity. Soil productivity is accompanied by nature's generation of water, temperature, and pests (gray diamonds) to impact people's food production.

(1) Climate/weather is represented by two weather diamonds on the left;
(2) Non-animate physical environment is represented by the lack of water diamond and the soil oval;
(3) Humans are represented by the rectangles;
(4) Supernatural Mother Nature is implied in one of the rectangles;
(5) Animals are represented in the agricultural output oval (plus pests are animals);
(6) Plants are represented in the agricultural output oval.

Thus, indeed, there are representatives of each of the six etic categories within the causal model of Nature. And this graphic causal model provides some insight into the core facets of a cultural model of Nature as well as the relationships among the six etic categories so that we can develop a broad view of what is at the heart of this causal model of Nature.

Hypothesized cultural model of Nature

The hypothesized cultural model or mental organization of knowledge relies on organizing the above results into the most important approximations of Nature held in the minds of these villagers. The propositions presented below are the primary cultural truths to the people of this village, at least from what can be evinced from the way they talk about their daily lives and the food production that their daily life entails. Again, these are my interpretations of their statements, and future research will involve the extent to which each of these statements is shared in the community.

1. Humans depend on nature, but specifically humans are given everything by Mother Nature and/or God;
2. Mother Nature responds positively to care of the earth, but specifically soil must be recharged and cared for and respected;
3. God responds to care of the earth and right living;
4. Sometimes Mother Nature and God are the same, sometimes they are not;
5. Taking care of family is the most important reason for living;
6. This specific region is protected by Mother Mount Cotacachi and Father Mount Imbabura;
7. Agricultural production is untenable, unlike in the past;
8. We are to blame for the situation with agriculture and nature.

The cultural model suggests not only causality, but it also indicates some potential overarching dimensions of importance. One dimension is that of 'give and take.' People take from Mother Nature, the soil, and God, and they give back through respect, ritual, and soil-enriching practices. Another potential dimension of the model is that of 'wet and dry.' Seasons are categorized by wet and dry, and great attention is paid to the timing of the rains, the shift in that timing, and to the amount of rain that falls.

One of our goals was to capture how plants, animals, landscape/non-biological features, weather, supernatural beings/activities, and people interacted, were grouped together, or stood apart. These six domains are ours as scientists and used to improve the systematicity of the research such that even coverage occurs in each of our sites. My understanding is that plants, animals, landscape, and physical entities besides celestial bodies, weather, some spirits, and rural-dwelling humans are inside Nature. Some saints and boogie-man-type spirits probably lie outside of Nature, and it appears that urbanites are also considered as outside of Nature.

Following on the model of causal relationships, my goal is to generate a very general understanding of how people view the relationship between the six domains of animals, plants, landscape features (or other aspects of the physical environmental), weather, supernatural, and people. I subsumed each of the enclosures in the above model into one of these six domains and collapsed the duplicative lines/ties between domains into a single line. Since the six domains are the scientists' domains, I have altered the domains in Figure 5.3 to fit local conceptualizations by splitting the spirit world into two parts (God and Mother Nature), splitting humans into two parts (rural

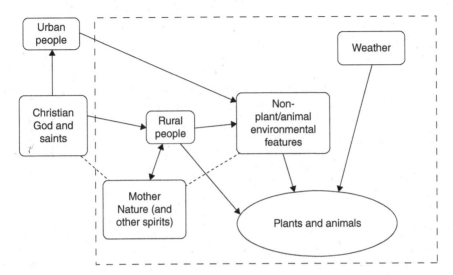

Figure 5.3 Summary cultural model.
Relationships between the general domains of Nature based on the causal logic in Figure 5.2.

dwellers and urbanites), and lumping plants and animals together, resulting in seven locally responsive domains (i.e., enclosures) instead of the scientific six chosen for our comparative project.

Having both God and Mother Nature seems to fit with another aspect of the local cosmo-vision—that the region is protected by the volcanoes Mama Cotacachi and Tata (father) Imbabura. This parallel between parental male and female gods and the mother and father volcanoes reinforces people's emphases on parenthood and caring for family. The split between urbanites and rural dwellers does not, however, result in a shared duality that is displayed by the gods. These rural dwellers did not make any connections between themselves and the people who live in big cities—even though many of the people who live in cities are family members, and even though there is a tradition of circular migration to and from the cities as well as a tradition of commuting to the nearby city of Ibarra.

My analysis of the interviews leads me to think that the local cultural model holds that urbanites and God are often outside the core group of entities and relationships in their cultural model of Nature. However, sometimes God and Mother Nature seem to some of the interviewees to be one and the same (designated by the dotted line between them). Additionally, God provides for people, which might make this deity part of Nature in some ways. I did not connect Mother Nature with the other entities of plants, animals, and weather, as Mother Nature is often equated with the soil and the earth (thus the dotted line) and thereby influences plants and animals through the soil and earth. Weather did not seem to be related to Mother Nature and, thus, it stands on its own. Mother Nature is not equated with humans in the same way that Christians sometimes say that God is in people. These Cotacacheños from Alambuela do see themselves as part of the earth and as part of nature, but Mother Nature is not in them, she is never manifest in people. This dualism is discussed in the next section, but for now suffice it to say that people can be integral or peripheral to the core of Nature, depending on their behaviors, and the supernatural world is similarly split between core and periphery in the model—particularly because of the relevance of Mother Nature to agriculture and the somewhat decreased relevance of God to agriculture.

Discussion and conclusion

The hypothesis I presented of a cultural model of Nature contains both causality among components of Nature, and dimensionality of the essence of being in the world, of being part of Nature. In the section 'Hypothesized Cultural Model of Nature,' I list several propositions that appear to be the most salient for my interviewees. Here, I combine them and whittle them down to capture the more general aspects of the hypothesized cultural model of Nature.

(1) Taking care of family is the most important reason for living.
(2) Humans are given everything by Mother Nature and/or God, both of whom can respond better when humans care for the earth.
(3) We have been to blame for the difficulties in nature (which is primarily seen as agricultural production) through not caring for the earth—particularly the soil—and not caring for people.

We have an interesting mix of mystical and animistic tenets here. Specifically, in (3), mystical retribution results from moral injunction where no particular god/spirit or person/witch generates the state of things. However, (2) clearly identifies animistic gods. And the background for (1) is that family life is under attack because of human failure, morally, and because of Mother Nature and God not responding favorably to pollution and poor agricultural practices. Animism, which holds that all entities are filled with spirit(s), is more conducive to the dualism of right vs. wrong than are mystical, magical, and non-animistic forms of belief. This dualism is evident in the cultural model of Nature, with the emphasis on right living, blame, and care.

So, what are we to make of the differences between the proposed cultural model(s) and what Campbell (2006) found—that less than 4 percent of the people named soil impoverishment as the greatest driver of problems in agricultural production (but over 30% saw climate change as the greatest driver of agricultural production problems)? Despite people not overtly saying that soil impoverishment technically was the problem, Campbell arrived at the conclusion through interpretation of survey data, participant observation, agricultural transects, and ethnographic interviews (but not cognitive procedures for cultural models) that people indeed perceived the soil as tired.

In addition, Campbell's analysis compared five communities near Cotacachi and also found that small land parcelization to individual households vs. communal rights of households to larger pieces of land helped explain how people saw their situation. Is it possible that the metaphor here is that people are tired and thus talk about the soil as tired? Could the formation of the metaphor be due to the perceived erosion of community ties that would have provided more energy and meaning in people's lives? This would be interesting to investigate further. Also, since farmers, like other producers, likely vary in their perceptions of change based on roles played (e.g., gendered work roles) and resources available (e.g., irrigated or not, plot size). Future efforts with this study's data will involve exploration of roles and resources as sources of variation in the cultural model(s).

At the foundation of this research—which involves the exploration of these domains—the question was: How do each of the six domains we chose interact, group together, or stand out? The goal of answering this question is to characterize producer cultural models and to compare causal models (which are included in cultural models) to those causal models of Nature set out in the Introduction to this book: God-centered, God/human-centered, and holistic causal models of Nature. In this case, preliminary results suggest that nature can exist without cities, and nature can exist with or without the Christian God. This splitting of the spirit world between Christian spirits and Mother Nature (and other spirits), as well as the splitting of humans into urbanites and rural dwellers undoubtedly creates some cognitive dissonance and may partially be influenced by the common Christian and Western/urban dualisms. However, such differentiation between kinds of spirit worlds and kinds of human worlds also gives the opportunity for people to be able to switch from one type of living (i.e., different cultural milieus) to another, or to identify their existence with the cultural model that is convenient or appropriate at a given time. This perhaps occurs in many or all societies, but it may also be indicative of the social and ecological changes these informants are experiencing.

The types of causal models of nature proposed by Bennardo in the Introduction are God-centered, God/human-centered, and holistic. The causal model for smallholder agriculturalists in Alambuela, this village near Cotacachi, appears to be close to the holistic model, although perhaps a slight revision of that general causal model is in order. These Quichua speakers do indeed highlight humans and the Christian God in ways that puts those two components outside the core of Nature. In other words, this causal model might be something more like a nature-centered (i.e., biophysical environment-centered) causal model of Nature.

Acknowledgments

Heartfelt thanks to Alicia Guaján for the invaluable assistance in the field, to the people of the village of Alambuela, to the area's umbrella organization for the villages—UNORCAC—for easing my entry into the community, and to the family of Rumiñahui Anrango for their hospitality during my stay with them. Thank you to Kristina Skarbø and Kristen VanderMolen for providing additional tips and insights about the fieldwork. The National Science Foundation (BCS 1330070) funded the data collection for this project.

Notes

1 The project is led by Giovanni Bennardo, but the specific award for the Ecuador portion of the research is NSF-BCS 1330070.
2 Mother Nature, '*Pachamama*,' is the goddess of the world (earth and time) and is key for fertility. In this community, people's conceptualization of her is that of a semi-personalized supernatural being as in an animistic belief system.

References

Campbell, B. C. (2006). Por que esta cansada la tierra? Un analisis comparativo del cambio y la intervencio en la agricultura en el Ecuador Septentrional. In Rhoades, R. E. (ed.), *Desarrollo con identidad: Comunidad, cultura, y sustentabilidad*. Quito: Ediciones Abya-Yala, 391–412. (Also published in English as *Development with Identity: Community, Culture and Sustainability* (2006). Cambridge, MA: CABI Publishing.)

Flora, G. (2006). La migración circular y la identifad comunitaria: Su relación con la tierra. In Rhoades, R. E. (ed.), *Desarrollo con identidad: Comunidad, cultura, y sustentabilidad*. Quito: Ediciones Abya-Yala, 413–434. (Also published in English as *Circular Migration and Community Identity: Their Relationship to the Land* (2006). Cambridge, MA: CABI Publishing).

Jones, E. C. (2002). The role of wealth and cultural heterogeneity in the emergence of social networks and agricultural cooperatives in an Ecuadorian colonization zone. PhD diss., University of Georgia.

Kempton, W., Boster, J. S., and Hartley, J. A. (1996). *Environmental Values in American Culture*. Cambridge, MA: MIT Press.

Rhoades, R. E. (ed.). (2002). *Bridging Human and Ecological Landscapes*. Dubuque, IA: Kendall Hunt. (Also published in Spanish as *Tendiendo Puentes entre los Paisajes Humanos y Naturales* (2001). Quito: Abya-Yala.)

Rhoades, R. E. (ed.). (2006). *Development with Identity: Community, Culture and Sustainability in the Andes*. Cambridge, MA: CABI Publishing. (Also published in Spanish as Desarrollo con identidad: Comunidad, cultura, y sustentabilidad (2006). Quito: Ediciones Abya-Yala.)

Rhoades, R. E., Martinez, A., and Jones, E. C. (2002). Migration and the landscape of Nanegal. In Rhoades, R. E. (ed.), *Bridging Human and Ecological Landscapes*, 57–83. Dubuque, IA: Kendall Hunt. (Also published in Spanish as *Tendiendo Puentes entre los Paisajes Humanos y Naturales* (2001). Quito: Abya-Yala.)

Rhoades, R. E., Zapata Rios, X., and Aragundy, J. (2006). El cambio climatico en Cotacachi. In Rhoades, R. E. (ed.), *Desarrollo con identidad: Comunidad, cultura, y sustentabilidad*. Quito: Ediciones Abya-Yala, 109–123. (Also published in English as *Climate Change in Cotacachi* (2006). Cambridge, MA: CABI Publishing.)

Skarbø, K. (2006). Viviendo, mermando, perdiendo, encontrando: El estado y los cambios en la agrobiodiversidad de Cotacachi. In Rhoades, R. E. (ed.), *Desarrollo con identidad: Comunidad, cultura, y sustentabilidad*. Quito: Ediciones Abya-Yala, 191–213. (Also published in English as *Development with Identity: Community, Culture and Sustainability* (2006). Cambridge, MA: CABI Publishing.)

Skarbø, K. and VanderMolen, K. A. (2014). Irrigation access and vulnerability to climate-induced hydrological change in the Ecuadorian Andes. *Culture, Agriculture, Food and Environment* 36(1): 28–44.

Skarbø, K., VanderMolen, K., Ramos, R., and Rhoades, R. E. (2012). The one who has changed is the person: Observations and explanations of climate change in the Ecuadorian Andes. In Brokensha, D. A., Castro, P., and Taylor, D. (eds.), *Climate Change and Indigenous Knowledge: Perceptions and Adaptations of Threatened Communities*. Rugby, UK: Practical Action Publishing, 119–128.

Viviroli, D., Archer, D. R., Buytaert, W., Fowler, H. J., Greenwood, G. B., Hamlet, A. F., Huang, Y., Koboltschnig, G., Litaor, M. I., López-Moreno, J. I., Lorentz, S., Schädler, B., Schreier, H., Schwaiger, K., Vuille, M., and Woods, R. (2011). Climate change and mountain water resources: Overview and recommendations for research, management and policy. *Hydrological and Earth Systems Sciences* 15: 471–504.

6 Cultural Models of Nature and divinity in a rain-fed farming village of Punjab, Pakistan

Stephen M. Lyon and Muhammad A. Z. Mughal

Introduction: Cultural knowledge of nature

This chapter[1,2] examines the relationship between complex, generative conceptual cultural models and the actions and decisions farmers make in their agricultural lives. It is part of an international collaboration that focused specifically on primary food producers in different parts of the world. In part, the motivation was to develop a better understanding of the significance of idea systems and their practical manifestations. Lurking beneath the esoteric anthropological questions about knowledge production and its impact on behaviors, however, were very practical concerns about the effects of changing context of primary food producers.

The contexts include: the climate; local flora and fauna; soil and water quality and availability; local, national, and international politics; economic and cultural systems; energy systems; and the availability of agricultural products and equipment. The collaboration is ambitious and grand in scope, but the strength of anthropology is routinely found in the analyses of very local-level phenomena. By generalizing from the particulars of micro-level phenomena, anthropologists have argued we can develop more realistic explanatory and predictive models for human behavior at meso and macro levels.

This collection sets out to demonstrate the effectiveness of employing cross-cultural, comparative micro studies for developing robust analytical tools for addressing complex global challenges. In this chapter, we use a subset of our data to illustrate some core foundational conceptual idea systems that underpin agriculturalists' beliefs and behaviors in rural northern Punjab, Pakistan. Using data elicited through free-listing exercises, and semi-structured interviews, we suggest that there are clear conceptual models that partially map onto a local concept called *kudruti mahole*, which articulates the relationship between the supernatural and the natural worlds that, in practice, enable the farmers in our study to exhibit extraordinary resilience in the face of volatile political, economic, and environmental change.

In recent decades, Pakistani farmers have had to contend with accelerated levels of economic growth and instability coupled with changes to the

DOI: 10.4324/9781351127905-7

natural environment. In many cases, the changes have been so dramatic that farmers may lack suitable cultural frames of reference to effectively adapt their farming practices. Until relatively recently, local farmers in northern Punjab were only marginally impacted by many of these changes because they were still effectively locked into persistent relationships of subsistence dependency with one another. This is no longer the case. Farming has arguably changed almost beyond recognition in many parts of Punjab in the past twenty years.

Remittances from overseas have significantly affected parts of the Punjab as a consequence of a number of factors, not least increased labor migration, particularly to the Middle East from the 1970s onwards, and the UK from independence (see Donnan, 1997; Kaur, 2006; Khalidi, 1998; Noman, 1991; Talbot and Thandi, 2004). Political instability and environmental problems in Afghanistan, the Federally Administered Tribal Areas (FATA), and parts of Khyber-Pukhtunkhwa have triggered large-scale movement of economically active people across Pakistan that has had a notable impact on the kinds of farming practices that take place. Traditional agriculture in rain-fed areas of northern Punjab was based on mixed farming with two main crops (wheat and maize). Various fodder crops were used for rotation, but these were entirely consumed by local livestock (buffalo, cows, goats, and sheep). With the introduction of diesel-powered generators and electric pumps, groundwater irrigation became possible from the 1980s and is now a feature of all large farms. All these changes bring into question the relevance of local farmers' environmental knowledge and its utility in informing critical agricultural decisions.

Ecological anthropology has long sought effective ways of understanding the complex interplay between environmental and cultural phenomena. The early anthropological adopters imported invaluable conceptual tools that expanded the evolutionary systems theory of Steward (1955). Rappaport's (1968) ground-breaking ecological anthropological study of a Tsembaga Maring community in Highland Papua New Guinea, for example, demonstrated the power of integrating information systems theory into an analysis of the interplay between human ritual and the environment. Vayda argued that ecological studies should begin with concrete events. This is well illustrated in his explanations of the causes of warfare in Borneo and Papua New Guinea (Vayda, 1969, 1971, 1989). Vayda and Rappaport's contributions to ecological anthropology have been significant, but the field has diverged in important ways since the 1970s. Vayda and Walters (1999) argued that at least some proponents of political ecology, for example, argued a priori that the political, particularly external, wider political-economic system, is always important and should always be given priority in the analysis of the complex interplay between social, cultural, and environmental factors. They repeated Vayda's earlier call for a focus on concrete events and then adapting the theoretical assumptions to fit the empirical data.[3]

The concept of nature has, like seemingly everything else in anthropology, been problematized. Ingold's (1987) edited collection, *The Appropriation of Nature*, attempted to disentangle the significance of human production of nature and the distinctions between material and social aspects of the environment. While some aspects of this argument may appear overly dualistic, and it is not always clear how Ingold's material/social distinctions might actually allow the development of useful models of nature, the premise that human ecology, and by extension other forms of ecology in which humans are present, must meaningfully incorporate social relations is sound. Ellen and Fukui's later edited volume (1996), which included a contribution from Ingold, was equally thought-provoking in arguing for a middle ground between seeing culture as the derivative of the imperatives of reproduction or as the principle constructor of nature. Instead, they argue that culture and nature are mutually constitutive.

If cultural models of nature are key to decision-making for primary food producers, then we need to know what these are in order to assess ways in which behavior might adapt. Humphrey et al. (1993) identified important cultural models in the way nomadic Mongolians accessed and used available resources that might have important implications for their success in the event of significant environmental change. Specific anthropological studies of the relevance of cultural models in times of change suggest that issues of adaptation are complex.

Horowitz (2001) describes the layered composition of Kanak identity ideologies in New Caledonia that inform subsistence decision-making. The dramatic environmental, economic, and political changes that have occurred in recent decades have caused young Kanak, especially, to say that Western economic activities are destroying their culture, and they cannot maintain traditional subsistence practices. Neisheim et al. (2006), in a study of Quetzal-speaking return migrants in Guatemala, found that changes to location and economic use of plants affect local knowledge; in particular, commercialization leads to an understandable investment in knowledge production around commercially rewarding species, which can correspond with a reduction in active use of traditional subsistence species. Their study does not suggest that Technical (sometimes Traditional) Ecological Knowledge (TEK) becomes irrelevant as a consequence of physical relocation and changes to economics, but rather that TEK is dynamic and responds to such changes. In particular, the study suggests what has long been argued: that TEK is an iterative result of empirical engagement with the local environment. Similarly, Fernández-Giménez and Estaque (2012) found that, despite the radical environmental and economic changes to Pyrenean pastoralism, local TEK could contribute to sustainable stewardship and resource monitoring of upland pasture lands in Spain.

Beyond the specific TEK of plant species and how to manage and cultivate them, however, there are fundamental questions about core cultural models[4] that inform the production of TEK as well as shape the relationships between categories of TEK and nature more generally. In this chapter, we focus on some of the most important cultural models for local farmers in rural Punjab and the ways in which they underpin observable behaviors and attitudes about nature in times of significant political, economic, and environmental change. If farming decision-making has adapted to local environments, then understanding the cognitive models that inform those processes may be critical for determining the extent to which local primary food producers' core cultural models are fit for purpose. To be sure, we are not arguing that culture is a *barrier* to adaptation, rather that the resilience of different conceptual models of nature may vary in ways that could be harnessed to deliver more effective, targeted intervention that makes sense to local farmers and enables them to adapt more quickly and successfully.

This research was undertaken as part of the project, Cultural Models of Nature across Cultures: Space, Causality, and Primary Food Producers. The research for this project was conducted by several scholars in more than a dozen countries to understand how primary food producers understand nature and environmental change. One of the major propositions of the project is that human agency in nature has spiritual, moral, and behavioral aspects. Although similar data-collection techniques were used, each country and area had specific local conditions that resulted in focusing the topics in different ways. An important objective of the project was to document how plants, animals, landscape, or non-biological features, weather, supernatural beings or activities and people interacted within and or outside of nature. Like all the contributions in this volume, we seek a more comprehensive understanding of the relationship between primary food producers' environments, practices, and cultural models that shape, and are in turn shaped by, nature.

The field site

The fieldwork for this part of the collaborative project was carried out in Tehsil[5] Fateh Jang, Attock District, northern Punjab, Pakistan. Pakistan has retained many of the administrative boundaries inherited from previous regimes. While the boundary lines for the northernmost Punjabi District, Attock, have shifted in places and the district has been situated within both the North-West Frontier Province (now Khyber-Pukhtunkhwa) and Punjab, it is largely recognizable as the British District known as Campbellpur. It is perhaps not best described as a politically important district in the grand politics of Pakistan or South Asia, but it has seen the movement of important armies and migrants for thousands of years.[6]

Attock District is in the Potohari dialect speaking part of Punjab (Shackle, 1979). The linguistic variation across Punjab is testament to the fragmentation of this diverse province. In the subdistrict of Attock District in which the data for this chapter were produced, Fateh Jang, the linguistic variation can be considerable even between villages within 10 kilometers of one another. This reflects the historical level of competition that has existed in ensuring subsistence. The subdistrict has very little reliable surface water, and the villages surrounding the one that was the base for this research have no year-round surface water available. In the past, this has restricted agriculture to only two principle crops: wheat and maize. Farmers have relied on animal husbandry and the precarious annual harvests to maintain basic livelihoods. As a buffer region between the areas controlled more directly by the British Raj (followed by the Pakistan state) and the so-called tribal areas loosely regulated through tenuous agreements, Attock District has never been the target of large-scale infrastructural investment that might have offered local people viable commercial or manufacturing alternatives to subsistence farming.

We have described elsewhere, the historic rural composition of Fateh Jang, Attock District (Lyon and Mughal, 2017). Fateh Jang remains a majority rural subdistrict. The absence of diverse economic opportunities has resulted in particularly strong patron–client networks in the past (see Lyon, 2004a). While this has changed somewhat in the past decade, reliance on an economic elite for access to the few existing wage opportunities remains high. Coupled with an absence of naturally occurring reliable surface water, the economic precarity creates an environment in which competition between farmers, and especially landowners, can be intense. There are few circumstances in which the rewards for cooperation are compelling enough to persuade individual farmers to willingly cede control over their resources for collective enterprises. Landowners even seek to 'poach' good peasant farm workers from others and, although everything is less extreme than the situation described by Barth (1959), in Swat there are clear social continuities as well.

The challenges of delivering adequate irrigation for the range of crops local farmers have invested in are considerable. Farmers are visibly preoccupied with rainfall throughout much of the year, but particularly at the critical moments in the agricultural cycle in which crops require irrigation or, conversely, need to dry out prior to harvesting. The erratic nature of rainfall—by apparent consensus said to be worse now than in the past—leaves local people vulnerable to serious economic hardship unless they have the resources to invest in costly groundwater pumping irrigation.

It is therefore in the context of a farming village in a predominately rural region, with unpredictable and sometimes extreme drought and rain conditions, that this research was undertaken. There are, to be sure, parts of Pakistani Punjab that benefit from more reliable water and a longer history of planting diverse crops. Some of those areas have had clear rewards for greater cooperation, and some of the social antagonisms described by Lyon (2004a) elsewhere are more muted.[7] As Bennardo and others in this volume make clear, the findings of our study are specific to the people in the village in which the research was undertaken. Arguably, there are aspects of the cultural models of nature that are the same, or very similar, to many parts of Punjab and Khyber-Pukhtunkhwa, but we stop short of asserting this here. So, while we refer to Punjab throughout, when discussing the specific field data and their implications, we restrict our references to the farming villages immediately surrounding our central field site.

Categorizing nature in Punjab

The chapters in this volume have agreed a particular set of definitions for the term *nature*. In Bennardo's Introduction, he distinguishes between Nature with an upper-case N, and nature with a lower-case n. Here, we are concerned with the former, Nature, which might usefully be understood as the worldview of a group of people. Identifying a simple noun that encapsulates local cultural models of 'Nature' (hereafter nature) is potentially problematic in any society. Clearly, the term *nature*, in English, has a variety of meanings that shift depending on the context and have demonstrably shifted over time.

In rural Punjab, the Urdu word for nature, *kudrut*, is understood but does not mean much. In other words, people seem to understand the word, but give it little to no thought on its own. This is, nevertheless, the term for nature that is most widely understood and recognized locally. It is very much something that acts upon people. Locally, people render this noun into what would ordinarily be the adjectival form with an ending '*i*,' (*kudruti*) but this does not mean that the word has been rendered into an adjective. One of the remarkable characteristics of the way people speak in Punjab, and particularly in the rural areas, is the playfulness with which they twist and modify words. The use of nonsense rhyming words is widespread, and people happily modify standard words to suit their sense of aesthetics at the moment. Lyon once had on DVD a Bollywood film called *Zakhm* (Wound). He told people the name of this film, and they systematically referred to it as *Zakhmi* ('Wounded'). When he showed the literate men the title on the DVD to prove that in Urdu there was no ending '*i*' on the word, they shrugged and said that that was probably correct, but *Zakhmi* sounded better.

In Fateh Jang, the term *kudruti* includes trees, land, animals, rain, and so on, but it is not a passive thing around us. It is an active thing that impacts on people and has a personality. People have *kudruti* as well. So, when we ask for *kudruti*, we must narrow it down a bit to the *kudruti* of the 'atmosphere' (*mahole ka kudruti* or *kudruti mahole*) or a specific person's *kudruti* or a category of person's *kudruti*. This may suggest a more holistic concept of nature, one which integrates all of the animals, plants, weather, and people into a single system that is impacted by larger supernatural force—which, in this case, is clearly God, or Allah.

Methods

We carried out a number of tasks to elicit a range of information about nature. This included:

- Semi-structured interviews about the environment's changes over time;
- Free-listing task on pre-agreed categories of 'natural' things designed to facilitate comparison across all the sites:
  - Soil (n = 35);
  - Animals (n = 15);
  - Trees (n = 7);
  - Plants (n = 8);
  - Weather (n = 11).

The gender ratio of our participants was heavily skewed toward men in all tasks. We were not granted direct access to any women for these tasks. Although Lyon has worked in the same village for more than 20 years and is therefore given considerable freedom to enter the private areas of the households, normally reserved for related men (*mehram*), it would be inappropriate for him to seek an extended interview with all but a select number of women. Indeed, even when he has had the opportunity to carry out extended interviews with very old village women, he has subsequently been asked to refrain from publishing anything from these interviews.

It can be difficult for foreigners, especially Europeans and North Americans, to appreciate the delicacies of gender expectations in rural Punjab. Families and households are judged on the behavior of the individual members, and particularly on the reputations that develop around them. One of the many constraints on the breadth and quality of these data is, therefore, the absence of women. This is not surprising, and Lyon has previously reported on the notable segregation of genders in this village (Lyon, 2005, 2004b). Despite Lyon's unsatisfying previous attempts at addressing this absence by employing a female social scientist, we hope to address this issue in future research.

Semi-structured interviews

Like the other contributions to this volume, our semi-structured interview 'script' was negotiated both with the specific local people in mind as well as the need for comparable data. We therefore concentrated on asking local farmers about their own experiences of environmental change and their explanations for those changes (if indeed they existed). We asked them for more details about the relevance of the soils, crops, and animals they listed in the free-listing exercise and tried to probe the logical groupings that might exist between them. We sought to develop a better understanding of the supernatural forces that impact on farming and the daily lives of farmers.

The interviews varied considerably in length, something that is not at all unusual. Some farmers answered the questions politely but succinctly and offered little to no elaboration on the initial brief answers. Others were eager to seize the opportunity to deliver highly charged rants about morality, God, economic investments, and the political mistakes of the elite in the region, the province, and the country. The interviews are revealing in a number of ways and because of that are sensitive data. Since many farmers chose to stray from a narrow discussion of environmental change, farming practices, and farming resources, we wound up with a data set that must remain confidential in order to prevent embarrassment or other negative consequences for those involved.

A number of striking points emerge from the semi-structured interviews. First, there is a clear consensus among farmers of all ages that the climate has changed. Weather patterns are more erratic and rain, in particular, is less predictable. The village has endured periods of sustained drought as well as inundations of rain, both of which can result in catastrophic crop failure for small farmers. The largest landowners are able to survive in part through substantial investment in tube-well irrigation[8] and by selling parcels of land in poor years.

Farmers describe their powerlessness in the face of the changes to rain patterns. For example, a farmer in his forties in response to a question about changing rain during his lifetime said:

> Allah knows this all. Why should I tell you a lie that I have this experience when I have no idea why it's happening? This system is managed by Allah. We only know how to cultivate but we have no control or knowledge of these weather conditions. Even you see meteorology department says that there are chances/probability of raining (rain is expected) today. They don't say that the rain will definitely come today. They just say it's possible or chance [*imkaan*] to have rain today. Only my God knows when rain will come or not. This is his system.

Land in the area around the village has risen substantially in market value in the past decade. With the introduction of a modern motorway in the early part of this century, residential 'societies' have begun to spread from nearby urban centers, including the capital, Islamabad, which is roughly fifty kilometers away. Travelling to Islamabad in the late 1990s took about 1.5 to 2 hours by motorized vehicle. On the motorway today, the same trip takes about forty-five minutes. Since much of the land in the area is considered *banjr*, or uncultivable, landowners have reluctantly agreed to sell land they cannot afford to transform in order to either invest in other areas (such as orchards) or purchase modern technologies, cars, or build new homes and guest houses.

When queried about possible causes of climate change, illiterate and semi-literate farmers expressed a human cause, but not one that is entirely compatible with contemporary scientific models of climate change. The recurring theme revolved around Allah's wrath triggered by immoral human behavior. This was expressed in various ways. A farmer in his mid to late fifties got very animated in explaining the cause of the drought they were experiencing:

> Listen to me, Dr Sahib, Allah is angry at the people. Allah is angry about stupidities and sinful behavior. People in Islamabad are all sinners, especially the women. They expose this [motioning to his chest] and the sinful men let their ladies do this. That's why Allah doesn't give us rains—because people in Islamabad are sinners (harami).

Lyon took a local farmer in his forties with him to Islamabad for company while he met with urban-based businessmen on unrelated matters. The businessmen spent the evening drinking and watching modern Bollywood music videos with very scantily clad women dancing extremely suggestively. There was one video in which a woman poured champagne from the bottle over herself in a scene that can only be described as pseudo-porn (at best). In the morning, after some of the businessmen had gone home, and others were still sleeping off their hangovers, Lyon discussed the previous evening with the local farmer. The man, who had spent the majority of his life in a small farming village, said

> those men make Allah very angry. That's why we need someone like the Taliban in our country—to scare rich sinners into obeying Allah's law. If they followed sharia law, then we would have rain and peace of mind. Good Muslims don't like this scandalous Indian culture/behavior, and so it is understandable that some would turn to groups like the Taliban to try and maintain the moral standards that Allah wants for humanity.

He is not a man who condones or supports violent political action; however, he was deeply disturbed by both the videos and the behaviors of the wealthy Pakistani businessmen.

The single greatest change in the region in the past three decades has been the increase in irrigation. The first tube-well was sunk in the village-owned lands in 1981. That was on the site of the first citrus orchard, which was developed roughly a decade later. There has been little, if any, coordination in irrigation practices among those landowners with the resources to develop tube-well irrigation. Consequently, the water is poorly distributed, and the burden of investment is difficult to organize in ways that might generate economies of scale. The persistent land disputes have hampered village-wide irrigation cooperation, and these show no sign of diminishing, as the total amount of land available for agriculture is reduced, and landowners sell off parcels of land to housing developers.

The drive toward greater and more reliable irrigation has led to the adoption of non-native crops to the region. This has had some negative consequences on farm employment. Landowners report a lack of confidence in local Punjabi farmers' ability to carry out non-*desi* (indigenous/local) farming practices. Some landowners have consequently employed migrant Pukhtun/Pathan laborers.[9] Pukhtuns have a long tradition of migration and therefore are presumed to be more versatile in their ability to learn new farming techniques. Partly to address the perception that local farmers adapt poorly to new crops, government extension workers from the National Agriculture Research Centre have provided training for local farmers when landowners have agreed to participate in experimental trials of new crops (notably growing true potato seed and canola).

There continue to be a large number of local Punjabis employed in farming despite the desire to employ Pukhtuns. In addition, the rise in political instability has also led to a growing reluctance to have too many Pukhtuns living around the village. For the most part, Pukhtuns are not invited to live in the village itself but are provided housing that is several kilometers outside the village, where they can watch over and protect the fields for which they are responsible. Pukhtuns in the area for purely seasonal labor seem to stay with the Pukhtuns living outside the village. There is a surprising number of them around and, in addition to working as farm laborers, they are occasionally called on to act as hired guards to intimidate rivals.

While relations between Punjabis and Pukhtuns are courteous and cooperative when dealing with farm matters, this has caused considerable discontent among local farmers. Punjabis worry about what they say is an increase in kidnappings for ransom and, in particular, are worried for Lyon's safety. While in the late 1990s, Lyon was afforded more or less total freedom to interact with any man in the region, since 2007, local people have expressed a great deal of unhappiness about him interacting with Pukhtuns when outside of their presence.

Though we have no verifiable data on the number of kidnappings for ransom in the area, these are reported to have increased dramatically. Lyon has met with family members and victims of those involved. The sums of money demanded are well-researched and correspond with the amounts that a family can generate within about two weeks. The victims report being reasonably well treated in standards that are clearly tied to their socioeconomic status (i.e., wealthy kidnapping victims say they are locked into comfortable bedrooms with televisions and newspapers; poor victims may be kept in disused animal stables). Despite the reports of reasonable treatment, all victims are aware that the consequence of not paying is serious and typically means death.

The frequency of reported problems, political, climatic, economic, and others, reflects a growing sense of frustration and dissatisfaction among farmers. Throughout all conversations, most farmers repeatedly muttered praise or gratitude for Allah when discussing difficult times (*Mashallah, Allah ka shukr, Alhamdulillah*, etc.). In one interview about the nature of

Allah's creation, one literate farmer in his early fifties explained the relationship between different types of creatures:

> *Insahniyat* 'humanity' is Allah's greatest creation and all other creations are there to serve *insaan* 'man/human.'

The reliance on divine support extends beyond direct prayers to Allah in the mosque. Ritual devotion at shrines is a widespread tactic for dealing with misfortune beyond people's control. Mini pilgrimages to the local saint buried at the top of the mountain on the outskirts of the village are common. Further afield, local farmers will travel considerable distances to meet directly with renowned saints (*pir* or *fakir*, locally referred to collectively as *pir-fakir*) for help with serious health problems or to get a person who has a proven positive relationship with Allah to ask for rains on their behalf (see Lyon, 2004b, for a more detailed description of the importance of saints).

In addition to frequent direct references to Allah as the supreme controller and creator of everything, local Punjabis also occasionally mention lesser supernatural beings, *jinn*, who can play tricks on people and cause misfortune on a small scale. *Jinn* cannot, however, alter in any way the intentions of Allah. So, ultimately, the reason given for poor rains or floods or crop failure is linked directly to Allah's will rather than to other supernatural forces or the climate-science explanation of accelerated carbon emissions.

The centrality of Allah in people's accounts of nature in Attock District are not distinct from other parts of Pakistan or the wider Muslim world. They are, in fact rooted in orthodox understandings of Allah and nature. The Quran is explicit in placing Allah at the center of all creation and tells that the purpose of nature is, ultimately, to serve Allah and His creations, particularly humans (see Golshani, 2000, for a theological account of Islam and the sciences of nature).

Cultural models and interview data

Interview data can be an important opportunity for allowing local people's own ideas about something to be heard. Giving people a voice outside of their own communities is an aspiration in anthropology that is both admirable and highly problematic. The interview data that we have included speaks directly to ideas about the role of God in relation to people. The ideas refer to divine plans and expectations and to human fallibility and weakness and the consequences. Were we to expand our analysis here to include data produced elsewhere in Punjab or include significantly more of the earlier work done on local shrines and religious practices, we are confident that we would demonstrate even more persuasively the primacy of God in the dominant local cultural model of nature.

The cultural model is not so crude that it can be reduced to a single all-powerful divine entity (Allah) and His creations, but that would appear to be a critical a priori assumption embedded deeply within the model. The fact that this is strongly reinforced through formal religious education and in daily ritual practice might make this less of a 'local' cultural model in origin, but no less relevant or powerful for 'local' people as a result. One of the potential outcomes of this kind of research is to assist in identifying ways that local technical and environmental knowledge may be harnessed for more effective resource management in changed (and changing) conditions. To that end, we suggest that the ways in which local farmers articulate their understanding of the changes they have seen, as well as their explanations, provide an invaluable source for tailoring more-effective strategic interventions and non-interventions.

Free-listing results

Free-listing exercises serve a number of important functions in social science research. At their simplest, they offer a useful technique for building up a comprehensive local glossary of terms on defined topics. Somewhat more ambitiously, free listing can be an integral step toward understanding the salient cultural domains in diverse cultural contexts. Bernard (2011) argues that interrogating cultural domains has its origins in the earliest empirical research in anthropology, at least as far back as Morgan's studies of kinship systems in the nineteenth century. Interrogating the terms that people know on a specific topic allows researchers to probe beyond the contingent recall that may arise in a conversation (2011: 225–226) and can increase the documentation of the semantically relevant vocabulary within a cultural domain. In part, this simple technique allows researchers to ask *better* questions in other contexts, because developing a better grasp of the ways in which local people logically group ideas and terms can ensure that the interviewer and interviewee are not unintentionally confusing culturally dissimilar categories.

Free lists give researchers a sense of what goes together. We do this by looking not only at the total list and the frequency of terms generated, but also by looking at the ordering of the terms. Some terms can be understood as 'triggers' for the terms that follow because having thought of one, the terms that are closest in 'group' are then easier to recall. So, among English speakers, cats and dogs are likely to be listed close together, as are sheep and goats (see Bernard, 2011: 226–227). We do not address this aspect of our free listing results here, but it is one of many reasons for eliciting free lists as part of our interviewing repertoire in anthropology.

One of our objectives in the project was to establish the locally salient 'natural' categories of nature. Free listing was therefore an instrumental tool in populating the categories that we had reason to believe were relevant within the broader umbrella category of nature. The comparative goals of the project meant that we could not generate our subcategories of nature entirely based on local cultural imperatives, however. We needed to ensure that the data produced in each site were comparable across *all* sites. So as a collaborative team, we agreed on a fixed set of subcategories of nature that we would all elicit data about. This helped us to identify the contents of the subcategories and the relationships of those elements within them. Coupled with the interview data, these groupings reinforce an overall cultural model of nature that defines clear responsibilities and opportunities for humans in relation to the resources provided by a unitary divine force.

The free-listing tasks proved very useful in our field site, despite the challenges of carrying out such an exercise among a largely illiterate or semi-literate population. We could not give participants a sheet of paper and pen and ask them to list all terms associated with an idea. Instead, we asked them to verbally tell us types of land, or types of trees. They were clearly able to provide lists, but typically wanted to provide a context for each term. So, when we asked about land types, the participants often provided us with examples of where we might find the specific land or soil type. They used terms like, *lepara,* and told us which specific fields that we had seen were examples of that soil type. While somewhat frustrating at first, this proved an invaluable source of information that was far richer than the simple lists of terms we sought.

We carried out free lists with men born in the region who have lived most of their lives in and around the village, though many have spent various periods of time as wage laborers outside of the village. Determining ages is imprecise at best, but we estimate that the ages ranged from late teens to mid-eighties. Participants included men who own land as well as those who work exclusively on the land of others. There were two landlords (*zamindar*) included in the sample as well, since they are not absentee landlords and work regularly with the peasant farmers. So, while they do not tend to carry out actual manual labor, they are intimately involved in all the tasks performed and spend much of their time advising and overseeing their farm laborers.

Soil and land types

Since the late 1990s, Lyon has been collecting data from experts on soil types. These experts include farmers who are said to be knowledgeable, soil scientists from the Pakistan Agricultural Research Centre, and the published literature on rain-fed agriculture in Punjab. The lists have varied a bit, but have included the following terms:

- *Retlee*—sandy land;
- *Patrelee*—stony land;
- *Hulky zehree*—white land (also called *kamzour*);
- *Ruhkr*—uncultivated, unbalanced land;
- *Ruhtee*—red land;
- *Sufaid*—white land;
- *Surukh*—red land in Urdu;

This is not, however, a comprehensive list, because a specialized vocabulary for cultivated land is also used that includes words like

- *Mera*—powerful land (people describe this as *achi* (Urdu) or *changi* (Punjabi), both terms for good;
- *Luss*—near the village where the land gets animal fertilizers;
- *Lepara cheri*—this is said to be the best land;
- *Hulky mera*—weak land;
- *Banjr*—forest, uncultivated;

In practice, soil experts working in rain-fed areas of northern Punjab, have reduced these land types down to two salient categories: *lepara* and *mera* (Byerlee, Sheikh, and Azeem, 1992). This reflects, in part, the focus of experts on soil that is most likely to produce high agricultural yields.

Our free-listing task was carried out with 35 men, ranging in age from mid teens to a man in his 80s (probably). In Table 6.1, all terms listed by two or more farmers have been included. It would appear that agricultural

Table 6.1 Soil types (all terms listed 2 or more times)

Item	Frequency (%)	Average rank	Salience
chitti 'white'	80.0	3.25	0.439
kaali 'black'	77.1	2.78	0.515
retlee 'red'	60.0	3.57	0.357
banjar 'barren/uncultivated'	17.1	6.50	0.069
pathreelee 'stony'	14.3	3.00	0.104
sakhat 'hard'	11.4	1.75	0.097
kallar	8.6	3.67	0.055
naram	8.6	2.33	0.059
khushak	8.6	1.33	0.071
surukh	8.6	6.33	0.034
Sem	8.6	6.00	0.022
ruhkr	8.6	5.33	0.046
seekra	8.6	6.33	0.015
tibbay	8.6	4.67	0.029
zarkhez	8.6	2.00	0.066
baraani	8.6	2.33	0.063
mera	5.7	8.00	0.024
matt	5.7	1.50	0.054
luss	5.7	9.00	0.019
pathar	5.7	5.50	0.021
ghulabee	5.7	4.00	0.026
changi	5.7	2.00	0.046
hulky-zehree	5.7	3.00	0.048
kassi	5.7	6.00	0.021
kanjur	5.7	5.00	0.025
lepara-cheri	5.7	10.00	0.014
hulky-mera	5.7	11.00	0.010

experts and local farmers are employing different categorical criteria for classifying land. Although they are both driven by concerns with fertility, local farmers employ color terms to distinguish highly fertile soil (*kaali* 'black') from less-fertile soil (*chitti* 'white' and *retlee* 'red'). Farmers know a great many terms for soil and employ numerous synonyms, including some very playful ones that combine nonsense rhyming words on the end of the soil type (for example *chitti-shitti*). The use of nonsensical rhyming words beginning with *sh* is very common in this part of Punjab, and the principle is found across a number of South Asian languages.[10]

After the three most-common color terms for soil (*kaali, chitti,* and *retlee*), the terms drop considerably in frequency and salience. The remaining terms describe a range of physical properties of the soil, such as rocky (*pathreelee*) or hard (*sakhat*). Many of the soil types provided do not exist in the local region, but farmers are aware of neighboring areas where these can be found.

Animals

We asked 15 male farmers to list animals that were present in the local area. Some men included camels (*oont*), which do not live anywhere in the village or in immediately neighboring villages but pass through the area periodically and exist in villages within a 20-minute drive. One person listed the camel as a camel-horse (*oont-gora*), suggesting that, while known, camels are not particularly important categorically in the local contexts.

The top three animals listed are, unsurprisingly, the most ubiquitous animals present in the area: buffaloes, cows and goats (see Table 6.2). Each was present

Table 6.2 Animals (all terms listed 2 or more times)

Item	Frequency (%)	Average rank	Salience
beins 'buffalo'	93.3	2.00	0.874
bakri 'goat'	93.3	3.29	0.778
gai 'cow'	93.3	3.07	0.782
kutta 'dog'	73.3	7.73	0.357
gudda 'donkey'	66.7	6.10	0.391
billi 'cat'	60.0	7.89	0.263
chiri 'sparrow'	60.0	11.56	0.204
kava 'crow'	53.3	11.00	0.177
doomba 'ram'	53.3	5.75	0.381
bheyr 'ewe'	53.3	4.50	0.386
gora 'horse'	40.0	6.00	0.244
seyr 'boar'	40.0	9.33	0.184
teetr 'partridge'	40.0	15.00	0.063
battaira 'quail'	40.0	14.50	0.072
saor	33.3	9.60	0.144
kongi	33.3	11.00	0.107
lumbr	33.3	11.00	0.105
loali	33.3	9.80	0.133

Table 6.2 (Cont.)

Item	Frequency (%)	Average rank	Salience
pagyar	26.7	8.50	0.138
dand	26.7	7.25	0.162
bad	26.7	9.50	0.121
sanp	26.7	12.00	0.065
chani	26.7	13.00	0.046
lama	20.0	14.33	0.055
oont	20.0	7.00	0.119
gargo	20.0	13.67	0.028
chitti_kiri	20.0	17.00	0.023
kunde_wale	20.0	8.33	0.103
khargosht	20.0	8.00	0.109
prindi	13.3	10.50	0.064
seya	13.3	12.00	0.036
bada	13.3	3.00	0.117
gidr	13.3	7.00	0.080
babl	13.3	2.00	0.117

in 93.3 percent of the lists and came early in most peoples' lists. Very few of the animals listed were not domesticated farm animals, though some pests were included (for example *kundey-wala* 'a type of insect' and *seyr* 'wild boar'). There were birds included, though in no case did any farmer begin his list with a type of bird. Animals of prey (quail, partridge, and rabbit) and burden (donkey, horse, bull/ox) were included. Sheep and cows were listed by sex (*doomba* 'ram,' *bheyr* 'ewe,' *gai* 'cow,' and *dand* 'bull' or 'ox'). Animals that do not have different root terms for sex difference were not listed separately (e.g., *gora* 'horse,' *gori* 'mare'). There were no terms for animals that had been castrated, which is not surprising since this is not a common practice in the village. They do not keep male animals in large numbers, and those that are present (like rams) are used for reproduction before being slaughtered for meat.

Trees

We free listed trees with fewer farmers because most farmers claimed to draw a blank on trees. While we could successfully encourage them to name trees by prompting them with some suggestions, we discarded all free lists that included terms that we had suggested. Consequently, these terms were generated from only seven farmers. Despite this low number, there were 59 tree terms listed, so those farmers who did know trees, tended to know rather a lot of them (see Table 6.3). There were far fewer terms listed two or more times, however, suggesting that there is not as much shared knowledge of trees as either animals or soil types.

Perhaps the most interesting thing about this list is the frequency of *malta*. This is an imported variety of citrus tree that has become extremely important part of wealthier farmers' attempts to generate more income from cash crops.

Table 6.3 Trees (all terms listed 2 or more times)

Item	Frequency (%)	Average rank	Salience
malta 'Malta orange tree'	71.4	6.60	0.375
kikr	57.1	2.75	0.494
kava	57.1	4.50	0.364
pilai	42.9	5.67	0.298
kander	28.6	14.00	0.040
kikri	28.6	3.50	0.222
aru	28.6	8.00	0.152
tali	28.6	6.00	0.163

Only very wealthy farmers can afford to introduce any type of orchard because the initial investment is very high and the subsequent demands for irrigation are ongoing, both in terms of energy (either electricity or diesel to power the pumps at the tube-wells) and maintenance. The first orchards in the area were citrus trees. These were introduced beginning in the early 1990s and there was one well-established orchard when Lyon first arrived in the village in 1998. At that time, two other farmers were investing in citrus orchards outside the village. In the past ten years, wealthy farmers have invested heavily in more-diverse varieties of orchard (primarily peaches and grapes). Although *malta* is the most frequently cited tree, it had a lower average rank than all but two of the eight most-frequently cited terms. This may suggest that, while it is a well-known tree, it is not particularly important for peasant farmers.

Plants

We initially attempted to collect plant lists by meaningful groupings: trees, cultivated crops, wild plants. This was reasonably successful with trees but did not generate particularly good results when we distinguished between cultivated crops and wild plants. The distinction is clearly there but, in a free-listing context, farmers seemed unable to remember plants by such categories. By the time we asked farmers to generate these lists, they had already done a number of free lists on other categories of nature, so it may have been task fatigue. To their credit, they tried to carry out every task to the best of their ability, but none of the men we asked to do this task had attended school. We suspect that asking illiterate farmers to do repeated tasks that feel like academic tests or exams, may be more distracting than we had anticipated. It is perhaps necessary to ask a single individual to do only one or two free-listing tasks in one sitting.

   In the end, we wound up with usable free lists on plants from eight men. The most frequently cited terms (*maki* 'maize' and *jondra* 'a fodder plant') did not have the highest average ranking. Wheat (*gundum*), although only mentioned by four out of the eight men, had the highest average rank of all the terms. There were more than 60 terms listed in total, and many of these were certain varieties of specific plants. In particular, several people each

Table 6.4 Plants (all terms listed 2 or more times)

Item	Frequency (%)	Average rank	Salience
maki 'maize'	62.5	2.80	0.521
jondra 'fodder plant'	62.5	4.20	0.422
gundum 'wheat'	50.0	1.00	0.500
bajra 'millet'	50.0	5.50	0.328
aloo 'potato'	50.0	7.75	0.224
jawar 'sorghum'	50.0	5.00	0.348
sarey	37.5	5.00	0.279
jaon	37.5	4.00	0.301
mangni 'lentil'	37.5	10.00	0.129
matr 'peas'	37.5	7.67	0.125
bangen 'aubergine'	25.0	13.00	0.074
kanok	25.0	2.00	0.235
jamiyan	25.0	8.50	0.133
masoor 'lentil'	25.0	12.00	0.082

listed more than one type of lentil though, interestingly, only two varieties of lentil were mentioned by two or more farmers (*mangni* and *masoor*). Grains and fodder appear to be the most important plants listed, though potato also appeared in 50 percent of the lists (see Table 6.4 for the complete list of all terms mentioned by two or more farmers).

Unfortunately, the usable number of lists from this exercise is low. This probably means that there are few, if any, inferences possible about priorities, distribution or organization of plant knowledge among this population of Punjabi farmers. This may be something that can be dealt with more adequately at a future time.

Weather

Perhaps the most surprising results were those regarding weather terms. After collecting 11 free lists on weather, we realized that respondents not only found this task confusing, but they genuinely seemed not to be able to list weather terms without prompts. There are, to be sure, considerably more terms for weather than those we collected, and both Lyon and Mughal have heard local farmers use these terms, but respondents appear to have found it difficult to recall the terms in the abstract. Since the total number of listed terms was seven (once synonyms were collapsed), we have listed all terms even if mentioned by only a single respondent (see Table 6.5).

All respondents listed two categories of weather: *sardi* 'cold' and *garmi* 'hot.' In some ways, this reflects the range of weather experienced in the region. Winters are very mild, and temperatures rarely drop below 5°C. Summers are very hot and can reach the high 40s and even into the low 50s on occasion (°C). Rains are reportedly less predictable than in previous decades and do not occur in all months. The fifth term on the list, *bahar* 'spring,' was the season in

Table 6.5 Weather (all terms listed)

Item	Frequency (%)	Average rank	Salience
garmi 'hot'	100.0	1.36	0.883
sardi 'cold'	100.0	1.91	0.706
barish 'rain'	54.5	3.67	0.185
saf 'clean'	18.2	3.50	0.076
bahar 'spring'	18.2	5.00	0.052
acha 'good'	18.2	3.00	0.083
sourij 'sunny'	9.1	3.00	0.061

which the free-listing exercise was conducted. The term *acha* 'good' is almost a synonym for *garmi* 'hot.' When asked what constituted *acha* weather, farmers replied *garmi*, however, this must be understood as a contextualized answer. We are not confident that they would reply that *acha mosam* 'good weather' equals *garmi mosam* in June or July, when the heat is at its peak.

Cultural models and free-listing data

The free-listing data taken in isolation are of limited use. It is clear that farmer recall is heavily skewed toward animals, soils, trees, weather, crops, and other plants that are of use to them. This is particularly true of their categorization of the weather, which was striking both by its brevity as well as the complete consensus of the two most important terms, that is, hot and cold. Taken with the interview data, however, what emerges is a picture of a population that has an instrumental relationship with nature. Nature is 'provided' for utilization by a higher power. God, referred to as Allah, has *made* all of the surrounding natural resources available to His favored creation (people). Term recall is intimately connected to material advantage and this is not solely driven by historical importance or significance but can, in fact, be the result of recent innovations. Among the terms for trees, for example, note the first-place ranking of a tree that has only existed in the area since the 1980s and remains the exclusive prerogative of the most wealthy landowning farmers, the citrus tree, *Malta*.

Buffalo (*beinz*) remain highly ranked despite their cost and the fact that many farmers do not actually *own* a buffalo. These animals are integrally linked to all aspects of farming and subsistence and provide critical fuel, food, and fertilizer. Goats and cows, equal in frequency to buffalo, are ranked lower—perhaps because they are materially less advantageous. Cows provide the same fuel, food, and fertilizer as buffalos, but they are more difficult to handle, and their milk is less fat, so seen as less 'tasty.' Goats (and sheep) offer the additional advantage of being a relatively low-cost sacrificial animal so if the exercise were carried out immediately around the time of *Eid-ul-Adha* (the ceremony marking the sacrifice of

Abraham's son), then it may be that goats and sheep would rise in the rankings.

Among the cultivated crops listed, maize, fodder plants, and wheat score very high. Maize and fodder are more frequently cited, but those who listed wheat systematically listed it first, suggesting its relative importance for some people. All the top-six listed crops except potatoes are those that are suitable for rain-fed agriculture. This is to be expected given the population of farmers interviewed for this study. Most of them have only a small fraction of irrigated land at best and must continue to rely on the unpredictable rains for their irrigation and so immediate recall is, unsurprisingly, focused on the crops they know best. The presence of potatoes may be a good indication of the labor power required for producing potato crops. Even though most peasant farmers are not able to sow potatoes, they would invariably find themselves recruited for periods of intense wage labor on larger farmers' potato fields.

These data together begin to form a coherent picture of a model of nature that is resilient and adaptive. It is instrumental, to be sure, but has the capacity to retain clusters of relevant information within durable subcategories of nature. The umbrella category, *kudruti mahole*, is of only marginal use in the area for a number of reasons. The free-listing data suggest a coherent organization of materially relevant resources necessary for subsistence survival without recourse to an articulable parent category of 'nature.' As the interview data suggest, the parent category is subsumed within a higher-order cultural model of the divine, which furnishes the subcategorical resources directly.

Conclusion

The richest source of data about the relationship between humans, nature and God, thus far has arguably been the interview data, in which it is possible to begin to develop a coherent cultural causal explanation of identified problems of climate change. Although the local causal model is at odds with global scientific explanations, it nevertheless places the blame squarely with human beings. Like the dominant scientific model in the West, it attempts to incorporate technical and moral explanations.

In the Western model, excessive carbon production and emission has led to changes in the composition of the Earth's atmosphere which disrupt patterns of heat flow. Excessive carbon emissions are a consequence of lavish energy consumption which many of the world's governments are attempting to frame as morally questionable. For local Punjab farmers in this part of northern Punjab, the mechanism for disrupting rains, in particular, is rooted in the omnipotent Allah who has the power, and authority, to deprive humans of rain or flood them with excessive rain at will. He does this because he is angry about the behavior of humans.

The dominant reason given for Allah's anger is immorality in the cities which is being adopted by rural people (see Jones, this volume for a comparable attitude among Qichua speakers). Some farmers blame Indian and Western cultures for spreading immoral, un-Islamic ideas and behaviors to the rural areas and triggering Allah's anger. The typical response to this anger is to say that people should pray more, both in the mosque an in local and regional shrines. The latter locations for praying are themselves cited as part of the cause of Allah's anger by farmers more heavily in line with Wahabi- or Salafi-influenced schools of Islam, including the Deoband school,[11] which is the majority among Pukhtun groups. This remains a minority in rural areas and is correlated with higher education levels. The less formal education a person has, the more likely he or she will be a follower of Barelvi Sunni Islam, a South Asian variety of Sufi Islam.[12]

Free listing tasks produced mixed results. The free lists on soil types, animals, and trees were reasonably extensive and informative. The one for plants is probably insufficient for inclusion in comparative analyses within this project. The free listing on weather, although clearly an inadequate reflection of the range of weather terms that Lyon and Mughal have heard in the village, is telling. The relatively short lists and the unanimous inclusion of the terms *garmi* 'hot' and *sardi* 'cold,' suggest that weather may be something that is not emphasized or prioritized by farmers because it may be perceived as too far beyond their control. The more elaborated vocabularies elicited on other topics all refer to domains in which individual farmers can make reasoned choices, but weather must be endured regardless of the impact on one's crops or comfort. This, like other matters, requires further study to generate and test plausible hypotheses for the drivers of such apparently restricted vocabularies.

The evidence suggests that the most widespread model of the natural world involves a powerful supernatural domain, which includes Allah, as a sole God, plus, various non-human spirits or *jinn*, who can be both benign and malicious, and a bewildering array of spiritually powerful saints, or *pir-fakir*, to whom individuals can pray and seek some form of intervention. These *pir-fakir* typically do not themselves perform miracles, but they are beloved by Allah and are somehow in a position to sway His actions in some people's favor. For Barelvi Sunni Muslims, this influence continues even after death, which means that the gravesite of powerful *pir-fakir* themselves become sites of religious worship and devotion. While this is arguably contrary to a literal interpretation of doctrinaire Islam, it is nevertheless remarkably widespread across the Muslim world and constitutes majority practice in South Asia. The remainder of the 'natural' world, including animals, plants, weather and non-human entities, appears to be part of the benevolent offering from God. So, while there remain a number of questions to be answered in how inanimate and animate entities are related, there is no evidence to suggest widespread animist models of such things having independent relations to one another, as opposed to being the product of a single deity.

Notes

1 Parts of this chapter were published in a special issue of *World Cultures* on Primary Food Producers, Climate Change, and Cultural Models of Nature (see Lyon and Mughal, 2017).

2 We are aware of the ambiguity of the term *nature* in English. The multiple meanings and contexts are addressed, in part, later in this chapter, but also see Bennardo's Introduction to this collection.

3 See also Vayda (2006) for a refutation of what he considered spurious assertions of causality in relation to Indonesian forest fires. He was consistent in calling for research to focus on events rather than preconceived drivers of systemic change.

4 Core cultural models are akin to Leaf's foundational idea systems. See Leaf's development of this concept in Leaf 1971, 1972, 2005, 2008; Read et al., 2013.

5 Tehsil refers to the Pakistani subdistrict administrative units. These have little authority and few resources, but they serve as important venues for managing local disputes and to a lesser extent as a source of geographical social identity in their regions.

6 See Lyon (2004a) for a concise history of the region from the stories of Alexander the Great's (Sikandar-i-Azam) famous peaceful stay in nearby Taxila to the greatness of the Buddhist Gandharan civilization to the more recent waves of successive Central Asian invaders and occupation by Ranjit Singh's Sikh armies.

7 Though, we are not convinced that there exists any farming village, or indeed any community, anywhere with a *complete* absence of antagonism.

8 Tube wells, or borehole wells, are a type of well in which a long, steel tube or pipe is bored into an underground aquifer to pump water to the surface.

9 The interchangeable terms, Pathan, Pukhtun, and Pushtun all refer to the dominant ethnic group in Khyber-Pukhtunkhwa, Pakistan and Eastern Afghanistan. They typically refer to themselves as Pukhtun or Pushtun, but beyond KP, in other parts of India and Pakistan, they are referred to as Pathan. Pukhtun/Pathan migrants have spread across Pakistan for a variety of reasons. The ones who come to Attock District are diverse and have often come to escape the violence that has been on the rise in the Tribal Areas, or the harsh sharecropping arrangements of some parts of Khyber-Pukhtunkhwa (KPK). Attock's history as a buffer district between Punjab and KPK has meant that there is a long history of Pukhtuns passing through and settling in all of the subdistricts of Attock.

10 See Abbi (1985) on the distribution of reduplicative structures (RS) present across all South Asian language groups. Abbi argues that modernization is 'killing' RS in more 'developed' languages like Punjabi, so this pattern of nonsensical rhyming may be a residual consequence of an earlier semantically meaningful RS.

11 See Metcalf (1982) for a historical account of the rise of reformist Islam in South Asia, especially the Deoband School. See also Metcalf (2010) for a discussion of the forms of educational instruction that allowed it to spread so effectively.

12 Sufi Islam is a form of devotion that arguably is rooted in the emotional experience of Allah and the divine, rather than in a strict interpretation of the orthodox texts. In South Asia, there are two dominant schools of Islam, Deobandi and Barelvi. Barelvi adherents are more inclined to establish elaborate shrines around living or deceased saints. In this part of Punjab, most Muslims would describe themselves as Sunni, by which they mean Barelvi (see Choudhary, 2010, for

an ethnographic account of the ritual practices of Sufi Islam in Punjab and see Ewing, 1990, for an interesting account of how Sufis loosely guide adherents through dream interpretation).

References

Abbi, A. (1985). Reduplicative structures: A phenomenon of the South Asian linguistic area. *Oceanic Linguistics Special Publications* 20: 159–171.

Barth, F. (1959). *Political Leadership among Swat Pathans*. London: University of London, Athlone Press.

Bennardo, G. (2009). *Language, Space, and Social Relationships: A Foundational Cultural Model in Polynesia*. Cambridge: Cambridge University Press.

Bernard, H. Russell. (2011). *Research Methods in Anthropology: Qualitative and Quantitative Approaches*. Lanham, MD: AltaMira.

Byerlee, D., Sheikh, A. D., and Azeem, M. (1992). Food, fodder, and fallow: Analytics of the Barani farming systems of Northern Punjab. In Byerlee, D. and Hussain, T. (eds.), *Farming Systems of Pakistan*. Lahore: Vanguard, 155–189.

Choudhary, M. A. (2010). Religious practices at Sufi shrines in the Punjab. *Pakistan Journal of History and Culture* 31(1): 1–30.

Donnan, H. (1997). Return migration and female headed households in rural Pakistan. In Donnan, H. and Selier, F. (eds.), *Family and Gender in Pakistan: Domestic Organization in a Muslim Society*. New Delhi: Hindustan Publishing Corporation, 111–131.

Ellen, R., and Fukui, K. (eds.). (1996). *Redefining Nature: Ecology, Culture and Domestication*. Oxford: Oxford International Publishers.

Ewing, K. P. (1990). The dream of spiritual initiation and the organization of self representations among Pakistani Sufis. *American Ethnologist* 17(1): 56–74. www.jstor.org/stable/645252

Fernández-Giménez, M. E., and Estaque, F. F. (2012). Pyrenean pastoralists' ecological knowledge: Documentation and application to natural resource management and adaptation. *Human Ecology* 40(2): 287–300. www.jstor.org/stable/41432991

Golshani, M. (2000). Islam and the sciences of nature: Some fundamental questions. *Islamic Studies* 39(4): 597–611. www.jstor.org/stable/23076115

Horowitz, L. S. (2001). Perceptions of nature and responses to environmental degradation in New Caledonia. *Ethnology* 40(3): 237–250. https://doi.org/10.2307/3773967

Humphrey, C., Mongush, M., and Telengid, B. (1993). Attitudes to nature in Mongolia and Tuva: A preliminary report. *Nomadic Peoples* 33: 51–61. http://www.jstor.org/stable/43124052

Ingold, T. (ed.). (1987). *The Appropriation of Nature: Essays on Human Ecology and Social Relations*. Iowa City: University of Iowa.

Kaur, R. (2006). The last journey: Exploring social class in the 1947 Partition migration. *Economic and Political Weekly* 41(22): 2221–2228.

Khalidi, O. (1998). From torrent to trickle: Indian Muslim migration to Pakistan, 1947–1997. *Islamic Studies* 37(3): 339–352.

Leaf, M. (1971). Baking and roasting: A compact demonstration of a cultural code. *American Anthropologist* 73(1): 267–268. www.jstor.org/stable/671831

Leaf, M. J. (1972). *Information and Behavior in a Sikh Village: Social Organization Reconsidered.* Berkeley: University of California Press.

Leaf, M. J. (2005). The message is the medium: Language, culture, and informatics. *Cybernetics and Systems: An International Journal* 36(8): 903–917.

Leaf, M. J. (2008). Indigenous algorithms, organizations, and rationality. Structure and dynamics. *Structure and Dynamics.* http://escholarship.org/uc/item/996031cv

Lyon, S. M. (2004a). *An Anthropological Analysis of Local Politics and Patronage in a Pakistani Village.* Lampeter, Wales: Edwin Mellen Press.

Lyon, S. M. (2004b). Putting social engineering on the back burner: Teaching priorities in formal education in rural Punjab, Pakistan. *Anthropology in Action: Journal for Applied Anthropology in Policy and Practice* 11(1): 35–44.

Lyon, S. M. (2005). Culture and information: An anthropological examination of communication in cultural domains in Pakistan. *Cybernetics and Systems* 36(8): 919–932.

Lyon, S. M., and Mughal, M. A. Z. (2017). Categories and cultural models of nature in Northern Punjab, Pakistan. *World Cultures* 22(2). https://escholarship.org/uc/item/77w806mp

Metcalf, B. (1982). *Islamic Revival in British India: Deoband, 1860–1900.* Princeton, NJ: Princeton University Press.

Metcalf, B. (2010). The madrasa at Deoband: A model for religious education in modern India. In Lyon, S. M. and Edgar, I. R. (eds.), *Shaping a Nation: An Examination of Education in Pakistan.* Karachi: Oxford University Press, 30–53.

Nesheim, I., Dhillion, S. S., and Stølen, K. A. (2006). What happens to traditional knowledge and use of natural resources when people migrate? *Human Ecology* 34(1): 99–131.

Noman, O. (1991). The impact of migration on Pakistan's economy and society. Donnan, H. and Werbner, P. (eds.), *Economy and Culture in Pakistan.* London: Macmillan, 77–96.

Rappaport, R. A. (1968). *Pigs for the Ancestors: Ritual in the Ecology of a New Guinea People.* New Haven, CT: Yale University Press.

Read, D., Fischer, M., and Leaf, M. (2013). What are kinship terminologies, and why do we care? A computational approach to analyzing symbolic domains. *Social Science Computer Review* 31(1): 16–44. https://doi.org/10.1177/0894439312455914

Shackle, C. (1979). Problems of classification in Pakistan Panjab. *Transactions of the Philological Society* 77(1): 191–210. https://doi.org/10.1111/j.1467-968X.1979.tb00857.x

Steward, J. H. (1955). *Theory of Culture Change: The Methodology of Multilinear Evolution.* Urbana: University of Illinois Press.

Talbot, I., and Thandi, S. S. (2004). *People on the Move: Punjabi Colonial, and Post-Colonial Migration. The Subcontinent Divided: A New Beginning.* Karachi: Oxford University Press.

Vayda, A. P. (1969). The study of the causes of war, with special reference to head-hunting raids in Borneo. *Ethnohistory* 16(3): 211–224. https://doi.org/10.2307/481584

Vayda, A. P. (1971). Phases of the process of war and peace among the Marings of New Guinea. *Oceania* 42(1): 1–24. www.jstor.org/stable/40329969

Vayda, A. P. (1989). Explaining why Marings fought. *Journal of Anthropological Research* 45(2): 159–177. www.jstor.org/stable/3630332

Vayda, A. P. (2006). Causal explanation of Indonesian forest fires: Concepts, applications, and research priorities. *Human Ecology* 34(5): 615–635. www.jstor.org/stable/27654144

Vayda, A. P., and Walters, B. B. (1999). Against political ecology. *Human Ecology* 27(1): 167–179. www.jstor.org/stable/4603312

7 The salience of woodland in the Dolomites (Italian Alps)

Anna Paini

In this chapter I discuss how the people living in Vinigo, a mountain village situated in the Belluno province of the Veneto Region, Italy (see Figure 7.1),[1] perceive changes in their environment. I also provide indications on how villagers interpret the effects of these changes. In their reasoning, they attribute agency to elements of the close physical environment and emphasize engagement and interaction with them. They indicate the causes that have brought about these changes and the risks involved as well as their anxieties about the future. Their perception of the environment is filtered by local knowledge, which highlights salient reciprocal and asymmetrical relationships among fundamental components of Nature such as humans, plants, and animals. In the chapter, I report how the data was acquired and analyzed. I focus on the results of a thematic analysis and a metaphor analysis carried out on the texts of the semi-structured interviews we conducted. Overall, four themes emerged as most prominent: (1) woodland is neglected; (2) woodland is encroaching the village; (3) cultivated fields are considerably reduced; (4) more wild animals are coming into the village. The results of the linguistic analyses allowed me to hypothesize a cultural model of Nature, which I revise through the results of the analysis of free-listing tasks. Fundamentally, because of the way they attribute agency to different components, it appears that they hold a holistic approach to the concept of Nature.

Introduction to the field site

Vinigo, at an elevation of 1,025m (3,363 feet), is one of the oldest settlements in the Ladin area (*Vinego Paés Laden*) in the Dolomites, which were included in the Unesco World Heritage List in 2009 (Seville, June 26, 2009), when nine areas were designated as 'Serial Heritage Sites.'[2] Although the Dolomites have been recognized as the heritage of humanity, the role of local inhabitants is neglected in the Unesco declaration, as several authors have highlighted, stressing the underlining assumption of a rigid boundary between natural space and human space (Varotto and Castiglione, 2012). The geographer Mauro Varotto remarked that such

DOI: 10.4324/9781351127905-8

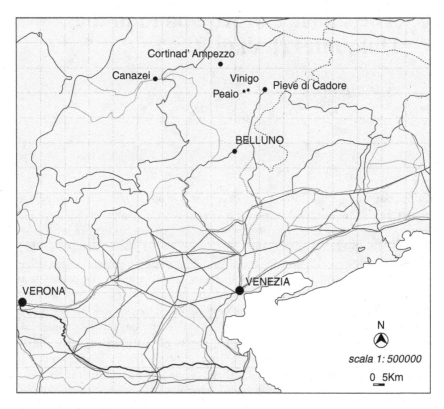

Figure 7.1 The field site: Vinigo in the Veneto Dolomites.

little or no consideration of the role of the people and local communities appears all the more jarring, even in the face of the fact that the legal ownership of the Unesco heritage in some cases belongs to the people themselves, through the *regolieri* institutions and ASUC (Amministrazioni Separate Usi Civici). During the nomination process, the promoters stressed the difficulty of bringing about an understanding of the positive role of the human presence in preserving the same environment, thanks to the management systems developed by a secular agro-pastoral civilization (Guichonnet 1986), of which one has become less and less aware, since the same local society has embraced new models of development and behavior.

(2012a: 288)

Cesare Lasen of the Fondazione Dolomiti-Dolomiten-Dolomites-Dolomitis Unesco clarifies that the nine sites have been recognized on the basis of two criteria: aesthetic–landscape and geologic–geomorphologic components. The Italian dossier included two further criteria, the biological–naturalistic and ecological–succession components, however, 'for these last two aspects, it was impossible to demonstrate their uniqueness, a fundamental requirement together with that of integrity' (Lasen, 2012: 273).

Vinigo is included in the area called Cadore, an historical region that borders Austria. The nearest town is Vodo, in the Boite Valley, home to the municipality that also includes Peaio and Vinigo.[3] The village lies between two creeks, the Rudan (to the west) and the Ruinian (to the east); the latter was in the past home to three windmills. Vinighesi (as local people are called) say that Rudan (*ru* = creek) means '*torrente/fa danno*,' 'creek/makes damage,' while Ruinian means '*torrente/fa rumore, e non fa danno*,' 'creek/ makes noise and not damage.' Even the most recent event of a *roa* 'landslide' in the area (August 2015) caused by heavy rain, has provided evidence that this seems to be the case. The Rudan is a tributary of the Boite, a right tributary of the Piave,[4] a river that flows entirely in the Veneto Region and one of the most artificial waterways in Europe (creeks and rivers harnessed, artificial lakes, dams). Both streams originate on the Antelao (the second highest peak in the Dolomites, 3,234m), which is located to the north of the village. The other imposing mountain (to the west) is the Pelmo, 3,168m, locally named *el caregon del Padreterno*, 'the throne of God.' (Figure 7.2). Both mountains are relevant to the life of the people of Vinigo and in their

Figure 7.2 The Pelmo seen from Vinigo, November 2014 (Photo © A. Paini).

daily talk they often make reference to them. To the south lies Mount Rite (2,160 m). and to the east is Col Maò (1,470 m).

Vinigo is connected to the rest of Cadore by a paved road. One of our interviewers recalled how in the past people from Vinigo would be preparing to get off the bus in Peaio and the bus driver would announce in an ironic way: 'For Vinigo. You change here: Eagle service.' In times of heavy snow the road, with a steep slope and sharp turns, is closed as was the case for the unexpected snow storm at the end of January/early February 2014: The village remained isolated, cut off from electricity for 48 hours, and cell phones became useless.

Analyzing the relevant issues concerning contemporary Alpine spaces, Varotto underlines the role of 'intermediate spaces that act as buffers between protected areas and areas of strong touristic and agro-industrial development' (2012b: 325).[5] Vinigo could be considered one of such intermediate spaces.

In the first half of the twentieth century Vinigo was entirely surrounded by cultivated fields: wheat, rye, corn, potatoes, barley, and hemp. A cultivated landscape that is still alive in people's memory and documented by old photographs. Then meadows took over in order to produce hay to feed the cattle. Nowadays, no local family raises cows or pigs, and fields are fallow. 'Everyone had animals: cows, goats, and also pigs' recalls Riccarda. And Mario adds: Few families, 'the more wealthy ones,' also had one or two horses. As Dario says: *'Stalla e bosco'* 'stable and woodland,' from these two sources came what you needed to survive. As the *bosco* 'woodland' is no longer maintained and used for woodcutting, it is expanding and encroaching the village. The Alps are an 'exceptional wealth of biodiversity compared to the entire European continent' (Lasen, 2012: 273). The spread of the woodland involves a loss of such biodiversity (Varotto, 2012a). Retreating glaciers are also participating in creating an unfamiliar landscape in the area.

Until the 1960s and 1970s, Vinighesi derived their main source of livelihood from agriculture, breeding, and timber. Itinerant activities such as *calderai*, 'coppersmiths,' and *vetrai*, 'glaziers,' were added as an essential source of income. The village felt the dramatic impact of different waves of emigration in the 1900s. In some cases, they were seasonal movements, in others (particularly between the two world wars) migration was definitive and permanent (e.g., to the United States and Argentina). People also emigrated to Germany, Holland, and the former Czechoslovakia to be ice cream makers. However, they always stress that they left to be *gelatieri* 'ice cream makers' and not *gelatai* 'ice cream sellers.'

Vinighesi of a certain age remember the *colonie di vacanza* 'holiday camps' that enlivened the village in the summertime during the 1950s and early 1960s. For example, la Locanda dal Gobbo, the village inn Emma Pivirotto opened in 1957 and was in business for almost thirty years, also hosted guests in rented rooms in private homes, a forerunner of the 'albergo diffuso' 'diffused hotel,' as one of our interlocutors put it. As her daughter recalls: 'Parents came to visit their children, and then they used to come back bringing their friends.' People have very fond memories of that period. The arrival of young people, often from the cities, animated the life of the village during the summer; it allowed the making of new acquaintances, which sometimes turned into long-lasting friendships; the locals found out about things and practices of the city, and for families, being hosts was a way to acquire some revenue. People remember those summers when their parents made them and their siblings give up their bedrooms in order to host guests. Ettore, in his mid-seventies, adds that for the holiday of *ferragosto*, 'August 15,' even the barns were used to accommodate guests.

When *occhialerie*, 'manufacturers of glasses,' opened in the area in the late 1960s, these factories provided a major source of income for many families from Vinigo. To get a better understanding of the importance of this industry, one needs to be reminded that 80 percent of the lenses and frames made in Italy are produced in Cadore. Yet, depopulation has continued; today, the village has only 115 inhabitants (58 males and 57 females)[6] compared to 359 in 1929; and during wintertime they are down to less than a hundred residents. Some houses are abandoned, some have become *seconde case*, 'vacation homes.' The archival data kept in the town hall show that in the early 1900s Vinigo had 177 heads of families. When we consider that the average family was made up of four or five people, we get an idea of the strong impact of depopulation. The last grocery store closed its doors in December 2013, a few months after our first fieldwork. In the past, there were five *osterie*—small taverns—and a 'family restaurant.' Today none survive. One element stressed by several interviewees as characterizing the Cadore, is that in the past both boys and girls went to primary school. 'The school in Cadore was ahead of the school of the plain,' says Enrica, born in the early 1950s. A consideration backed by historical studies (Piseri, 2012: 55).[7]

Mapping the village of Vinigo

The village has a circular shape. The central area—locally called *pias*—is traditionally dedicated to small, privately owned plots for the cultivation of *capuże* 'cabbage,' and it is of a very fine variety that is considered the most prestigious produce of the village. Today, other vegetables are also grown in these plots. The historical *destinazione d'uso* 'intended use' of this central area has remained remarkably similar through time. In fact, no development project has been allowed in this area.

This central area is enclosed by two streets forming a kind of oval. Locally, one street (via Savilla) is considered *via par davante* 'street in the front' and one (via della Grotta) *via par daos* is the 'street in the back.' The more formal side of the village (the front) is where the Church of San Giovanni

Battista (the oldest section dates to 1506), and the former primary school—today home of the local chapter of the Associazione Nazionale Alpini (Italian Association of Former Alpine Veterans)—are located. The back—the more informal side—is where the Latteria Sociale 'Communal Dairy' used to be (the building still stands, but the dairy closed in the mid-1970s). These distinctions are locally drawn. As one of our interviewees, in her sixties, told us: In order to take the front side one should be properly dressed. Most people still adhere to this. A third street (*via pias*) cuts through the village, and it is called *via par mezzo* 'middle street' by the locals. At the northern edge of the village, the path to Greanes starts, a close-by locality used in the past by Vinighesi for pasture.

Space is an important and multifaceted dimension in Vinigo. If some interlocutors recognized a 'front' and a 'back' side, which follows a north/south axes, all the old inhabitants of Vinigo acknowledge a further distinction, which follows a different criterion: the low half vs. the high half of the village. People remember a strong sense of belonging to either Festin (low) or Savilla (high) as well as (in the past) the local rivalry. Today, people still speak of *do Festin* 'going down to Festin' and *sun Savilla* 'going up to Savilla.' However, this distinction is less marked these days, and people tend to recall more the sense of belonging than of competitiveness. As one can see in Figure 7.3, this distinction is expressed through a dotted line, which follows an east–west axis and splits the village in two halves. The Church of Saint John is located in the Festin half, whereas the Chapel of Saint Lorenzo is in the Savilla half. Another line indicates the road descending to Peaio.

A social institution that cuts across this distinction is *coscritti* in the past 'an age class' of young men joining the Army, today men and women born in the same year or in years with close proximity. On the façade of a wooden

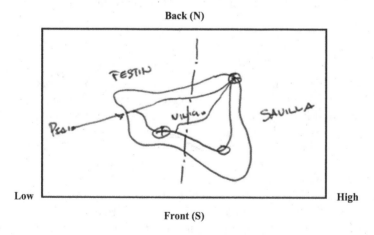

Figure 7.3 Drawing of the lower/upper area of the village, made by an interlocutor.

Figure 7.4 Via alla Grotta, Graffiti, January 2014 (Photo © A. Paini).

building in via della Grotta the prominent white graffiti '1950 51 52,' written in the 1970s by the *coscritti* of the year 1951, has not been removed. Today it stands as 'traditional' graffiti (see Figure 7.4). Seven men and women of this age group still live in Vinigo (one of them only part of the year) and still engage in communal activities.[8] It was their idea to clean the inside of the

Communal Dairy in the spring/summer of 2014 as a part of a project for a new cultural association.

Most of the houses have at least a small fenced garden (locally called *orto* or *al brolo*), where carrots, celery, beetroot, garlic, onion, and lettuce are grown; sometimes also fruit trees. The plots in the *pias* are, instead, called *cianpo*. This large central area, which comprises small private plots still owned by various local families, is dedicated to the cultivation of the *capuże*, 'cabbage,' for which Vinigo has earned renown. All Vinighesi explain this continuity by stressing that 'it was a piece of land suitable for that kind of work.' We have questioned them in order to understand what 'being suitable' means. Some of them speak of the soil, which has good nutrients and the right amount of water, and it is at the right altitude; others refer to the fact that wild animals love cabbage, so in the past it was a way to protect the produce from being eaten by animals. As one among them put it, '*l'é l'altitudine, l'é la terra e l'é la conca, se vede che l'é protetta.*' 'It is the altitude, it is the soil, it is the gully, one can see that it is protected' (Gianna).

In the past, Vinighesi kept *capuże* for consumption at home and exchanged some of them with people from other communities. Today, some sell, others donate them to friends. As one of our female interlocutors told us, they are *troppo preziosi* 'too precious' to be sold. In more recent times, due to different climatic conditions as well as to wanting to try new food, new cultivations have been introduced, such as artichokes. Both elements of continuity and discontinuity surface from the interviews. In fact, some of the women interviewed, when asked how they choose what and where to plant in the *cianpo*, speak of a continuity with the choices made by the women who planted crops there before them (usually mothers, grandmothers) in terms of a form of showing *rispetto* 'respect' toward those women.

Land-use management

> If there were no Regole, the environment in Cadore would have been devastated.
>
> (MDB)

A very important local institution in the Dolomites region is *La Regola*, 'The Rule.' It is a traditional communal way of governing community life and managing land, woodland, and resources—a tradition that goes back to the thirteenth and fourteenth centuries. The 'communal properties' have through the centuries become a residual phenomenon (Lorenzi and Borrini-Feyerabend, 2009), all of which makes the land-use management in the Dolomites even more unique. As *terre civiche* 'civic lands,' they are characterized by being inalienable, indivisible, *inusucapibile* 'non-usucaption,' *inespropiabile* 'cannot be confiscated,'—guaranteed by the immutability of their agro-forestry designation.

La '*Regola Grande*,' the 'Big Rule' includes Vinigo, Peaio, Vodo e Cancia; their first *laudo*, 'common written charter' goes back to 1289. At the time, Vinigo was part of the Centenaro of Venas, one of the ten constituencies that made up the *Magnifica Comunità* 'Magnificent Community' of Cadore. The story of the *Regole* is very complicated, especially in the nineteenth century. The new Napoleonic municipalities were generally grafted onto these old constituencies. There was not a total affirmation of private property in the 1800s, and this was followed by a rebirth of the *Regole* system in the 1900s. In spite of continuing tension between the two systems of land tenure and management, in the twentieth century, the *Regole* was revived and with it the 'Magnificent Community.' Today, Vinigo with Vodo and Peaio, form the *Regola Grande*. The *Regola Grande* has been able to get back 95 percent of their land (5% remains with the municipality). In the past, also a *Regola Piccola* 'Small Rule,' which included Vinigo and Peaio, had functioned, but it dissolved (Belli, 2007: 21). Woodland around the village became private property; however, none of the inhabitants is able to remember when this reorganization of land management took place.[9]

For centuries people of this Alpine area have operated in strict compliance with both private and collective property rules. Relying on the work of Giuseppe Richebuono, Giandomenico Zanderigo Rosolo (2012) reports that on October 30, 1226, the Vinigo di Cadore's *regolieri*—'members of the Regole,' who, at the time owned the Cimabanche, pasture land, (which today belongs to the *regolieri* of Ampezzo)—donated a parcel of this land for building a small church dedicated to wayfarers. On the occasion of the church's consecration, the *regolieri* made clear to the authorities who had come for the ceremony that they should stay within and not cross the well-defined boundaries of the given pasture. In a document from 1289,[10] the *regolieri* made a list of the people who had the right to access the mountain, specifying that, '*isti sunt consortes montis et alii non*'; 'only these, and no others, can access the mountain' (2012: 35).[11]

The *regolieri* used to be only males. Nowadays, in the case of no male descendants, a woman originating from a *regolieri* family, and married to a *regoliere*, can also become a member according to the *Regole Ampezzane* 'Rules of Ampezzo.'[12] Another proposal under discussion at the *Magnifica Regola Grande dei Monti di Vodo* 'Magnificent Great Rule of Vodo Mountains' is that a woman can become/maintain her role even if married to a *regoliere* as long as, and even if she undertakes to transmit to her son her family name (Mario [MDB] January 29, 2014). In any case, a *regoliere* must descend from one of the ancient families or one that has been living in the area for at least a hundred years.

An example of the importance of the *Regole* and of what the *regolieri* can achieve can be seen in the mountain Pelmo having no ski slopes. They opposed any development projects of this type on the mountain. While the Vinighesi speak with respect for the *Regole*, they also stress that they have no confidence in the national government. Thus, confidence in local, traditional, *Regole* is counter-posed to mistrust in wider forms of government.

Family names

Four historical family names are found among Vinigo inhabitants: De Lorenzo, Della Bona, Marchioni, and Pivirotto. These are matched by nicknames: An individual named De Lorenzo, 'Tomea,' belongs to a different family subgroup from a De Lorenzo, 'Frates,' or De Lorenzo, 'Nanete' or 'Fortunes.' Local people often use these family nicknames rather than last names—for example, *ie de chi dei Vece*, 'they are from the Vece subgroup,' referring to a family among those carrying the Pivirotto last name. This usage is also followed in the *foglio di famiglia* 'family sheet' of the *Registro di Popolazione 1896–1902*, 'Register of Population 1896–1902,' concerning the village of Vinigo, for example, Maria Marchioni (1857–1904), widow of De Lorenzo Flaminio 'Medego' (sheet 30).[13]

Climate and environmental changes

Phenomena related to climate and environmental changes affect the Dolomites in general; the perception of global warming is an experience shared by its inhabitants. For all of them, the memory of past very cold and snowy winters is quite vivid. Their family memories highlight the changes taking place. They remember that during the early years of the last century some *frazioni*, 'hamlets,' experienced true isolation—that is, they were often blocked by layers of snow several meters high, sometimes even for weeks. The local highest mountain, the Antelao, used to have three glaciers, but today the upper and the lower glaciers are in regression, while the third has disappeared. The other 3,000m high mountain, the Pelmo, had a *nevaio* 'permanent snowfield,' which is no longer there.

At the altitude of Vinigo (3,300 feet), the increased temperature has paradoxically had 'positive' effects on agriculture: New cultivations (definitely not alpine) like tomatoes are now possible in the most sunny areas. On the other hand, the increasing wild woodland (no longer cultivated) is changing the micro-climate and raising the level of humidity. This is making wild animals (mainly deer) come closer to the village searching for food, especially at night. Fencing individual parcels of the *pias* is a very recent practice to which Vinighesi resort hoping to protect their crops from being decimated in the night.[14]

Methodology

Focusing on the relationship between local knowledge and climate change, the data were collected by Elisa Bellato and myself during our fieldwork in Vinigo between October 2013 and July 2015 for a total of 7 weeks.[15] Our visits were planned on 'the cabbage calendar,' that is, on the main activities connected to the *cavolo cappuccio* 'cabbage,' bearing in mind that the seed for the cabbage is prepared in autumn, sown in spring (April–May) close to

Figure 7.5 Cabbages ready to harvest and to be stored, November 2013 and October 2014 (Photos © A. Paini).

home, planted in the *pias* around June 24, St. John's Day—the patron saint of the village—and the cabbages are collected and stored in early November (see Figure 7.5). We also spent a couple of weeks in Vinigo during winter time (January–February 2014) in order to get a better understanding of daily life in the village. Because of the snow storm that struck Vinigo at that time, we were isolated from other communities for a couple of days, and this allowed us to acquire a more in-depth perception of what local people mean when they speak of feeling/being isolated—while at the same time it allowed local inhabitants to become more familiar with us (Bennardo and De Munck, 2014: 60–61).

We collected our data by using a number of different methods: participant observation, informal conversations, nature walks, open and semi-structured interviews, and free-listing tasks. As Bennardo and De Munch, among others, have argued (2014: 57–58), the qualitative versus quantitative methodology distinction does not correspond to the complexity of this type of research: Data are 'hybrid.'

Three types of data were collected: ethnographic, linguistic, and cognitive. Although we made use of semi-structured interviews, which fitted better our goals, we also had many informal conversations that helped us to get a closer understanding of what people considered salient issues and how these relied on the cultural model they hold. Since by definition cultural models are shared, it is appropriate to conduct semi-structured interviews with a sample of the population. This type of interview allows the researcher to ask the same questions of the interviewees, thus tapping into common knowledge, while at the same time allowing each interviewee the freedom to express their ideas in the way they think appropriate.

The interviews were structured around a series of questions (in Italian, see Appendix) that we considered culturally appropriate/relevant. These questions were organized around six main topics, taking as a starting point the list of questions agreed upon with the other research units (see Appendix A in the Introduction to this volume). The free-listing tasks (n = 30) and the semi-structured interviews (n = 14) were recorded. Later, Iolanda Da Deppo, a local research assistant from the nearby community of Domegge di Cadore, transcribed them. This was necessary because we had asked interviewees to speak/respond as much as possible in their Laden language.

The analyses of the linguistic data focused on the discovery of themes, and also of salient metaphors. The results of the linguistic analyses allowed me to hypothesize a cultural model, which I revised through the results of the analyses of the free-listing tasks. The fundamental idea behind a free-listing task is that the first names mentioned are more salient and constitute the most important concepts that participate in the construction of a cultural model. I present suggestions based on the data collected and the results of the analyses.

Results of analyses of some of the data collected

Semi-structured interviews: 'It was like velvet.'

We conducted and recorded 14 semi-structured interviews with 7 men and 7 women based on a series of questions in Italian; we also had many other informal conversations while in Vinigo. Our interlocutors often switched back and forth from Ladin to Italian and vice-versa. The interviews were transcribed after each period of fieldwork so that we could rely on them for the next research period.

I now consider various interactions and relationships of our interlocutors with their environment. I first examine ideas about changes in climate and environment through a choice of relevant passages of the collected and transcribed material. How do the people of Vinigo perceive them? Then, I look at how they understand/interpret the perceived changes. Further, I introduce a number of relationships that can be inferred from these passages.

In presenting their idea of 'nature,' our interlocutors foreground the changes that have taken place in the environment close to themselves. They first state that snow, ice, and glaciers are not part of the yearly landscape as they were in the past. They also point out that fields around the villages are no longer cultivated. Then, they affirm that woodland, although it has always been part of the landscape, is today taking a more prominent position. So, their first responses point to some components of their environment that withdraw or disappear, and then to others that are now taking a place more front-stage.

Lino, a man in his sixties who has spent most of his life in Vinigo, expresses in these terms his concern for the changes affecting the local environment: 'Certainly the temperature has increased. The glaciers that I used to know are there no more. And ... not even the year-round snowfields. For example, the lower glacier on the Antelao now is all gravel; there is no longer a permanent snowfield on the Pelmo.'

Most of our interlocutors refer to the time when fields around the villages were cultivated and those further away were used for pasture. When asked, they refer to these different parts of land outside the village using different specific local terms (*pràs, vàres, bosche*). Most of these elements of the environment have disappeared. Vinighesi associated these spaces with stories, some of which appear to be more detailed than others because of richer memories and a willingness to share. The environment has changed and, along with this, so have all the narratives associated with hard working, sharing, and sociality. Marilena, a woman in her fifties, with a university degree, who has chosen to live in the village, points to that difference when she says, 'The hay has a memory for me that the lawn does not.' She explains that it was her mother who carried the hay 'because for my mom going back and forth from the barn to the lawn with the sled was something she took in her stride.'

People mention other changes connected to the loss of agricultural land. In fact, there is a loss of memory and knowledge about their environment. Ettore, for example, refers to part of the woodland that he inherited from his father, but he cannot recall its location. He explains: 'When you were cutting the grass you also knew where the boundaries were; now we no longer know where the boundaries are.' Marilena, although younger than Ettore, makes a similar remark: 'In the past the boundaries between fields, you could see them, really you could see them.' So the change in the environment has brought along also a change in the ability to recall, the knowledge of boundaries is lost.

While they notice elements missing from their environment, at the same time they highlight new ones that have appeared. Marilena adds: 'Compared with the past, the woodland has been allowed to encroach into the field. It would have been better if this had not been allowed to happen, unfortunately, however, it has an air of abandonment about it' (see Figure 7.6). The idea of an environment that has not been taken care of, that has been 'abandoned,' 'neglected' emerges in other interviews, and I will return to

Figure 7.6 Woodland encroaching on the village, November 2014 (Photo © A. Paini).

them. The presence of deer is another notable new feature of the local environment, a new phenomenon to which many make reference. To mention but one: 'Deer have been hostile to roes because deer also inhabit the dense forest, while roes need clearings to live. And there are few clearings today, because the woodland has become so thick' (Riccarda, a woman in her sixties).

So, the woodland is expanding while at the same time it is becoming more dense—two important changes because of the fact that the land is no longer cultivated. However, Lino remarks that, among the conifers, the *larice* 'larch' is disappearing. He is stressing that although the woodland is expanding and becoming more dense, some traditional salient species such as the larch are disappearing, and he is convinced that the *Forestale*, 'Forest Rangers,' the institution in charge of giving permission to cut down trees, is not taking this change seriously.

Weather is another component to which Vinighesi refer when talking about changes in the environment. For some of them, in the past it snowed more often, whereas today it rains more often. Weather is considered more unpredictable compared to the past (*le stravaganze del tempo* 'the strangeness of the weather,' Gianpietro). However, some of the elderly men mention the Christmas Eve of 1940, when a fire destroyed a section of Vinigo, burning to the ground many timber houses, and drawing attention to the fact that it was a snowless Christmas, which made it more difficult to contain the fire. To them the weather has always been unpredictable.

Local interpretation of climate/environmental change

I will now discuss how people explain the changes they mentioned. For some, the weather is the king, whereas for others it is human activity that is all important. A human intervention that does not speak the language of domination, but that of care, taking care of the woodland. Still, for others these two rationales combine (see Strauss, 1999) as Rino's comments suggest: 'Everything depends on the weather.' '*Il tempo è quello che comanda tutto.*' 'The weather is what rules everything.' 'In the past there was sun, a lot more than today. Now in the same day, the weather changes one thousand times … because the weather has changed.' He goes on to remark:

> The bark or the cones, the dry ones, were burned, and some branches as well, if we were allowed to collect some wood, because in the past the woodland was treated like a kitchen. It was really clean; now one cannot even walk because now it is a disaster, but at one time it was taken care of with respect, those who were cutting firewood were cleaning up after themselves.

Rino, a Vinighese in his sixties, who has worked most of his life outside the village, but has always kept his home in the village, points out the concerns that emerge from many of the interviews, that is, the 'neglect' in which the woodlands are left today.

I am struck by the passage: 'In the past the woodland was treated like a kitchen,' as Rino connects the woodland, an open space, with a kitchen, a domestic space. My interpretation of this metaphor, given the context in which it is advanced, is that the kitchen refers both to a place kept clean and where nothing went to waste. A place that required looking after. In the past, in many homes the kitchen was the only room kept warm during the cold season, thus a place lived in by people. As Lino explains: 'If you had little food in the kitchen you could survive, but if you could not heat the kitchen you would die.' The metaphor can also refer to the fact that in the past the woodland was less thick and one could find clearings they used and that reminded them of their living space.

The sense of a place well-kept looms large. Gianna, for example, is quite explicit about it: 'The fields were spectacular. Flowers everywhere. The flowers disappeared when they stopped cutting the grass. In some places where they started cutting again, the flowers came back.' If some components are not present anymore in the environment, nevertheless their disappearance is considered reversible; it is not an absence without the possibility of a coming back. And in both cases, it is human intervention ('when *they* stopped cutting the grass' and 'when *they* started cutting again'), that is responsible for it. The sense of a place well-kept is associated with the idea of 'spectacular' fields and the aesthetic of the place.

Questions that have been central to this research are how do Vinighesi perceive the features of their environment? Do they attribute them intentionality? Some, such as Marilena, seem to attribute agency to elements of the close environment: 'That is how things are, this year the Antelao wanted to move around' (Her comment came from a telephone call after a landslide affected a lower nearby village in summer, 2015). Others, such as Lino, prefer to stress interactions with the environment: 'When I go for a walk …, I come and go, and a year later I pass the same place I was before. If I go to Milan, no ... a street, a house does nothing for me, but in the woodland, I remember, a plant, a stone, the root of a tree.'

As Tim Ingold underscores: 'Ways of acting in the environment are also ways of perceiving it' (2000: 9). Two local perspectives connected to humans and their relationship with the woodland emerge: (1) One should read the woodland, and (2) one should act on it appropriately. Our interviewees, in fact, associated two different types of needs and skills: One needs to have knowledge about the woodland and one must also have the capacity to listen to it. Lino emphasized that 'A woodland is like a book, is a book ... it says it all. The important thing is to read it. But clearly before reading it, you need to know how to read it. And take the time to read it.' And this explains that you need to have 'passion' for this.

Some of our interlocutors seem to stress an 'earpoint' more than a 'view-point' (Feld, 1996: 95).[16] While Fantino points out that in the woodlands there was 'more noise' compared to today, Lino underscores: '*Se io sono in mezzo al bosco sento l'aria, il profumo delle cose, sento ... mi sento a casa*': 'If I am in the middle of the woodland, I sense the air, the smell of things, I feel ... I feel at home.' And again: '*Dute i camina de corsa, dute i core. Nel bosco si cammina piano, ci si ferma, si annusa l'aria, si sente ...*' 'Everyone rushes, everyone hurries. In the woodland you walk slowly, you stop, you sniff the air, and you take it in ...' The earpoint overlaps with the smell of things in bringing back memories. As anthropologist Daniela Perco points out, 'What is crystallized in the memory is the smell of berries, herbs ... that is largely similar to the flavor (the scent of strawberries is also the flavor of the strawberries)' (2013: 241). Everyone agrees that in the past the woodland had a very rich *sottobosco* 'undergrowth,' for example, a high production of blueberries, which today is gone. Whatever is left is considered of a lesser quality: Mushrooms, for example, are less flavorful than what they used to be.

Thus, there is a way of acting in the environment that requires a specific posture. Yet, to act rightly also implies the possibility to act wrongly. Flavio, during our first nature walk, clearly stated: 'A woodland must be cleaned up; otherwise the following year there will be no firewood.' Short water-drains crossing the path leading to the top of the hills should also be kept clean, otherwise this might cause devastating effects (Figure 7.7). Again, this comment seems to point to a kind of reciprocity between elements of the environment and humans.

We should remember that, as Sara points out, 'to collect firewood everyone has his/her own places, because everyone has their own property, and you cannot go onto other people's property.' As I have already mentioned, Vinigo woodland, which used to belong to the *Regola Piccola*—thus, common property—has been transformed into private properties. Humans must tend to the woodland to keep it healthy, and a healthy woodland benefits humans. Otherwise, as Maria states: '*Il bosco si "mangia" tutto*' 'The woodland eats everything,' a concern that reveals also some kind of anxieties about the future.

Figure 7.7 Nature walk, a blocked drain, uphill (left), and neglected woodland (right), November 1, 2013.

I want to leave the last word to Gianna; speaking in Ladin about what she considers a dramatic alteration that has affected the close environment. She brings out memories of when she was young, and the fields were well groomed: '*Era duto bel neto, era i bosche nete. Nos autre riedes deane co i scarpete fate in cèsa e basta*' 'Everything was well-kept, the woodlands were well-kept. We, the children, went around in our home-made soft-soled shoes.' And, she adds, '*I pra i era come al veludo*': 'The grasslands were like velvet.' Another strong metaphor that points to a tactile sensation in perceiving the environment by associating the land to the feel of a fine textile. The environment of the past brings back memories of long hours of hard work for the women and the men, though mitigated by images of softness, care, good tastes, closeness, and solidarity among people. The memories of a strong interaction with the environment loom large.

Free-listing tasks

I now turn to the discussion of the results of the free-listing tasks that contribute to some understanding of how the cultural model works. The free-listing tasks were administered to 30 subjects and were based on 6 categories—*piante*, 'plants,' *animali*, 'animals,' *territorio*, 'physical environment,' *tempo atmosferico*, 'weather,' *persone*, 'people,' *esseri fantastici*, 'supernatural.' The last category proved to be the most difficult to elicit. During our first visit we used the category, *supernaturale*, 'supernatural,' but we soon realized it did not generate any result. We tried *esseri fantastici*, 'supernatural beings,' and although we were not completely satisfied with it, we realized it proved a more appropriate way to put the question. The very limited responses we received attested to a lack of interest in this domain. Ten out of 30 did not reply and only one woman mentioned the Christian god.

The two longer lists of terms elicited were those concerning plants and animals. These data are currently under analysis.[17] Under 'animals,' our participants inserted wild animals, domestic animals, quadrupeds and bipeds, birds, reptiles, and one respondent a fish. Under 'plants,' they included wild plants, domestic plants, edible plants, fruit trees, and flowers. In general, women seemed more patient than men in listing the different items. The men would mention a few items and then start to narrate stories connected to one or more of those items.

The results of the free-listing task allowed us to make the point that women have maintained a deeper local knowledge than men. Gianna (f), in her late sixties, recalled 46 names of plants and 51 of animals; Fanny (75 years old f), mentioned 22 plants and 25 animals; Lino (m), instead 17 plants and 19 animals; Dario (m), 10 plants and 19 animals. On the other end, Artelio (m), born as Gianna in the 1940s, was able to name 26 plants and 42 animals. This difference may be due to the fact that in the presence of migratory (seasonal or definitive) movements involving mainly men, women had more interaction and experience with the local environment. They had to carry out all the work.

However, since in the interviews local people had called into question and highlighted two domains, that is, plants and physical environment, I decided to investigate them further, and the free-listing data provided an opportunity to do so. I will thus focus on the analysis of the free-listing concerning these two domains and see what we can infer from the results.

Looking at the results of free-listing task about the physical environment (Figure 7.8), the five most frequent items are *cianpo*, 'field,' *pra*, 'meadow,' *vara*, 'hayfield,' *orto*, 'vegetable garden,' *bosco*, 'woodland.' What connects these most salient items is that they all point to means of support. In fact, hay, grass, and woodland provide livelihoods to animals (domesticated and wild) and to people, thus playing a central role in their lives—a kind of triangle that includes human activities. Although *bosco* 'woodland' is not the most frequently mentioned element, if we add *bosco* as a general term to include *types* of *bosco*, then the term becomes more salient. This latter finding is in line with the results of the analyses of the interviews. It is interesting to note that the salience of woodland as a general term is the same for men and for women.

Regarding the results of the free-listing of plants (Figure 7.9), those that are found in the woodland are the most salient. Woodland seems to be the focus of a higher level of attention, even though the current characteristics of woodland contrasts with the characteristics of the cultivated environment. In fact, the people of Vinigo suggest that woodland should be kept in order, clean, and not left to go wild. The content of the graph indicates a difference between men and women—the former tend to recall better the plants that make up the woodland, whereas the latter tend to recall better fruit trees—and also provides supporting evidence for woodland to be more salient than other words listed.

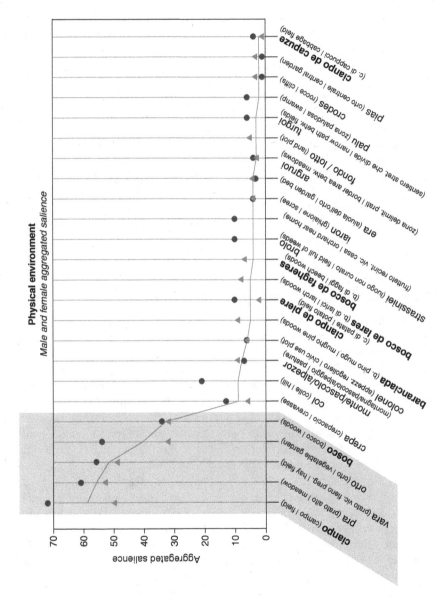

Figure 7.8 Physical environment (the line gives the aggregated salience for both men and women [stress is omitted]).

Two reasons can be foregrounded: Woodlands were historically important as a very valuable resource; they provided wood for building houses, heating kitchens, making tools, sleds; they were used for hunting, for collecting produce from the *sottobosco*, 'undergrowth' and, recently, the Vinigo woodland has become even more salient because it is encroaching on the village—although in this latter case its saliency is connected to a value loss. Also, for plants, the results in the graph show a difference between men and women (Figure 7.9). So, woodland emerges as a multifaceted element of their environment, which is still highly appreciated although its neglect is associated with a loss of value on the part of the local people. 'Woodland' appears to be an umbrella concept, which includes trees, bushes, animals, human activities, weather, and spirits. The literature on the Italian Alps supports the salience of woodland in this area (Perco, 2002).

The spread of woodland also causes a loss of biodiversity. Local people rarely mention biodiversity, although when they speak of *bosco misto*, 'mixed woodland,' as being the best woodland, they refer to a woodland made up of different types of vegetation and different species of trees, bushes, grass—that is, they are indirectly referring to biodiversity. Further, when they mention that woodland is becoming wider (quantity) but is losing in quality, they are again referring to biodiversity without mentioning it.

Hypothesis about the Cultural Model of Nature

The field material and the examples presented foreground a number of relationships that are parts of a Cultural Model of Nature. Vinighesi seem to attribute agency to elements of the close environment and to stress engagement and interaction (symmetrical/asymmetrical) with them. Both men and women hold a rich image of woodland and highlight its importance in local daily life. If human activity causes the expansion and thickness of woodland—fields are no longer cultivated—the relationship between humans and woodland emerges as being reciprocal. In fact, Vinighesi speak of the significance of the lost relationship between the woodland and themselves. This lack of relationship causes a loss of balance that needs to be restored. When everything is interconnected, a balance could be achieved. A point of view well summarized by Mario: 'The land was worked so much ... now trees, trees ...' meaning that the interaction with the land is lost and today trees are everywhere creating disorder and imbalance.

Causal relationships can be inferred from different passages of the interviews. Different human activities—depopulation, changing subsistence practices, technologies—'cause' diminished farming and the closing of barns, which in turn 'cause' diminished human activities in the woodland. This latter 'causes' woodland to become wider and denser and to encroach the village. The expanding of the woodland results in increasing

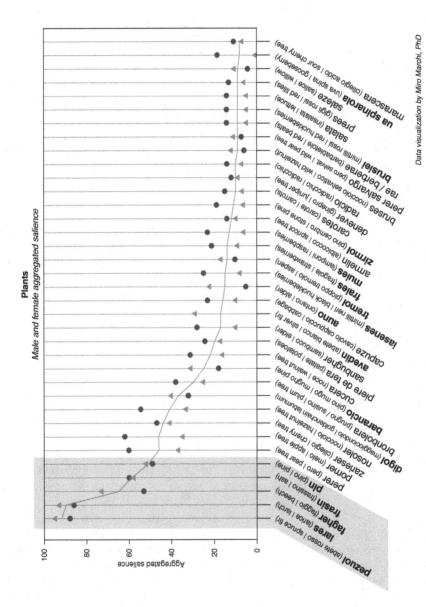

Figure 7.9 Plants (the line gives the aggregated salience for both men and women [stress is omitted]).

moisture and, consequently, the 'air is not clean and dry as before' stresses Giuliana. Further, the number of deer, which have replaced roes, is significantly increased, and they are often coming into the village and 'causing' the ravaging of the cultivated area in the center of the village.

It is difficult to locate the place animals have in this causal network. Although, in the free-listing tasks, some men provided long lists of animals in the interviews, people from Vinigo did not talk much about animals; places were more salient. Today's families no longer have active stables. In addition, our interlocutors, when asked about the activities connected to taking the animals to the higher fields in the past, focused more around moments of sociality with the elderly or with peers or around the heavy work required to harvest hay—which would be used to feed animals once it was taken back to the village—than about narratives centered on animals. Further investigation is needed to build on this preliminary assessment.

When one focuses on giving and receiving, would the notion of reciprocity fit the way Vinighesi think about these interactions? The view endorsed by many in Vinigo is that 'humans and land are connected.' What do they mean by that? What does it mean 'to take care of the land'? It is likely that they mean that when humans are in a closer relation with woodland and plants, then the woodland and the plants give back.

In conclusion, we can suggest a number of relationships as constitutive parts of their cultural model of Nature: (1) a *reciprocal* relationship between humans and woodland; (2) an *asymmetrical* relationship between woodland and wild animals, for example, increasing woodland leads to an increasing presence of deer. However, deer do not influence the woodland; rather they are getting acquainted with coming into the village, thus, eliminating the barrier between wild animals' space and human space; (3) an *asymmetrical* relationship between weather and human activities, for example, the weather influences agricultural produce such as cabbage's growth, whereas humans do not influence weather.

Fundamentally, because of the way they attribute agency to some of its components, it appears that Vinighesi hold a holistic approach to the concept of Nature. A type of holism that so far seems to include some supernatural elements but does not include the Christian god. In the interviews, this latter had little resonance. Further supporting this conclusion, the yearly procession, *dintorno iei*, 'to go around the countryside' to bless the countryside that in the past saw a great participation of people alongside the priest, has not been carried out since the 1970s. A woman born in the early 1960s, remarked: 'In the past there were many people, but not during my time. The last time it was carried out was when I was 11 or 12.' An additional domain that needs to be further investigated. It also appears that this cultural model of Nature included a causal model number 2 (see Figure 7.10).

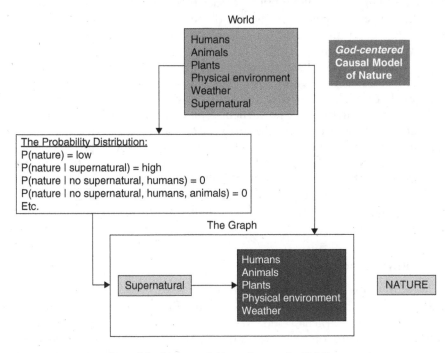

Figure 7.10 Causal Model of Nature 2 (from Bennardo 2014).

Conclusions

The research conducted in Vinigo (Italian Alps) foregrounds how local people perceive changes in the environment and interpret them. Vinighesi pay more attention to the changes taking place locally than to outside changes. Their primary focus is on the woodland; their views emphasize that it was through human activities that the woodland was kept in order and clean, whereas, today, the woodland is in a state of neglect, disorder. As a result, it is not a valuable resource for people anymore; on the contrary, it has become the cause of anxieties because the woodland is encroaching the village. Changing types of human activities had a profound effect on the environment and on the human's capacity to deal with it and to take care of it. Thus, Vinighesi's perception of environmental changes makes clear reference to the fact that a strong relationship exists and should be properly restored between humans and the woodland. In the words of a male interviewee: 'The woodland must be cultivated as a field.'

Interviewees did not talk directly about climate change but, when asked about it, they pointed to radical changes taking place. They also did not speak the language of biodiversity, yet they named mixed woodland as being the best type and referred to the woodland as becoming wider and at the same time diminishing in quality, which is another way to refer to biodiversity without mentioning it.

Combining the results of the interviews and the free-listing tasks proved to be beneficial. In addition, using insights obtained from the results of the analyses of the free-listing tasks, salient concepts were identified that allowed me to arrive at a more articulate description of the cultural model already hypothesized. From the analyses of the material collected—texts of interviews and results of free-listing tasks—a holistic approach to the concept of Nature emerged. The Vinighesi attribute agency to different components of their environment, although they emphasize some elements and downplay others. The relationship, a reciprocal one, which stands out as being the most salient is without any doubt that between the humans and the woodland.

Acknowledgments

I want to thank the people of Vinigo (*Graie ai paesane de Vinigo*) for welcoming us and accepting to share time and knowledge with us. My thanks go to Stefano, Marilena, Lino, Maria, and especially to Giuliana. I also thank Elisa Bellato for her help in collecting the data and for the many hours spent together in Vinigo. Many thanks are also due to Iolanda Da Deppo for her excellent work in transcribing the collected material. I am grateful to Giovanni Bennardo for stimulating conversations on the analysis of the data and to Miro Marchi for data visualization.

Appendix

Interview questions

LAVORO AGROSILVOPASTORALE

(1) Fai qualche lavoro legato alla terra o al bosco?*
(2) Ci racconti queste attività
(3) Quando sei impegnato/a con queste attività? (stagionali, annuali, continuative, saltuarie ecc.)
(4) Ci racconti cosa hai fatto ieri (questa settimana)?
(5) Ci sono delle attività che si fanno solo in un certo momento della giornata o della notte? (ad es. nel passato si falciava l'erba al mattino presto per via della rugiada che la rendeva più tenera; oppure certe attività legate all'orto)
(6) Ci sono modalità di lavoro e tempi che sono specifici di questo paese? (es. cavolo)
    * lavoro legato alla terra (attività principale-secondaria-saltuaria)

COMPETENZE NEL LAVORO

(1) Quali ritieni siano conoscenze essenziali per ottenere dei risultati positivi/buoni nel tuo lavoro? (es. nell'orto seguire ciò che fanno gli altri)
(2) Cosa consideri 'attività produttive' legate alla terra? (es. raccolta mirtilli o prodotti del sottobosco; rispetto all'orto)
(3) Quali sono le aree/terreni produttivi?
(4) Cosa influisce sulla produttività/crescita? Quali forze (umane, naturali, sovrannaturali) influenzano il successo di una produzione? (es. orto: concimazione, acqua)
(5) In che modo si capisce che una pianta/albero cresce bene? Cosa contribuisce alla crescita della pianta?

CONOSCENZE NECESSARIE

(1) Quali decisioni hai preso tu (tua famiglia) per ottenere risultati positivi?
(2) Quali informazioni/conoscenze sono stati utili per prendere delle decisioni (tramandate, apprese a scuola, in corsi di formazione, dai media, da conoscenti, autoformazione ecc.)
(3) Ci fai un esempio?
(4) Come scegli le colture da coltivare (anche nell'orto), ciò che cacci, ciò di cui vai alla ricerca (es. prodotti del sottobosco)?
(5) Quali problemi incontri e quali limiti/vincoli devi tenere in considerazione in queste attività? (es. periodi in cui piantare, questioni economiche, Regole, dopo san Marco non potevi passare sui terreni degli altri perché l'erba stava crescendo)

EFFETTI SULL'AMBIENTE

(1) Chi produce effetti maggiori sul tuo ambiente (campi, bosco)?
(2) Cosa e/o chi fa succedere le cose? (forze naturali o soprannaturali; umani, animali, piante, santi, spiriti ecc.)
(3) Il ruolo del governo e dei vari enti amministrativi (Comune, Comunità montana, Regione, Regole)?
(4) Qual è la cosa migliore/peggiore che gli umani possono fare nel cacciare, coltivare (orto o campi), raccogliere prodotti del sottobosco (es. solidarietà/litigare; incuria, abbandono del territorio)

SODDISFAZIONE RISPETTO ALL'ATTIVITA' LAVORATIVA SVOLTA

(1) Che cosa ti piace/non ti piace di ciò che stai facendo (soddisfazione)?
(2) Ci sono cose che devi fare che sono distruttive ma che non vorresti fare? (es. uso prodotti chimici nella coltivazione)

(3) Le conseguenze del tempo/clima, governo, guerre, gente sulle attività legate alla terra/ambiente
(4) Quali sono le forme alternative a questa per guadagnarsi da vivere. (Tu come ti guadagni da vivere? Vivi dei prodotti dell'orto?)

CAMBIAMENTI CLIMATICI

(1) Hai riscontrato **cambiamenti nell'ambiente** e nella tua attività legata al lavoro agrosilvopastorale? (ad es. modifica nelle aree destinate a pascolo)
(2) Che tipo di cambiamenti?
(3) Ci sono dei **cambiamenti climatici**? Quali? In che modo si sono verificati?
(4) A cosa ritieni siano dovuti le variazioni (ad es. stagioni più brevi) e i cambiamenti (assenza di stagioni intermedie)?
(5) Che cosa gli umani possono fare al riguardo?
(6) Ritieni che gli umani, come collettività o anche singolarmente, possono produrre effetti sulla natura e sul clima?
(7) Hai notato cambiamenti nella presenza o nel comportamento di una specie dovuti alla presenza di un cambiamento nell'ambiente o climatico (ad es. dovuti al bosco che sopravanza o alla presenza di una specie animale o di un cambiamento climatico)?

Notes

1 In Italy, the region is the main administrative subdivision followed by provinces, which have been stripped of powers in the recent administrative reform (Delrio law, 7 April 2014).
2 Among them the Pelmo–Croda da Lago System. 'The nine components of The Dolomites World Heritage property protect a series of highly distinctive mountain landscapes that are of exceptional natural beauty.' (http://whc.unesco.org/en/list/1237).
3 The relationship between Vinigo and Vodo has not been an easy one. The nicknames used to refer to the inhabitants of each village are telling : 'dogs' for the former, referring to the high altitude of Vinigo and the role of guardians of the territory historically played by its inhabitants [this is what the Vinighesi say] and 'cats' for the latter (De Ghetto 2009: 48).
4 It must also be mentioned the very important role played by the river during World War I.
5 For an overview of the most relevant issues facing the Alpine regions, see Varotto and Castiglione, 2012.
6 Source: Registry Office at the Town Hall of Vodo, February 6, 2014.
7 See Pier Paolo Viazzo (2012) and the sociocultural and demographic paradoxes that have emerged from research conducted in the Alps in the last two decades of the twentieth century, bringing forward a rethinking of the relationship between the mountains and the plains.
8 The eight components of this age group, a woman, is married and lives far away.

9　There is also the *Regola Staccata* 'The Detached Rule,' to which the families from Vodo belong.

10　Both documents are transcribed by Richebuono (1962).

11　The term *consortes* (literally co-participants) refers to the people who had rights to access the mountain, to be distinguished from mere residents (personal communication, Gian Maria Varanini, August 23, 2016).

12　In April 2016, the Assembly of the 'Rules of Ampezzo' voted 416 yes, 18 votes less than the needed quorum, to the proposition that women can become *Regoliere* and remains also if married to a non *Regoliere*.

13　I consulted this document in the Registry Office at the Town Hall of Vodo.

14　'Deer are getting more and more acquainted with villagers' (Giuliana, phone call, March 28, 2018).

15　Periods of fieldwork: October 30–November 4, 2013; January 28–February 11, 2014; May 19–May 22; June 27–July 5; October 28–November 3; June 30–July 5, 2015.

16　Although Marilena, referring to the vegetable garden, emphasizes that 'In the vegetable garden, you see if things are rotting. You do not have to go, *dai un occhio*, you just quickly look at it [from a distance].'

17　Miro Marchi, who has recently joined our team, has been working on cleaning the list from noises, that is, double entries or terms that are different but refer to the same animal or plant. He is the author of the data visualization, see Figures 7.8 and 7.9.

References

Belli, M. F. (2007). Alla scoperta del mondo ladino e della gestione del territorio montano attraverso i secoli—Comunità di villaggio e proprietà collettive. In *Ladini Oggi*, vol. 2. Cortina: Istituto Ladin de la Dolomites, 13–28.

Bennardo, G. (2014). The fundamental role of causal models in cultural models of nature. *Frontiers in Psychology*. October 10, 2014, http://dx.doi.org/10.3389/fpsyg.2014.01140.

Bennardo, G., and De Munck, V. C. (2014). *Cultural Models: Genesis, Methods, and Experiences*. Oxford: Oxford University Press.

De Ghetto, P. (2009). *An tin par sòrte. Stòries e Storièles*. San Vito di Cadore: Grafica Sanvitese.

Feld, S. (1996). Waterfalls of song. An acoustemology of place resounding in Bosavi, Papua New Guinea. In Feld, S., and Basso, K. (eds.), *Senses of Places*. Santa Fe: School of American Research Press, 91–135.

Ingold, T. (2000). *The Perception of the Environment. Essays on Livelihood, Dwelling and Skill*. London: Routledge.

Lasen, C. (2012). La promozione del bene Unesco. In Varotto, M., and Castiglione, B. (eds.), *Di chi sono le Alpi? Appartenenze politiche, economiche e culturali nel mondo alpino contemporaneo*. Padova: Padova University Press, 271–276.

Lorenzi, S., and Borrini-Feyerabend, G. (2009). Community conserved areas: Legal framework for the Natural Park of the Ampezzo Dolomites (Italy). http://cmsdata.iucn.org/downloads/ampezzo.pdf.

Marchioni, M., and Pivirotto, T. (2002). *Vinigo nel '900*. San Vito di Cadore: Grafica Sanvitese.

Perco, D. (2002). Riflessioni sulla percezione e sulla rappresentazione del bosco in area prealpina e alpina. In Lazzarini, A. (ed.), *Disboscamento montano e politiche territoriali. Alpi e Appennini dal Settecento al Duemila*. Milano: Franco Angeli, 319–329.

Perco, D. (2013). Sapori selvatici. In Da Deppo, I., Gasparini, D., and Perco D. (eds.), *Montagne di cibo. Studi e ricerche in terra bellunese*. Belluno: Museo Etnografico della Provincia di Belluno e Parco Nazionale Dolomiti Bellunesi, 241–295.

Piseri, M. (2012). La scuola di montagna nelle Alpi Orientali nell'inchiesta napoleonica 1810 (Dipartimenti del Piave e del Passariano). In Piseri, M. (ed.), *L'alfabeto di montagna. Scuola e alfabetismo nell'area alpina tra età moderna e XIX secolo*. Milano: Franco Angeli, 37–64.

Richebuono, G. (1962). *Ampezzo di Cadore dal 1156 al 1335*. Belluno: Tipografia Vescovile.

Strauss, C. (1999). Research on cultural discontinuities. In Quinn, N., and Strauss, C., *A Cognitive Theory of Cultural Meaning*. Cambridge: Cambridge University Press, 210–251.

Varotto, M. (2012a). Oltre il recinto Unesco: le sfide del territorio dolomitico. In Varotto, M., and Castiglione, B. (eds.), *Di chi sono le Alpi? Appartenenze politiche, economiche e culturali nel mondo alpino contemporaneo*. Padova: Padova University Press, 285–294.

Varotto, M. (2012b). Riflessioni conclusive/Concluding remarks. In Varotto, M., and Castiglione, B. (eds.), *Di chi sono le Alpi? Appartenenze politiche, economiche e culturali nel mondo alpino contemporaneo*. Padova: Padova University Press, 317–326.

Varotto, M., and Castiglione, B. (eds.). (2012). *Di chi sono le Alpi? Appartenenze politiche, economiche e culturali nel mondo alpino contemporaneo (Whose Alps Are These? Governance, Ownership and Belongings in Contemporary Alpine Regions)*. Padova: Padova University Press.

Viazzo, P. P. (2012). Paradossi alpini, vecchi e nuovi: ripensare il rapporto tra demografia e mutamento culturale. In Varotto, M., and Castiglione, B. (eds.), *Di chi sono le Alpi? Appartenenze politiche, economiche e culturali nel mondo alpino contemporaneo*. Padova: Padova University Press, 185–195.

Zanderigo Rosolo, G. (2012). Montagna, "res derelicta". In Varotto, M. and Castiglione, B. (eds.), *Di chi sono le Alpi? Appartenenze politiche, economiche e culturali nel mondo alpino contemporaneo*. Padova: Padova University Press, pp. 32–46.

8 Human nature of nature

Cultural models of food production and nature in the Northern Kanto Plain of Japan

Hidetada Shimizu and Chisaki Fukushima

Introduction

While the Japanese islands have been prone to a variety of natural disasters throughout their history, the magnitudes of some of these omnipresent threats are observed to have increased in recent years. Our informants, for example, anecdotally spoke of perceived increase in the temperature throughout the years. The relatively cool rainy season that lasted from the middle of June into July, which used to require heating equipment, turned into 'wet summers.' They also talked about orange trees they planted that used to produce sour fruits now yielding sweeter flavors, presumably due to the warmer climate.

Relatedly, storms of many kinds are reported to have intensified in recent years. In the past, tornados were unheard of, but today they are common and frequent occurrences. Other severe storms are accompanied by larger hailstones than in the past. In fact, in the winter of 2014, the year this fieldwork took place, eastern Japan, including Tokyo, experienced record-breaking snowfalls. As a result, many of the informants' greenhouses were destroyed.

Yet the informants appeared composed and nonchalant about the effects of the changing climate on their food production. Most of them did not bring up the topic during the interviews until they were asked specifically about it. What could be some of the reasons for this? For one, the general increase in temperature and the intensity of the rain and snowfall have not significantly affected the informants' outdoor crops, which are predominantly rice and wheat. The majority of other products, mainly vegetables, are produced indoors. The destruction of the greenhouses due to the record amounts of snow (over two feet) was a major loss. Nonetheless, the informants seemed to have accepted the incidents as long-gone, and showed a sense of gratitude toward the Japanese government, which helped cover about 90 percent of the loss. Such is a reminiscence of the way the people of northern Japan reacted calmly to the calamity of the tsunami in 2011 (Kingston, 2012).

What implications do these preliminary observations offer in terms of 'cultural models' that are purported to have influenced the informants'

DOI: 10.4324/9781351127905-9

narratives about food production? We hypothesize that the informants relied on an overarching cultural model in which nature[1] can be 'humanized' to enhance human endeavors, particularly in the areas of self-cultivation and associated interpersonal relationships. Using this cultural model works as a buffer against, and around which to circumvent, the perceived and real harms of raw and untamed nature (野生). According to this cultural model, raw nature is *un*-natural. Nature is 'natural' only when it is humanized to enhance human existence and relationships (Pelzel, 1974; Lebra, 1976).

To arrive at this hypothesis, the first author collected data through nature walks (videotaped and hand-written as filed notes) and semi-structured interviews (Bennardo, this volume, Chapter 1), which were then transcribed in Japanese by Japanese-speaking research assistants in the field. Then, he analyzed the data *ethnographically*. This means that he utilized (1) his cultural and linguistic expertise as a native of Japan and a native speaker; (2) his theoretical perspective as a psychological anthropologist trained in the tradition of 'culture and personality study' (see LeVine, 1982, as a representative of this theoretical framework); and (3) his broad experience about Japanese culture as an area specialist who has conducted extensive research in Japan (e.g., Shimizu and LeVine, 2001).

Looking through such interpretive and theoretical lenses, he underlined sections of his notes and the transcript that for one reason or another stood out for him. Then he jotted down tentative explanations. Finally, he reviewed all his analytical notes and made conceptual and theoretical inferences about what the informants were trying to communicate about the contents of their work (food production) and, subsequently, how these descriptions seem to presuppose some basic assumption (i.e., cultural models) about nature on which their work depends.

After making such holistic observations and inferences, we sifted the interview data through a set of linguistic analyses, which involved different interpretations than the 'ethnographic' analysis. These were: (1) words frequency and keyword analysis, and (2) reasoning analysis (See Bennardo, this volume, Introduction). Specifically, ethnographic information gives initial, overall insights into relevant information about the informants' cultural model of nature. The results of the word frequency and keyword analysis provide building blocks of the cultural model in terms of some of the most frequently appearing words, or conceptually relevant terms, or both. Once such building blocks are identified at the singular words level, reasoning and causality analyses discover relationships among them. This sequence of analyses is described in the findings section below.

Research site

The fieldwork took place during a four-week period in 2014, between May 21 and June18. The data were collected in Gunma Prefecture (see Figure 8.1, highlighted in the center), which is in the northwestern tip

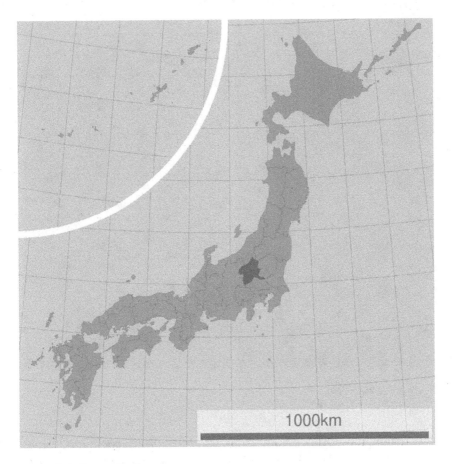

Figure 8.1 Gunma Prefecture.
(Courtesy of Lincun, CC BY-SA 3.0)

of Kanto Plain (see Figure 8.2)—the largest region of flat land in Japan, spreading southeasterly toward the Pacific Ocean. The southern section of Kanto Plain includes the Greater Tokyo Metropolis, the largest urbanized and industrialized region of the nation. Gunma's climate, location, and landscape make it an ideal place to produce many types of agricultural products (Shimizu, 2012).

Gunma's topsoil consists of volcanic ashes that accumulated over the centuries. The mountain range on the north blocks the moisture traveling from the Sea of Japan, creating much precipitation—in the form of rain in the summer and snow in the winter—on their 'back' (northern) side, giving Gunma the most sunny days per year in the nation. Gunma also has varying levels of altitude, offered by the mountain range gradually tapering down to the Kanto Plain. This allows food producers to alter growing temperatures

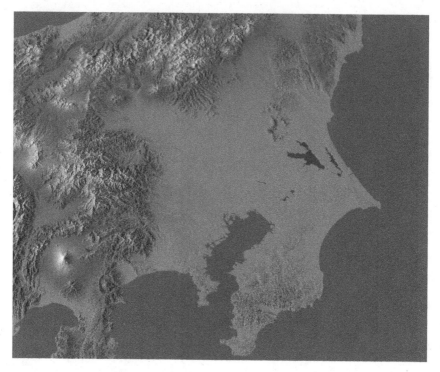

Figure 8.2 Kanto Plain.
(Courtesy of Σ 64, CC BY-SA 3.0)

by switching the altitudes where crops are grown. When combined, the fertile volcanic soil with rich minerals, the temperate climate, and the terrace-like farming fields produce nearly ideal condition for growing a variety of agricultural products. As one informant said, Gunma is a 'farmer's heaven,' where 'you can produce many different kinds of products within a relatively small proximity.'

Participants

The participants come from two of the most populous cities in the prefecture: Takasaki and Maebashi, which border each other and are centrally located in the prefecture. The sample was drawn via personal connections of the first author—his two high school friends and his mother. There were a total of 18 participants. The sample was skewed toward older males with high school education (i.e., the modal pattern): 13 males and 5 females; ages 29 to 66 with a mean of 55 (11 out of 18 reported). Of the 8 of 18 who reported their educational backgrounds, one had a four-year college degree, one had a junior-high degree, and the rest (6) had high school degrees.

About half of the participants grow rice and wheat (collectively referred to as *bei baku*, i.e., rice and wheat). All the rice and wheat farmers also grew a variety of other vegetables (e.g., cucumbers, lettuce, tomatoes, *daikon*, etc.) because rice and wheat require relatively little care in between the planting and harvesting seasons. The remaining half of the participants produced specialized products that included plums, pears, tomatoes, and pigs. One specialized in farming a variety of organic vegetables.

Ethnographic analysis and findings

Japan is a highly industrialized society with complex economic systems. The informants, therefore, did not engage in subsistence farming, as is the case in other chapters in this volume. They do not rely directly or solely on *raw* nature—for example soil conditions or weather patterns—to do their farming. Instead, they utilize state-of-the art, indoor facilities and technologies to raise plants and animals (e.g., pigs). They also take advantage of the wealth of current and research-based farming knowledge provided by municipal and national farmers' organizations such as Japan Agricultural Cooperatives (JA). They also exchange ideas and tips with other farmers, who have acquired them through experience or from the sources just mentioned.

Two patterns to successful farming

As to what makes plants and animals thrive, informants shared basic knowledge that they saw as fundamental to successful farming, that is, knowledge about optimal soil conditions (via appropriate fertilizers for plants and foods for animals), light, wind, temperature, timing of planning and harvesting, and other maintenance activities (e.g., pruning), and ways to prevent diseases. Some farmers said that such knowledge comes from experience, while others, including their parents and family members, said it comes from the government-based local and national farm bureaus such as JA. No one mentioned supernatural factors such as 'gods' or 'spirits' as factors contributing to successful farming.

In terms of their commercial success, informants' responses focused on two distinctive yet complementary types of activities. The first pattern may be called rational and profit-oriented activities. Here, the food producers work in concert with the information provided by JA about the crops and seed types and how to prevent the kinds of diseases that are prevalent, thereby maximizing productivity. The JA also organizes chains of marketing outlets into which the farmers can distribute their product in a timely fashion. Most of the large-scale rice, wheat, tomato, plum and pear farmers rely on such a support system.

The second pattern, which may be termed non-rational and relational, and even 'moral' and 'spiritual,' consists of seeking higher levels of meaning and satisfaction from farming than merely profiting from it. Informants often used the terms *kodawari*, 'to be particular about being unique, authentic, and/or perfect in one's pursuits,' and *tsunagari*, 'to be authentically connected with others' to express this view. To *kodawaru* (the verb form of *kodawari*) means to produce foods that bear one's 'signature' heart/effort. Many of the consumers who taste such foods become 'repeaters,' loyal customers who develop a special and lasting tie to the food producers. Many famers noted that they gained the most satisfaction out of their work from such special relationships. In short, the first pattern to farming success is essential because without it farmers cannot sustain their livelihood. The second pattern complements the first as it helps farmers find deeper and more personalized meaning in their work. Below are some examples of the second perspective extracted from the texts of the semi-structured interviews and of the 'nature walks.'

Individual cases of a relational path to success

Michiko Sekiguchi is a sixty-four year old woman, married into a multi-generational farming family. While her husband takes charge of the rice and wheat, which provides the family's main income, she grows green-house tomatoes along with a variety of other green vegetables. She says her operation is 'small and not profitable,' but she has continued it for the last 18 years. Asked why, she responded, 'It's [my] *kodawari*.'

Asked to explain to non-Japanese what *kodawari* means, she said, 'It means to be particular [about your mission] and not to compromise (*kotte iru*).' In a practical term, 'it means to ... wake up at three or four in the morning every day' to take her vegetables to the local stores. 'That way, people say when they eat my vegetables, *oishii*! (delicious). I pick them first thing in the morning and have people eat that way. I especially want young children to know how great they taste.' She also sells the vegetables she produces at low prices.

Another expression of Michiko's *kodawari*, in addition to always hand-delivering her vegetables fresh, is the farm stand she created for herself, which she named, *Daichi No Megumi* (The Earth's/Land's Blessing/Abundance), and which is the brand name given to the rice they produce. The space is filled with wall hangings and gifts she has received from her (female) friends. Many of them contain words of appreciation for the relationships they cultivated over the years. She said that the room symbolizes her connection with other women farmers.

It is also worth noting that this farm stand is located next to the family grave. Michiko is grateful that she and her husband inherited the land from their (the husband's) ancestors. She says, 'I know how our ancestors were attached to this land, so I would never let it go. When I think of their feelings, I, too, cannot let go of this land.' During our 'nature walk' around the family grave, she said, 'this [having the grave next to their farm] is a reminder that our ancestors are always watching over us.'

Shinji Amada is a 32-year-old pig farmer who also took over the business from his father, who inherited it from his own father forty years ago. As a third-generation entrepreneur, Shinji strives to create a brand that is unique to him. He said that such goal is a norm in Japan's farming business, which contrasts with the quantity-over-quality emphasis of the Western farmers—that is, American and Danish.

> Japanese pig farmers seek 'artistry' in their work. They put their 'soul' into their products so they naturally become expensive. In the United States and Denmark, they produce one 'national' brand. But here we have over four hundred brands of pork. Each farmer wants to produce 'something that only [they] can make' (*jinbun shika dekinai*). It's our *kodawari*. This is what is so unique about Japanese pig farming.

As with Michiko, Shinji said he 'grows food to make people happy.' He continued: 'I don't even want to make money unless everyone else is happy … I recently read a book that says never lose the sense of gratitude, and that the only way to get that gratitude is through seeing other people rejoice and smile.'

One way to achieve his goal is through the 'farm tour' designed for school-age children. He wants them to 'eyewitness the birth of baby pigs.' He said the reason for this project is both 'philosophical' and 'educational.' For him, 'to eat means to "be given someone else's life (*itadaku*)."' He elaborated: 'Pigs are like people. They are cute and friendly. To understand that we eat them to be alive is to understand the preciousness of both their and our lives. Hopefully, knowing this creates a sense of gratitude in all of us [to be alive at the expense of pigs' lives].'

Hikaru Hoshi, age thirty-nine, is another entrepreneur who dropped out of a corporate job in Tokyo to start organic farming in Gunma's isolated countryside. He grows vegetables free of chemical fertilizers and pesticides. But his *kodawari* is not merely to grow organic food, but 'to connect with people [since] there is still a gap to be filled between the farmers and people who eat what we grow. What future farmers need to do is to reduce the gap between them.' He visits restaurants and demonstrates how and what to cook with his vegetables: 'First, I cook and eat what I grow myself. I try to come up with my own methods of cooking [which I believe makes food taste good]. Then I go to a restaurant, get inside the kitchen and demonstrate what they can do [with my vegetables]. Sometimes I [go out of the kitchen and] converse with customers. I am a "talking" farmer.'

Connection to culture and personality theory

During the 'ethnographic' analysis of the data, the first author noticed a close parallel between the two types of activities mentioned earlier—the rational-profit oriented and the non-rational-moral/spiritual activities—and

Kardiner's (1939) and Whiting's (1966) notions of the primary and secondary institutions. The primary institutions are a society's adaptations to the environment to ensure its members' physical and economic survival. The secondary institutions are the products of culturally constituted personalities formed as the outcome of, or in relation to, the primary institutions. LeVine (1982) details this idea as follows:

> Kardiner and Whiting divided institutions into two classes, those that form personality and those that are formed by it. A group's ecology, economy, settlement pattern, social stratification system, and other 'hard' institutions that seem to act as constraints on individual behavior fall into the first class; and its religion, magical beliefs, disease therapies, art, folklore, and other 'soft' institutions that seem to permit expression of individual needs fall into the second class. *The 'hard institutions represent reality, which must be adapted to; the 'soft' institutions represent fantasy, the cultural expression of individual motives....* [Moreover] Whiting et al. (1966) have [added] a third class of institutions, *values, which serve as defensive beliefs to reduce the cognitive inconsistency between motivational goals and reality demands* (86, Italics added).

In short, one may hypothesize that while the rational–profit-oriented activities correspond with the primary institutions, the non-rational-moral/spiritual correspond with the secondary institutions. That is, the primary institutions include the 'hard' aspects of food production such as basic knowledge and skills of food production and associated marketing activities to remain economically competitive, and the secondary institutions, the 'soft' aspects, make the farmers work in a meaningful and motivating way, such as with the commitments to the originality and authenticity of their products (e.g., *kodawari*) which, in turn, enlarge and deepen the farmers' relationships with their customers. In addition, the potential gap and inconsistency between the market-oriented, profit-seeking (i.e., reality demands) and the psychological motives to connect with the food they produce and customers they serve (i.e., motivational goals) seem to be bridged by a cultural model that insists there be defensible moral and spiritual *values* in humans intervening upon and, hence, taking advantage of nature to satisfy their subjective desires. This hypothesis is tested further against the results of the linguistic analyses presented below.

Linguistic analyses and findings

After the initial ethnographic analysis, the second author conducted the following linguistic analyses in consultation with the first author: (1) word frequency and keyword analysis, (2) reasoning-causal analysis and (3) gist analysis. The results of the three analyses seem to point in the same direction as the ethnographic analysis, which is the importance of the idea of *hito*, or humans and relationships among them as singularly the most prevalent and salient point of reference across all the results generated by varied analytical processes.

Words frequency and key word analysis

Procedure: Unlike Indo-European languages, written Japanese words are not separated by spaces. For example, the following sentence in Japanese— 種苗会社から品種改良した株を買ってきて、増やしていきます。'We/I *buy selectively bred seedlings from nursery companies in order to propagate them*'—would be written with the English alphabet, or 'Roman letters,' as follows:

Shubyokaishakarahinshukairyoshitakabuokattekite, fuyashiteikimasu.

Therefore, we first separated the words into grammatically meaningful or functional units:

種苗会社　　から　品種改良　　した　　株　を　買って　きて、
増やして　いき　ます。
Shubyokaisha kara hinshukairyo shita kabu o katte kite, fuyashite iki masu
Nursery from selective did seedling buy come to propagate is going to
　　company breeding.

Some of these grammatical units had the same meaning and varied only in terms of suffixes. These units were grouped and counted as a combined, single unit. For example, the verb 増やす (*fuyasu*) 'propagate' can be expressed differently within a sentence depending on its grammatical connective functions with adjacent words (see 'variations' in Table 8.1). The frequency for each variation was added up and produced a total of 6.

We then transferred the data to a spreadsheet, after which we winnowed and grouped the data according to our analytical purposes. First, we eliminated words we judged to be intrinsic properties of the Japanese language. The language-specific elements were prepositions, particles, conjunctions, progressive verbs, negatives, relative clauses, and any other units that only played

Table 8.1 Grouping words with the same meaning into one unit with 増やす fuyasu 'increase, multiply, propagate' as an example

Common meanings	Variations	Frequency
増やす	増やし（て）fuyashi (te)	1
Fuyasu	増やす fuyasu	3
	増やせ（ば）fuyase(ba)	2
Total		**6**

ancillary roles to the meaning/grammatical function already identified. Of the remaining words, we eliminated those that appeared as direct, elicited responses to questions asked such as *nogyo* (agriculture, farming) or *seisan* (production). The remaining words, we reasoned, pointed us toward culturally salient terms because they (1) appeared even though we did not ask directly about these topics, and (2) were used with high frequency. In other words, we reasoned that the first characteristic was a result of our successful strategy of asking questions that could indirectly activate a cultural model that is 'out of awareness' (see Bennardo, Introduction to this volume). We considered the second characteristic as related to the fact that cultural models are 'shared' (used by many and often). Both these characteristics are key features of cultural models. We thus termed these words *cultural key words*. We present below the list of those that were mentioned ten or more times.

Cultural key words results

Japanese – English – Frequency (10+ times frequency)

1. 人	*hito*, person, people, others	99
2. 自分	*jibun* (my) self	86
3. 思う	think	72
4. 私	'I'	57
5. 日本 Nihon/Japan お客さん、お客様、お客	customers (with honorifics)	50
7a. もらう	receive/given	47
7b. される	be done to	47
9. くれる	be done to (from/via good will of others)	46
10. 農家	farming household	42
11. 人間	humans	40
12a. 違う、違った、違って	different	39
12b. 大きく、大きい、大きな	large	39
14. 気	'*Ki*' spirit/feelings/mind	33
15. 農協、	Japan Agricultural Cooperatives (JA)	32
16. 美味しい、美味しく	delicious/good tasting	27
17. アメリカ	America	25
18. さん	honorific/personifier	24
19. 自然	nature	21

20a. 国	nation	19
20b. 受ける	receive	19
20c. 人達	people	19
20d. 主人	husband	19
24. 収入	income	18
25. 生産者	producer	17
26a. 幸せ	happy/happiness	15
26b. 家族	family	15
26c. 仲間	peers/friend/fellow	15
29a. 義父	father-in-law	13
29b. 直売所	farm stand (small farmer's market)	13
31a. 息子	son	12
31b. 思い	thought/feeling	12
31c. 外国	foreign country	12
31d. 喜ぶ	be pleased/happy	12
35a. 細かく、細かい、きめ細かい	detailed	11
35b. 気持ち	feelings	11
37a. 頂く	receive	10
37b. 東京	Tokyo	10
37c. 日本人	Japanese	10

The most interesting finding is the dominance of human-related terms such as 1, *hito* 'other/s or human,' 2, *jibun* 'I, myself,' and 4, *watashi* 'I,' which together exceed 20 percent of all the words that appear more than five times. When we add other human-related terms with collective points of reference such as 11, *ningen* 'human beings' and 26b, *kazoku* 'family,' and others, they make up about 40 percent within the same category (i.e., counted more than five times). This is noteworthy in light of the fact that, although we asked the participants to talk about activities related to food production, the words used related to humans exceed the words used related to 19 *shizen* 'nature'—in fact, terms like 'water' are at the bottom of the list. This seems to corroborate the observation we made in the introduction of this chapter that nature is not the most salient feature in the food producers' descriptions of their work.

Furthermore, when we examined the human-related words as a whole in more detail, three subcategories emerged: (1) *watashi* 'I' also 'self,' (2) *hito* 'people' or 'people other-than-me,' and (3) *kazoku* 'family.'

Table 8.2 Human category (10+ times frequency)

Category	Japanese term	
Human	person, others *Hito* human *Ningen* people *Hito-tachi*	158
I	*Jibun* *Watashi*	143
Family	*Nohka (farmer household)* *Shujin (husband)* *Chichi (father/-in-law)* *Musuko (son)*	86
Customer	*Kyaku, Okyaku, okyaku-san,*	50
Producer	*Seisansha*	17
Colleague	*Nakama*	15
Japanese	*Nihonjin*	10
	Total	621

Reasoning-causal relation analysis: Motivation and schema

Procedure: In order to uncover causal-reasoning examples from the texts on food production, we had to go beyond the conventional English linguistic markers, such as 'because,' 'if,' 'therefore' and other grammatical sign posts, and look for the agent/patient relationship embedded in the sentences (see Bennardo's Introduction to this volume for a more complete discussion).

The first step was to look for linguistic markers for reasoning, such as the Japanese particle '- *to*' 'therefore,' or '- *te/tara*' 'and then,' '*yotte/de*' 'due to,' '*moshi ... temo/nara*' 'if, even if,' and so forth. These words indicate the semantic causal relation between two entities. However, it is sometimes not easy to find the causal relation when these linguistic markers are absent. The reasoning may be embedded across several sentences or be expressed in euphemism and metaphorical phrases. By looking for causal indices in semantic roles, we are able to broadly grasp who/what (the *subject/agent*) does something or causes something to whom/what (the *object/patient*).

The second step is to discover the subject and the object of propositions. Both are often missing in Japanese dialogue since they are conventionally dropped when the information is obvious to both speakers.[2]

Example: 風評被害が 一番の 問題で 、 売り上げが 半減した
Romaji: *Fuhyo-higai ga ichiban no mondai de, uriage ga hangen shita.*
Literal translation: Rumor-harm number-one problem, sales reduced half
Translation: The rumors of the harm of radiation has become the number-one problem, which has reduced crop sales by half.

Table 8.3 Groups of frequent words (>5 times frequency)

Human(s)	*Nokyo* JA, people, husband, family, peer/colleague, father in law, *musuko*, child/ren, ancestor, parents, group, neighbor, human, myself, I, customer(s), *Nohka*, (farming family), human being, producer, ego, others, part-time worker, *Saba* (name), leader, *salary-man* (the employed), young people, repeater (repeat customer), we, parents, father, mother, study group, company, Japanese people
Feeling & emotion	think, feel, suspect, guess, presume etc. *ki* (chi; mental energy), happy or happiness, thought, be glad, feeling, heart, effort, labor and time, be happy, preference, hard task, have, difficulty, fine, healthy, notice, recognize, easy, *kodawaru*, adherence work hard, strange, wired, cheering up
Hierarchy & exchange	be given to, be done to, be done to (out of good will of others), *san* (honorific title), receive receive *itadaku*, watering/ being watering, benevolence, loan/lend
Politics and state	Japan, America, country/state, foreign country, government, China
Physical/Geographical environment	*Tokyo*, mountain, large scale farms, prefecture, place of production
Natural environment	nature, leaf, tree, wind
Economic factors	income, price, financing, consumption

The third step is to group the words that are recognized as either agents or patients into common themes. This process required the use of a categorization strategy of the terms in order to find out their shared attributes. We employed a clustering technique suggested by Quinn (2005) that involves the use of small cards with the 327 terms that appeared five times or more. Each word was printed on a single card and grouped with conceptually similar words. Words with distinct meanings were placed further apart. This produced clusters of words grouped by shared themes (see Table 8.3).

While the technique has many advantages, there remains some ambiguity in the results. We could not, for example, unambiguously assign every term to a unique theme because some terms have many connotations and their meaning is context-dependent. There are, therefore, a small number of terms that fit within multiple themes. In addition, this clustering is *not* the participants' conceptual mapping, but rather the analysts.' Despite the imprecision and the fact that this is an analytical technique, rather than an ethnographic elicitation technique, it is helpful in finding the attributes of each cluster. For example, in our data, 'human' was the most frequent theme in our key words analysis. As we sorted the terms, different aspects of humans, individuals, local groups and national institutions were mentioned. While there were significant differences between terms, they all expressed some attribute of human activity or existence.

We then tagged the agent–patient relations within a sentence. In the example about the damage caused by *rumors* about the dangers of radiation, *fuhyo-higai*, 'rumors' is the agent and the decline in sales is the patient. However, it implies that the primary cause to declining sales is the people who manipulate the public's opinion, not the rumors themselves. Moreover, the patient also tacitly includes the speaker himself, a farmer who has been affected. This sentence was coded as 'Group of Humans influencing an (individual) Human's economic status.'

We then added the frequency of the same reasoning type in the spreadsheet (Table 8.4). Within each category, we also devised subcategories in which the agent–patient relationship with the same subjects were reversed (e.g., human as agent with market/economy as patient, or market/economy as agent and humans as patient).

Results: We found 269 reasoning sentences in total, ranging from 8 to 29 sentences in each interview. There was a striking abundance of human factors; 83 percent of the farmers' reasonings (n = 225) was about human categories, while the remaining 17 percent covered everything else (notably nature, politics and all other categories). The strongest causal tie was human–human (39 percent) of the total reasoning sentences, followed by human-product (14 percent) and human–market and economy (13 percent). We interpreted this to mean that the human group/others terms were articulated most frequently in the causal relationship implied while talking about farming.

In examining the sentences that involved human relationships (n = 225), 76 percent (n = 172) of the reasoning overwhelmingly attributed humans a patient role rather than an agent role. Specifically, there were three types of roles for humans: (1) humans as patient, such as with human groups/others or the natural environment; (2) mutual relationship, human either patient or agent at approximately the same frequency; and (3) humans as agent. The first type of reasoning sentences with humans as patient accounted for 61 percent of all human factors. The second type was limited to product or market and economy in which the farmer sees the relations as mutual. In addition, there were a small number of expressions of farmers as agents—the third type—in relation to weeds, vermin, disease, and wild animals. However, it is a limited number, and it is not always clear that farmers conceive of their actions as agentive in these contexts. Thus, the focus on humans stands out in this reasoning-causal analysis as it did in the results of the key words analysis.

As for the contents of the reasoning, the relation with customers (people who purchase the farmers' crops) was the most frequently and meticulously narrated:

Table 8.4 Frequency of reasoning sentences

Cause/Agent	Result/Patient	Frequency	Total
Human	Group of humans & other people	11	88
Group of humans & other people	Human	77	
Human	Product (crop & animal)	16	32
Product (crop & animal)	Human	16	
Human	Market & economy	14	31
Market & economy	Human	17	
Human	Climate, season & time	0	19
Climate, season & time	Human	19	
Human	Natural environment (soil, resource, mountain etc.)	5	19
Natural environment (soil, resource, mountain etc.)	Human	14	
Human	Politics	1	13
Politics	Human	12	
Human	Ancestor & supernatural (spirit, God & unidentifiable power)	0	10
Ancestor & supernatural (spirit, God & unidentifiable power	Human	10	
Product (crop & animal)	Market & economy	6	9
Market & economy	Product (crop & animal)	3	
Market & economy	Market & economy	7	7
Human	Physical environment (space & distance)	1	6
Physical environment (space & distance)	Human	5	
Human	Weed, disease & vermin	4	6
Weed, disease & vermin	Human	2	
Physical environment (space & distance)	Product (crop & animal)	5	5
Product (crop & animal)	Physical environment (space & distance)	0	
Product (crop & animal)	Climate, season & time	1	5
Climate, season & time	Product (crop & animal)	4	
Physical environment (space & distance)	Market & economy	4	4
Market & economy	Physical environment (space & distance)	0	
Physical environment (space & distance)	Natural environment	3	3
Natural environment	Physical environment (space & distance)	0	
Physical environment (space & distance)	Weed, disease & vermin	3	3
Weed, disease & vermin	Products (crops & animal)	2	2
Human	Wild animal	1	1
Natural environment (soil, resource, mountain, etc.)	Politics	1	1
		Total	264

Example 1: お客さんに喜ばれて、ようやく苦労も報われる
という感じ。

Translation: I feel my hardship is finally rewarded once my customers
are happy.

This farmer's description of his/her feeling, for example, implies that they
are in an exchange relationship with their customers that goes beyond a
simple monetary transaction. In fact, the customers' happiness rewards the
farmer for the investment, suffering and hard work. Initially, this farmer was
asked about the work routine and replied that the work he did was tiresome
and meticulous. Then the topic shifted from the work to the reward from
his work. He suggested that, unlike the less guaranteed monetary reward, he
believes he will be able to satisfy his customers and hence receive his most
prized compensation. This confidence keeps him working towards the goal
(customer's happiness) regardless of the trouble and hard work.

Further examination of the interviews with other farmers reveals some
additional understanding of this reciprocal exchange:

Example 2: 人を喜ばせることによって対価収入を得ている。
他人の幸せによって満足する。

Translation: By making the others [the customers] happy, I earn the
equivalent payment (*taika-shu-nyu*). I satisfy myself by others' happiness.

Exchange that is predicated on non-economic values is foundational for
social relations in Japanese society (Lebra, 1976 and Hendry, 1999). As
such, as stated in the previous example, it is clear that feelings play a critical
part even in the material economy. This interviewee goes far beyond a simple
reflection, however, and abstracts his working ethic by articulating a cultural logic of social reciprocity that is added to the logic of his commercial
transactions. The two sentences complement one another. The first asymmetrical explanation about 'pleasing others' leads to the 'other's happiness,'
which leads to 'earn(ing) the price,' which enables 'satisfy(ing) myself.' The
taika-shu-nyu, the equivalent return for the hard work he put in, needs to be
fulfilled. The above sentences suggest that money is not a sufficient return
by itself. Rather, the customer's happiness meaningfully contributes to the
level of the farmer's satisfaction. In many propositions mentioned in the discussion of agricultural productivity, the main emphasis seems to be on self-
fulfillment via human relations, which is expressed in words like *kodawari*
and *tema*.

Gist analysis

The gist analysis consists of the simplifications—omitting unclear and
ambiguous terms and expressions—of the propositions produced by the

interviewees. Thus, a closer look is achieved at the reasoning used. The first step eliminates repetitions and redundant information in the utterances. After several reiterations of this process, that is, winnowing, we were able to access more clearly the logic behind the propositions.

When winnowing was nearly completed, we could identify similar sentences sharing the same gist. We combined them together in a single gist, which reduced further the whole number of propositions, so that we obtained a manageable dataset of 'gists.' Together, these gist propositions could be classified into two categories: descriptions about 'humans' and about 'nature.' Once we had divided our gist sentences into these two groups, we identified subtopics within each group. For example, we identified the subgroup about the family/household within the group 'humans.' Then, we connected key ideas from the gist propositions within each subcategory to compose coherent paragraphs reflecting the underlying logic used by the food producers.

For the first group about humans, the followings are the key examples of the gist propositions we generated.

- We descendants benefit from our ancestors' (to whom we are directly related through patriarchal line) input/investment (*tema*) into the land.
- The farm is run by a household unit based on patriarchal inheritance.
- The household has division of labor.
- It's important for offspring to learn farming.
- In a group, one has to take collective responsibility for an individual making a bad product.
- Farmers always look for something new or different in order to avoid competition inside their farming community.
- A communal tie is strengthened through social events.
- Farmers acquire information through social networks.
- The government protects and regulates the farmer at the same time.
- There is something farmers cannot trust about government.
- Japanese farmers cannot win by quantity but can win by quality.
- Productivity is influenced by the ancestor's input such as labor, effort and thought.
- *Kodawari* is essential for farming.
- One should not waste products into which human labor and effort were invested.
- You can make more and better products with labor and effort.

Using the gist propositions at hand, we composed the following paragraphs that reflect the logic behind the gist propositions in each of the five subcategories for humans we had identified.

(1) *Household*:
The primary production unit is the household. In the Japanese farming households, each generation invests in the farmland and passes it on to the

next generation through the male line. Maintaining land requires more than one individual, so labor is divided among household members. The expectation is that farming skills and knowledge is to be learned and continued by the offspring.

(2) *Food production community*:
The information source is critical for farming. The information is exchanged through social ties that are strengthened by social occasions (*yoriai* shared *ba* is important). The occasion consists of 'same-quality' farmers, sharing similar value/situation/interest. Such events can offer a wide range of information, which is productive. Farmers like/enjoy such social interactions.

(3) *Relation with customer*:
Giri 'obligation'-*ninjo*, 'sentimental desire and the tolerance of such desire in others' (Lebra, 1976) is what helps the business thrive instead of single-minded capitalist pursuit of profit. The monetary compensation does not equal the high price paid by the farmer (including actual cost and labor), but mutual empathy (as in *omoiyari*) does. One needs to consider the [business] relationship in terms of mutual empathy with customers because feelings of interdependency between the two parties is what lies at the basis of sales relationships.

(4) *Institution*:
Nokyo (JA) ensures sales and income using connection with the government, thus a farmer needs *Nokyo* to earn a living. On the other hand, *Nokyo* mixes each product with those of others, and it does not matter how much better the products an individual farmer makes with more input and investment. This withers the farmer's motivation.

(5) *Government, nation, and states*:
In the relationship between farmers and government, a farmer is protected in the exchange of compliance (mutual dependency). The relation appears to be not always mutual, and the farmers are not happy.

   For the second group about nature, the followings are the key examples of the gist propositions we generated.

- Farmers notice that climate has changed in the recent past.
- There is nothing farmers can do about environmental change.
- Nature damages human livelihoods.
- Farmers are awed by nature and can only obey and adapt to it.
- People attempt to adapt to nature by circumventing its harmful effects.
- Nature is beautiful by itself, which humans appreciate.
- You have to appreciate the precious life of produce that you consume.
- All livings are dependent on each other.

Using these gist propositions, we composed the following paragraphs for each of the three subcategories for nature we had identified.

(1) *Relationship*:
Nature gives human benefits as well as damage. There is nothing a human can do about what nature does, but to fear and be awed by it. People can prevent or minimize secondary damage, and that is the only way to adapt to nature.

(2) *Consumption*:
There is life in other living beings (including plant crops), therefore people have to be grateful for the loss of life when they consume it. The feeling and time of devotion, *tema* and *omoi*, are necessary for growing. Without them, they do not grow healthier so as to sell better. The more it sells, less excess and less wasteful is for the farmer.

(3) *Aesthetic*:
Nature is beautiful, and its beauty is to be appreciated.

Summary of findings

Focusing on a small sample of food producers residing in two main cities of Gunma in central Japan, we sought to discover the cultural models of nature they utilize to produce and talk about their farming activities. Through a blended methodology of ethnographic and linguistic data collection and analyses, we constructed a coherent cultural model of nature, as well as an associated cultural model of Nature, which seem to complement each other.

At the level of the cultural model of nature, there was a clear indication about the centrality of human intervention to 'naturalize' nature. We started our analysis based on the first author's ethnographic participant observation and interview data. In this analysis, he identified two main themes that were repeatedly emphasized or elaborated, while giving an overall picture of farming activities in the region: (1) farming is conducted as part of complex systems of interpersonal relationships and social organization, which seem to keep the food producers from being dependent upon conditions given (or not given or destroyed) by 'raw' nature, that are very unpredictable to guarantee successful food production; (2) farming has the twofold goal of supporting economic livelihoods and of pursuing personal meaning and satisfaction. An example of the latter theme is *kodawari*, 'perfectionism in personal authenticity,' and was illustrated in three case studies.

The subsequent linguistic analyses also supported these two themes. The word frequency and the keywords analyses showed what words, that is, the 'building blocks' of cultural models, appeared most frequently and relatively independently of the contents of the questions they were asked. That is, words that remained salient even after such 'reflexivity' factors—that is, the impact of the researcher and the research methods on the data collected, including the nature of the interview questions—were strategically removed. First, among the words mentioned more than 10 times, 40 percent were related to 'human' factors. These human-related words could be divided into further subcategories, which denoted *hito*, 'humans generally,' *jibun*, 'self,' *ie*, or *ka*, 'family' and 'family members,' *kyaku*, 'customer,' *seisansha*, 'producer,' *nakama*, 'colleague,' and *nihonjin*, 'Japanese.'

An associated finding is a relative absence of words related to *raw* natural phenomena (water, land, temperature, weather), except for those achieved through human engineering (e.g., controlling the temperatures of greenhouse). Altogether, farming is framed primarily as interpersonally and socially organized *human* activity, rather than an activity that is taking place in relation to raw, untamed nature.

The reasoning-causal analysis was conducted to discover cause/agent and result/patient relationships. Not only did the results show an overwhelming emphasis on the human factor, but they also revealed subcategories within this factor and causal relations about them. First, we selected words that were mentioned more than five times in the word frequency and key words analyses. Then, we classified them into categories by using the card-sorting method (see Quinn, 2005). This enabled us to obtain the following subcategories: (1) Humans; (2) Feelings and Emotions; (3) Hierarchy and Exchange; (4) Politics and State; (5) Physical/Geographic Environment; (6) Natural Environment; and (7) Economic Factors. Other than 5 and 6, all else relates to human affairs.

When we examined the agent/patient relationship, we discovered that the vast majority, 87 percent, suggested human-related causal links, while the remaining 17 percent included 'nature.' Of the three possible causal patterns involving humans—that is, humans as agent, patience, or neither agent nor patient—patient was the most frequent. This finding dovetails with the focus on humans already indicated and, at the same time, it adds an important new detail: It is other humans and not ego that are the center of attention.

Conclusion and suggested cultural model of nature

Nature, with the capital N, in this volume refers to a cultural 'worldview' (Bennardo, Introduction, this volume). Attributing to Nature such a meaning is conducive for us to make inferences about culturally mediated ontological views about the world in which the food producers live and work. We can hypothesize a cultural model of Nature that includes three subsets of ideas that corroborate existing theoretical perspectives. First, there appears to be a fundamental divide between nature—what exists naturally—that is altered in some way by and for humans, and the rest, which is untouched by, unrelated to, or even out of control of humans. To understand this binary distinction, we call attention to the two separate meanings of the word *nature* in Japanese: nature as existing world and nature as what is 'natural.' Second, the findings suggest a quasi-religious view about the world that is 'benevolent' and the role of a person in it, which consists in an effort to reduce and overcome self-centeredness. Finally, the results of the analyses suggest a view about an inside and outside, which corresponds to the view of what is 'good and virtuous' versus 'unknown and dangerous, albeit powerful and overwhelming.'

Two meanings of 'nature.' The Japanese word for nature, *shizen* (自然), has two basic meanings: to be 'natural'—that is, to be 'spontaneously or naturally so' (Tucker, 2003: 161)—and that which pertains to the natural world—the environment and creatures in it (Tucker, 2003; Shimizu, 2012). Consequently, we generate an hypothesis about what constitutes 'natural' (meaning 1) ways to produce foods via 'nature' (meaning 2).

Using both meanings, we propose this proposition as a relevant part of the cultural model of Nature—'nature' is not 'natural' until it is 'humanized.' An analogy here may be that of tending a *bonsai* tree, the art of producing miniature trees that 'mimic' the way they 'naturally' grow. This view contrasts with the two other alternative views—that nature is 'below' human to be used as *the means to* achieve utilitarian gain, or 'above' them in that it is too powerful and beyond human control (e.g., natural disasters).

Takie Lebra (1976), a Japanese-born cultural anthropologist, citing Pelzel (1974), describes this 'humanization' of nature as follows: 'Humanism, Japanese style [is where] all elements of the universe be *related horizontally and mutually* [italics added], that they share the same "human" status, rather than being hierarchically controlled with the ultimate keeper of the order at the top' (10). Hereby the 'task of [humans] was to make nature civil, removing from it the troublesome qualities of speech, mobility, and violence' (Pelzel, 47, quoted in Lebra, 1976: 11).

Below are some examples from this study that support this first propositional content of the cultural model. As Hikaru Hoshi and I drove away from his organic farm after the 'nature walk,' he muttered: 'Being out there (where his field is) late in the evening, I hear wild animals begin to make noises. At a time like that, I feel that there is a "natural" [that is, untamed] world out there that is beyond human affairs. I feel that I need to leave there to give it respect.'

Supporting evidence comes also from what Mr. Terada says. He is Mr. Hoshi's business partner and his job is to facilitate the close producer-consumer relationships mentioned earlier by Mr. Hoshi. He states that there is a stigma attached to 'strict organic farming ... People tend to see organic farmers as religious fanatics of sorts ... It's a perception unique to Japan ... Organic farmers are seen as being too "stoic" (*suto ikku*), and not in sync with the sentiment of the rest of people.' This 'sentiment,' as we interpret it, suggests a belief that food production and consumption must be a two-way, mutually interdependent process between the food producers and the consumers. To produce foods according to an abstract principle held by the food producer alone, that is, growing foods devoid of chemicals, is a less 'natural' way to produce and consume foods than that which is embedded in the close, interdependent relationships between the food producers and their consumers.

'Spiritual' ways to produce food. In his classic work on Japanese religion (1985), the cultural historian Robert Bellah argued that what is at the foundation of the astonishing economic development of post-feudal, modern Japan are certain religious and spiritual attitudes prevalent during the Tokugawa time, the era that preceded the modern era. Of relevance to our current findings are two basic views (i.e., worldview or Nature) that permeated the religious attitude of the people during Tokugawa time, namely, 'gratitude toward nurturant beings' and 'identification with the ground of being' (14). The first view posits that the basis of one's exist- ence is dependent on the goodness of others who sustain and nourish it, as reflected in the

> view of a man as weak and helpless by himself. Only with the help of benevolent beings can he live, and the blessings he receives are so much greater than his ability to return them that actually he can only return an infinitesimal amount. By devoting himself utterly to returning these blessings he assures to himself the continuation of them, and in some sense he is thereby saved from his weakness. (73)

Likewise, our findings support a quasi-religious view that at the root of the food producers' activities is their being recipients of benefits intrinsic to inter- personal relationships. The clearest example of this is the sentiment expressed toward the ancestors who laid the groundwork, both literally by working on the soil as well as establishing and preserving the farming family. At the most 'secular' level, this view is consistent with the findings from the semantic role analysis in which food producers tended to frame themselves as patients rather than agents in describing their work activities. It is also consistent with the first author's past work that showed *omoiyari* 'empathy for others' as the basic virtue of selfhood among adolescents (age 12 to 18) in a Japanese school (Shimizu, 2001). Finally, it corroborates the basic spatial orienta- tion that causality originates in others and not ego in self-other relations in Japanese socialization and educational discourses (Shimizu, 2011).

In addition, Bellah (1985) notes 'identification with ground of being' as another tenet of a persisting spiritual worldview. As a religious practice, this orientation is associated with various meditative, spiritual ascetic training wherein a person strives 'to destroy the self as an ontological entity, to des- troy the dichotomy between subject and object (74).' For our purpose, it can be stated as an attempt to transcend the boundary of an ego-centered self via transforming the self-calculating, profit-oriented activities into those that serve 'higher' purposes than mere self-serving productivity and achievement. An example of this would be Shinji Amada's almost 'redemptive' effort to use his pig-farming business as a spiritual education opportunity for school children.

Uchi 'inside,' *soto* 'outside' and far out. Ethno-psychological (Doi, 1973, 1986) and ethno-sociological (Lebra, 1976; Hamaguchi, 1985) research in Japan have documented the centrality of knowing the distinction between *uchi* 'inside' and *soto* 'outside' spheres of society, and the ability to navigate the two worlds skillfully (Lebra, 1976; Doi, 1986) as a the basic requirement for being a mature and 'normal' person in Japanese society. We draw on this basic binary model to shed new light on our current findings.

Briefly, the world familiar to oneself is the world of insiders (*mi-uchi*) such as one's family members, co-workers, fellow citizens (e.g., Japanese). Conversely, the world outside of this sphere is that of outsiders (*tanin*, or 'other' people) such as strangers, members of groups other than one's own, or foreigners. Generally, the inside world is where one does not have to adhere strictly to the formal rules of group-oriented behaviors (e.g., bowing, using respect words for elders and superiors). The outside world, as already indicated, is where one must apply appropriate rituals, rules and language to respect the formality of situations.

Lebra (1976) extends this model to indicate that there exists the outermost realm beyond the *soto* 'outside,' which is inhabited by beings who are not only outsiders, but also out-*caste* as far as they are completely cut off even from knowing and respecting this insider-outsider distinction. Lebra (1976) offers Japanese tourists' offensive behaviors, which were prevalent in the 1960s, as an example of what happens when the tourists perceive them to be in a situation 'outlawed' by Japanese norms of interpersonal conduct. Also, in a popular Japanese festival of *setsubun*, children throw soybeans while voicing, *Oni wa soto, fuku wa uchi* 'Oni, leave here (inside) and stay outside, good fortune, come in and stay with us.'

We believe that at least two examples that emerged from the current study belong to this outermost sphere of the informants' cosmology—the contrast between farming within Japan and foreign countries, and between humanized nature and untamed nature. We suggest that for our participants, Japan, as a geographic and cultural entity, is a notable and useful point of reference indicating characteristics that are distinctively separate and unique from those of some Western countries such as the United States and Denmark.

Support for this suggestion comes from the cultural key word results where the word 'Nihon/Japan' is the fifth most frequently mentioned word, while 'America,' 'foreign country,' and 'Japanese' also made the list at the 17th, 31st, and 37th place, respectively. Related findings are the two gist-propositions, 'Japanese farmers cannot win by quantity but can win by quality,' and '*kodawari* is essential for farming.' These propositions were taken from the original interviews where the participants said high quality products brought on by *kodawari* 'perfectionism' is what gives them a competitive edge over the quantity based marketing methods of the United States and Denmark. In this instance, participants perceived two foreign countries as places where what constitutes 'natural' for them—food production that includes a human network and *kodawari*—clearly does not apply.

Another category that seemed to constitute the 'far out territory' is that of 'raw nature' (野生) Support for this comes from the remark by Mr. Hoshi, the organic farmer, that his customers consider that produce untouched and uncared for by human effort is outside of their normative standards. On the same day this interview took place, when we left his field deep in the woods and darkness started to set in, he also noted, as mentioned earlier, that the field at night belongs to the wild (i.e., raw nature), not to humans.

We would like to propose that the above examples of demarcation between the inside and the 'far' outside apply also to the known fact that throughout Japanese history there has been a strongly held view about which people qualify as 'normal' Japanese and which do not. The Ezo, considered and named 'barbarians,' who inhabited northern Japan, and the Burakumin, descendants of 'outcast' classes during pre-modern Japan, are cases in point. In the case of the Ezo, one needs to think of the sentiment toward Ezo, literally meaning 'foreigners.' This population was considered too 'wild' to be incorporated into the central government of Japan during the rise of the warrior class as the ruler of the nation. In fact, the name given to the head of the government was 征夷大将軍 *Sei-i Taishōgun* 'Commander in chief of the Expeditionary Force against the Barbarians' (Wikipedia, https ://en.wikipedia.org/wiki/Sh%C5%8Dgun). Similarly, Burakumin have been subject to discrimination against them for fear that they are too 'defiled' to be part of mainstream Japanese society, since they dealt with the 'wild' part of nature by being butchers and tanners: two of the historically main occupations among the Burakumin (DeVos and Wagatsuma, 1967; Kawamoto and Shimizu, 2004).

The three above-mentioned elements of the cultural model of Nature lead us to the following conclusion. The ethnographic and linguistic data we presented regarding our participants' way of producing foods via their work with nature hinge on the worldview that there exists a binary distinction between the world of insiders (*uchi*) and outsiders (*soto*). This knowledge is essential for normal interpersonal transactions in mainstream Japanese society (Doi, 1973, 1986; Lebra, 1976). This view supports a related belief that raw nature must be humanized because the humanization process transforms it into more culturally acceptable forms for 'insiders' that make up one's day-to-day interactions and experiences: one's fellow farmers, family members, and customers. At the root of this motivation, we propose, is a deep-seated fear and contempt for that which is raw and untamed, which parallels the sentiments expressed toward Ezo and Burakumin. The 'spiritualization' of their work seems to help them rationalize or transcend the problem of coming into contact with raw nature and using it for utilitarian purposes since there is 'something more' in what they do than simply taking advantage of nature for egotistic (i.e., personal profit) purposes.

In sum, the three ontological orientations complement one another. Food producers work with nature to establish both their livelihoods and personal meaning by humanizing it. This intervention has a moral and spiritual value, in the same sense that Whiting et al. (1966) see 'values' mediating the practical and expressive sides of institutional behaviors. Nonetheless, the humanization of nature and its rendering into a spiritual path still appears to rest uncomfortably, emotionally, and morally, upon the fear of raw nature that resides at the periphery of their cultural model of Nature.

Notes

1 Small letter 'nature' refers to the physical environment, plants, animals and weather. We will be using the word nature with this meaning throughout the chapter.
2 Native English speakers often find it surprising how infrequently Japanese speakers actually need to articulate the subject or object of a sentence.

References

Bellah, R. (1985). *Tokugawa Religion: The Cultural Roots of Modern Japan.* New York: Free Press.

D'Andrade, R. (2005). Some methods for studying cultural cognitive structures. In Quinn, N. (ed.), *Finding Culture in Talk: A Collection of Methods.* New York: Palgrave, 83–104.

DeVos, G., and Wagatsuma, H. (1967). *Japan's Invisible Race: Caste in Culture and Personality.* Berkeley: University of California Press.

Doi, T. (1973). *Anatomy of Dependence.* Tokyo: Kodansha International.

Doi, T. (1986). *Anatomy of Self.* Tokyo: Kodansha International.

Hamaguchi, E. (1985). A contextual model of the Japanese: Toward a methodological innovation in Japanese studies. *Journal of Japanese Studies* 11(2): 289–321.

Hendry, J. (1999). An Introduction to Social Anthropology: Other People's Worlds. Basingstoke: Macmillan.

Kardiner, A. (1939). *The Individual and His Society.* New York: Columbia University Press.

Kawamoto, Y., and Shimizu, H. (2004). 'Burakugaku' (Buraku study): A paradigm shift for education. *Mid-Western Educational Researcher* 17(4): 27–33.

Kingston, J. (2012). *Natural Disaster and Nuclear Crisis in Japan: Response and Recovery after Japan's 3/11.* New York: Routledge.

Lebra, T. W. (1976). *Japanese Patterns of Behavior.* Honolulu: University of Hawai'i Press.

LeVine, R. A. (1982). *Culture, Behavior, and Personality: An Introduction to the Comparative Study of Psychosocial Adaptation.* New York: Aldine.

Nakagawa, M. (2005). *Two Worlds (Seken and Sekai) from the Perspective of Kango.* Iwanami Publisher.

Pelzel, J. (1974). Human nature in the Japanese myth. In Lebra, T. S. and Lebra, W. P. (eds.), *Japanese Culture and Behavior: Selected Readings.* Honolulu: University of Hawai'i Press, 3–26.

Quinn, N. (2005). How to reconstruct schemas people share, from what they say. In Quinn, N. (ed.), *Finding Culture in Talk: A Collection of Methods.* New York: Palgrave, 35–81.

Shimizu, H. (2001). Japanese cultural psychology and empathic understanding: Implications for academic and cultural psychology. *Ethos* 28(2): 224–247.

Shimizu, H. (2011). Cognitive anthropology and education: Foundational models of self and cultural models of teaching and learning in Japan and the United States.

In Kronenfeld, D. B., Bennardo, G., de Munck, V. C., and Fischer, M. D. (eds.), *A Companion to Cognitive Anthropology*. London: Blackwell, 430–449.

Shimizu, H. (2012). Cultural model of nature and environment in an agricultural region in central Japan: A preliminary proposal. In Bennardo, G. (ed.), *Cultural Models of Nature and the Environment: Self, Space, and Causality*. DeKalb, IL: Northern Illinois University, Institute for the Study of the Environment, Sustainability and Energy.

Shimizu, H., and LeVine, R. A. (2001). *Japanese Frame of Mind: Cultural Perspectives on Human Development*. New York: Cambridge University Press.

Tucker, J. A. (2003). Japanese views of nature and the environment. In Selin, H. (ed.), *Nature Across Cultures: Views of Nature and the Environment in non-Western Cultures*. Boston: Kluwer.

Whiting, J. W. M., et al. (1966). The learning values. In Abert, E. (ed.), *People of the Rimrock: A Study of Values in Five Cultures*. Cambridge, MA: Harvard University Press.

9 Domesticating categories of the wild environment

Eliciting cultural models of nature among Hai//om

Thomas Widlok

Introduction: The domestication of culture

A key point of concern in the discussion of *cultural* models of *nature* is the in-built distinction between culture and nature that continues to be problematic in comparative anthropology. Research in this domain therefore not only provides new insights into the diversity of cultural models around the world but also the opportunity for recalibrating what 'culture' is and what it is not in this debate.

The culture concepts since the nineteenth century have been strongly influenced by the ages of 'discovery' and colonization during which 'culture,' denoting a collective with a separate way of life and a distinct view of the world, became an important tool for making sense of encounters with people who appeared to be different (see Wagner, 1979). However, there is an older notion of culture that has been subdued but has never quite disappeared. This old European culture concept is typically traced back to etymological roots in the Latin word *colere* 'to cultivate/to nurse,' linked up with an old sense of 'economy' as derived from the Greek *oikos* 'house' and *nomos* 'rule,' managing the house, as exemplified by 'house-based societies' of today and the recent past (see Därmann, 2011: 112). What is highlighted here is that there are transgenerationally learned patterns that matter for the way in which human life on this planet is taking place. However, it is not difficult to discern a certain bias here that ties culture to a rather narrow horticultural worldview.

The question that I want to pursue in this chapter is whether the repertoire of human ways of perceiving, of maintaining, and of changing the environment is in fact much broader than the image of 'man the gardener' and 'man the householder' suggests. I base my argument on empirical field research with people in northern Namibia, more specifically with a majority population of Khoesan-speaking ≠Akhoe Hai//om who are nationally subsumed under the minority group category of San (formerly known as Bushmen).[1]

Environmental and social changes

The last 25 years have seen considerable changes in both environmental and social conditions in northern Namibia. Therefore, a major challenge

DOI: 10.4324/9781351127905-10

to social science studies of environmental perception of climate change and its implications is the attempt to bring together changes that occur in the natural environment with changes of cultural ideas and practices of agents living in this environment. Although it is generally assumed that there is no immediate or tight fit between environmental changes and changes to cultural models, we urgently require more data and better theories that explain the interrelation between ecological environmental changes and the transformations of cultural models. Comparing the results of the most recent field research with earlier visits to the field sites over the years (see Widlok, 1999) shows that there has been considerable change in almost all domains of life. On the one hand many local people are today much less mobile, restricted by land enclosure and the privatization of land while they are, on the other hand, confronted with an influx of neighbors who intensify their agro-pastoral use of the land and make it more difficult to cultivate other land uses such as hunting and gathering. As a first step toward investigating cultural perceptions of the environment I have carried out some free-listing tasks covering the domains of animals, plants, and people.

The purpose of the free-listing task was to get a first impression about what locals, using their own language, consider to be salient elements that are relevant in environmental change. The instructions were kept simple in that I asked (in their own language) a variety of respondents who were already known to me: 'What are the entities that belong to x ...?' (or 'What is it that is part of x?') whereby I would consecutively insert for 'x' vernacular labels for the categories 'animals,' 'plants' and 'humans' (and later on, 'the supernatural,' 'the weather' and 'the environment'; see further below). The idea was to get an impression of both the diversity and the consensus in ecological knowledge with regard to the relevant agents and forces that effect environmental change.

In the Namibian field site, the first two categories, animals and plants, were largely unproblematic in the sense that in these domains respondents generated more or less long lists of terms for plants and animals. One of the most striking results was that, although the Hai//om in question now live in an area that for some thirty years has been depleted of game animals and has been subject to massive influx of cattle, sheep, and other domesticated animals, the category of 'animals' (*xamanin*) was still almost exclusively filled with names of wild animals from the bush. The fact that cows, chicken, goats, and dogs were visible and audible all around us—whereas the animals they listed were not—did not have an effect on the content of their lists. Only two (young) individuals included some of the domesticated animals, and only very late in the sequence. Similarly, only few mentioned domesticated garden plants, while everyone's listings were dominated by trees, bushes, and other wild plants.

How are we to explain this discrepancy? The respondents were leaving out the animals and plants that were so prominent in their here and now, and in the life-worlds of their dominant agro-pastoralist neighbors.

When subsequently questioning respondents, they were happy to include domesticated animals in the *xamanin* 'animal' category but, like insects, these animals were clearly not the prototypical animals that constituted the category. It may be suggested that the term *xamanin* should be translated as 'wild animal' instead of 'animals' (as the compilers of dictionaries of neighboring groups suggest; see Haacke and Eiseb, 2002), but if that was a strict categorical difference, then no extension toward domesticated animals should occur. Furthermore, the same phenomenon was observed with regard to the plant category (*hain*) which, when respondents were being prompted in the free-listing tasks, was readily extended to include all kinds of domesticated plants and still produced a very marked preponderance toward 'wild' plants.

I draw two conclusions from this evidence: First, the case study from northern Namibia underlines (once more) that the categorization of animals into wild and domesticated species, land into natural landscapes and cultural landscapes (see below), and uses of the environment into productive versus appropriative is not universal. Second, the results are also an indication that respondents were indeed abstracting from what has been their everyday situation for several decades (and in some cases for their whole lives). There seems to be no immediate feedback effect from environmental change to the cultural categories.

Cultural strategies of categorizing the environment

Free lists for animals and plants (and the sequences of these lists) differed across subjects in terms of length, but the overall tendency of highlighting undomesticated species was robust across subjects. Results differed much more with regard to the other domains investigated in which the diversity was such that there were very fundamental differences in the strategies of categorization.

The free lists for the category 'humans' (*khoen*), is a good example because it showed a strong bifurcation. While many respondents produced a list of ethnic groups living in the country (varied in terms of the number and comprehensiveness of categories), there were several respondents who produced a very short list, consisting only of terms for their own ethnic group ≠*Akhoe* and that of the neighboring *!Xû*. Both strategies follow well-known patterns of categorizing people in southern Africa: The categorization according to ethnic groups has been a dominant feature throughout the colonial period, in particular in South Africa's sphere of influence, where the apartheid policy tried to cement ethnic categorization. The second strategy responds to the widespread tendency for autonyms to translate as 'real people/humans' and to implicitly or explicitly categorize other people as being outside that group, a tendency observed widely in sub-Saharan Africa and with regard to other small-scale societies (Bird-David, 2017).

At least over the last 25 years since Namibian independence, considerable educational and media effort has gone into the broadening of the 'people' category beyond ethnicity, and the mobility of the population has been such that one would expect longer and more diverse lists to emerge under the key word 'people.' Therefore, again, although people live in a wider social surrounding made up of many ethnic groups, and while they are dominated by other ethnic groups and by groups that are no longer defined only in ethnic terms but in terms of professions and in terms of holding office in the state or in NGOs, the respondents would limit their free lists to the two closely related local hunter-gatherer groups as constituting the category 'people' in their social environment.

While some respondents produced what we may want to call a birds-eye view, trying to cover all groups in the region, others produced an ethnocentric view. The informal interviews carried out immediately after the free-listing suggest that many respondents feel at ease shifting between the two perspectives, sometimes spontaneously, or when reflecting on the issue. In either case, it seems that a few decades of social change were not sufficient to change the pre-independence model premised on ethnic identities and oriented toward a foraging subsistence. We may take this as an indicator that cultural models are not particularly quick in adapting to environmental change of the type that recent climate change and current political change produces. One working hypothesis for the ongoing research is therefore to see whether cultural models have a conservative bias in the sense that they are kept unaltered in a situation of change and that, only in the long run, may this new situation eventually change the model. A few decades may be long in terms of the effects that man-induced climate change can have, but typically it is not long in the context of established cultural models that usually change at a much slower pace. The incongruence of the two transformations is a problematic that is important to take account of, not only in the practice of people confronted with environmental change, but also in the social theories that investigate these situations.

The other indication the data provides is that changes to the cultural model are not of an on/off binary type, but rather are of 'gracious' transition in which different responses are latently present, co-occurring with one another. This has important practical implications because these latent (partial) models can be (re)activated when a situation comes up in which they are of relevance. Talking to people in conversation after the free-listing task, I repeatedly noted that they were ready to agree that there were indeed other animals, plants, and people that could also be included in these categories— but only when being explicitly prompted to do so. In other words, there were many more latent members of the categories animals, plants and people than those that were spontaneously realized when compiling the lists. It seems that elements may fade in or fade out of a category, and they can exist in a 'dormant' state for considerable time. This is a major difference from the actual occurrence of natural species, which may also increase or decrease, but which in many situations of radical environmental change also disappear without the possibility of returning to the environment.

The natural-selection metaphor that many natural scientists have whole-heartedly internalized, and which they often extend also to cultural features that go 'extinct,' shows its limits here, a point to which I shall return in the conclusion. The next point to consider is not only to ask what the environment consists of, how items are classified, but also what are the causal factors involved in environmental change.

Talking about weather and climate

A point frequently made in recent discussions of climate change is that local people may note and discuss changes in weather that should not, however, be confused with changes in climate, which are more long-term and often not as clearly perceptible as changes of weather. Tim Ingold has (2015: 76) criticized the modernist tendency to consider weather as 'localized instantiations' of climate and to divide the notion of atmosphere into measured meteorology and aesthetical metaphors. However, all of these notions (weather, climate, and atmosphere) are abstract and need to be translated into sensuous features that affect people and about which they feel comfortable talking. Moreover, during field research in Namibia, even the common assumption that 'talking about the weather' is always an easy strategy, in fact does not hold.

It is noteworthy that Hai//om do not talk about the weather (let alone climate or the atmosphere) as an agent, but rather about 'the sun burning,' 'the rain(s) failing' or 'the wind(s) blowing.' The weather category in Hai//om (and other, related languages) that is being used as a translation of, say English media and international policy discourse, is itself simply a compound of these agentive forces. The term /nanutsi//haotsi≠ôab literally translates as 'rains-and-clouds-and-wind,' that is, it contains a list in itself. Not surprisingly, when doing free listings for 'weather,' I received exactly the features that were contained in the compound term. The only additions to the list of three (rain, clouds, wind) were sun and moon in some of the free lists. Moreover, the term /nanutsi//haotsi≠ôab itself is hardly used in everyday discourse, and it only comes in because it is used in radio broadcasting as a translation for the English term 'weather.'

The same holds for the notion of 'the environment,' which Hai//om people have heard of, largely because these terms are used extensively in the national radio and by teachers, development workers, and bureaucrats. There are terms such as ≠namibeb and!ha!hais that were originally coined by official language committees and recommended for official usage (Haacke and Eiseb, 2002: vii), but which are not commonly used in vernacular speech. In everyday conversation these learned constructions are not widely spread. In free lists and interviews I have used these terms interchangeably, confident that respondents would know roughly what I was interested in. The main results of these elicitation exercises is that respondents consistently produced rather short lists, but which typically included items such as 'houses/huts' and 'fire places.' Thus, while the English meaning (and the official language policy in Namibia that is mapped onto it) primarily considers environment to be the natural environment with a latent extension to the man-made environment, I found the exact opposite with Hai//om respondents who were focusing on the man-made environment as that 'which is around you' and extending it only into matters of 'the land' when being prompted to do so in further conversation.

In sum, interview data suggest that no abstract notion of 'weather,' and even less so of 'climate' or 'environment,' are being used in everyday conversation, and that technical terms that have been created in Khoesan languages by the media, by government, and non-governmental agencies are slow to enter local language use. Not surprisingly for a region of the world with highly erratic rainfall and serious problems of drought, there is a lot of talk about rain (or its absence), but this is usually connected to the planning of specific activities. The same holds for 'winds,' which are strongly associated with disease and danger. In other words, weather (and the environment at large) is not a problem or a challenge in the abstract, but something that one needs to take account of whenever planning an action, any action, or as Ingold (2015) would have it, 'simply for leading one's life.'

For instance, forays into the bush are often not carried out under overcast rainy skies during the wet season because it is known that snakes are very active under such conditions. Conversely, the onset of rains at the very beginning of the rainy season is an important factor for successfully harvesting swarming termites. However, all of these situations can be handled effectively and routinely without any reflection or conversation about the weather or the climate in overarching terms. In parallel to what I pointed out above for the categorization of animals and plants, there is no categorical distinction between, on the one hand, the 'wild' vagaries of sun, winds, and rains, or the 'natural' environmental features such as hills, dunes, and rivers, and on the other hand human environmental action such as going hunting, moving camp, putting up a hut or making a fire and the results of these actions that are visible in the environment. Unlike many agricultural people in Africa (and the urbanized elites of today) who rigidly separate the (hostile) bush from the cultivated land, no such a separation was detectable in interviews or in the free-listing exercise nor in participant observation. ≠Akhoe Hai//om seem to have a seamless perception of their surroundings as one environment that combines both 'natural' and 'man-made' features.[2]

In fact, this matches the results of an inquiry into the last domain of agents that feature in this research and that may be expected to influence the environment, namely supernatural forces. There is little to no discussion of supernatural entities in everyday Hai//om conversations. As with many groups in Africa the creator God (*!xub*) is seen as otiose and as not actively interfering with human affairs. There is the notion of a so-called lesser god (*//gãuab*), glossed by missionaries as 'Satan' who is said to be present in sickness and healing, but again this is relevant only when dealing with concrete illnesses that require concrete measures, as for instance carrying out a trance healing dance (Widlok, 2001). The appropriate means of dealing with these powers is through ritual activity (above all through trance dancing) but this is left out of propositional discourse. As a consequence, the category of 'supernatural' is very hard to convey to respondents. In free listing, various attempts consistently produced a one-entry category (*!xub* 'God'). I think the parallel ways of dealing with the 'natural' forces of weather and of dealing with the 'supernatural' forces once again underlines that distinguishing the two is not very productive or relevant in Hai//om everyday life.

When discussing related matters, Hai//om does not provide a cover term for 'supernatural.' When attempting to fall back to descriptors such as 'things that you cannot see or touch' would occasionally provoke reactions such as 'You mean like when you are blind?' or 'Lions! You hear them but I never see one since I run away as soon as I hear them.' As already mentioned, a number of respondents named 'God' (and 'God' only) but there were other isolated responses that included 'dreams' and 'the wind.' The most marked pattern that emerged is that most respondents professed to lack knowledge of what cannot be seen and refused to speculate about it. There was no sense of anxiety or fear to talk about the domain, as one may suspect, but rather one of ignorance and a lack of ready-made propositions that people could rely on.

Although most respondents are nominally Christians, at this stage, there is little evangelization taking place so that the temptation to use 'borrowed discourse' of religious specialists with theological training is not pronounced. Rather, the category of the supernatural was effectively turned into 'that which we [by definition] do not know much about.' It is noteworthy that, in other parts of Africa, ethnographers were able to elicit much longer lists of what constitutes the 'supernatural' domain (see Lienhardt, 1961). However, across all these cases respondents emphasize the degree of unpredictability and of conflicting forces within that domain that may prevent or provoke human life (or suffering) (see Widlok, 2014). The conclusion that I draw from this is, again, twofold: Cultural models seem to differ not only in the ways in which they carve up or categorize the world, but also in terms of how much they are pragmatically used as a *model* for exhaustively explaining the world and as a *model* for changing or maintaining that state of the world.

Conclusions

The Namibian case study shows remarkable stability of orientation toward 'wild' plants and animals despite ongoing ecological and economic changes. Undomesticated animals and plants are still named as prototypical examples for these categories, even though many animal species that used to be hunted have disappeared, and many undomesticated plants are no longer used as intensively as they used to be. The ≠Akhoe Hai//om case suggests that cultural models and their features do not die out or get selected in the same way as natural scientists tend to think about the destiny of species in environmental change. Rather, it seems that human environments as cultural constructs are always limited selections from the surroundings. Instead of a one-to-one correspondence between environmental conditions and cultural models, there appears to be a considerable degree of freedom in constructing different cultural models in one and the same environment.

It also questions the assumption that humans are inescapably trapped in a cultural model of their environment in a way similar to how biologists tend to talk about animals that are said to be 'embedded' in their natural niches. The evidence suggests that Plessner had a point when he insisted that humans differ from animals in that they are not centered in their environment, but regularly take on an ex-centered position towards their 'co-world' (Plessner, 1983: 86). If the creation of new representations of that world is an open process, then the task ahead for future research is to investigate how such new representations emerge and how existing cultural ideas that may have stayed dormant for considerable time are re-established. For as far as we can see now in the results of this project, ≠Akhoe Hai//om seem to readily switch between alternative models in their everyday pursuits. Or, more precisely, they seem to cultivate ways of dealing with the environment that look very unlike the strategy of planning authorities, who produce a model so that it can be realized (more or less mechanically) according to a preconceived plan derived from that model.[3]

Returning to the issues I raised at the beginning of this contribution, I suggest that the Hai//om case study helps to develop a wider notion of culture as 'cultivation': Cultivation in this sense clearly not only applies to the land (things, materials) or to challenges provided by external natural changes such as climate change. Rather, cultivation—in the sense of creating, maintaining and altering cultural categories and the cultural ways of dealing with causalities—seamlessly involves social relationships and man-made conditions. Humans have to relate to animals and plants independently of whether they are 'wild' or 'domesticated'; they have to deal with an environment that is at the same time beyond control (sun, rains, wind) as well as a product of previous actions by humans (who make fires, build houses, kill animals, and so forth).

The Hai//om notion of 'environment' prototypically includes elements of the man-made environment and seamlessly merges with elements that elsewhere are considered to be part of the natural environment. For Hai//om there is no reason for separating two categorical domains from the start, in that they are interwoven. Such a wider culture concept would allow us to see cultivating and nurturing relationships across the board. It would also, importantly, introduce the idea that cultural models not only differ in their internal categorizations, but also in the way in which any cultural model can be expected to be able to structure and shape the world. As I have shown, the Hai//om case defies an image of the environment as abstract and passive substance 'out there' upon which humans act. At the same time the uncertainties and limitations that environmental forces set for human activity are not considered to be entirely external to what humans think and do, but are built into what we elicit as cultural models of nature.

Notes

1 Field research has been carried out in this area intermittently since 1990. Much of the data discussed in this chapter was collected in 2014 in the Oshikoto Region in northern Namibia, more specifically at several places around a farming area called 'the Mangetti-West' farms. Support for this research was received from the NSF (Award 1330637) and the Collective Research Centre 806 funded by the German Research Council (see www.sfb806.de), which is gratefully acknowledged. My sincere thanks go to all ≠Akhoe Hai//om who supported this work in Namibia.
2 In this respect they are in fact very close to the state-of the art scientific community in which this separation is also increasingly questioned.
3 It may be noted in passing that there is a parallel here in the way in which spatial orientation works in these settings. Hai//om solve spatial orientation problems differently from Bantu-speaking residents of the same environment since they use absolute orientation systems (Neumann and Widlok, 1996; see also Levinson, 2003). However, another striking feature is that many responses need to be classified as 'inconsistent.' This means there is not a clear and 'clean model' understood as mechanistic blueprints that allow only a single strategy to individuals. Rather, this underlines the point that there is considerable freedom in the way in which humans use cultural templates (Widlok, 2007).

References

Bird-David, N. (2017). Before Nation. Scale-Blind Anthropology and Foragers' Worlds of Relatives. Current Anthropology 58(2): 209–220.

Därmann, I. (2011). Kulturtheorien zur Einführung. Hamburg: Junius Hamburg.

Haacke, W., and Eiseb, E. (2002). *A Khoekhoegowab Dictionary*. Windhoek: Gamsberg Macmillan.

Ingold, T. (2015). *The Life of Lines*. Oxford: Routledge.

Levinson, S. (2003). *Space in Language and Cognition. Explorations in Cognitive Diversity*. Cambridge: Cambridge University Press.

Lienhardt, G. (1961). Divinity and Experience. The Religion of the Dinka. Oxford: Clarendon Press.

Neumann, S. and Widlok, Th. (1996). Rethinking some universals of spatial language using controlled comparison. In Dirven, R. and Pütz, M. (eds.), *The Construal of Space in Language and Thought*. Berlin: de Gruyter, 345–369.

Plessner, H. (1983). Über das Welt-Umweltverhältnis des Menschen. In Plessner, H., Conditio Humana. Frankfurt/M.: Suhrkamp, 77–87.

Wagner, R. (1979). The Invention of Culture. Englewood Cliffs, NJ: Prentice-Hall.

Widlok, Th. (1999). *Living on Mangetti. Hai//om 'Bushmen' Autonomy and Namibian Independence*. Oxford: Oxford University Press.

Widlok, Th. (2001). The illusion of a future? Medicine Dance rituals for the civil society of tomorrow. In Widlok, T. and Sugawara, K. (eds.), *Symbolic Categories and Ritual Practice in Hunter-Gatherer Experiences*. African Study Monographs Supplementary Issue. Kyoto: The Center for African Area Studies, 165–183.

Widlok, Th. (2007). Conduction cognitive tasks and interpreting the results: The case of spatial inference tasks. In Wassmann, J. and Stockhaus, K. (eds.), *Experiencing New Worlds*. New York: Berghahn Books, 36–57.

Widlok, Th. (2014). Agency, time and causality. *Frontiers in Psychology* 5: 1264. doi: 10.3389/fpsyg.2014.01264.

10 The earth is getting old

Personification of climate and environmental change by Tagalog fishermen

Katharine L. Wiegele

Introduction

San Andres barrio is an old, traditional fishing community located along the Verde Island Passage in the Philippines, one of the most important and diverse marine ecological zones in the world. Family-owned small-scale commercial fishing enterprises have over generations helped build this densely populated community on the shore of Batangas Bay. From San Andres it is just a five-minute ride by motorized tricycle on a paved road through rice paddies and new subdivisions to the city center of Bauan, of which San Andres barrio is part. Numerous industries line the Batangas Bay, an area busy with shipping vessels coming and going from Batangas Pier.

Dozens of large outrigger boats called *pukotan* (small-scale baby purse seiners with gill nets) crowd the narrow strip of beach between the water's edge and the houses that front it. A crew of 15–20 men using ropes and logs need half a day to push a *pukotan* out of the water onto land. Launching or beaching these boats are not decisions a captain makes lightly.

Moving these large boats from water to land used to happen seasonally with the shift in winds and the onset of typhoon season. *Pukotan* were beached to be out of harm's way until the wind shifted again and calm summer seas signaled the arrival of the deep-sea fishing season. Once the *pukotan* were moved from land to water, when not in use they would stay anchored in the water for most of the summer. During the warm months, fishermen would net different species of schooling fish, the migrations of which they could usually predict depending on the month. Fishermen also timed their capital-intensive fishing expeditions with phases of the moon.

But now the *pukotan* seem to be parked on shore more often than not, no matter what the season. It has become a losing proposition to launch such a large fishing vessel and to maintain the *pukotan*, hire the necessary crew of 15 or more, and employ the smaller boats that assist the enterprise (see Russell, 1997). This is because in recent years, typhoons now batter the area willy-nilly off season—for example, during what the fisherman call the calm season (summer). Long stretches of calm are no longer assured. The weather is erratic, and boat owners cannot afford to beach and launch their

DOI: 10.4324/9781351127905-11

pukotan repeatedly. Furthermore, sometimes no fish at all appear in the bay for weeks or months during the fishing season. When they do, captains can no longer predict the migration of the various fish species they normally capture. And they say timing the fishing according to the phases of the moon, a system they have used for generations, no longer works.

Because of fish scarcity and weather unpredictability, small-scale commercial purse seining is no longer economically viable in San Andres. Besides, the beach has been shrinking by a few meters every year. The beached *pukotan* are almost up against the houses now, and community members believe the large boats will soon have to go. How do these experienced captains, who now sit idly cutting their losses, and their crew, understand the climate and ecological changes that are radically altering their community?

East of Batangas Bay, along the same Verde Island Passage, another coastal community called Olo-olo in the municipality of Lobo confronts some of the same conditions. But their fishing is less capital-intensive; their boats are smaller and operate close to shore, and much of what they catch is for subsistence. They can adjust their fishing strategies when storms arrive out of season. But many rely on agriculture in some capacity for subsistence or cash, and cultivation has been affected by intensifying heat and other weather extremes. Furthermore, fishing is restricted in their community's protected marine area. The municipality has been transitioning to an eco-tourism strategy, restoring and protecting both the land and the marine environment and, at times, educating community members as collaborators. However, the livelihoods of these fishermen may be equally at risk due to this conservation strategy. How do these fishermen understand climate and ecological changes and human-environment relationships compared to the fishermen in San Andres?

The present work is based on six weeks of research at these two field sites in Batangas province, the Philippines, from March to April, 2014, as well as prior research experience in San Andres beginning in 1990. The primary goal of the research is to discover the cultural models of nature held by full-time and subsistence fishermen in this important marine ecological zone, the Verde Island Passage (see Figure 10.2). Developing a picture of the cultural models of nature these food producers use to understand the changes in livelihood that affect them directly could help policymakers and conservationists at all levels, from municipal to international, design implementable strategies that might simultaneously preserve the valuable ecology of the area while maintaining livelihood activities and, hence, the communities themselves.

The fundamental questions driving the research therefore are (a) What is the local knowledge about how and why the climate and the natural environment are changing? (b) How and why are local food-production activities changing? (c) How do fishermen understand human relationships to various elements in the natural environment, including weather, climate, fish, animals, and the supernatural? (d) Are there differences between the two communities in regard to all of the above?

Methodology

I conducted 18 semi-structured interviews about subsistence and food-production activities, and 36 free-listing tasks using a set of components from the research protocol—plants, animals, geographical features, weather, the supernatural, humans (see Introduction, this volume). In the interviews, informants also discussed local environmental conditions and climate and weather patterns, changes in these conditions and patterns, and the possible causes of these changes.

I analyzed these topics conducting a gist analysis, a metaphor analysis, and to a lesser extent a key word analysis on the texts of the semi-structured interviews to identify features of a cultural model of Nature present in the two communities of fishers. Research methods also included analyzing free listing and nature walks with informant narration. Lastly, participant observation was done in the contexts of community life in general, fishing expeditions (including the larger-scale purse-seining and smaller-scale inshore fishing), snorkeling with the volunteer community sea patrol (*bantay dagat*), and activities associated with artificial coral reef construction, sea patrol, and fish marketing.

My observations benefit from a longitudinal perspective in San Andres, where I conducted qualitative ethnographic fieldwork in the early and mid-1990s on rituals and beliefs associated with fishing luck and success and other phenomena.

The field sites

The two fishing communities in Batangas province—San Andres (Bauan municipality) and Olo-olo (Lobo municipality)—were chosen for their variation in terms of the influence of non-governmental and governmental conservation education efforts, the presence of tourism and protected marine areas, the methods of fishing subsistence used, the proximity of industry, and the relative health of the land and the marine habitat. The two communities are part of the southern Tagalog region, where Tagalog is spoken.

Both communities (San Andres and Olo-olo) are located along the Verde Island Passage, a part of the Philippines known as one of the most important marine ecological zones in the world. The entire Philippines is part of the Coral Triangle (see Figure 10.1),

> a marine area located in the western Pacific Ocean. It includes the waters of Indonesia, Malaysia, the Philippines, Papua New Guinea, Timor Leste and Solomon Islands. Named for its staggering number of corals (nearly 600 different species of reef-building corals alone), the region nurtures six of the world's seven marine turtle species and more than 2,000 species of reef fish. The Coral Triangle also supports large populations of commercially important tuna, fueling a multi-billion dollar global tuna

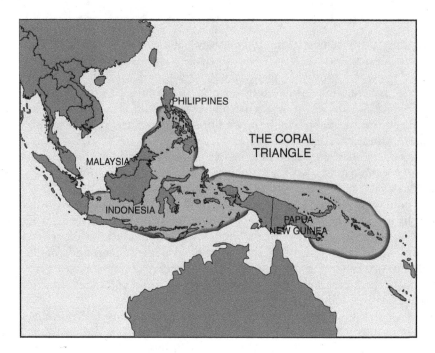

Figure 10.1 The Coral Triangle.

industry. Over 120 million people live in the Coral Triangle and rely on its coral reefs for food, income and protection from storms.

(World Wildlife Fund)

The Philippines is widely recognized as a global priority for marine conservation. There are more marine animals in a meter of ocean water in the Philippines than anywhere else in the Coral Triangle. The Verde Island Passage is between southern Luzon and Mindoro islands (see Figure 10.2). It has the greatest variety of shore-fish species in the Coral Triangle, indicating that a vast wealth of other species resides there as well. For that reason, the Verde Island Passage has been dubbed 'the center of the center of marine biodiversity' in the global context (Carpenter and Springer, 2005).

Bauan, Batangas, the municipality San Andres belongs to, is a community of 81,000 (2010) located on the shore of Batangas Bay around 10 kilometers from Batangas Port. San Andres as a barrio (*barangay*) is known for its high concentration of small-scale baby purse seiners with gill nets (*pukotan*) (see Figure 10.3), but various other types of subsistence and smaller-scale fishing methods are employed with a variety of smaller vessels.

Batangas Bay itself measures around 85 square miles in surface area with 290 miles of coastline. Bauan is the most industrialized municipality in Batangas

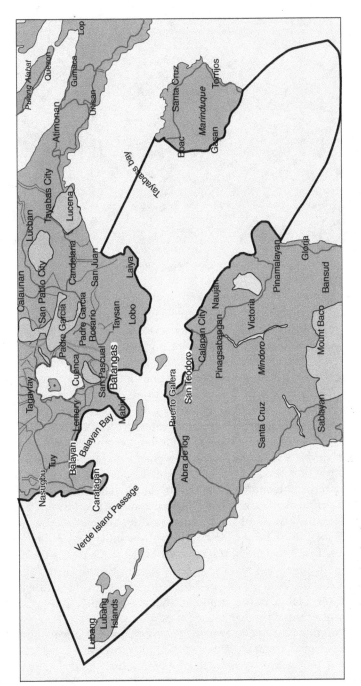

Figure 10.2 The Verde Island Passage.

Figure 10.3 Pukotan: Baby purse seiner, Bauan, Batangas.

Province. The municipality's development priority appears to be industrial-izing and capitalizing on its strategic location with regard to Batangas Port. However, the municipality is home to a number of marine protected areas that are used by local beach and dive resorts for tourist snorkeling and scuba diving. The San Andres area does not have one of the protected areas. The bay in general is a heavily trafficked shipping route. Deep-sea *pukot* fishermen, whose expeditions take them to all areas of the bay, must be careful to steer clear of these large freighters. Numerous industries and communities line the coast. Much of the marine and land habitat has been heavily compromised.

My interviews focused on captains, crew members, and vendors associated with the large fleet of small-scale baby purse seiners. Changes in seasonal weather patterns, including the increasing unpredictability of weather and storms, affects them greatly. The boats, nets, and other equipment are expen-sive to maintain because of the large size of the vessels and nets. Crew of around 15 men must be retained along with smaller vessels that assist in fishing trips. Costs to launch the boat, to beach it, or to engage in fishing expeditions include fuel, municipal fishing permits, and boat registration. As mentioned, the vessels must be beached during stormy weather and re-launched later, a labor-intensive and costly proposition.

Uncertainty caused by changing climate and weather patterns or declines in fish populations can spell permanent economic collapse for a boat owner and his crew. Smaller-scale fishers (for example those who use smaller boats and crews of 1–5 men) have more flexibility in terms of altering their fishing patterns in response to unusual and unexpected weather variation; they also have lower economic stakes with less capital investment.

Pukot fishermen have always dealt with a degree of unpredictability, not to mention uncertainty and danger. In addition to expert knowledge of seasonal winds, storm and weather patterns, lunar cycles, and fish behavior, fishermen have used economic and organizational strategies, kinship networks, luck rituals, charms, and Roman Catholic rituals such as boat blessings (Wiegele, 1991). However, their traditional coping strategies appear to be losing effectiveness given the increase in weather-related uncertainty and unpredictability, and the scarcity of fish.

Lobo, Batangas, the municipality Olo-olo belongs to, is a city of 37,000 (2010) approximately 60 km east of Bauan. In contrast with some areas of Bauan, its entire coastal area is a relatively pristine marine and shoreline environment. There are no large industries in the area, and its location outside Batangas Bay means it is relatively unaffected by major shipping traffic. The municipality has a progressive agro-tourism vision of growth that emphasizes ecological balance, sustainable growth (social, cultural, and economic), and food. There are many beach and dive resorts. In 2005, the Lobo municipal government declared one area of its shoreline a fish sanctuary, and now the entire three kilometers of shoreline and 300 meters (980 feet) fronting the shore have been declared a protected area. As stated, fishermen in this field site area do primarily part-time subsistence fishing (they also farm). They use a variety of fishing techniques and boats, but in no way as large as the *pukot* fishing found in Bauan. Artificial reefs have been installed in some areas, and exposure to governmental and non-governmental conservation training among locals is more common in Lobo compared to Bauan. Olo-olo is one of the town's small coastal barrios (*barangay*).

General normative understandings of seasons and moon phases

Seasons: In both communities, informants' direct experiences with the seasons and seasonal weather variation were primary topics of concern in the semi-structured interviews about subsistence. Fishermen need expert knowledge of seasonal winds, storm and weather patterns, and lunar cycles (as these correspond to fish behavior and seafaring conditions) in their fishing activities. Those whose activities are more associated with the land and farming are more attuned to temperature and rainfall and to a lesser extent, lunar cycles. The word for season, *panahon,* which also means era, weather, and climate, was the second most salient word after *isda* 'fish' in the key word analysis of the semi-structured interviews. The word for month and moon, *buwan,* was the third most salient word, with *dagat* 'sea' coming in fourth.

Although the calendar months of the year (January, February, and so forth) were used secondarily as reference points; informants primarily described two seasons in terms of (a) temperature and rainfall or (b) wind direction. *Tagulan* 'rainy seasons' and *taginit/tagtuyo* 'hot/dry season' are common terms, however among fishermen and to some extent in fishing communities generally, seasons are primarily labeled in reference to the prevailing monsoon wind directions: *habagat* 'west or southwest wind' and *amihan* 'northeast wind' seasons. Fishermen occasionally referenced seasons according to wind/sea current strength: *lakasin/taglakas* 'strong season' and *kalmahin* 'calm season.'

The full-time fishermen in Bauan were more likely to characterize the seasons according to wind direction and wind strength/sea current strength than were the part-time fishermen, who also cultivate. As mentioned, these latter were more likely to include use temperature and rainfall designations to distinguish seasons.

Many changes in annual seasonal patterns were noted by fishermen and other locals (see below). The free-listing results support the saliency of wind direction and strength (and hence the importance of typhoons and their timing) for the small-scale, full-time commercial fishermen in San Andres, Bauan, and the additional saliency of heat and rainfall for the more casual fishermen in Olo-olo, Lobo, whose subsistence depends both on cultivation and fishing. Both the results of the free-listing tasks and key-word analysis confirm the saliency of typhoons, wind, wind direction, heat, and rain.

Fixed calendar months of the year were used primarily as reference points when fishermen and other community members were comparing changes in weather patterns over time. For instance, typhoons now arrive sporadically in March and April, while twenty years ago this was unheard of and, in recent years, the rainy season extends into the traditional start of the school year, prompting school administrations to delay the school year starting date.

The moon and fish behavior: In both communities, fishermen use the phases of the moon to time fishing trips, at least until recently. In addition, and perhaps tangentially, some farmers noted a positive connection between rice seedling growth and a waxing moon phase, while crabs in the sea and sometimes fish were noted to grow more during a waxing moon in perhaps a parallel fashion (see also Bennardo and de Lima, this volume, for similar concepts in Tonga and Amazonia). However, in San Andres especially, many fishers observed that the traditional system of using the moon to time fishing expeditions is now 'broken.' In other words, timing fishing with phases of the moon is no longer an effective technique for increasing catches. This was attributed either to the general lack of fish due to pollution in the bay, changes in weather patterns, or unknown/unknowable reasons.

Changes in the environment, climate, and weather patterns

Locals in both communities noted many changes in the natural environment and the weather (often climate and weather were used interchangeably). Many of these changes had a direct impact on their livelihood as fishers and cultivators. The following are translated informant gist statements created using the informants' words.

San Andres, Bauan

> The beach is smaller by 50 meters (thus the houses are closer to the sea).
> The seasons are more unpredictable (typhoons during dry season, delay of seasons).
> The weather changes more abruptly (from hot to cold, rain to shine).
> The weather is 'stronger' (extreme heat, extreme rain, more powerful storms).
> More rain comes with storms, there is more flooding.
> We are more 'exposed.'
>> The mountains are deforested.
>> The houses are closer to the sea (due to sea level rise).
> There are no corals or plants in the bay.
> There are fewer fish per catch and throughout the year.
> The bay water is warmer.
> The behavior and presence of fish in Batangas Bay is unusually unpredictable with regard to
>> Seasonal presence of species
>> Seasonal quantity
>> Presence during phases of moon
>> Length of time specific species stay in the bay
>> Quantity of fish available for capture annually
>> Annual variety of schooling species typically caught (number down from 10 to 2–3)

Changes in seasonal weather patterns, especially the onset of rainy seasons, were so pronounced that officials were contemplating a shift in the school year calendar at the time of this fieldwork. In addition, there had been several years recently in which *pukot* fishermen caught no fish for the entire year.

Olo-Olo, Lobo

> The storms come out of season (typhoons come during dry season).
> The cold season extends longer.
> The hot season extends longer.
> The environment has become 'stronger.'
> The heat and cold are more extreme.
> There are more abrupt changes in temperature.
> The thunder and lightning are more frightening now.
> The weather is hotter, dryer, more windy.
> There is more flooding, erosion.

A few informants in Lobo reported no changes in the weather, environment, or climate. A few reported that their environment was being gradually restored because municipal laws regarding the use of land and marine resources were being enforced.

Causes of changes in climate, environment, and weather

Among informants' explanations of the changes in climate, the environment, and weather patterns they had observed, the following themes emerged in a causality analysis of gist statements, suggesting some patterns in the relationships between humans, the natural physical environment, and weather.

Climate and weather are beyond human agency

The tendency to view climate and weather as beyond human agency in general was noted in both field sites. The following are examples of gist statements to this effect.

> There is nothing humans can do [regarding changes in weather patterns].
> Humans cannot know why the climate changes, we can only observe the changes.
> The climate affects us, we do not affect the climate.
> The climate changes and we have to adjust.
> We can adjust, but there will come a time when we can no longer adjust.

Some of these statements might reflect the concepts of balance and equilibrium as fundamental elements of life as described by Jocano (2001) in his ethnographically non-specific, long-term comparative studies of Philippine culture and worldview. This traditional conception, while not explicitly articulated in my field sites, may contribute to understanding some of the unconscious aspects of the cultural model of Nature I am investigating, and deserves further discussion.

In this model, as Jocano explains, life processes involve a balance of positive and negative forces such as hot/cold, growth/decay, male/female, and so forth. This balancing process, which applies to all living things, inherently involves temporary imbalance that brings about growth (similar to a metabolic process) necessary to keep things developing. Humans should remain neutral in this process (2001: 27). The role of humans is one of adjustment or adaptation in order to maintain balance. Adjustment is part of the dynamic of human-natural world relations. Adjustment may involve change in values, attitudes, and relations. However, it is possible to have unfavorable disequilibrium that can bring disaster or destruction so great that it cannot be repaired (see Zhang, this volume, for a similar concept among the Kachin in southwest China). This model implies that humans are part of nature and are in a dynamic relationship with nature.

The general tendency to view climate and weather as beyond human control may stem from this underlying model of human-nature relations. In the statements above, humans adjust to climate (and weather) changes but do not change the climate. There is also a recognition here and in other statements (see below) that weather and climate changes may eventually reach a tipping point at which they are broken beyond repair and/or humans can no longer adjust.

Human activities in this area destroy the Bay habitat

While informants generally do not conceive of weather and climate as within human agency, many reported that people create pollution that destroys the natural environment, specifically the nearby, immediate environment and the people who live in or exploit this environment. This activity was often linked to the health of the Batangas Bay habitat. A few also connected pollution to increased heat and lower fish stock in the bay. Many attributed the rise in sea level to activities of industries in Batangas Bay. None spoke of human activities generally or on a global scale as causing environmental destruction (although three people blamed shortcomings in Filipino national character). The following gist statements illustrate this point.

> Industries here dumped soil in the bay causing the water level here to rise. (Bauan)
> Corporations, ships, refineries pollute Batangas Bay. (Bauan)
> My neighbors dump garbage in the bay. (Bauan)
> Bay pollution makes the water hotter. (Bauan)
> Developments here leave no space for mangroves. (Bauan)
> Illegal fishing methods scare the fish away. (Bauan)
> Factories destroy corals. (Bauan)
> The destruction of the environment causes too much heat. (Bauan)
> The weather is hotter because there's too much development now. (Bauan)
> Fish cannot reproduce when the weather is too hot. (Bauan)
> Fish die/go away when it is too hot. (Bauan)
> Deforestation causes flooding. (Lobo)
> Filipinos are 'hard-headed' by nature; they will never stop. Some people are just greedy. Others are only supporting their families. (Lobo)

You cannot blame people, corporations, or the government

Although industry and development in the immediate vicinity cause habitat destruction, health problems (air pollution), and a decline in the fishing industry in Batangas Bay, many of the Bauan fishermen state that these activities are inevitable and unavoidable due to the inherent roles and responsibilities of family members, industry, and government, as these gist statements illustrate.

> Corporations ruined the bay, but we rely on them for jobs to support our families.
> Working for the companies cannot be avoided.
> The government sells the land to corporations, but the government must develop the country.

People use illegal fishing methods, but they are also trying to support their families.

Explanations referencing God

Though not a dominant theme, some informants offered Christian-based understandings of weather and climate change. These statements combined aspects of other explanations mentioned here, including human culpability (and agency by implication), lack of human agency, the weather/climate as a human metaphor (see below), the weather/climate as a cycle metaphor (see below), and the unknowability of weather/climate. The following gist statements and direct quotes place God in a variety of relationships to humans and the climate.

Maybe the weather changes because God is punishing the people.
God is mad at the people because they are getting wiser than God, they are bad, crazy.
People lack faith, prayer, going to church.
'Only God can know why the weather reverses.'
'The environment is having a tantrum. Even God is having a tantrum.'
'Personally, I don't know why the weather changes because neither we nor God make the weather, but the natural environment does it.'
'They said that the weather (climate) from before will soon return. The past will return according to the Bible.'

Fishermen in San Andres in the early 1990s described to me strategies for increasing fishing success, luck, and safety that went beyond financial investment, personal skill, and diligence. These included boat-blessing rituals and the boat *compadre* 'god-parenthood' system within the colonial Spanish Catholic tradition, and *anting-anting*, secret charms that increased fishing luck. *Anting-anting* took many forms, all inanimate, both man-made (such as an old coin) and natural. The latter were spontaneously 'found,' sometimes in a forest nearby that was considered 'wild.' Often *anting-anting* took forms homologous to aspects of fish capture, for example, a (dead) hummingbird caught in a spider web or a part of a plant that resembled a noose (Wiegele, 1991).

As *anting-anting* are charms, they can account for fishing luck but are not evoked to explain scarcity or unfavorable fishing conditions. During my 2014 stay, for example, since *pukot* captains were sitting idle and not taking fishing expeditions (no one was having success at the time), I offered to pay for fuel and other expenses if one of the captains would launch an excursion and bring me along as an observer. During that excursion, the crew took in a fairly sizable catch, going against the long, unsuccessful streak all fishermen were having at the time. Seizing upon the fact that I was somehow good luck, the crew set out a second time in the same night and invited me along. I declined, but they went anyway and, using the rest of fuel I had purchased, they took in an additional, but lesser catch. They reasoned the second time that my luck still lingered on the boat, perhaps through the fuel. However, the general decline in fishing success in the community was not attributed to supernatural entities, charms, or the lack thereof.

Both *anting-anting* and Christian rituals (e.g., blessings) involve reciprocity between the entity and humans. Traditionally, as they were described to me in 1990, *anting-anting* needed to be maintained through secrecy and prayers; Catholic rites required faith in God and due respect to communal Catholic expectations. In addition, environmental animate beings such as *duwende* (small invisible dwarfs or goblins that live in houses, in trees, in mounds, or underground) provided humans good luck or misfortune depending in part of how they were treated by humans.

Because in Tagalog the concept of 'supernatural' is not present as a cover term or idea, the free-listing task based on it was not successful. Informants could list 'spirits' if asked to do so, but even this term excluded many animate entities, not the least of which are Christian-based (such as God, the Holy Spirit, saints) even though the informants were all Christian and mostly Catholic. Environmental entities such as *duwende* were not included in lists of spirits although knowledge of *duwende* is widespread. Even so, it is fair to say from these few examples from 1990 and 2014 that humans, God, and other supernatural entities are connected reciprocally in a variety of ways to the physical environment (geographical features, plants, and weather) and animals (including fish) (see also Magos, 1994).

Metaphors used to explain climate and weather pattern change

In both communities, two metaphors were used to understand and talk about climate and weather changes: (1) the climate/weather as human, and (2) climate/weather change as a cycle.

Personification of weather/climate (weather/climate as human metaphor)

In this metaphor, the weather has moods, reactions, idiosyncrasies, and a life cycle similar to those of humans. The most widespread application of this metaphor is that the weather, the earth, or the climate is getting old. It was used often to explain changes in climate and weather patterns, as the following quotes, translated from Tagalog, illustrate.

> The weather is like a human. It gets mad. It gets silent.
> The people can't be stopped, that's why the environment is having a
>   tantrum.
> The weather gets wild even when it's not the time for it to be wild.

The weather gets bored and we make our adjustments.

The weather here is kind to us [in reference to the typical climate of the area].

The weather [pattern] changes because it is getting old. An old person changes his mind a lot.

Personification metaphors also emerged when informants spoke of animals' lives. Certain sea animals have sentient lives, knowledge, feelings, fears, altruism, and guardian roles. These include especially whales, dolphins, sharks, whale sharks, turtles, and octopus. Fish have some of these capacities to a lesser degree. Young and old animals are qualitatively different and may react differently to things (pollution, heat, noise, illegal nets). Larger species of fish are sometimes considered older. Personification metaphors emerged in the free-listing tasks as well as the interviews.

The free-listing tasks I administered in these fishing communities, which elicited word lists from informants about suggested components of Nature from the research protocol (plants, animals, geographical features, weather, the supernatural, humans), revealed a wealth of knowledge and categories in the area of sea life. The original components for the listing tasks were modified during the course of the fieldwork after successive interviews, in response to interactions with informants. The component 'animals,' for example, elicited only land animals at first. Therefore a 'sea animals' component was added to the listing tasks (see Bennardo, this volume, for a similar issue).

When 'sea animals' elicited mainly non-fish (especially dolphins, turtles, and whales) and occasionally the word 'fish,' it was determined that fish comprised, not surprisingly, a salient component, and needed to be asked about directly. Lists of fish tended to be recalled in subgroups, the most salient of which were fish for capture and other fish, as might be expected since the majority of informants were fishermen, and secondarily, fish vendors.

Combining the qualitative ethnographic observations made during this task with the content of the semi-structured and unstructured interviews reveals that other salient categories based on a variety of criteria might be contained within the fish and sea life categories, and within the fish for capture/other fish categories. For example, dolphins, turtles, and whales, salient in the category of 'sea animals,' are all creatures that tended to be personified to a great extent in stories informants told. They were often ascribed human emotions, such as sea turtles that showed sadness at human actions by crying; human-like motivations such as a whale that sacrificed its own life to save a drowning human; octopus who will only be caught if they want to be caught; and personified roles, such as whales and dolphins as guardians of the sea. In addition, stories described human interactions with these animals in terms that mimicked human-to-human relationships.

Fish were rarely if ever personified, however the category of fish needs to be explored in more detail through sorting tasks. Categories suggested by the ethnographic observation of the free-listing task include 'young' and 'old' fish species, sea creatures legally prohibited from capture, seasonal/migrating fish, and fish for capture, but more are likely to exist.

In Olo-olo, Lobo, a community with a healthier land habitat where many informants had close contact with an intact and protected forest environment (in addition to the marine environment), people have more extensive knowledge of the animal and plant life within the forest compared to people in San Andres, Bauan. The notion of 'young' versus 'old' deserves more exploration, as this concept appeared with reference to forest animals as well. More targeted investigation into these rich areas of local knowledge is called for based on the results of this research.

Weather and climate change as cyclical

The 'climate/weather change as a cycle' metaphor used by Batangas fishermen has two subtypes, (a) and (b) below.

(a) The climate and the earth have a human-like life cycle with an end. This metaphor is widespread in both communities. It is an aspect of personification connected to the 'climate/weather as human' metaphor, as in 'the earth/weather/climate is getting old.' It is illustrated in the following quote:

> It will end, but gradually, from hunger, from difficulties in work, in the system of work in the sea. Maybe that's what they call the end of the earth. Maybe it's almost like the earth getting old. It's normal that it gets old. It will die. It won't become young again. It will get even older. Nothing will be young again. Because the people here can't be disciplined anymore. They're hard-headed.
>
> (Bauan fisherman)

(b) The earth's climate and the annual weather cycle are changing in a continuously turning cycle. This metaphor evokes small and large continuous cycles and is also used to describe a fisherman's economic life.

—Weather Cycles (small)
'Ever since I was a child the weather cycled between hot, cold, hot, cold and it always returned.'

—Climate and Earth Cycles (large)
The earth turns. It's just their time to get typhoons now.' [referring to people who live in areas not normally effected by typhoons, but who are now experiencing typhoons]

The earth turns differently [now].

[Researcher: Did the weather during your childhood get bored, too? (see above)] No, because that's how the environment is, it doesn't stay the same, it just comes and goes.

They said that the weather [climate] from before will soon return. The past will return according to the Bible.

—Fishermen's cycles (small)

The life of a fisherman is like a wheel. Sometimes you're up, sometimes you're down.

Every day, sometimes we have some, sometimes we don't. It goes around, returns.

Possible features of a cultural model of nature

Humans, animals, weather, climate and the earth are linked by shared characteristics. The notion of a human steward role is found mostly among people who have been exposed to conservation education. It is stronger in Lobo where more people have attended conservation seminars (see Austin, 2014 for a similar observation among fishermen in Palawan, the Philippines). The changes in weather patterns and the local natural environment people are experiencing seem to be understood in various ways:

- The earth, like a human, has a natural life cycle and is entering the end of it.
- The earth is returning to a previous phase in a continuous cycle.
- In both cases, humans can do nothing about changes in weather patterns and climate (and by extension do not cause them); humans can only adjust to these changes.
- There will come a time when the environment is 'broken' beyond repair and humans won't be able to adjust.
- Human activities in the immediate vicinity are responsible for local environmental degradation, the depletion of fish supply, and the rise in sea level.
- These changes (above) are mostly inevitable.
- For the most part, people cannot hold other people accountable for environmental degradation because people, corporations, and governments are just performing their roles.
- Filipino national character (hard-headedness) is partially to blame for local environmental degradation but it cannot be changed.
- Humans, animals, weather, climate and the earth are linked by shared characteristics.
- Supernatural entities, the weather, the physical environment, people, plants, and animals are reciprocally related.

This list of propositions suggests that the major components of Nature (humans, plants, animals, weather, physical environment, and the supernatural) are related to each other holistically. In this approach or model humans are the source of a personification metaphor that explains how Nature in general and the earth (holistically) work—through cycles of life moving naturally from young to old (to death), or cycles of life that involve continuous regeneration. God may act through nature (especially the weather and the earth in general) or the weather and the earth may have a 'life' of their own; either way they have moods and emotions that parallel those of humans (see Boyer, 2008). Furthermore, humans, God, and other supernatural entities are connected reciprocally in a variety of ways to the physical environment (geographical features, plants, and weather), and animals (including fish). Even global concepts such as 'the earth' and 'the climate' are at times conceived in human terms.

I consider this list of propositions to be significant parts of a cultural model of Nature held by San Andres and Olo-olo community members. This model reflects the complex mix of traditions and contemporary situations of people who have multiple historical and cultural influences (Wiegele, 2005, 2011; Austin, 2014). In addition, the fishermen in these two communities have vastly different experiences with their environment in terms of preservation and degradation, as well as changing weather patterns, both of which present challenges to their livelihood. Taking into consideration the cultural model of Nature these food producers use to understand the changes in livelihood that affect them directly could help policymakers and conservationists at all levels, from municipal to international, design implementable strategies that might simultaneously preserve the valuable ecology of the area while maintaining livelihood activities and, hence, communities.

References

Austin, R. (2014). Environmental values and cultural models among fisherfolk and NGOs in Honda Bay. In Eder, J. and Evangelista, O. (eds.), *Palawan and Its Global Connections*. Quezon City: Ateneo de Manila Press.

Boyer, P. (2008). *Cognitive Aspects of Religious Symbolism*. Cambridge: Cambridge University Press.

Carpenter, K. E., and Springer, V. G. (2005). The center of the center of marine shore fish biodiversity: The Philippine Islands. *Environmental Biology of Fishes* 72: 467–480.

Jocano, F. L. (2001). *Filipino Worldview: Ethnography of Local Knowledge*. Quezon City: Punlad Research House.

Magos, A. P. (1994). The concept of *Mari-it* in Panaynon Maritime Worldview. In Ushijima, I. and Zayas, C. N. (eds.), *Fishers of the Visayas: Visayas Maritime Anthropological Studies*. Quezon City: University of the Philippines Press, 305–355.

Russell, S. D. (1997). Class identity, leadership style, and political culture in a Tagalog fishing community. *Pilipinas, a Journal of Philippine Studies* 28: 79–95.

Wiegele, K. (1991). Luck and Ritual in a Philippine Fishing Community. Unpublished MA thesis, Northern Illinois University.

Wiegele, K. (2005). *Investing in Miracles: El Shaddai and the Transformation of Popular Catholicism in the Philippines*. Honolulu: University of Hawai'I Press.

Wiegele, K. L. (2011). Everyday Catholicism: Expanding the Sacred Sphere in the Philippines, in Adams, K. and Gillogly, K. (eds.), *Everyday Life in Southeast Asia*. Bloomington: Indiana University Press.

World Wildlife Fund website. www.worldwildlife.org/places/coral-triangle.

11 Flowing between certainty and uncertainty rhythmically

Spirits' power and human efforts in a Kachin Cultural Model of Nature and environment in southwest China

Wenyi Zhang

Introduction

One hot afternoon in 2015, my Kachin friend and I walked to his walnut field on the mountainside along a road that leads to Burma and is locally called the business road because it was built particularly for the China–Burma trade. My friend, a college graduate in the 1960s from a local university and now in his early sixties, had worked in the local government for about ten years and came back to his village as a peasant in the 1980s. He told me that five years earlier he had planted a lot of *amomum tsao-ko* (a spicy ingredient favored by many Chinese) and earned a lot of money. The amomum tsao-ko requires a shaded (cool) and damp environment.

'Previously, my field was perfect for it. It is close to a rivulet and well shaded by big trees; more importantly, it is also near the business road, making my work much easier.' He is considerably nostalgic for his good life with a decent income in the old days, when the temperature was not so high in this region. 'Now, the weather climbs up along the hills, and our village and field become hot. My amomum tsao-ko grows very well but bears no fruit. This year, my son's father-in-law earned big money from his amomum tsao-ko field.' His son's father-in-law lives in Xima, a village about three hours' bus away, where it was known for its poverty and for the cold weather on the top of the mountain. No crops grew well there, 'even the ears of corn did not bend down! But now, our weather has moved up there, while the weather of the valley moved up to our village and field.' He sat on a stone on one side of the road, seeming to become too weary to walk. 'It seems that the altitude of my place has been lowered down. The weather has moved away, and animals have done so, too. They went to Xima or Burma. Plants cannot move. They die or grow rapidly without bearing fruit. Before, we Kachin moved along too, but now we are stuck here [by the Chinese Hùkǒu system],' he concluded.[1]

He explained that nature and climate move rhythmically. Previously, humans read signals from nature and followed the rhythm. 'We read our divination table (see Table 11.1) no matter what we did, so we knew the right time for the right thing.' Nowadays, humans have excessive desires and

DOI: 10.4324/9781351127905-12

do not follow nature. Nature is still rhythmic and knowable, while human desires are endless and unpredictable. Humans follow their desires, and the gap between the certainty of natural rhythm and uncertainty of human desires is increasing continuously.

As my fieldwork proceeded, I came to realize how my friend's view of nature and climate change illustrates the local views of nature and environment here in southwest China. In this chapter, I elaborate on these views using the concept of the cultural model (Bennardo, 2009; Bennardo and De Munck, 2014; Kronenfeld, 2008; Strauss and Quinn, 1997). I base my examination upon Kachin villagers' basic notions and principles of the local religious and medical tradition of animal sacrifice, which serves as the primary resource for attributing causes for major problems. Animal sacrifice saves human life by sacrificing animal life to spirits that make people ill. Spirits penetrate people's lives. They allocate preordained fates to individuals, shaping the latter's life, death, achievements, and even the afterworld life. They circumscribe details of people's activities, such as when and where one might go so as to avoid bad luck. In this regard, animal sacrifice captures basic causal relations among a number of fundamental and constitutive categories of Nature, such as people, animals, plants, weather, physical environment, and the supernatural (Ho, 1999; Atran and Medin, 2008). I describe this causality in terms of the local scheme of time, according to which the Kachin regulate their activities rhythmically. In specifying this scheme, I then propose a Kachin cultural model of nature and environment. In particular, I will phrase the model as three propositions, according to which the remainder of the chapter will be organized.

Before I move to the details of the Kachin view of nature and environment, I need to specify the meanings of terms words used in this chapter. The English word 'nature' does not have an exact Kachin translation, though my informants definitely have a clear idea of nature. For them, nature does not refer to a thing, but rather to a process or a condition. During interviews, most villagers said they believe that there must be a Kachin word for 'nature' (as a noun), but nobody could remember it, including those who often write in Kachin (one of the Tibeto–Burman languages of the region). Instead, villagers talked about 'nature' as a verb or an adverb. On the one hand, in daily conversations they say something exists naturally ($sha^{31}hkai^{55}$ $bing^{31}$ ai^{33}),[2] meaning that its existence is predetermined and beyond human control. Villagers pay more attention to the process of creating things or of how things change, rather than the things themselves. On the other hand, they use two words to refer to things naturally formed in the world, namely, the components of nature (as a noun): $ma^{31}tut^{31}$ refers to plants produced by the motherland (nam^{33} $ma^{31}tut^{31}$ refers to wild plants, and $ma^{31}tut^{31}$ to cultivated plants. In the language of Kachin, the land is always called the motherland), and $nhprang^{31}$ refers to wild animals and minerals that are not directly produced by the motherland. A couple of villagers also used these two words as a translation of the Chinese word for 'nature' (*ziran*, meaning 'naturally' on its own as an adverb, or 'nature' as a noun). Most villagers in my fieldwork sites speak some Chinese and some of them use the English word 'nature' (a couple of villagers from Burma know some English). In particular, weather is called $la^{31}mu^{31}$ $ma^{31}rang^{33}$ ($la^{31}mu^{31}$ 'the sky' and $ma^{31}rang^{33}$ 'rain'), and both weather and climate are called $ga^{31}tsi^{33}$ $ga^{31}htet^{55}$ (literally, 'cold and hot'). Weather follows its natural rhythm ($a^{31}hka^{33}$ $la^{31}do^{31}$: $a^{31}hka^{33}$ 'things related to season and weather,' $la^{31}do^{31}$ 'stages'). Based on these explications, below I will use the word 'nature' to refer to the process/state of the surroundings the Kachin live in (e.g., weather, climate change, people, and spirits), and use the word 'environment' referring to the physical objects/components of the surroundings.

The Kachin and my fieldwork

The Kachin live astride the borders of Burma, China, and India.[3] They have been a well-known case in the literature of anthropology regarding historical transformation of their marriage and political systems (Leach, 1954, Robbine and Sadan, 2007). Kachin in China were politically, economically, and culturally controlled by the Chinese owing to their intermediary position in the caravan-trade of China, Tibet, and Southeast Asia (Ho, 1997; Wang, 1997), and to their disassociate relations with the states or kingdoms in Southeast Asia largely in times of war (Fernquest, 2006). From the late eighteenth century, major Chinese caravan trade routes passed through the Kachin Hills. The trade, largely attributed to the rise of kingdoms in Yunnan such as Nanzhao and Dali (sixth to thirteen centuries), which shaped ethnic configurations of the region (Backus, 1981).

Various theoretical models of political and sociocultural transformation based on the Kachin case have been generalized for understanding the politics between lowland polities and upland chieftainships in mainland Southeast Asia (Leach, 1954; Friedman, 1979; Lehman, 1989; Nugent, 1982; Zhang and Chitlaing, 2013). Currently, the Kachin case is intensely discussed by scholars with a Southeast Asian perspective, who consider ethnic groups in Yunnan (including Kachin, Wa, Dai and so on) a politico-economic and sociocultural intersection between China and mainland Southeast Asia, playing the role of middlemen (Chit Hlaing, 2009; Giersch, 2001). Kachin have been playing such a role among Chinese, Dai, Burmese and many others in the China-Burma border areas for centuries, and so the most of Kachin individuals are multilingual (Hill, 1998).

From 2003 to 2011, I conducted 32 months of fieldwork, mostly in Sama Village and its four neighboring villages in the Tongbiguan Village Tract, Yingjiang County, Yunnan Province. These villages have been interconnected by marriage for hundreds of years. There are about five hundred adults, over 90 percent ethnic Kachin. Sama is a Kachin cultural center in China. One of the two greatest specialists of animal sacrifice in Tongbiguan Village Tract lives there. Before 1953, when the Chinese Communists took the Kachin Hills, Sama was the headquarters of the most powerful Kachin chief in China (the *Nhkum*[31] *Du*[33] *Wa*[33]), who controlled most areas of today's Yingjiang and Longchuan counties. Currently, the Jianbian Administrative Office (the lowest local governmental office) is in Sama. It governs Sama and its four neighboring villages. In 2014, I also conducted intensive interviews with sixty villagers (including eight religious specialists, three government officials, and people who are fluent in Chinese and Kachin, and those who speak only Kachin, male:female = 2:1, Christians:non-Christians = 1:2).

Most interviews were conducted while I stayed with people, meeting with them in their fields, focusing on natural objects and phenomena I could see and think of during my fieldwork. I asked about names of, and daily expressions regarding, objects and phenomena in the Kachin language, whether and how people use the objects or deal with the phenomena in their daily life, and what will they do if the objects or phenomena do not appear as expected. Based on preliminary analysis of interview data, I conducted dozens of semi-structured interviews with religious specialists and oral-history tellers, relating the objects/phenomena I observed to their belief and cosmologies. I asked about rituals for tackling problems caused by people's inconsistency with their environment, and how and why they specify time and space for conducting the rituals. During the years of fieldwork, I have attended most of the rituals mentioned in our conversations and, in the interviews I also focused on details I observed in rituals relating them to other details concerning the Kachin genesis stories and daily life. In particular, I also conducted a few semi-structured interviews with officials in charge of development projects managed by the local county government, and I asked about the impact of the projects on the local environment.

During fieldwork in 2014–2015, I spent at least one day every week to preliminarily analyze the data I had collected. I first looked for key words and metaphors based on the frequency of use by villagers, and I designed further questions for follow-up interviews. Then, I worked to discover relations among these key words through reasoning and thematic analyses of the interview data. From the results of these analyses, I designed questions for further interviews to either verify or disprove the relations discovered. I often told villagers the relations among key words I thought I had found and asked for their comments. I also resorted to religious specialists for understanding comments in relation to the Kachin use of time. In particular, my previous fieldwork on the Kachin tradition of animal sacrifice and their use of the div-ination table (see Table 11.1) helped me specify the local way of conceiving causality regarding the relations between humans and their environment.

The first proposition

Following the certainty of nature

I specify the first proposition of the Kachin cultural model of nature and environment from the local views of temporal rhythm. During my interviews and daily conversations, I found that 'rhythm' is the first and most-used key word when villagers talk about their relations with things in the world. This word appeared in almost all semi-structured interviews and daily conversations, and people often talked about it by using a metaphor: Things move as if sliding over joints of a bamboo pole. People have to go past each joint one by one—avoiding a joint might mean falling off the bamboo pole. Ordinary villagers always refer to the time/rhythm of the world, while religious specialists refer to the divination table.

The second and third salient key words are 'spirits' and 'flow,' and they appeared more frequently in daily life conversations with ordinary villagers than in semi-structured interviews with religious specialists and oral history tellers. My understanding of the relation among these three key words is based on the local rhythmic alternation of the rainy and wet seasons and, concomitantly, the people's activity pattern I observed.

A year starts with the dry season, and alternation of the dry and wet seasons establishes the local cycle of agriculture. The twelve months of a year are evenly allocated into six units, with three in the dry season and three in the wet season. The first unit, $Ma^{31}ji^{33}$ $Ma^{31}ka^{55}$ Ta^{33} (October and November in the Chinese Lunar calendar), is for harvest and celebration ($ma^{31}ji^{33}ma^{31}ka^{33}$: to celebrate; ta^{33}: month). The second unit, $Hkru^{55}$ $Ra^{33}Ta^{33}$ (December and January), is the period in which everyone has enough food for celebrating the New Year and always feeling full following the harvest ($Hkru^{55}$: being full; ra^{33}: being ordinary or average as all people get almost the same amount of rice). The third unit, Wut^{31} $Sha^{31}la^{31}$ Ta^{33} (February and March), is the period for planning and starting a year's agricultural work (wut^{31}: to plan a whole year's work; $sha^{31}la^{31}$: to begin the work with cutting a swidden field). The dry season is dry and cold, when things fade and die. It is the male's time, beginning with men's killing of small animals (chickens and small pigs) in making sacrifice to spirits and praying for fortune and protection for their trading trips. During most of the dry season, men conduct business far from home. The dry season ends when males come back home and sacrifice large animals (pigs and buffalos) to the spirits, thanking them and seeking blessings for a new cycle of cultivation in the coming rainy season. As important parts of these rituals, males narrate history, chant genealogy, and read the divination table to identify proper periods for specific activities.

As people finish planning their cultivation, the rainy season comes. Its first unit, $Ja^{31}htum^{33}$ $Sa^{31}ngang^{33}$ ta^{33} (April and May), is the period for planting seedlings in the paddy fields and corn in the swidden fields ($ja^{31}htum^{33}$). When seeds germinate, people will tell how well they may grow ($sa^{31}ngang^{33}$). In the second unit, Shi^{33} $Ma^{31}ri^{33}$ Gup^{31} Shi^{33} ta^{33} (June and July), it rains hard, making the work in the field difficult. Initially, the rain flies with the wind, and crops do not head (shi^{33} $ma^{31}ri^{33}$). Later, the rain falls perpendicularly helping crops head, and people who plant early can anticipate the harvest (Gup^{31} shi^{33}). The third unit, Gup^{31} $Tung^{33}$ $Ka^{31}la^{55}$

Ta^{33} (August and September), is the period in which crops fully head (gup^{31} $tung^{33}$), and people feel satisfied when a harvest is anticipated (-la^{55}: 'happy'). The rainy season is wet and hot. It is the time when women grow gardens, gather wild vegetables, exchange agricultural products in the local market and gifts among relatives. A female is thus considered the guardian of all kinds of corn seeds (n^{31}'$hpro^{31}$ n^{31}'$hkye^{33}$ $ga^{31}nu^{31}$: n^{31}'$hpro^{31}$ and n^{31}'$hkye^{33}$, respectively, white corn and red corn; $ga^{31}nu^{31}$, mother). As most rituals for planning cultivation have been conducted by males at the end of the dry season, the rainy season, short of rituals, depends on divination and ritual activities conducted in the dry season.

During the year, most people follow the seasonal alternation maintaining a synchronization between their activities and the environment. In other words, they organize the relations among the three key words (rhythm, spirits, and flow) in the following way: Everything in the world flows following its rhythm, gradually and continuously, and humans are supposed to follow this rhythm. I consider this relation to be the first proposition of the Kachin cultural model of nature and environment.

The second proposition

Regulating the uncertainty of human desires

I specify the second proposition of the Kachin cultural model of nature and environment based on villagers' use of the local divination table and animal-sacrifice rituals. The divination table is used to maintain synchronization between humans and nature, while animal-sacrifice rituals are conducted for mending broken synchronization.

In daily life, females and ordinary males referred to seasonal rhythm in talking about their relations with things in the world, while religious specialists (mostly men) and other knowledgeable men mentioned the divination table more frequently. In using the table, these men add a fourth keyword to the Kachin view of nature and environment: human desires. Based on reasoning and thematic analysis of my semi-structured interview data with religious specialists, I summarize their thinking in the following way: Humans have desires and expectations, and how should we regulate desires by the natural rhythm? It is easy to follow the seasonal rhythm of the world, but how should we act in our daily life? The divination table tells the secret by which humans influence luck, 'manage their desires, and regulate their activities.'

The divination table derives from the local oral history that constitutes the ultimate source for legitimizing villagers' daily life. History is called $la^{31}bau^{55}$ in Kachin, and history-telling is to 'trace the origin of things' ($la^{31}bau^{55}$ $hkai^{31}$; $hkai^{31}$: 'to tell history by tracing the origin'). The genesis chanted by the specialist of the highest rank in a 'feast-of-merit' is referred to as 'history from the beginning to the present' ($gin^{31}ru^{31}$ $gin^{31}sa^{31}$ $la^{31}bau^{55}$). Lasting three days and nights with interruptions only for eating and drinking, it narrates the creation of the sky, the earth, and everything in between.[4] Each phase of creation is marked by the procreation of a couple consisting of spirits and/or humans. Accordingly, genesis is essentially a 'Genealogy of Everything'; everything is hung on a certain position in the genealogy and so is set in a web of relations with everything else.

As all things are genealogically, or mythologically, connected, history (as genesis) is considered the source of human development. It possesses power that legitimizes practices, reason that justifies current life conditions, and sources that facilitate life experience. Therefore, the Kachin are prone to attributing everything back to history, tracing back to its position in, and relations with, all other things within the 'Genealogy of Everything.' However, in reality, only a religious specialist of the highest rank could specify these complicated relations among everything. In daily life, ordinary villagers resort to knowledgeable men who can read the divination table, a categorical elaboration on the 'Genealogy of Everything,' to acquire information on the rhythmic activity pattern of everything in the world so as to plan their activities accordingly.

As shown in Table 11.1, the divination table classifies relations among everything into five categories (represented by five symbols: one circle, two circles, a cross, four circles, and a blank). The five symbols capture five sets of relations prescribed for all possible existences in the world, and each symbol is associated with an unlimited number of properties, meanings, or relations—such as time, directions, colors, shapes, spirits, order, and numbers. A real-life event results from a specific configuration of these factors. As the combination of factors are unlimited, the number of their configurations is also infinite (the number of permutations among factors increases at an exponential rate as the number of factors increases). The table thus provides a categorical outline that classifies countless real-life events in the Kachin cultural world into five kinds of interactional patterns and correlations.

In addition, the table maps the recurrence of the five categories onto the cycles of five days of the lunar calendar (without considering months and years). In the table, a column represents a day and a night, and a row represents the period of about two and a half hours; therefore, a cell represents a period of time within a specific day. A day and a night are further divided into two sets of five periods (one set from the first row going up to the fifth, and the other, going down from the fifth to the first). In reading the table, the diviner sits facing East, the direction of life and of sunrise, as opposed to the West, the direction of 'going back to the old home (of the ancestors).' The order of the reading is as follows: It starts from cell 11 (about 8 a.m. of the first day of each month), moves up to cell 51 (8 p.m. of the same day), and down again to cell 11 (before 8 a.m. of the following day). The time of 8 a.m. of the following day starts from cell 12, and so on iteratively. Once a cycle of five-days has been completed, the calculation starts again from cell 11.

Table 11.1 The divination table

		West				
		1st, 6th, 11th, 16th, 21st, 26th	2nd, 7th, 12th, 17th, 22nd, 27th	3rd, 8th, 13th, 18th, 23rd, 28th	4th, 9th, 14th, 19th, 24th, 19th	5th, 10th, 15th, 20th, 25th, 30th
5	17:36 – 20:00	O Hpung Chyut Ten	00 Hka Long Ginsup Ten	Tsa Na Ten	X Hkai Li Hkai Ten	00 Ding Hku Li Ten 00
	20:00 – 22:24	Time for asking each other to go home	Time for hurting people by using sorcery	Drunken time	Time for planting seeds	Time for being pregnant
4	15:12 – 17:36	00 Baren Num Lu Ten	Hpyen Sum Ten	X Lu Sat Ten	00 Shingai Lu Ten 00	Lawa Shan O Sha Ten
	22:24 - 24:48	Time for having a dragon wife	Time for being defeated	Time to kill	Time for baby-delivery	Time when wild people eat meat
3	12:48 - 15:12	Htong Hkat Ten	X Jo Sat Ten	00 Hka shaton Ten 00	O Mason Chyu Ten	Hkring Ga 00 Nong Ten
	24:48 – 3:12	Time to be imprisoned	Time to kill by using poison	Time when water is level in all directions (in a balanced state)	Time to be jabbed by a spear	Time for religious chanting
2	10:24 – 12:48	X Hpyen Rot Ten	Hko Hkam 00 Mying Lu 00 Ten	Sharo Shan O Sha Ten	Ganu Gawa 00 Hkong ten	Nam Dum Hkrat Ten
	3:12 – 5:36	Starting time for a war	Time for naming a prince	Time when a tiger eats meat	Time for meeting parents	Time for falling into a latrine
1	8:00 – 10:24	Hko Ya 00 Hko La 00 Ten	Hko Hkam O Tai Ten	Gumhproi 00 Bum	Ntq Du Wa Ten	Htung X Pru Ten
	5:36 – 8:00:	Time for giving each other benefit	Time for enthroning a prince	Silver mountains	Time for going home	Time for being set free from a prison
		1	2	3 East	4	5

Each cell is associated with a symbol and a cell meaning (expressed by words contained in the cell). The meaning of a symbol is fixed, representing the recurrence of the five sets of relations. Cell meanings, by contrast, were added long after the table was constructed. The meanings are subject to personal interpretations. An event is thus programmed in terms of known factors (associated with a symbol) and the contextual factors (personal interpretations of the cell meanings). Enabled by the table, people infer future events from known patterns of event occurrence, both rigorously (due to fixed symbol meanings) and contingently (because of personal interpretations).

In particular, the table provides a means for divination, or for identifying a proper time for activities. If the purpose of a planned activity matches the relations and properties of a symbol and a cell meaning, people who carry out the activity in a period associated with that symbol and cell meaning will gain benefit and avoid bad luck. The divination table thus specifies one's life and death, sickness and health, fortune and fate, all of which are determined by the temporal features of human activities. In other words, the table constitutes the local idea of causality. The Kachin use the table to manage their desires and regulate their activities so as to maintain synchronization between humans and nature.

The time scheme characterizes the relations between humans and nature/environment into a rhythmic pattern: The seasonal rhythm defines human activities within a year, and the divination table specifies those within a day and a night. According to these rhythms, people plan their activities and formulate their relations with the surroundings, generating a synchronization among humans, other creatures, and the physical environment. In this process, as human desires may expand easily so as to collapse the synchronization, Kachin have developed techniques to maintain, or to mend, the synchronization through animal sacrifice. In bad situations, when the synchronization has been broken too deeply, nature will move away, and humans will be left behind. As many villagers claimed, this is why the Kachin in the past always moved around chasing the climate and the environment.

In villagers' daily life, misfortune and disease are considered a signal of broken synchronization, which animal sacrifice rituals are intended to restore. To achieve this purpose, a ritual officiant should enter into an enhanced state of consciousness so as to negotiate with spirits, who manifest the rhythm of the world. The key to negotiation is the officiant's enhanced state of consciousness based on the Kachin view of the human soul and consciousness ($woi^{33}nyi^{31}$) which, together with the body and the life cord ($sum^{31}ri^{31}\ sum^{31}dam^{33}$, it connects the body to the soul indicating one's life expectancy), constitute the four essential components of a complete human life. The soul exists in both the living and the other worlds respectively in two different forms: $num^{31}la^{33}$ (the soul of the living) and $tsu^{31}\ nat^{55}$ (the soul of the deceased; Tsu^{31} is the ritual name for the afterworld). The former is attached to the body while the latter is independent of the body and it is essentially the same with all other spirits.

According to the Kachin linguist and anthropologist Maran La Raw (2010), the Kachin word '$woi^{33}nyi^{31}$' (consciousness) came as a loan-word from the neighboring ethnic Shan who in turn received it from the Burmese-Pali, *wi-nyan*, originally meaning consciousness. Its essence is to express the spirit as a positive force of life, *contra* the force of the spirit of death (the soul). To enter into an enhanced state of consciousness, a ritual officiant should activate the duality of his soul in the chanting so as to have a dialogue with spirit(s): His soul in the living world represents the living to pray to spirit(s) and his soul in the other world embodies spirit(s) to negotiate with humans. In this virtual space of an enhanced state of consciousness, words are not simply words, but they constitute effective actions (they are performative in Austin's term, 1955). What the chanter promises to offer to spirit(s) should be rigorously enacted by his assistant. Through such negotiation, broken synchronization is supposed to be repaired.

Based on villagers' use of the divination table and animal-sacrifice rituals, I specify the second proposition of the Kachin cultural model of nature and environment: Humans follow the temporal rhythms regulating their desires and expectations accordingly. When desires expand out of control, they need to repair the synchronization between humans and nature, and this is achieved through animal-sacrifice rituals.

The third proposition

Humans are left behind by nature if synchronization cannot be resumed

In this section, I specify the third proposition of the Kachin cultural model of nature and environment by examining what would happen if synchronization between humans and nature has been broken so deeply that it could not be repaired through animal-sacrifice rituals. Based on my interview data and my observation of villagers' daily life during the past ten years, two sociocultural processes since the 1990s have continuously undermined such synchronization—the decline of the tradition of animal sacrifice, and the Chinese government-sponsored development projects for eradicating poverty.

Following the Chinese Cultural Revolution (1966–1976) that intended to eliminate all religions in China, the tradition of animal sacrifice started to decline. In particular, the tradition was modified in its internal core in two fundamental aspects. First, the Kachin now use the Chinese Lunar Calendar, while the divination table is designed according to the Kachin traditional calendar. The Kachin calendar classifies its twelve months into six units, with three in the dry season and the rest in the rainy season. This classification corresponds with the local agricultural cycle within the alternation of the dry and rainy seasons. The Chinese lunar calendar is instead constructed around the alternation of four seasons. As the calendar defines the fortunes of the living and their relations with spirits, adopting the Chinese lunar calendar dis-enables the Kachin traditional time scheme. Consequently, relations between humans and spirits set according to the traditional scheme do not synchronize with using the lunar scheme. As a result, people lose the ability to anticipate spirits' activities and fail to plan their activities accordingly.

Second, another basis for the synchronization of the divination table has also been undermined, and the table loses its capacity to embody the power of life and death and so, too, its usefulness for divination. The power of life of the table is realized by the way it is drawn. Each cell should be drawn in the period it represents so as to embody the fortune of that period. Drawing a table thus takes five days. This synchronizes the table with the fortune of a five-day cycle, by which the table embodies the (mis-)fortune of the world. The power of death of the table is realized by the material on which it is drawn. An effective table should be drawn on a particular part of the skull of a 'bad-death' person (those who die violently, such as being killed by a tiger). The deceased is touched by the power of death, and the part of his/her skull that is used should not touch the earth when s/he dies and falls to the ground. That part is touched by the power of death while not yet belonging to the afterworld, thus mediating between the living world and the after-world. However, many specialists today do not understand the origin of the power of the table. They draw the table on paper at their convenience, depriving it of its power for divination.

In the late 1990s the cooperative team in the village of Sama allocated to households plots (now government-owned) on the mountainsides, with each getting about two hundred 'mǔ' (a Chinese unit of area, 1 mǔ = 1/15 hectare) in 2007. The local government encouraged villagers to cultivate cash crops (such as walnuts and coffee) and commercial woods (like the Chinese fir), providing free seedlings. In 2008, the local county government issued usufruct certificates to ensure villagers' possession of what they had planted. These projects brought villagers a more comfortable material life. At the same time, the projects broke villagers' attachment to their motherland and to the balance between humans and everything else in the world. In a short time, the allocation changed the local yearly cycle of work and rest.

Before the allocation, the rainy season was the time for the motherland to produce, and the dry season was for cultivation, harvest, and trading products of the motherland. After the allocation, villagers became extremely busy in cultivation during the rainy season. They did not leave time for the motherland to produce and restore her vitality. Worse, allocation and their cultivation stimulated people to extract money and profits from the motherland in all possible ways. Villagers seemed to take the motherland as their own and destroyed all other creatures' reliance on her. Whenever they deemed it necessary, all trees in a field would be felled, and shrubs burned with only a small amount of cash crops left. Large animals have run into Burma, and small ones have become fewer and fewer. Pesticides, which were never used in the mountains, have become widely used. Villagers were surprised to find that one single sick plant might wipe out all plants in a plot, whereas they had seen in the old days one type of dying plant would not harm all others around it.

'Now, we do not care about the time/rhythm; we focus only on money. So, the weather moves away, so do animals.' This is what most villagers frequently say when talking about the current climate change. The market has expanded their desire excessively. 'The market is a wandering witch spirit!' Many villagers cite this interesting metaphor in talking about the market. As the witch spirit enables its mediums to gain power while estranges them from all others, the market generates similar ambivalence between the development of economy and the degeneration of the world.[5] In addition, the market is always wandering around, expanding everyone's desires.

To make sense of the broken synchronization, villagers have come to claim that the climate of the valley moved up to the mountainside, and that of their home village moved up to the mountain top. For instance, there were so many leeches in the mountainsides before, and even so in villages, as buffalos and oxen wandering in the mountains carried them back. But a couple of years ago when people started to use herbicide in their fields, leeches disappeared. Villagers said that leeches had moved either up to the mountain top or down to the valley. 'Who knows. I miss them. It makes me feel weird without leeches stinging me when working in the field during the rainy season.' A villager said this during an interview, seemingly to be humorous, while I could sense his sad mood. Worse, herbicides do not kill weeds; a specific herbicide may clear weeds for a few weeks and make the earth dark, but after a while weeds will come back and the same herbicide does not work anymore. Another herbicide might clear weeds again, but the earth becomes darker. 'I know there is something seriously wrong, but I don't know what is wrong. One thing I am certain that we have been left behind by the motherland. She produces only weeds and those plants that do not bear fruits.' As evidence, he pointed out that the production of *amomum tsao-ko* decreased tremendously in the past five years. In 2010, one family in the Sama, who planted a lot of *amomum tsao-ko*, earned about RMB 20,000 (USD 3,333), while in 2014, the income plummeted to less than RMB 5,000 (USD 833).

In a melancholic tone, villagers told me a widely circulated story full of moral lessons. Before the construction of the business road from Yingjiang County seat to Burma in 1993, one of the reasons that prevented villagers going to Burma was malaria. Suffering from and surviving malaria had even become a symbol of Kachin masculinity. A village located on a mountain road to Burma and close to the border was named after malaria: Almost everyone passing the village would suffer from malaria on their way back from Burma. As one villager narrated, 'Every time I passed the village of malaria, my shoulders suddenly started to quiver, out of control. It was like that you were suddenly thrown into a cold and foggy forest on a very dark night. Then I knew malaria had jumped on me, and I was sick when arriving at my village.'

All this has changed since the early 2000s, about ten years following the construction of the business road from China to Burma. The road enabled people to transform Burma into a place where they can fell trees and plant bananas, teaks, and other commercial woods. '[There have been] too many trucks, too many people, and less and less animals and trees. Our motherland then moves away, so do animals, even malaria!' My informant seemed to be possessed by his nostalgia, even hoping malaria to come back. 'When I caught malaria, my wife was kind to me. I did not need to work. I wandered around the village chasing the sunshine. I found that I begin to miss the sense of being hot and cold.' He and his wife divorced in 2011.

To sum up, when synchronization between humans and spirits is broken and irreparable, nature, following its rhythm, will move ahead; also, the climate will climb up the hills, so will animals, and humans will be left behind. I consider this the third proposition of the Kachin cultural model of nature and environment.

Conclusion: A Kachin cultural model of nature and environment

The concept of cultural model is a scholar's' construction of local understandings. In this chapter, I presented the Kachin cultural model of nature and environment based on the local scheme of time that captures the causal relationships among people, the supernatural, and the physical environment. I hypothesize the model as being made up of the following three propositions: (1) All things flow according to the temporal rhythms of the world. (2) Humans follow these rhythms, regulating their desires and expectations accordingly; when desires expand out of control, they need to repair the synchronization through animal sacrifice. (3) If synchronization cannot be resumed, nature will flow away, and humans will be left behind. In other words, I consider such a flow between the predictable, rhythmic nature and the uncertain human desires as a Kachin cultural model of nature and environment.[6]

The key to the model is the idea of rhythmic flow, and villagers told me a couple of social phenomena that illustrate their idea of flow. Climate climbs up the hills, animals move away, and cash crops move along. Kachin girls prefer to marry Chinese men in the city, and boys have to take wives from Burma. Wealthy Chinese come into the mountain areas building their nice houses and enjoying the environment, while the poor Kachin migrate into cities doing hard manual labor. 'Humans and things always move. Before, we Kachin followed the motherland wandering in the mountains. Now, we chase money and go to the city.' A villager so concluded.

Acknowledgments

Fieldwork in 2009–2011 was supported by a Doctoral Dissertation Improvement Grant from the National Science Foundation (09-18290 DISS), a grant from the Lewis and Clark Fund for Exploration and Field Research. Fieldwork in 2014 and 2015 was supported by a National Science Foundation grant (#BCS-1330637).

Notes

1 The Chinese system of Hùkǒu was established in 1951 and extended in 1955 to regulate the movement of people within China and the redistribution of economic and social resources such as legal residency, housing subsidies, land, medical care, and education.

2 The Kachin Orthography used in this work is consistent with the standard Kachin, namely, *nhkum³³ ga³¹* (Kachin spoken in the political domain of the *Nhkum³³* chief, in today's Tongbiguan Village Tract, Yingjiang County; *ga³¹* means 'language'). Four tones of Kachin are marked by 33 (mid-level); 31 (low falling); 55 (high-level); 51 (high falling). Details, see Xu et al., 1983.

3 Traditionally, the term 'Kachin' is used in English and French to refer to people who call themselves Jinghpaw across the borders of China, Burma, and India, and currently the term, used as a multi-ethnic category by the Jinghpaw elites, involves a number of other ethnic groups (such as Lisu in China). The word Kachin is the transliteration of the Kachin term Gachye (the spelling is Ga-Khyen) meaning 'red land,' referring to the Kachin origin place in their genesis legends (for a history of this term, see Wang, 1997, chapter one). The term Jinghpaw is written in the Chinese Pinyin orthography as Jǐngpō, and is pronounced in the Kachin dialect in India as Singhpo. In China, they are known as one of the nation's 55 officially identified ethnic minorities (mínzú). Both the term Kachin and Jǐngpō include the same six branches of the people, while in China it also includes ethnic Lìsù who live together with Jǐngpō, and in Burma it includes Hka Hku branch (for details see Sadan, 2013). The biggest branch of Kachin is also called Jinghpaw. The language of the Jinghpaw is used as the ritual language, and their political system is treated as a model for all the other branches. In this chapter, I focus on the Jinghpaw branch in China, most of whom live in Tongbiguan and Kachang Townships, Yunnan Province. When I say Kachin, I refer to the Jinghpaw branch unless otherwise specified. All personal names used in the article are pseudonyms.

4 The whole legends were published in both Chinese (Li et al., 1991; Xiao, 1992, 2008) and Kachin (Htoi man, 1987; Xiao, 2008).

5 The Kachin idea of witch spirit implies a hereditary bad fate. The spirit transmits from parents to children and between sex partners. Possessed people are said to have evil eyes or hands, and the possessed families have a hereditary bad fate. When a possessed person envies others, by pointing at, or watching, people or something else with interest, the witch spirit will 'bite' the envied person or kill

his/her livestock at night, either spontaneously or sent by its medium. To recover, the victim has to make a secret sacrifice to it. However, the sacrifice only temporarily relieves diseases, rather than removing the spirit's surveillance. To sever the surveillance means to kill the whole possessed population, which Kachin ancestors had tried to do but failed. The only practical way to eschew the spirit while not provoking it is to prohibit marriage with the possessed people. In this sense, the metaphor of the market as a witch spirit indicates villagers' ambivalent views toward the market; though the market brings them money and a new life-style, it endows a new bad hereditary fate to them—they are now captivated by their desires.

6 Kachin in my fieldwork sites are currently influenced by three knowledge systems: the Kachin animal sacrifice, the Chinese folk beliefs, and Christianity. Traditionally, the Kachin played an intermediary role in the caravan trade between the Chinese and Southeast Asia, and so the Kachin in China were politically and economically controlled by the Chinese (Maran, 1967; Nugent, 1982). The influence from the Chinese is found in two aspects: the naked power of the Chinese government and the fusing of southwest Chinese folk beliefs with the Kachin animal sacrifice. Kachin animal-sacrifice makers treat Chinese folk belief as a resource for daily life regarding relations between humans and spirits. From the Chinese, the Kachin learned to associate catastrophic environment changes with social-historical changes. The Chinese have a long tradition in which environmental and weather changes (such as floods and earthquakes) foretell great socio-historical changes. In particular, in Chinese traditional medicine, weather changes are treated as the final reason for epidemic and collective health deterioration because they break the unity between humans and their surroundings. For instance, in the eyes of ordinary Chinese, recent natural disasters, like the Wenchuan earthquake in 2008 in southwest China, the Yushu earthquake in northwest China in 2009, and severe snow storms in early 2010, are all signs from the Universe that indicate possible future big socio-historical vicissitudes.

Christianity started to influence the Kachin from the late 1890s, and in my fieldwork sites, one-third of the population had been converted by 2010. Christians intend to convert each Kachin into a child of God, irrespective of cultural differences among His children all over the world. They provide an alternative knowledge system about nature and environment, adding moral implications to the catastrophic environmental changes. They attribute the current crisis of HIV/AIDS among Kachinto to a betrayal of God/s teaching, and the drought in 2009–2010 was interpreted as further evidence of the outcome of betrayal of God's teaching.

References

Atran, S., and Medin, D. L. (2008). *The Native Mind and the Cultural Construction of Nature*. Boston: MIT Press.

Austin, J. A. (1955). How to Do Things with Words. The William James Lectures delivered at Harvard University. Cambridge: Harvard University Press.

Backus, C. (1981). *Nanzhao and Tang's Southwestern Frontier*. London: Cambridge University Press.

Bennardo, G. (2009). *Language, Space, and Social Relationships: A Foundational Cultural Model in Polynesia.* Cambridge: Cambridge University Press.

Bennardo, G. and DeMunck, V. (eds.) (2014). *Cultural Models: Genesis, Methods, and Experiences.* Oxford: Oxford University Press

Chit Hlaing (Lehman, F. K.). (2009). The central position of the Shan/Tai as 'Knowledge Brokers' in the inter-ethnic network of the China–Burma Borderlands. *Journal of Contemporary Buddhism* 10(1): 17–30.

Fernquest, J. (2006). *Crucible of War.* Bangkok: Bangkok Post.

Friedman, J. (1979). *System, Structure, and Contradiction: The Evolution of 'Asiatic' Social Formations.* Copenhagen: National Museum of Denmark.

Giersch, C. P. (2001). The 'Motley Throng' social change on southwest China's early modern frontier, 1700–1880. *Journal of Asian Studies* 60(1): 67–94.

Hill, A. M. (1998). *Merchants and Migrants.* New Haven: Yale Southeast Asia Studies.

Ho, T. (1997). Exchange, Person and Hierarchy. Unpublished PhD diss., University of Virginia.

Ho, T. (何翠萍) (1999).《生命、季节和不朽社会的建立－论景颇、载瓦时间的建构与价值》（Life, season, and the creation of an immortal society: A discussion of time and value among the Jingpo and Zaiwa）. In《时间，历史与记忆》（*Time, History and Memory*）。黄应贵主编，，157–228。Taibei: Zhongyang Yanjiuyuan Minzuxue Yanjiusuo.

Htoi man (1987). Wunpong Kachin Ginru Ginsa: Hkungran Jaiwa (*The Kachin Genesis Legends*). Kunming: Yinnan amyu laika lajang dap.

Kronenfel, D. (2008). *Culture, Society, and Cognition: Collective Goals, Values, Action, and Knowledge.* Berlin: Mouton de Gruyter.

Leach, E. (1954). *Political System of Highland Burma.* London: Athlone Press.

Lehman, F. K. (1989). Internal inflationary pressures in the prestige economy of the Feast-of-Merit Complex. In Russell, S. D. (ed.), *Ritual Power and Economy.* DeKalb, IL: Northern Illinois University Center for Southeast Asian Studies, 89–102.

Li X., Shi R., and Shang C., trans. (李向前，石锐，尚晨宏) (1991).《目瑙斋瓦》 (*Manau Jaiwa: Jingpo Genesis Legends*). Mangshi: Dehong Minzu Chubanshe.

Maran, L. (1967). Toward a basis for understanding the minorities of Burma. In Kunstadter, P. (ed.), *Southeast Asian Tribes, Minorities and Nations.* Princeton, NJ: Princeton University Press.

Maran, L. (2010). personal communication.

Nugent, D. (1982). Closed systems and contradictions: The Kachins in and out of history. *Man NS* 17(3): 508–527.

Robbine, F., and Sadan, M. (eds.). (2007). *Social Dynamics in the Highlands of Southeast Asia: Reconsidering Political Systems of Highland Burma.* Leiden: Brill.

Sadan, M. (2013). *Being and Becoming Kachin: Histories Beyond the State in the Borderworlds of Burma.* London: OUP/British Academy.

Strauss, C., and Quinn, N. (1997). *A Cognitive Theory of Cultural Meaning.* Cambridge: Cambridge University Press.

Wang, Z. (1997). *The Jinghpo.* Tempe: Arizona State University.

Xiao, J. (萧家成) (1992).《勒包斋娃：景颇族创世史诗》(*Labau Jaiwa: The Jingpo Genesis Epic*). Beijing: Minzu Chubansh.

Xiao, J. (萧家成) (2008).《勒包斋瓦研究：景颇族创世史诗的综合性文化形态》(*A Study on Labau Jaiwa: A Synthesis on Cultural Form of the Creation of Kachin People*). Beijing: Shehui Kexue Wenxian Chubanshe.

Xu X., Xiao J., Yue X., Dai Q. (徐悉艰,肖家成,岳相昆,戴庆夏) (1983).《景汉词典》(*Kachin-Chinese Dictionary*). Kunming: Yunnan Minzu Chubanshe.

Zhang, W. and Chit Hlaing, F. K. L. (2013). The dynamics of Kachin 'Chieftaincy' in Southwestern China and Northern Burma. *Cambridge Anthropology* 31(2): 88–103.

12 Conclusion

Comparison of Cultural Models of Nature and the role of space in cognition

Giovanni Bennardo

The fundamental characteristics of the research project conducted about cultural models of Nature and whose results have been presented in the chapters of this volume make it possible to draw comparisons among the communities investigated. All the scholars used the same three basic parameters in selecting their research sites: (1) communities needed to be characterized by food-producing activities such as subsistence, farming, fishing, herding, or hunting-gathering; (2) communities needed to be relatively small so that any sample of the population investigated would be highly representative of the communities themselves and of similar communities in those cultural areas; (3) communities were selected because it was ascertained that effects of climate change were saliently present.

In addition, the methodology chosen to investigate cultural models of Nature was kept uniform across the sites. That is, the data collection was initially conducted by similar ethnographic strategies such as nature walks, participant observation, and open interviews. Semi-structured interviews followed, conducted with a significant sample of members of the community. These latter interviews contained a set of questions that was replicated in each site, though slight variations occurred due to translation in the local language. The questions in the interviews were the same and indirectly addressed the cultural model of Nature targeted by mostly inquiring about daily food-producing activities (see Appendix 1 in the Introduction chapter). This topic was agreed upon as one that would require the engagement of cultural models of Nature held by the interviewees in order for these latter to be able to answer the questions.

The cognitive task chosen and administered was a memory task, that is, a free-list task in which members of the community were asked to remember and list words about the six components of Nature, such as plants, animals, physical environment, weather, humans, and the supernatural. However, the number of components of Nature slightly varied locally. Thus, researchers conducted as many free-listing tasks as the number of salient components of Nature were shared in each community. The major assumption behind the free-list task is that words first mentioned are more salient. Therefore, the

DOI: 10.4324/9781351127905-13

top commonly shared words represent likely building blocks for the cultural model we intended to discover.

As part and parcel of the common methodology, researchers conducted the same type of analyses of the linguistic and cognitive data collected. The linguistic data was analyzed at the word (key words), sentence (semantic role, metaphor, and source/target), and discourse (causality and reasoning) level. The cognitive data were analyzed for frequency, both within one informant's list and across informants' lists. Some researchers used the results of these tasks to complement their construction of the cultural model of Nature obtained from the analyses of the linguistic data (see for example Chapter 3 by De Lima). Others, instead, used mainly the results of the free list tasks to start building the model (see, e.g., Chapter 4 by De Munck).

Commonalities across the communities

From the Andes to the Alps, from the Amazon to the Kalahari, from Pakistan to Polynesia, from Ethiopia to Western China, and from Lithuania to the Philippines, members of the food-producing communities investigated perceived changes in their climate change–affected environment. Some mentioned weather patterns, others soil fertility, others changes in the availability of fish or game. All shared their concern about an environment whose predictability is now lacking, thus, generating the occurrence of unpleasant and unpredictable events.

The perceived changes were typically explained by and attributed to 'local' causes, including especially the actions of humans. And this was so even when the major responsibility of change was assigned to a supernatural being whose actions were in response to 'wrong' human doings. 'Global' causes were very rarely mentioned and occasionally suggested only by those few individuals who had undergone some kind of climate change 'training' in their community.

When considering the content of the various chapters of this volume, another commonality that emerges across the sites is the indication by the scholars of the presence of two or more cultural models of Nature used within individuals or across individuals in any specific community. These models often comprise a propositional content that might be considered contradictory across them. That is, where one model would assert, for example, the separation of the supernatural from the other components of Nature, another would emphasize that the supernatural is part and parcel of a holistic way of conceiving Nature.

Strauss had already pointed out the likelihood of this phenomenon in the use of cultural models and articulated some of the possible arrangements among different and at times contradictory cultural models as 'integrated,' 'compromised,' and/or 'compartmentalized' (2012: 98). The latter modality seems to prevail in the reported cultural models of Nature we found. In fact, whenever contradictory cultural models are employed by interviewees, there is no awareness of such contradiction. Each model is called upon in specific contexts and in order to address specific issues without any cross-over of information between the two. That is, the two models are 'compartmentalized.'

For example, Tongan subsistence farmers and fishermen typically use a model of Nature in which all the components are interrelated. They produce statements of this type: 'Humans are related to plants, animals, physical environment [i.e., soil], weather, and supernatural [i.e., traditional gods] and they could not exist if separate from them.' At the same time, when directly asked about the immanence of God, they state that God 'masters' nature. Thus, a separation is suggested between God and all the other components of Nature. They express these two positions in different contexts (i.e., different moments during the interviews) and do not seem to be aware of the contradiction that marks them: Thus, they hold the two models in a manner that we can labeled as 'compartmentalized.'

If we look further at the content of the suggested cultural models of Nature, then other commonalities also emerge that do not extend to all the communities but bind together some of them. A cultural model in which the supernatural, for example, God, is the focus of attention and is separated from the other components of Nature—plants, animals, physical environment, weather, and humans—is suggested by Lyon and Mughal (see Chapter 6) for their Pakistani community; by Adem (see Chapter 1) for his two Ethiopian communities; and by Jones (see Chapter 5) for his Andean (Ecuadorian) community. This separation of the supernatural, though, does not prevent the conceptualization of possible relationships between the other components of Nature and the supernatural.

In fact, on one side, the supernatural determines the changes in the factors contributing to food producing, such as soil productivity, weather, and plant and animal growth. Humans, on the other side, perform rituals that are intended to modify the current deteriorated status of their world by convincing intermediaries such as angels or saints (see Chapter 1 by Adem and Chapter 6 by Lyon and Mughal) to intercede for them with the supernatural (God). Such possibilities make the suggested separation of the supernatural from the other components of Nature to be a mendable one—that is, it is possible to establish a form of exchange that will be eventually mutually beneficial: Humans obtain corrections to their damaged food-production context, and the supernatural obtains respect and appropriate worship, as required, from its created subjects. Consequently, while the conceived separation is part and parcel of the model, it is also thought of as a starting point for a reconciled wholeness. It is interesting to point out how the agents of the reconciliation or reintegration are humans who mediate between the supernatural and the other components of Nature (see Manzoor, 2003).

Another cultural model that is definitely centered on humans is the one suggested by Shimizu and Fukushima (see Chapter 8) for their Japanese community. In their proposal, it is only humans who make nature—plants, animals, physical environment and weather—become part and parcel of what is considered an appropriate living space. If humans do not 'humanize' nature, then nature maintains and shows its 'raw' aspect and as such is dangerous and the bearer of unfortunate events. This dual aspect of nature and the way it relates to humans needs to be considered when conceiving Nature (whole) within which nature (part) and humans holistically dwell.

This human-centeredness is also apparent in the second model suggested by De Munck for Lithuanian farmers (see Chapter 4). A generalized Lithuanian cultural model of Nature is indicated as holistic. Humans are conceived as in a relation with the other components of Nature, and this is fundamentally and intrinsically holistic. That is, humans are 'in' Nature, and when they need to regenerate themselves from the world they have constructed, that is, urban, they seek a crucial communion by coming into close contact with other 'natural' elements, such as plants, animals, and the physical environment. The second model, held by farmers, instead, sees humans as in competition with those same natural components. Their goals are to tame the 'natural' world to their wills and needs in a confrontation that eventually results in successful food production. This differs from the Japanese model wherein the 'humanization' of nature is conducive to the construction of a holistic living space.

In a fashion similar to their Japanese and Lithuanian counterparts, the ≠Akhoe Hai//om people in Namibia are reported by Widlok (see Chapter 9) to rely on a cultural model of Nature in which humans are conceived of as deeply enmeshed with the other components of Nature, such as plants, animals, the physical environment, and weather. In addition, it is difficult to separate these components from the discourse about the people's food-producing practices, especially their traditional hunting-and-gathering activities. This holistic posture stops at the threshold of the Creator, who is thought of as separate and 'seen as otiose and as not actively interfering with human affairs.' It is hard to understand if this position is the result of Christianization or belongs to a traditional belief system.

The suggestion by Bennardo (see Chapter 2) for Tongans (Polynesians) also includes a duality, but of a different nature. Two models are presented: One model is detected as all-encompassing, that is, holistic—all the components of Nature, including the supernatural, are conceived as interdependent and impossible to be talked about as separate from each other. The other model, instead, contemplates a Creator who 'masters' nature, including humans. This discourse is clearly associated with the process of Christianization that took place in the islands during the nineteenth century. The resilience of the traditional way of conceiving Nature as the realization of *Mana*, that is, all-encompassing living force, and instantiated in the first model, is more deserving of attention in my opinion.

A different type of division characterizes the cultural model of an Andean (Ecuador) community suggested by Jones (see Chapter 5). In his case, the supernatural world is divided between Christian spirits and Earth Mother, and humans are divided between urban and rural dwellers. We have already seen that a similar duality is presented by De Munck (Chapter 4) when discussing Lithuanian food producers. Where Andean food producers separate themselves from the urban dwellers, Lithuanian food producers add to a common and holistic model of nature a different model specifically constructed about their farmland.

Members of three communities in different parts of the world—Amazonia (see Chapter 3 by De Lima), China (see Chapter 11 by Zhang), and the Philippines (see Chapter 10 by Wiegele)—share a common theme in their cultural model of Nature. They conceive of the relationships between the various components of Nature as regulated by a cycle. This latter has been put out of synchrony by a number of causes—mainly human actions—and, consequently, the components involved are also out of synchrony and moving in a dangerous direction.

The Kachin community in Southwest China (at the border with Myanmar) conceive of Nature as a rhythmic flow whose regularity is captured, and its content rendered, as a table that governs food-producing activities within specific yearly periods, months, and even days. Humans need to be in synchrony with such rhythmic flows to maximize crop yields and personal and social fulfillment. Contemporary human desires, especially of material things, lead to a break in the synchronic process and, as a consequence, nature moves away, leaving humans behind.

Pilipino fishermen in Batangas also conceive of the contemporary state of their world as part of a cycle. This cycle, though, is rendered as a metaphor that uses the human condition of birth, growth, aging, death, and decay as a way to interpret Nature. Like humans, everything is born, grows, ages, dies, and finally decays. Human actions may contribute to accelerate the process, but humans cannot do anything to stop it or change it significantly. In other words, they are aware of the contemporary deterioration of their environment, and they conceive it to be unavoidable. As for humans, though, the cycle restarts with another life and this is what will eventually happen to Nature.

Subsistence farmers in two riverine Amazonian communities also conceive of their food-producing activities as dependent on cycles rooted in 'time-frames' spanning from years to seasons, from months to weeks and days. These cycles have recently been upset, especially regarding rain that is less in quantity and unpredictable in occurrence, thus causing an unexpected number of hot days. This has had a serious impact on planting and growing activities and is conducive to humans having to reduce their work in the fields because of excessive heat and to plants rotting in an overly heated soil. Though each of these three cycles differs in its constitutive aspects and relative topical content, conceiving a salient characteristic of Nature as being realized by a cycle is commonly shared.

The cultural model of Nature held by a Dolomitic community in the Italian Alps (see Chapter 7 by Paini) includes reciprocal relationships among a number of components of Nature—a common feature in a number of suggested cultural models of Nature. Humans and woodland, that is, a mixture of plants and physical environment, woodland and animals are some of the components of Nature thought of as being in a strict relationship and bound by bilateral exchanges. Another set of components also in relationship are weather and plants, even though this time it is the former affecting the latter in a unidirectional manner.

Another clear indication of the salience of interrelationships among various components of Nature is. provided by unsolicited statements produced in Amazonian (see Chapter 3 by De Lima) and Tongan (see Chapter 2 by Bennardo) discourse about food production. Both communities stress the close relationship that exists between the phases of the moon and their planting activities. One should plant during the days preceding full moon because the waxing phase of the moon strengthens, and at the same time ensures the proper growth, of the newly planted plants. Such a deeply felt belief points to a taken-for-granted understanding that components of Nature—such as plants, the physical environment, and humans—are holistically connected in close relationships that make it impossible to conceive of them as separate from each other.

In bringing to a close this brief discussion, it is noticeable how five more themes in cultural models of Nature have emerged that are shared by a number of communities. The first is the one in which components of Nature—either all or some of them—are commonly conceived as in strict relationships with each other. These relationships generate a 'holistic' model. Other times a model is generated wherein the only separate component is the supernatural, while all the others components are in close association with each other. This separation of the supernatural represents the second emerging theme. A third theme is provided by the construction of a division in the supernatural that obtains a separation between the Christian God and Mother Earth in the Andes and Ecuador (and maybe Mana in Polynesia). Conceptualizing a division is also employed to distinguish between rural and urban dwellers. These latter do not adhere to Mother Earth's 'ways' and cause damage to food-production activities.

A focus on humans represents a fourth theme. This focus is differentially put on humans as mediators (Ethiopia, Pakistan) between the supernatural and nature, and as agent (Japan) without whose actions nature could not be rendered appropriate and approachable. A final theme is the salience of cycles, either the human life-cycle as a metaphor for Nature or the life-flow within which synchrony, among the various components of Nature, needs to be achieved. All of these cultural models of Nature includes casual relationships that have been either explicitly or implicitly indicated as major constituents of their structure. A typology of these causal models in presented in the following section.

Causal models: An extended typology

The content of the cultural models of Nature hypothesized for the communities investigated by the contributors to this volume allowed us to expand the preliminary typology about causal models within cultural models of Nature as suggested by Bennardo (2014). In fact, new articulations of types of relationships, specifically causal, among the basic components of Nature have emerged.

The original tri-partite typology for causal models in cultural models of Nature included (1) a holistic model, (2) a God-centered model, and (3) a God- and Humans-centered model (see Introduction to this volume). Given a specific world—in our case made up of six components: Plants, animals, physical environment, weather, humans, and supernatural (and local variations)—the results of the investigations presented in the chapters of this volume, especially the suggested cultural models of Nature, provide sufficient grounds to establish fundamental probabilities for the components of the world. These probabilities stand for the likelihood of a causal relationship between and among these components. Thus, a causal graph can be arrived at in which those probabilities are displayed by boxes containing groups of components and by arrows standing for causal relationships among them (see Figures I.3, I.4, and I.5 in the Introduction to this volume).

Three new types of causal models emerged from the intrinsic content of the suggested cultural models of Nature: (4) a Humans-centered model; (5) an Enchanted-centered model; and (6) a Mother Nature–centered model. The Type 4 model is found in Japan, where humans are at the center of the causality structure of the cultural model of Nature. It is human actions that make 'raw' nature become what Shimizu and Fukushima define as 'humanized.' The centrality of humans is found also in other models, for example, the Lithuanian, the Pakistani, and the Ethiopian models, but none of these display the exclusive role that characterizes the one in the Japanese community.

Causal model Types 5 and 6 represent subtypes of the supernatural-centered model. Type 5, found in Amazonia, introduces in the causality structure traditional beings called 'Enchanted' who dwell under the surface of the earth (that is, water and soil), and 'master' the existence of many components of Nature. Type 6, instead, introduces Mother Nature as a supernatural being who is symbolically represented by Mt. Cotacachi—Mt. Imbabura represents Father. In spite of centuries of Christianization, it is Mother Nature who generated and takes care of plants, animals and the physical environment. This separation between the Christian God and Mother Nature is also reflected in the separation between rural and urban populations who 'forget' to follow Mother Nature. In addition, the urban

Table 12.1 Scholars, communities, and causal models

	Scholar/s	Community	Food-producing activity	Causal model
1	Adem	Ethiopia	Subsistence: Gardening; Animal husbandry	2. God-centered; 3. God-humans-centered
2	Bennardo	Tonga	Subsistence: Gardening; Fishing	1. Holistic; 2. God-centered
3	De Lima	Amazonia, Brazil	Subsistence: Gardening; Fishing; Hunting	1. Holistic; 5. Enchanted-centered; 3. God-humans-centered
4	De Munck	Lithuania	Farming	1. Holistic; 4. Humans-centered
5	Jones	Andes, Ecuador	Subsistence: Gardening; Animal husbandry	6. Mother Nature-centered: 2. God-centered
6	Lyon-Mughal	Pakistan	Subsistence: Gardening; Animal husbandry	2. God-ccentered; 3. God-humans-centered
7	Paini	Dolomites, Italy	Subsistence: Gardening	1. Holistic; 2. God-humans-centered
8	Shimizu-Fukushima	Japan	Farming	4. Humans-centered
9	Widlok	Namibia	Subsistence: Hunting-gathering	1. Holistic; 2. God-centered
10	Wiegele	Philippines	Fishing	1. Holistic: Life-cycle
11	Zhang	China	Subsistence: Gardening; Animal husbandry	1. Holistic: Life-flow

population does not behave in ways that would be conducive to safeguarding the productivity of the soil as it was received by Mother Nature.

In Table 12.1, I present the various communities, that is, country, investigated by the authors in the volume. I also include the type of food-producing activity and the causal model type that was indicated in, or could be evinced from, the cultural models of Nature suggested.

In labeling the Pilipino and the Chinese (Kachin) communities as 'holistic,' I decided to add a qualifying reminder about the nature of their 'holism.' In fact, I added 'Life-Cycle' to the Pilipino holism and 'Life-Flow' to the Chinese one. I also want to draw attention to the fact that I labeled the Ethiopian and the Pakistani communities as holding both a God-centered (Type 2) and a God-Humans–centered causal model (Type 3). This is because the role of humans in their causality structure is that of mediating between God and the other components of Nature.

Finally, another comparative aspect of the research project focused on the role of space in cognition. All the scholars administered a space task in order to detect a specific preference for the mental representation of spatial relationships in their communities. This aspect of the research project requires a comprehensive treatment, and I devote the following sections to it.

Space and Cultural Models of Nature

The authors of the chapters in this volume have suggested a number of cultural models of Nature in communities all over the world. The availability of such proposals opens the possibility of investigating a significant aspect of human cognition, that is, the role played by space in the human cognitive ontogeny. Space is an ontological prime, and the internal structure of the mental spatial module is made up of what have been called 'frames of reference' (FoRs from now on; see Levinson, 2003; Bennardo, 2009). A preference for one of the logically possible FoRs has been called a 'foundational cultural model' by Bennardo (2009).

The typology of FoRs includes a Relative type and an Absolute type (see Levinson, 2003)—it also includes an Intrinsic type that I am intentionally leaving out of this discussion. The axes (front-back and left-right) organized by the Relative FoR are typically centered on the speaker and instantiate a focus on ego, thus, standing also for a separation of ego and its spatial field. The axes organized by the Absolute type of FoR are centered instead on a chosen 'point' or 'points' (e.g., Mecca, land-sea or cardinal points) in the field of ego, thus, standing for a focus on other-than-ego—this latter includes the physical environment. Then, a more inclusive/holistic mental posture is realized regarding space—ego and its field are conceived as inherently related (see Bennardo, 2009 for a discussion of this point).

The scholars participating in the research project reported in the chapters of this volume—in addition to the data they presented—collected cognitive data aimed at discovering a mental preference for one of the FoRs in their communities. If a preference is detected, and it correlates positively with a certain cultural model of Nature—specifically with the causal model that characterizes its content/structure—then, the possibility of the participation of space, that is, a preferred FoR or a foundational cultural model, to the construction of molar cultural models, in our case, a cultural model of Nature could be substantiated, or at least positively advanced.

The constructive role that space plays in cognitive architecture and development has been extensively suggested and demonstrated (Gattis, 2001; Jackendoff and Landau, 1992; Jackendoff, 2002; Lakoff, 1987; Levinson, 2003; Mandler, 2004, 2008; Mix, Smith, and Gasser, 2010; Schubert and Maas, 2011; Slobin et al., 2010; Talmy, 2000a, 2000b). For example, Clark (2010) argues that space and language perform similar cognitive functions, namely, they reduce the complexity of the environment. Space grounds language, and Spivey, Richardson, and Zednik (2010) convincingly show how abstract verbs are understood in terms of spatial relations (2010: 33). In addition to the contribution of space to the construction of language, the idea that 'abstract concepts are connected to space at a deep, unconscious level—literally the product of neural juxtaposition' (Mix, Smith, and Gasser, 2010: 5)—leads one to expect a very early reliance on spatial information in cognitive development. This is exactly what Mandler (2004, 2008) demonstrates in her research about cognitive development in pre-verbal children.

Once established that space (i.e., spatial relationships) plays a fundamental role in the development of cognition, in the formation of concepts (see the relationship between space and time, e.g., Boroditsky, 2000; Bender, Beller, and Bennardo, 2010; Ramscar, Matlock, and Boroditsky; 2010), and in the construction of language; researchers have focused on the role it plays in social cognition. 'The results converge in the insight that much of social thinking builds upon spatial cognition' (Schubert and Maas, 2011: 3). In other words, it is now being demonstrated that 'space plays a role for thinking that goes far beyond a medium for communication. Indeed, it seems that it can become the medium of thinking itself, with spatial and social cognition being closely and intrinsically intertwined' (ibid.: 3). Since space—and the relationships that constitute it—is a very early contributor to the development of cognition, concepts formation, and language, and since the same perception-action couplings are at work in both spatial and social cognition (see Tversky, 2011), then, it is plausible to expect that it may play a relevant role in the construction of knowledge representations as cultural models. Thus, we can find the preference for a specific type of spatial relationships, for example, a FoR, replicated in the construction of other domains of knowledge, that is, a cross-domains homology.

A relevant finding in support of the role of space in mind is the one presented by Shimizu's (2000a, 2000b, 2011) work on the construction of self (i.e., proprioception). Shimizu shows how the cultural model of self in the United States, Japan, and China reflects spatial features (e.g., focus on other-than-ego instead of on ego) in their structural compositions that correlate well with the respective preferences about the representations of spatial relationships (Shimizu, 2009; see also Nisbett, 2003; D'Andrade, 2008). In addition, in 2009, Bennardo showed how a Tongan preferential organization of the representation of spatial relationships is replicated in a good number of other domains of knowledge, for example, time, possession, kinship, and social relationships (see the results of two NSF grants #0349011 and #0650458; PI Bennardo). He proposed that a preference for organizing knowledge about space, that is, a foundational cultural model, contributes to the generation of cultural models in other domains (Bennardo, 2009; see also Shore, 1996).

I restate here the distinction between a foundational cultural model and a molar cultural model already presented in the Introduction to this volume. The former refers to simpler and more abstract models that organize only a few bits of knowledge during the earliest stage of cognitive development, such as within ontological domains, for example, space, time, quantity. They are out of awareness, and it is very difficult to bring them to consciousness. The latter refer to larger and less abstract models that encompass knowledge from a variety of domains. They are also mostly out of awareness but can be brought to consciousness either by others (e.g., researchers) or on occasion by oneself (see Bennardo and De Munck, 2014). Foundational cultural models participate in the construction of molar cultural models. For example, a preference for organizing spatial relationships in a radial manner—that is, organized around a point other-than-ego with consequent backgrounding of ego and foregrounding of other-than-ego—is replicated in other domains of knowledge, for example, kinship relations constructed by starting from a sibling and not from ego. Bennardo and Read (2011) demonstrated empirically that this preference in the Tongan kinship domain resulted in performances on kinship tasks that were more correct and faster when a task required an individual to start reasoning from a sibling ('if your brother, etc.') instead of from ego ('if you, etc.').

Thus, we are convinced that a preferential way in organizing the representation of spatial relationships, for example, use of relative or absolute FoR—hence, a foundational cultural model (Bennardo, 2009)—can play a salient role in the organization of molar cultural models and, specifically, a cultural model of Nature. After all, the conceptualization of nature, and of the relationship of primary-food producers to nature for production, rely on a spatial dimension of knowledge and perception. The availability of the cultural models of Nature hypothesized in the many communities investigated makes it possible to find supporting evidence toward the hypothesis just advanced. The findings about space can be used for a comparison with those about cultural models of Nature.

Collecting data about preferences for frames of reference

Data was collected about a possible preference in representing mentally spatial relationships, that is, the use of a FoR in long-term memory. The task used is called 'Animals-in-a-Row' (from now on 'space task') and was developed by the Cognitive Anthropology Group at the Max-Planck Institute, Nijmegen, The Netherlands, and used by many scholars, including Levinson (2003), Bennardo (2009), and Dasen and Mishra (2010). Participants in the space task are required to stand in front of a table (or an available surface). On the table they are shown a set of three small plastic farm animals—a cow, a pig, and a horse (the animals may differ in each field site to match locally familiar ones)—standing in a row and all facing the same direction, either to the right or to the left on the transverse axis in front of the informants. Participants are asked to memorize the position of the animals. When they are ready to go to the next step (typically, after a few seconds), the animals

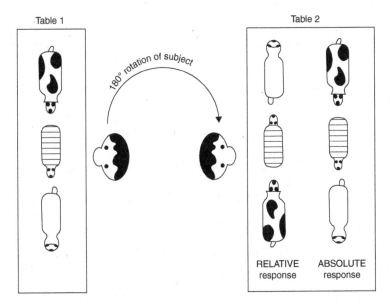

Figure 12.1 Animals-in-a-row task (from Levinson, 2003: 156).

are taken away and a minimum of 60 seconds need to elapse in which some conversation takes place between the informant and the researcher (this is done to engage long-term memory).

Thereafter, the participant is directed to another table opposite the first one requiring a 180-degree rotation from the previous position (see Figure 12.1). The researcher then hands the three animals to the participant and asks that they be placed on the new table in the sequence and direction memorized. The trial is repeated five times for each participant, and each time the sequence and direction of the three animals changes randomly (a variation of this task was introduced in Levinson (2003) and used by Dasen and Mishra, 2010).

The way in which the participants set down the animals provides a cue towards which FoR has been used to remember the spatial arrangement observed. If participants use a relative FoR, the direction of the animals would stay the same as the way they were seen, that is, either to the participant's left or right. If participants use an absolute FoR, the direction of the animals would stay the same relative to some landmark or cardinal point, but not to their own left or right (see Figure 12.1). The stimulus involves only visual perception, and the response only motor activity. Between the exposure to the stimulus situation and the response, some coding of spatial relationships by means of a FoR in non-perceptual memory is involved. The nature of this coding is exactly the target of the task.

Data collected and results of the tasks

All the scholars who authored a chapter for this volume—except for Adem, because he became part of the team at a later stage—administered the space task to a sample of the local community they investigated. Each scholar designed the sample based minimally on the following parameters: gender, age, kinship, education, activity/job, and social status. The average composition of the sample is 27 individuals, with a range of 10–43. Table 12.2 contains the distribution of the various samples by scholar, field site, and number of subjects.

The task was submitted five times to each participant. Thus, in addition to each response being possibly coded either Relative or Absolute, each subject can also be coded as an absolute or relative coder once s/he uses the same FoR three or more times. It is insightful, first, to see what type of preference is shown by all the responses in each sample. In Table 12.3, I introduce the total responses for each field site (i.e., country) and the distribution of those responses according to the use of the Absolute (Abs) FoR or the Relative (Rel) FoR. Then, I look at what type of preference is elicited for the sample by considering subjects with a minimum of 3 responses out of 5 as either Absolute or Relative coders. Since 3 out of 5 same responses represents only 60 percent of responses of one type (a statistically low preference), I decided also to base the relative versus absolute coding of the participants on 4 out of 5 same responses because this result represents 80 percent of responses of one type (a statistically high preference) for each subject.

Three of the results introduced in Table 12.3—columns: Abs FoR; Subjects/Abs 3/5; and Subjects/Abs 4/5, that is, percent of Abs responses, percent of Abs in 3 out of 5 subjects, and percent of Abs in 4 out of 5 subjects—allowed me to code the various communities using the following key: 45–54 percent = Mixed; 55–62 percent = low Absolute or low Relative; 63–74 percent = Absolute or Relative; 75–100 percent = high Absolute or

Table 12.2 Scholar, field site, and sample size

	Scholar	Field site	Sample
1	Giovanni Bennardo	Tonga	27
2	Leandro Mahalem de Lima	Brazil	32
3	Victor de Munck	Lithuania	43
4	Eric Jones	Peru	22
5	Stephen Lyon/ M. Mughal	Pakistan	10
6	Anna Paini	Italy	28
7	Hidetada Shimizu	Japan	19
8	Thomas Widlok	Namibia	25
9	Katharine Wiegele	Philippines	36
10	Wenyi Zhang	China	31
		Average	**27**

Table 12.3 Preferences for the absolute FoR by responses and by subjects

Field site	Responses			Subjects			
	Subjects	#	Abs. FoR	Abs. 3/5	Code 1	Abs. 4/5	Code 2
1 Tonga	27	135	65/48%	54%	Mixed	33%	Relative
2 Brazil	32	160	103/64%	81%	High absolute	89%	High absolute
3 Lithuania	43	215	153/71%	72%	Absolute	79%	High absolute
4 Ecuador	22	110	71/65%	77%	High absolute	91%	High absolute
5 Pakistan	10	50	27/54%	50%	Mixed	62%	Low absolute
6 Italy	28	140	79/56%	61%	Low absolute	64%	Absolute
7 Japan	19	95	25/26%	28%	Relative	16%	High relative
8 Namibia	25	125	85/68%	84%	High absolute	90%	High absolute
9 Philippines	37	185	112/60%	61%	Low absolute	72%	Absolute
10 China	31	155	87/56%	65%	Absolute	63%	Absolute
Average	27	137	81/57%	63%	70%/Abs.	66%	80%/Abs.

high Relative (see the 2 columns under Subjects, titled Code 1 and Code 2). The ranges for the coding were generated by the distribution of the percentages present in the results. The average for all the field sites is 63 percent at 3/5 or 66 percent at 4/5, that is, an overall good preference for the use of the Absolute FoR.

The coding of the communities has this frequency distribution (when considering 3/5): 3 High Absolute; 2 Absolute; 2 Low Absolute; 2 Mixed; and 1 Relative. It is apparent that the three different types of Absolute preferences—high, normal, and low—represent the majority of the recorded types of preferences across the various sites (7/10, that is, 70%). The size of the communities investigated and the nature of the activities the members engage in—primary food production—may lead one to speculate that it is the extensive and daily contact with the outdoor that might have produced such a generalized preference (see Pederson, 1993, for an early detection of this phenomenon; but see also Dasen and Mishra, 2010). In other words, it might be the nature of the communities chosen that produces such a result.

Leaving this speculative realm, what emerges from the results is that no communities are exclusively using one FoR over the other. On the contrary, since both FoRs are cognitively possible and linguistically expressible in all the communities, the subjects actively choose to use them both during the performing of the tasks. Relevantly, there is for sure a detectable overall preference for the Absolute FoR. However, in one community (Japan) the Relative FoR is the preferred one and in another two communities the Relative FoR is used almost as much as the Absolute FoR (Mixed) with no detectable statistical preference (see in Table 12.2 results for Pakistan and Tonga). Significantly, the 2 Mixed results move toward a clearer preference once the responses to code a subject as Absolute or Relative is raised to 4 responses out of 5. In fact, Pakistan shows a final Low Absolute FoR preference and Tonga shifts to a Relative FoR preference.

All the other results (except for China) become stronger in their already-detected preference once one compares the results for 3 responses out of 5 with those of 4 responses out of 5. In fact, the new coding (see column labeled Code 2 in Table 12.2) has this frequency distribution: 4 High Absolute; 3 Absolute; 1 Low Absolute; 1 Relative; and 1 High Relative. Again, it is apparent that the three different types of Absolute preferences—high, normal, and low—represent the great majority, this time higher, of the recorded types of preferences (8/10, that is, 80%).

Discussion: Foundational cultural models in molar cultural models of Nature

I called a preference for a specific FoR a 'foundational cultural model' (see Bennardo, 2009). We know from Cultural Models Theory (see Introduction to this volume) that foundational cultural models can participate in the

Table 12.4 Food-producing activities, preferences for FoR, and causal models

	Field site	Food-producing activity	Preferred FoR	Causal model
1	Tonga	Subsistence: Gardening; Fishing	Relative	1. Holistic; 2. God-centered
2	Brazil	Subsistence: Gardening; Fishing; Hunting	High absolute	1. Holistic; 5. Enchanted-centered; 2. God-humans-centered
3	Lithuania	Farming	High absolute	1. Holistic; 4. Humans-centered
4	Ecuador	Subsistence: Gardening; Animal husbandry	High absolute	6. Mother Nature-centered; 2. God-centered
5	Pakistan	Subsistence: Gardening; Animal husbandry	Low absolute	2. God-centered; 3. God-humans-centered
6	Italy	Subsistence: Gardening	Absolute	1. Holistic; 2. God-humans-centered
7	Japan	Farming	High relative	4. Humans-centered
8	Namibia	Subsistence: Hunting-gathering	High absolute	1. Holistic; 2. God-centered
9	Philippines	Fishing	Absolute	1. Holistic: Life-cycle
10	China	Subsistence: Gardening; Animal husbandry	Absolute	1. Holistic: Life-flow

construction of molar models. We now have obtained distinctive spatial preferences for many communities around the world—that is, preference for the Relative or for the Absolute FoR. In addition, we also have available cultural models of Nature, that is, molar models, for each community investigated, including the internal causal models that contribute to the overall structure of the molar models. Then, it is now possible to see how the two results relate in an attempt to detect a participation of foundational cultural models in the domain of space to the construction of molar cultural models.

In Table 12.4, I present the various communities (i.e., country) investigated, the food-producing activities that characterize each of them, the preferred FoR detected, and the causal models that have been presented or evinced from the cultural models of Nature suggested in the chapters of this volume. Typically, from one to three causal models are indicated for each community. This finding dovetails with the one presented in the previous section regarding the use of FoRs. In fact, both possible FoRs were used during the performance in the space task. Thus, favoring one FoR or a specific causal model does not preclude the presence and use of others in the mind of the members of the community.

A close examination of the content of the two columns in Table 12.4 labeled 'Preference for FoR' and 'Causal Model' reveals a good correlation of the Absolute FoR and the Holistic causal model. The Holistic causal model appears six times (60%) when a preference for the Absolute FoR is present—in Brazil, Lithuania, Italy, Namibia, Philippines, and China. The remaining two cases of preferred Absolute FoR, in Ecuador and in Pakistan, need some clarification. The Andean community prefers the Absolute FoR but does not have a holistic causal model in its molar model. I am convinced that the 'traditional' cultural model of Nature, including causal model Type 6, with Mother Nature as the supernatural component, is in its fundamental characteristics a 'holistic' way of conceiving Nature. In fact, Mother Nature is in close relationship with all the other component of Nature, she generates them. It is because of this that humans can modify their behavior to rekindle that unity between generator and generated in a holistic manner that ensures positive consequences also for plants, animals, physical environment (i.e., soil), and weather.

The Pakistani case is of a different kind. Originally the preference for a FoR was 'mixed' and it is only when I made more stringent the coding of participants—from 3 out of 5 to 4 out 5, see Table 12.3—that the preference for the Absolute FoR emerged. In addition, the number of participants (n = 10) is low compared to the average sample size (n = 27). Thus, it is likely that an extended sample might modify the results. At the same time, features of holism are always present in a God-centered (Type 2) and a God-Humans-centered (Type 3) causal models that characterize their molar cultural model of Nature. This may have generated the preference for the Absolute FoR in spite of the small sample. This lack of clarity for this case requires further investigation in the future.

The only two communities with a preference for the Relative FoR are the Tongan and the Japanese ones. They represent two different cases as well. For the Japanese community this preference is related to a causal model that is Humans-centered (Type 4). It appears that the strong focus on humans correlates well with the preference for the Relative FoR that is by definition centered on ego (see Levinson, 2003; Bennardo, 2009). The Tongan preference for the Relative FoR instead is associated with two causal models, a holistic one (Type 1) and a God-centered one (Type 2). I have already discussed in the section titled 'Commonalities across the communities' how Christianization in the late 1800s is responsible for the introduction of the Type 2 causal model in the Tongan milieu. Type 1, the holistic causal model, could be considered 'traditional' and related to the pan-Polynesian concept of *Mana*, a life force that is found underlying any form of existence. Why is there a preference for the Relative FoR contrary to almost any other community where a holistic causal model correlates with a preference for the Absolute FoR?

I must point out that the Tongan community I investigated in 2015 is the same one in which I had administered a number of space tasks in 1994, including the Animals-in-Row task. In 1994, the results had been very different, in fact, I had detected a strong preference for the Absolute FoR (80%). In a recent presentation at a Conference in Berlin (Bennardo, 2017), I have suggested that a number of factors might have contributed to this change. First of all, the shift in preference is mainly present in younger participants (less than 45-years-old). On the contrary, older ones (more than 45-years-old) of both genders maintained the previous preference (this is true more for females than males).

Second, a large emigration wave from Tonga to New Zealand, Australia, and the United States in the last five decades has made the population of Tongans living abroad to be larger than those living in the Islands. Third, the close contact with this population (e.g., remittances and returning individuals and families) has brought a great number of economic and cultural changes, including funeral and wedding practices, dress codes, speech giving, song writing and also a higher salience of economic status compared to traditional status. Fourth, television broadcasting, use of cellular phones, and access to the Internet have also contributed to make a once distant and different world—using a foreign language, that is, English—much more familiar and frequently accessible.

Fifth and finally, English has become the compulsory medium of instruction in middle and high school and this added knowledge and experience is matched by the influx of English-related cultural themes already mentioned. In major towns, the use of a language called 'Tonglish' is publicly acknowledged and this is the result of these two latter factors, schooling and English-based media and experiences. All these factors have contributed to cultural changes and they are all based on coming to close contact with a language—English—and cultures—New Zealander, Australian, and American—who prefer the Relative FoR (see Levinson, 2003; Dasen and Mishra, 2010). This might explain the change that occurred from the preference of the Absolute FoR to the Relative FoR.

Even though plausible, this suggestion is difficult to substantiate empirically. I would like to focus instead on the resilience of the holistic causal model that points in the direction of a lack of change in mental organization of knowledge (see also Chapter 5 by Jones about an Andean community). In other words, while converting to Christianity, old traditional thinking patterns have been preserved and endure. Similarly, while apparently succumbing to the flood of English—and its accompanying preference for the use of the Relative FoR—the traditional preference for the Absolute FoR still persists and is witnessed by its co-presence with the now slightly prevalent Relative FoR. This might explain the correlation for Tonga of the holistic causal model with the Relative FoR and not with the Absolute FoR since the latter is now less frequent.

In closing this discussion, I feel confident in stating that the presence of a preference for the Absolute FoR, that is, a foundational cultural model, points toward a co-presence of a holistic causal model, that is, a relevant part of a molar cultural model of Nature. On the other hand, the presence of a preference for the Relative FoR (a foundational cultural model) points toward a co-presence of a Humans-centered causal model (part of a molar cultural model of Nature). Thus, even though not fully and sufficiently supported, a relationship between the two types of cultural models (foundational and molar) has been detected. Once we contextualize this finding within the literature presented in the section titled 'Space and cultural models of Nature' about the role played by the content of the domain of space, that is, types of FoRs, within cognition, I would consider our finding as further supporting evidence for the significance of this role.

Conclusion

The authors in this volume have all adopted Cultural Models Theory and the common methodological path it entails (in some cases, part of it) as a fundamental aspect of their research. The results about cultural models of Nature presented in all the chapters, then, became comparable across the various communities investigated. A common result that needs to be pointed out is the contemporary use in each community of two or more cultural models in perceiving and interpreting the changes in their environment due to climate change. We have seen how this multiplicity is also reflected in the use of more than one FoR during their performance in spatial tasks.

This lack of an exclusive use of either knowledge organizations—FoRs, foundational cultural models, and cultural models of Nature, molar models—adds empirical support to the flexible, creative, and adaptable nature of human knowledge. The overall focus of the research project is knowledge organization, that is, cultural models, then it is relevant that salient aspects of this knowledge emerge so prominently. In addition, the type of knowledge we have looked for, cultural models of Nature, is such that can be considered crucial in communities heavily impacted by the effects of climate change. In fact, these models play an essential role in perceiving and interpreting reality and thus contribute to the generation of behavior. Thus, once these models are made available, they can be used to interpret behavior.

We are already working to counteract climate change and we need to do it even more in the near future. It is abundantly evident that planning and implementing policies about the effects of climate change should take into consideration local knowledge. This move would enhance the chances of collaboration with and active participation of the members of the communities interested by the policies and may avoid the generation of hostility and antagonism or even resentment. Local knowledge is constituted of cultural models and saliently by a cultural model of Nature, a molar cultural model. The results of our research illustrated in the chapters of this volume can be seen as a contribution toward this collaborative goal. We presented commonalties, discussed peculiarities, and examined characteristics of local knowledge in a number of communities all over the world. It is now time for policy makers to become more aware of, acknowledge, and take advantage of this knowledge. We would all benefit from such wisdom.

References

Bender, A., Beller, S., and Bennardo, G. (2010). Temporal frames of reference: A conceptual analysis and empirical evidence from English, German, and Tongan. *Journal of Cognition and Culture* 10(3–4): 283–307.

Bennardo, G. (2009). *Language, Space, and Social Relationships: A Foundational Cultural Model in Polynesia.* Cambridge: Cambridge University Press.

Bennardo, G. (2014). The fundamental role of causal models in cultural models of nature. *Frontiers in Psychology.* October 10, 2014, http://dx.doi.org/10.3389/fpsyg.2014.01140.

Bennardo, G. (2017). Culture in mind, cultural models, and a changing Tongan self. Paper presented at the *3rd German Anthropological Association Conference,* Berlin, October 5.

Bennardo, G., and de Munck, V. C. (2014). *Cultural Models: Genesis, Typology, and Experiences.* Oxford: Oxford University Press.

Bennardo, G., and Read, D. (2011). Salience of verticality and horizontality in American and Tongan kinship terminology. In Milicic, B. and Jones, D. (eds.), *Kinship, Language, and Prehistory: Per Hage and the Renaissance in Kinship Studies.* Salt Lake City: University of Utah Press, 173–191.

Boroditsky, L. (2000). Metaphoric structuring: Understanding time through spatial metaphors. *Cognition* 75: 1–28.

Clark, A. (2010). Minds in space. In Mix, K. S., Smith, L. B., and Gasser, M. (eds.), *The Spatial Foundations of Language and Cognition.* Oxford: Oxford University Press, 7–15.

D'Andrade, R. (2008). *A Study of Personal and Cultural Values: American, Japanese, and Vietnamese.* New York: Palgrave Macmillan.

Dasen, R. P., and Mishra, R. C. (2010). *Development of Geocentric Spatial Language and Cognition: An Eco-Cultural Perspective.* Cambridge: Cambridge University Press.

Gattis, M. (2001). *Spatial Schemas and Abstract Thought.* Cambridge, MA: MIT Press.

Jackendoff, R. (2002). *Foundations of Language: Brain, Meaning, Grammar, and Evolution.* Oxford: Oxford University Press.

Jackendoff, R., and Landau, B. (1992). Spatial language and spatial cognition. In Jackendoff, R., *Languages of the Mind: Essays on Mental Representation.* Cambridge, MA: MIT Press, 99–124.

Lakoff, G. (1987). *Women, Fire, and Dangerous Things: What Categories Reveal about the Mind.* Chicago: University of Chicago Press.

Levinson, S. C. (2003). *Space in Language and Cognition.* Cambridge: Cambridge University Press.

Mandler, J. M. (2004). *The Foundations of Mind: Origins of Conceptual Thought.* Oxford: Oxford University Press.

Mandler, J. M. (2008). The spatial foundations of the conceptual system. *Language and Cognition* 2: 21–44.

Manzoor, P. S. (2003). Nature and culture: An Islamic perspective. In Selin, H. (ed.), *Nature across Cultures: Views of Nature and the Environment in Non-Western Cultures*. Boston: Kluwer, 421–432.

Mix, K. S., Smith, L. B., and Gasser, M. (eds.). (2010). *The Spatial Foundations of Language and Cognition*. Oxford: Oxford University Press.

Nisbett, R. E. (2003). *The Geography of Thought: How Asians and Westerners Think Differently … and Why*. New York: Free Press.

Pederson, E. (1993). Geographic and manipulable space in two Tamil linguistic systems. In Frank, A. U. and Campari, I. (eds.), *Spatial Information Theory: A Theoretical Basis for GIS*. Berlin: Springer, 294–311.

Ramscar, M., Matlock, T., and Boroditsky, L. (2010). Time, motion, and meaning: The experiential basis of abstract thought. In Mix, K. S., Smith, L. B. and Gasser, M. (eds.), *The Spatial Foundations of Language and Cognition*. Oxford: Oxford University Press, 67–82.

Schubert, T. W., and Maas, A. (2011). *Spatial Dimensions of Social Thought*. Berlin: Mouton de Gruyter.

Shimizu, H. (2000a). Beyond individualism and sociocentrism: An ontological analysis of the opposing elements in personal experiences of Japanese adolescents. *Human Development* 43(4–5): 195–211.

Shimizu, H. (2000b). Japanese cultural psychology and empathic understanding: Implications for academic and cultural psychology. *Ethos* 28(2): 224–247.

Shimizu, H. (2009). Multivocal visual ethnography: Comparative study of adolescents in Japan, the United States and Hong Kong. In Minoura, Y. (ed.), *Ethnographic Fieldwork: Analyses and Interpretations*. Tokyo: Minerva Press (in Japanese).

Shimizu, H. (2011). Cognitive anthropology and education: Foundational models of self and cultural models of teaching and learning in Japan and the United States. In Kronenfeld, D., et al. (eds.), *A Companion to Cognitive Anthropology*. London: Blackwell, 430–449.

Shore, B. (1996). *Culture in Mind: Cognition, Culture, and the Problem of Meaning*. Oxford: Oxford University Press.

Slobin, D. I., Bowerman, M., Brown, P., Eisenbeiss, S., and Narasimhan, B. (2010). Putting things in places: Developmental consequences of linguistic typology. In Bohnemeyer, J. and Pederson, E. (eds.), *Event Representations in Language and Cognition*. Cambridge: Cambridge University Press.

Spivey, M. J., Richardson, D. C., and Zednik, C. A. (2010). Language is spatial, not special: On the demise of the Symbolic Approximation Hypothesis. In Mix, K. S., Smith, L. B. and Gasser, M. (eds.), *The Spatial Foundations of Language and Cognition*. Oxford: Oxford University Press, 16–40.

Strauss, C. (2012) *Making Sense of Public Opinion: American Discourses about Immigration and Social Programs*. Cambridge: Cambridge University Press.

Talmy, L. (2000a). *Toward a Cognitive Semantics, vol. 1: Concept Structuring Systems*. Cambridge, MA: MIT Press.

Talmy, L. (2000b). *Toward a Cognitive Semantics, vol. 2: Typology and Process in Concept Structuring*. Cambridge, MA: MIT Press.

Tversky, B. (2011). Spatial thought, social thought. In Schubert, T. W. and Maas, A. (eds.), *Spatial Dimensions of Social Thought*. Berlin: Mouton de Gruyter, 17–38.

Index